GENDER AND STRESS

GENDER

and

STRESS

Edited by ROSALIND C. BARNETT

LOIS BIENER

GRACE K. BARUCH

THE FREE PRESS
A Division of Macmillan, Inc.
NEW YORK

Collier Macmillan Publishers
LONDON

The Free Press
A Division of Macmillan, Inc.
866 Third Avenue, New York, N.Y. 10022

Collier Macmillan Canada, Inc.

Printed in the United States of America

printing number

1 2 3 4 5 6 7 8 9 10

Library of Congress Cataloging-in-Publication Data

Gender and stress.

Includes bibliographies.
1. Stress (Psychology) 2. Sex differences
(Psychology) 3. Women—Psychology. I. Barnett,
Rosalind C. II. Biener, Lois. III. Baruch, Grace K.
[DNLM: 1. Sex Characteristics. 2. Stress,
Psychological. WM 172 G325]
BF575.S75G45 1987   155.9   87-12053
ISBN 0-02-901380-1

Contents

Acknowledgments

We are grateful to Laura Wolff, our editor at The Free Press, for her superb and sensitive guidance. The patient efforts of Nathalie Thompson and Elise Moore greatly facilitated the multiple tasks of manuscript preparation. Finally, we owe a great intellectual debt to the members of the Women and Stress Seminar at the Wellesley College Center for Research on Women.

Many colleagues provided helpful comments on drafts of chapters and, indeed, on the entire book. We are sincerely grateful for their efforts. Stylistic considerations and limitations of space, however, precluded individual acknowledgment of each of these valuable contributions.

Contributors

Carol S. Aneshensel is Associate Professor in the Division of Population and Family Health, School of Public Health, University of California, Los Angeles. As a medical sociologist she has published widely on the antecedents and consequences of depression in the general population. Her current research concerns intergroup differences in stress and depression, and adolescent stress, depression, and pregnancy.

Ilana Attie is a fellow at the Educational Testing Service, Princeton, New Jersey, and St. Luke's–Roosevelt Hospital Center in New York City. Her research interests include developmental psychopathology, eating disorders, and female adolescent development.

Rosalind C. Barnett is a Research Associate at the Wellesley College Center for Research on Women and, with Grace K. Baruch, codirects a longitudinal study on stress and well-being in women health professionals. She has coauthored, with Grace Baruch, *Beyond Sugar and Spice* and *Lifeprints: New Patterns of Love and Work for Today's Women*. Her research focuses on the study of stress and well-being in adult women and on men's family roles as stressors; she has published widely in these areas.

Grace K. Baruch is an Associate Director of the Wellesley College Center for Research on Women. In addition to coauthoring numerous publications with Rosalind Barnett, she is coeditor, with J. Brooks-Gunn, of *Women in Midlife*. Her current research focuses on women and gender in relation to stress and adult development.

Deborah Belle is Assistant Professor of Psychology at Boston University and William T. Grant Foundation Faculty Scholar in the Mental Health of Children. She is the editor of *Lives in Stress: Women and Depression*. Her current research focuses on social support for children, particularly those unsupervised after school hours.

Lois Biener is an Assistant Professor in the Department of Psychiatry and Human Behavior, Brown University Program in Medicine, and Director of the Worksite Smoking Program at the Miriam Hospital, Providence, R.I. Her research interests and publications center around smoking behavior and smoking policy as well as around women and the health care delivery system.

J. Brooks-Gunn is a Senior Research Scientist and Director of the Adolescent Study Program at the Educational Testing Service, Princeton, N.J. She holds clinical appointments in pediatrics at Columbia University College of Physicians and Surgeons and the University of Pennsylvania Medical School. Her research focuses on developmental, reproductive, and achievement issues of women and on the well-being of mothers and children in poverty. Recent books include *Girls at Puberty* (with A. C. Petersen), *Women in Midlife* (with Grace Baruch), and *Adolescent Mothers in Later Life* (with F. F. Furstenberg, Jr.).

Diane Mitsch Bush is Associate Professor of Sociology at Colorado State University. Her research interests are gender role socialization, the public/domestic split, and the politics of gender. She has published extensively on these topics.

Paul Cleary is an Assistant Professor in the Department of Social Medicine and Health Policy and the Division on Aging at the Harvard Medical School. His major research interests include psychiatric epidemiology, health services research, and quantitative research methods; he has published widely in these areas.

Irene Hanson Frieze is a Professor of Psychology and Women's Studies at the University of Pittsburgh. Her research interests and publications in the area of victimization concern female victims' reactions and cognitive theories of reactions to victimization.

Suzanne Haynes is Chief of the Medical Statistics Branch at the National Center for Health Statistics in Hyattsville, Md. Her research interests include women and heart disease; Type A behavior and coronary risk; the epidemiology of aging; patterns and correlates of dietary intake; the health of Hispanic Americans; and the effect of video display terminals on health in the workplace.

Ronnie Janoff-Bulman is an Associate Professor of Psychology at the University of Massachusetts, Amherst. She has written extensively in the area of victimization and was coeditor of the *Journal of Social Issues* volume on "Reactions to Victimization."

Ronald C. Kessler is an Associate Professor of Sociology at the University of Michigan. He has coauthored *Linear Panel Analysis: Models of Quantitative Change* and *Television and Aggression: The Results of a Panel Study*. He is recipient of a Research Scientist Development Award from the National Institutes of Mental

Health and, under the auspices of this award, does research on the relationship between stressful life experience and mental illness.

Nicholas Kirsch is a doctoral candidate in Clinical Psychology at Temple University and a staff member of Temple University's Stress Management Center. He is currently conducting research on the interrelations among personality style, situational factors, and recovery in primary care medical patients.

Suzanne C. Ouellette Kobasa is Associate Professor of Psychology, Social/Personality Subprogram in the Graduate School of the City University of New York. She is also affiliated with the Department of Community Medicine at Mt. Sinai Medical Center and the Department of Psychiatry at Cornell Medical School. Her research interests include health psychology, personality and social systems, and psychology of religion. Among her publications is *The Hardy Executive*, coauthored with Salvatore Maddi.

Andrea Z. LaCroix is an epidemiologist at the National Center for Health Statistics. She has conducted several investigations on the relationship of occupation and work environment characteristics to coronary heart disease and hypertension. Prior to 1980, she practiced public health nursing and held a position as occupational health nurse for the telephone company in Maryland.

Stephen B. Manuck is an Associate Professor of Psychology and Psychiatry at the University of Pittsburgh and Adjunct Associate Professor of Comparative Medicine at Bowman Gray School of Medicine, Wake Forest University. His research concerns the role of behavioral and psychophysiologic factors in the etiology and clinical expression of cardiovascular disease and encompasses both human clinical investigations and animal models.

Jane McLeod, a doctoral candidate in Sociology at the University of Michigan, is studying childhood environmental determinants of adult psychological functioning. Other current projects include event-history analyses of the relationship of life events to the onset of depression and the study of predictors of relapse and recovery from depressive episodes.

Suzanne M. Miller is Associate Professor of Psychology and Adjunct Associate Professor of Medicine at Temple University and Director of Temple University's Stress Management Center. She has published extensively on stress and coping, focusing on the interacting effects of dispositional styles and situational factors. She is co-editing (along with Michael Lewis) a forthcoming volume, *Handbook of Developmental Psychopathology.*

Leonard I. Pearlin is Professor of Medical Sociology in the Department of Psychiatry, University of California, San Francisco. His most recent publications concern the general area of stress, its mediation by coping and social supports, and its variations and changes across the life course.

Joanna M. Polefrone is currently completing her Ph.D. in Clinical Psychology at the University of Pittsburgh. Her dissertation research concerns the effects of gender and menstrual phase on cardiovascular response to behavioral challenge.

Roberta G. Simmons is Professor of Sociology and Psychiatry at the University of Minnesota. Her primary research interest is social structure and self-esteem. She has recently published a book, *Moving into Adolescence: The Impact of Pubertal Change and School Context.*

Elaine Wethington is a doctoral candidate in Sociology at the University of Michigan. Her research focuses on how gender roles buffer or enhance the impact of acute and chronic stressors. Other research interests include social support and coping, and methodological issues in the study of life events.

Introduction

Why do women live longer than men? Why do they succumb so much later in life to coronary heart disease? Why are men less beset by anxiety and depression than women? Why do they report fewer minor physical illnesses, sick days, visits to physicians? Such questions form the backdrop of research on gender and stress, research that is the topic of this book.

Although these questions seem straightforward, when we analyze the arguments that have been put forth to answer them, a number of paradoxes are revealed.

First, given that women enjoy a physical health advantage over men with respect to life span and time of onset of coronary heart disease, it has seemed to many researchers that men must be sorely afflicted by the stress[1] inherent in their workplace role. Women, it seemed to follow, were protected because of their lesser involvement in work. The logical prediction then emerged that as more women became employed, especially at more demanding, high-level jobs, they would lose their health advantage (Friedman & Rosenman, 1974). But this prediction has proved wrong; if anything, employment has been a benefit to women's health (Verbrugge, 1982; Waldron & Herold, 1984).

Perhaps, then, the next argument goes, men's and women's jobs differ in stressfulness; that is, even if women work, they may be less exposed to the stressors inherent in employment. But as subsequent investigations—many of which are reported in this volume—show, women are more likely than men to hold jobs characterized by stressful conditions. Studies indicate that it is not high-level managerial and professional positions that are associated with such health problems as cardiovascular risk but rather those jobs that are both highly demanding and low in autonomy and control (Karasek, Schwartz, & Theorell, 1982). The balance between demands and resources to meet the demands is usually better for a company pres-

1

ident or a surgeon than for a middle manager or a nurse; women, of course, are more likely to hold the latter jobs.

Clearly it is not sufficient to look at the workplace for answers. Yet when researchers turn to the examination of men's and women's family roles, they find, as several chapters in this book show, that here too women's roles are more stressful than men's. If this is so, how can we explain women's advantage with respect to mortality? The chapters in this volume offer a variety of potential solutions to this paradox.

A second paradox concerns men's greater mental health advantage, at least with respect to certain "classic" categories of disorder such as anxiety and depression. How can we account for this difference? One major argument has been that men's multiple roles as workers and family members protect them by offering a diversity and variety of challenges, gratifications, and resources, and by providing alternative arenas for the development and maintenance of self-esteem (Gove & Tudor, 1973). Yet until recently few researchers have suggested that if women were to take on multiple roles, their mental health would benefit. Quite the contrary: until recently, perhaps the most popular topics in the study of stress and women have been the role strain, dual role conflict, and role overload presumed to afflict married employed women (Long & Porter, 1984).

But to the surprise of many, as more women—especially married women with children—have taken on the role of paid workers, their mental health appears to have benefited (Kessler & McRae, 1982). The gender gap in mental health remains, however. Again, possible solutions to this paradox are offered at various points in this book.

In the 13 chapters of this volume, authors examine the variety of ways in which gender affects the stress process. Despite the diversity of discipline and viewpoint, several themes emerge.

First, many authors emphasize the importance of the social environment—its organization and structure—in understanding the gender-stress relationship at the workplace (Aneshensel & Pearlin; LaCroix & Haynes), in the family (Barnett & Baruch), in the community (Belle; Wethington, McLeod, & Kessler), in the school (Bush & Simmons).

Second, authors share a concern with highlighting the points in the stress process at which gender is particularly salient—such as in vulnerability and psychophysiological reactivity to stressors (Cleary; Polefrone & Manuck) and in the choice of coping responses (Biener; Janoff-Bulman & Frieze; Miller & Kirsch).

Third, authors point to stressors that have been overlooked because of gender-related biases and assumptions. With respect to social roles, for example, neglected areas include men's family roles and women's roles as providers of social support to a wide network (Barnett & Baruch; Belle; Wethington, McLeod, & Kessler).

Fourth, authors share a concern with the implications for methodology of a more sophisticated awareness of gender. Do measures of Type A behavior work similarly for men and women (Kobasa)? How does the meaning of a task to a subject affect the results of laboratory experiments in comparison to real life events (Miller & Kirsch; Polefrone & Manuck)?

Fifth, authors point to the need to carry out analyses in as fine-grained a way as possible: Which specific job atttribute may differentially impair men's and women's health (LaCroix & Haynes)? Which neuroendocrine may operate differentially under stress (Polefrone & Manuck)?

Finally, there is an emerging conviction that the ways in which stress is experienced by individuals, the so-called "subjective" aspects of stress, are the critical entry points for understanding gender effects. The nature of women's and men's experiences may diverge even in seemingly similar roles or situations. The meaning of being overweight, or of being the object of sexual abuse, is no more the same for men and women than is the experience of being a parent.

A strategic question often raised by researchers interested in gender is whether to concentrate on studying gender differences or to focus separately on men and on women. Some chapters in this volume examine differences between the sexes; others emphasize the unique characteristics of each. In both cases, of course, the insights gained reveal more clearly how gender influences the stress process—and our lives.

THE ORGANIZATION OF THIS VOLUME

This book is divided into three sections. The two chapters in Part I, Biosocial Background, address the issue of stress-related male-female differences in morbidity and mortality, and in psychophysiological reactivity.

In the first chapter, "Gender Differences in Cardiovascular and Neuroendocrine Response to Stressors," Joanna Polefrone and Stephen Manuck present new research on psychophysiological reactivity that bears on gender differences in cardiovascular disease. They review evidence that estrogens play a role in inhibiting women's physiological responses to stressors. They also emphasize the importance of understanding that men and women may differ in how they experience stressors, whether these are laboratory tasks or real-life situations. Polefrone and Manuck also argue that progress in this area requires a precise understanding of specific variables, since results vary dramatically across different but related variables. We need to know, for example, exactly which neuroendocrine, or which index of stress reactions, is being considered.

In his chapter "Gender Differences in Stress-Related Disorders," Paul Cleary examines epidemiological data on sex differences in mortality and morbidity and reviews the most recent findings, such as those from the

Epidemiologic Catchment Area Studies of mental health disorders. He evaluates a variety of explanations for such phenomena as the shorter life span of men and the greater vulnerability of women to depression. The contributions of genetic and hormonal factors, of social roles, of health care utilization are considered as possible sources of gender differences. Cleary also points to such methodological concerns as the possibility of sex bias in diagnoses, whether by symptom scales or by physicians.

These two chapters are data-packed and relatively technical, but the reader's close attention to this material will be rewarded by a detailed understanding of what is known and what is unknown.

In Part II, Social Roles, authors reexamine theories and data on the effects of social roles as stressors and as buffers against stress. The authors emphasize the importance of considering not only the roles men and women occupy but also the quality of their experience in a role. It is clear that men and women may experience quite differently roles that bear identical labels—parent, neighbor, worker; it is also clear that within each gender individuals experience roles differently.

Several chapters suggest ways in which the social context and recent changes in social roles affect the relationship between gender and stress. This section demonstrates that our understanding of this relationship has been influenced by assumptions and myths—for example, that work roles are not critical to women, that family roles have little impact on men.

In their chapter "Structural Contexts of Sex Differences in Stress," Carol Aneshensel and Leonard Pearlin ask whether gender differences in exposure to stressors account for gender differences in distress outcomes. Characteristics of the social structure such as occupational segregation shape both the nature and the quality of the roles men and women occupy, making it likely that men and women will encounter different stressors. Using data from their own studies, the authors illustrate these points by asking, for example, how men and women differ in the likelihood and/or frequency of encountering employment-related changes such as entering and leaving the labor force.

Andrea LaCroix and Suzanne Haynes, in their chapter "Gender Differences in the Health Effects of Workplace Roles," focus on gender differences in workplace-related stress—in exposure to stressors at work and in patterns of adapting to and coping with them. They review a variety of explanations for the gender differences found, from expectations about work to burdensome role demands outside the workplace. Turning to specific job strains, LaCroix and Haynes examine the models of Robert Karasek and others, and argue for the importance of longitudinal studies in assessing the usefulness of such models. The data they present from their own research reveal the complexity and sex specificity of relations between job strains and health outcomes.

In "Social Roles, Gender, and Psychological Distress," Rosalind Barnett and Grace Baruch challenge assumptions about which roles matter most to men and to women. They review data on how work and family roles, singly and in interaction, differentially affect the psychological well-being of men and women. They also review conflicting theories about the impact of gender on the relationship between social roles and psychological distress and about the impact of multiple roles on well-being. They argue that social changes are affecting men's behavior as fathers, increasing the level of demands on them, and thus potentially increasing the stressfulness of men's family roles relative to their work roles and relative to women's family roles.

In their chapter "The Importance of Life Events for Explaining Sex Differences in Psychological Distress," Elaine Wethington, Jane McLeod, and Ronald Kessler analyze women's reactivity to events in their social networks, seeking clues to women's higher levels of psychological disorders. They argue that women have wider fields of concerns than do men with respect to individuals significant to them, that they are more likely to be emotionally distressed by the problems of other people, and are more likely to provide help to them. Thus women are more burdened with respect to both acute and chronic interpersonal stressors.

In Part III, Specific Stressors, three chapters address specific stressors—particular life stages, events, and chronic concerns for which gender is especially salient. In their chapter "The Role of Gender in Reactions to Criminal Victimization," Ronnie Janoff-Bulman and Irene Frieze examine differential responses by males and females to violent assaults. They argue that gender roles shape the meaning of the violent event itself and the appropriateness of differing responses, thus influencing the choice of coping strategies. Women, for example, are more likely to withdraw socially following an attack; men are more likely to increase their own levels of aggressiveness. Our understanding of the experience of victimization and of reactions to it is impaired, the authors show, by the stigmatization of male victims, leading to a serious underreporting of attacks by males against males.

In "Gender and Coping with the Entry into Early Adolesence," Diane Bush and Roberta Simmons argue that adolescence is the key period shaping gender differences in how stressors are experienced and responded to. The authors describe adolescence as a time of "gender intensification" during which cultural constraints on females and the lower status of the female role become more visible. Bush and Simmons draw on their own research to analyze a major contributor to this situation: the structure of the junior high school. Its bureaucratic organization interacts with developmental issues of puberty to the disadvantage of girls, whose self-esteem throughout this period decreases relative to that of boys.

In their chapter "Weight Concerns as Chronic Stressors in Women," Ilana Attie and J. Brooks-Gunn challenge the prevailing view that eating is primarily a response to stress and that dieting is a healthy way of coping with being overweight. Rather, the authors argue, responding to weight concerns by dieting constitutes a further source of chronic stress to which men and women are differentially exposed, beginning in the critical period of adolescence. Primarily because of social pressures, females more than males are vulnerable to hypersensitivity about body weight and thus to lessened self-esteem, which taken together threaten both their physical and mental health. Thus the cultural imperative concerning thinness is more dysfunctional for women, as is revealed in the data the authors present on eating disorders and on the futility and dangers of chronic dieting.

In the fourth and final section of the book, Coping and Adaptation, authors reassess current beliefs about women's and men's resistance to stressors and their coping strategies. Deborah Belle, in "Gender Differences in the Social Moderators of Stress," reviews concepts and findings concerning social supports, demonstrating that girls and women participate in larger social networks and benefit from a greater variety of "confiding" relationships than men, who tend to rely on one support provider, the wife. Belle analyzes possible explanations for the gender differences found. She also shows how the specific types of stressors that social supports may buffer are often sex specific—for example the divorced mother's child care needs. Although women's patterns may serve them well in times of stress, Belle argues, a chronic imbalance of "giving and getting" often characterizes women's social roles in contrast to men's.

In their chapter "Sex Differences in Cognitive Coping with Stress," Suzanne Miller and Nicholas Kirsch ask whether gender differences in cognitive responses to stressors can explain gender differences in distress outcomes—for example, the differential vulnerability of men and women to depression or anxiety. They discuss six categories of cognitive coping strategies and assess their adaptiveness, challenging the prevailing view that women have more maladaptive coping patterns.

In her chapter "Stress Responses and Personality," Suzanne Kobasa examines personality characteristics as stress-resistant resources. Focusing on self-esteem, control, the Type A behavior pattern, and hardiness, Kobasa reviews evidence about gender differences in the ways these function to buffer or moderate the effect of stressors on mental and physical health. Noting the limited and contradictory studies available to date, she provides suggestions to improve both the research paradigm and specific methodologies.

Lois Biener, in her chapter "Gender Differences in the Use of Substances for Coping," asks whether women are more likely than men to turn to substance use as a strategy for dealing with stress. Existing research is incomplete on this question, but Biener provides data showing that there are substance-specific sex differences in the use of alcohol and of prescription psychotropic drugs, differences that are influenced by gender-related norms affecting opportunities for and sanctioning of substance use. With respect to smoking, women's patterns of greater difficulties in overcoming addiction may be linked to their weight concerns and may reflect attempts to deal with stressors by managing painful emotions rather than by taking direct action.

In the Conclusion, the editors build on the conceptual and empirical material presented in the 13 chapters to consider the different ways gender may affect the stress process. Diverse chapters demonstrate that stress is best viewed as a process: the core of that process, to paraphrase Richard Lazarus (1981), is the perception that the demands one faces exceed one's capacity to cope. Not only one's biological sex but the psychological and social meaning and consequences of being male or female are shown to affect each element in the stress process: the potentially stressful situations or conditions one encounters, the likelihood of perceiving these as stressful, the choice of coping responses, and the long-term physical and mental health effects of the experience of stress.

In sum, until relatively recently gender has been neglected in mainstream research on stress. This neglect has hampered our progress in understanding the stress process; so too has the tendency for researchers to focus on males. As in so many areas of social science, the neglect of gender and the failure to include women at all stages of theory building and empirical research have impaired the accuracy and comprehensiveness of our knowledge in several ways.

First, findings arising from the study of men may incorrectly be assumed to be true of women, as, for example, the notion that the greater the quantity of one's social contacts, the more beneficial the effect on one's health. Second, issues important to—or most clearly seen in—women's lives may be overlooked, such as the emotional costs of social ties. Third, social policies and intervention strategies based upon studies of men may fail to address the needs of women. Finally, when one begins to consider gender, a more subtle problem in prior research on stress emerges—a kind of sex-segregation of studies (Long & Porter, 1984). In some areas of research, such as that on workplace stress, men's experience has been dominant; in others, such as family/work role conflict, women have been the focus. Thus both the male and female experiences are overrepresented in some areas and underrepresented in others.

In short, a truly startling assortment of assumptions, biases, gaps, and myths may result from disregarding gender issues and overlooking the experience of women. This book attempts to address—and ameliorate—many of these.

Finally, during their work on this book, authors and editors alike were frustrated by the limitations of the data available to them. Are black women's weight concerns similar to those of white women? Do gender and social class interact in influencing how marital quality affects psychological well-being? Are gender differences in the self-esteem of black adolescents similar to those in whites? As in other areas of social science research, issues of race and class often could not be adequately addressed because of the sampling limitations in prior studies. Excessive reliance on all-white and/or all-middle-class samples persists even in studies sensitive to the variable of gender. Sexual preference is even more rarely addressed. We note also inadequate treatment of chronological age. Although some studies specifically focus on children or adolescents, those purporting to study adults rarely include the elderly: apparently understanding older adults is considered a problem for the gerontologists. The contributors to this volume agree that race, class, ethnicity, sexual preference, and age need to become habitual categories of analysis in research on gender and stress.

NOTE

1. The terminology used throughout this volume to discuss stress and the stress process is not rigorously consistent, although "stressor" always refers to a stimulus and "distress" to the effects of stressors. As so many others have noted, clarity and uniformity of terminology are badly needed but difficult to achieve.

REFERENCES

Friedman, M., & Rosenman, R. H. (1974). *Type A behavior and your heart*. New York: Knopf.

Gove, W. R., & Tudor, J. (1973). Adult sex roles and mental illness. *American Journal of Sociology, 78*, 812–835.

Karasek, R. W., Schwartz, J., & Theorell, T. (1982). *Job characteristics, occupation, and coronary heart disease*. Final Report, Contract No. R-01-0H000906, National Institute of Occupational Safety and Health, Cincinnati, Ohio.

Kessler, R. C., & McRae, J. A., Jr. (1982). The effect of wives' employment on the mental health of married men and women. *American Sociological Review, 47*, 217–227.

Lazarus, R. S. (1981). The stress and coping paradigm. In C. Eisdorfer, D. Cohen, A. Kleinman, & P. Maxim (Eds.), *Theoretical basis of psychopathology*. New York: Spectrum.

Long, J., & Porter, K. L. (1984). Multiple roles of midlife women: A case for new directions in theory, research, and policy. In G. K. Baruch & J. Brooks-Gunn (Eds.), *Women in midlife*. New York: Plenum.

Verbrugge, L. M. (1982). Women's social roles and health. In P. Berman & E. Ramey (Eds.), *Women: A developmental perspective* (Publication No. 82-2298). Washington, DC: U.S. Government Printing Office.

Waldron, I., & Herold, J. (1984). *Employment, attitudes toward employment and women's health*. Paper presented at Society of Behavioral Medicine, Philadelphia.

BIOSOCIAL
BACKGROUND

1

Gender Differences in Cardiovascular and Neuroendocrine Response to Stressors

Joanna M. Polefrone
Stephen B. Manuck

In recent years the relationship between psychophysiologic reactivity and the development of heart and vascular diseases has become the focus of both experimental and clinical research (Krantz & Manuck, 1984). The aim of this chapter is to draw together and evaluate the evidence bearing on these relationships. The relevant evidence, although often only indirect, pertains to these relationships in general as well as to the specific focus of this chapter, namely, gender-related differences in psychophysiological reactivity to stressors.

The question of gender differences in these basic response parameters is central to understanding the role of gender in the stress process. Much work in the social sciences focuses on social roles and their consequences for facilitating or mitigating stress reactions. It is clear, however, that social roles may influence the expression of underlying differences in physiological processes that impact directly on the experience of stress. This chapter presents the major hypotheses and pertinent data on the important issue of gender differences.

Preparation of this manuscript was supported, in part, by HL 29028 and HL 35221. Portions of this chapter were prepared for the NIH workshop "Coronary Heart Disease in Women" (sponsored by the NHLBI; 1986) and appear in the conference proceedings.

Many kinds of psychosocial stimuli (e.g., interpersonal interactions, cognitive and psychomotor tasks) elicit appreciable responses of the cardiopulmonary, somatomotor, gastrointestinal, electrodermal, and neuroendocrine systems of the body. Subsets of these physiologic reactions—when elicited repeatedly by stressful environmental stimuli—are thought to contribute to the development of certain physical disorders. Among the most prominent of these disorders are diseases of the heart and vasculature, and, in particular, elevated blood pressure and coronary heart disease. It is frequently hypothesized, therefore, that in susceptible individuals, acute cardiovascular responses to environmental events predict subsequent rises in blood pressure and participate in the etiology of arterial hypertension (Obrist, 1981). It has also been suggested that behaviorally elicited cardiovascular and neuroendocrine reactions promote the development of atherosclerosis in the coronary arteries, and hasten such clinical manifestations as angina pectoris and myocardial infarction in persons with existing coronary disease (Manuck & Krantz, 1984).

Gender differences in the incidence of cardiovascular disorders raise interesting questions regarding potential psychophysiologic influences. Among the industrialized nations, coronary heart disease accounts for the greatest proportion of all deaths occurring in both men and women, but females enjoy a relative immunity from coronary disease during their premenopausal years (Kannel, 1982). Similarly, age-related increases in the incidence of hypertension are significantly delayed in women, when compared to their male counterparts (Rowland & Roberts, 1980). Yet, this phenomenon of "female protection" and the rise in cardiovascular disorders among postmenopausal women cannot be accounted for adequately by concomitant differences in the traditional risk factors for cardiovascular disease, such as serum lipid concentrations and cigarette smoking (Kannel, Hjortland, McNamara, & Gordon, 1976). It is reasonable, therefore, to question whether women differ from men on variables other than the established risk factors. Insofar as individuals' physiologic responsivity to psychosocial stimuli may contribute to cardiovascular disease, for instance, it is pertinent to consider whether there are corresponding sex differences in psychophysiologic reactivity. Moreover, as menopause not only presages an increased risk of cardiovascular disease but is accompanied by profound hormonal changes, it may also be asked whether the psychophysiologic responses of women vary significantly with changes in ovarian function.[1]

We have taken here as a point of departure the well-established gender differences in cardiovascular disease incidence and current hypotheses relating behaviorally elicited cardiovascular and neuroendocrine responsivity to such pathology. Coincidentally, the preponderance of evidence germane to sex differences in psychophysiologic reactivity also derives from studies of the response systems thought to be implicated in cardiovascular disease. These include hemodynamic factors, such as heart rate and blood pressure, as well as the adrenal-medullary and adrenal-cortical hormones, epinephrine, norepinephrine and cortisol. However, studies contributing to this literature have tended to focus separately on either neuroendocrine or cardiovascular reactions to stress, and have only rarely examined both sets of response variables within the same investigation. For this reason, this chapter is organized into two corresponding sections; the first deals with aspects of neuroendocrine responsivity and the second with cardiovascular parameters. Considerations relevant to gender differences and to the influence of female reproductive hormones on psychophysiologic reactivity are discussed in each of the two topical sections.

The majority of the following studies involve laboratory investigations in which physiologic measures of interest are recorded during subjects' exposure to discrete experimental challenges, or stressors. The actual stimuli employed are quite variable, including simple aversive stimulation, such as electric shock, challenges of an interpersonal nature, and the performance of difficult cognitive and psychomotor tasks. The psychophysiologic "reactivity" of the individual is typically expressed as the relative difference between physiologic states recorded during "stress" periods and those observed under "baseline" conditions. The latter measurements are usually obtained in an environment free of notable behavioral stimuli and during periods of inactivity. In a few of the investigations cited, more naturalistic stressors are exploited; these include events such as physical examinations conducted in a hospital setting, or the recording of physiologic measurements while subjects react to challenges arising in their ordinary work environment. In such instances, baseline or control values are usually recorded at home (e.g., on weekends) or during more quiescent hours of the day.

The most frequently reported data pertinent to gender-related issues are simple comparisons of the psychophysiologic responsivity of males and females. Samples are generally obtained from populations of convenience (e.g., college students), with male and female subject groups selected for their comparability on attributes unrelated to gender. Other questions of interest have included the interaction between gender and situation or type of stressor, and the influence of female reproductive hormones on psychophysiologic reactivity. Examining effects of the major female reproductive hormones, estrogens and progesterone, on physiologic responses to stress obviously requires the comparison of women who differ in hormonal status. Among the strategies employed here are the study of pre- and postmenopausal women, and, among postmenopausal women, of effects associated with the administration of exogenous hormones (i.e., replacement therapy). More common, though, is the study of women who are at different phases of the normal menstrual cycle at the time of psychophysiologic testing. These investigations generally involve an examination of women at two or more discrete intervals, usually focusing on the early to midfollicular, ovulatory, midluteal and/or premenstrual phases.[2]

NEUROENDOCRINE RESPONSIVITY TO STRESSORS

Neuroendocrine responses to stressors include reactions of both the pituitary-adreno-cortical and sympathetic-adreno-medullary systems. Regarding the pituitary-adreno-cortical axis (which links the anterior pituitary and adrenal glands), physical and psychological stimuli promote the pituitary release of adrenocorticotrophic hormone (ACTH) into the bloodstream. In turn, ACTH stimulates secretion of a class of hormones known as the glucocorticoids (principally cortisol) from the cortex of the adrenal gland. In contrast to the adrenal cortex, the adrenal medulla is directly innervated by the sympathetic nervous system, which serves as a stimulus for adrenal-medullary release of the catecholamines—epinephrine and norepinephrine. The major proportion of the adrenal secretion of catecholamines (about 80 percent) consists of epinephrine (Asterita, 1985). Interactions also exist between the adrenal-cortical and adrenal-medullary systems. For instance, cortisol modulates the conversion of norepinephrine to epinephrine in the adrenal medulla, and heightened levels of circulating catecholamines may increase the pituitary release of ACTH (Goldstein & McDonald, 1986). It is not surprising, then, that positive correlations have been found among subjects' epinephrine, norepinephrine, and cortisol responses to laboratory stressors (Lundberg & Forsman, 1979a); however, the strength of these associations is only moderate, and responsivity of the individual measures varies under different stimulus conditions.

While other endocrine substances (e.g., growth hormone, testosterone, prolactin) may be responsive to stress, our discussion will be limited largely to cortisol and the catecholamines. Cortisol has wide ranging effects on body tissues, including alterations in lipid metabolism that are thought to increase risk for coronary artery disease (Herd, 1983; Troxler, Sprague, Albanese, Fuchs, & Thompson, 1977). Effects of circulating catecholamines on the body are similar to those produced by the release of norepinephrine at sympathetic nerve endings, and extend to the many organs whose coordinated pattern of stress-response is commonly termed the "fight or flight" reaction. It has been hypothesized that the catecholamines contribute to cardiovascular disease through a variety of intervening mechanisms. These include acute elevations in blood pressure and associated injury to arterial endothelium, mobilization of serum lipids, increased aggregation of blood platelets, and precipitation of cardiac arrhythmias (Clarkson, Manuck, & Kaplan, 1986; Krantz & Manuck, 1984; Schneiderman, 1983).

Gender Differences

There is now a considerable body of research regarding gender differences in neuroendocrine reactions to stressors. The findings of this research indicate quite consistently that, in response to standard laboratory stressors, females show a less pronounced elevation in the urinary excretion of epinephrine than do males. For example, Frankenhaeuser, Dunne, and Lundberg (1976) report that when young adult males and females were exposed to two experimental stimuli—repeated venipuncture and a frustrating cognitive task—only the males showed a significant rise in urinary epinephrine. In related investigations involving similar cognitive challenges (Lundberg & Forsman, 1979b; Johansson & Post, 1974), tests of reaction time performance (Frankenhaeuser, Lundberg, & Forsman, 1980), and a regularly scheduled school examination (Frankenhaeuser, Rauste-von Wright, Collins, von Wright, Sedvall, & Swahn, 1978), the epinephrine responses of males also significantly exceeded those of females. The same relationship has been observed among 12-year-olds (Johansson, 1972), and, occasionally, in children as young as 3 to 6 years of age (Lundberg, 1983; Lundberg, de Chateau, Winberg, & Frankenhaeuser, 1981). Yet interestingly, none of the investigations cited above has revealed a corresponding sex difference in the urinary excretion of norepinephrine (Collins & Frankenhaeuser, 1978; Forsman & Lindblad, 1983; Frankenhaeuser et al., 1976; Frankenhaeuser et al., 1980; Johansson, 1972; Johansson & Post, 1974). The failure of norepinephrine to discriminate male and female subject groups is consistent with the observation that norepinephrine responds most appreciably to physical stress (e.g., exercise), while epinephrine is more reactive to psychological stressors of the type represented in the foregoing studies (Dimsdale & Moss, 1980; Ward, Mefford, Parker, Chesney, Taylor, Keegan, & Barchas, 1983). Among the few studies that have also examined rates of cortisol excretion, some have found nonsignificant trends suggesting a higher responsivity in males (Collins & Frankenhaeuser, 1978; Frankenhaeuser et al., 1978), while others have observed no sex-related differences (Frankenhaeuser et al., 1980; Lundberg, 1983).

The specificity of this sex difference in epinephrine excretion is underscored by the findings of several studies in which subjects' heart rate responses were also assessed. These investigations revealed the heart rate reactions of men to be no greater than those of women (Frankenhaeuser et al., 1976; Frankenhaeuser et al., 1980), and, in one instance, females exhibited larger heart rate elevations than did males (Collins & Frankenhaeuser, 1978). That subjects' heart rate responses did not parallel gender differences in epinephrine excretion in these studies is not altogether surprising, as circulating epinephrine has a relatively minor effect on cardiac performance relative to sympathetic neural influences (Berne & Levy, 1977; Obrist, 1981).

It has been suggested that the enhanced epinephrine excretion exhibited by males may stem from their reported experience of greater "effort" during laboratory tasks, compared to female subjects. However, the behavioral performances of women have usually been similar or superior to those of their male counterparts (Collins & Frankenhaeuser, 1978; Frankenhaeuser et al., 1976; Frankenhaeuser et al., 1978; Johansson, 1972). Females, therefore, do not appear to have been less overtly "engaged" in tasks presented to subjects under the various experimental protocols in these investigations. Of course, it is still possible that males exerted greater effort than females (albeit without a corresponding increase in performance) and that such effort was associated with concomitant elevations in the urinary excretion of epinephrine. Since males' self-report of greater effort may conceivably reflect no more than a gender-associated reporting bias, though, this interpretation is speculative in the absence of corroborating behavioral data.

It should be noted that the index of catecholamine activity employed in all of the studies cited above was the rate of urinary excretion of epinephrine and norepinephrine. A reliance upon urinary indices of neuroendocrine response in psychophysiologic investigations is frequently criticized as potentially unrepresentative of the plasma concentrations of these substances. Much of the norepinephrine released at sympathetic nerve endings, for instance, is metabolized prior to its appearance in urine, and it is probable that a portion of the urinary excretion is determined by sympathetic release within the kidneys (Goldstein & McDonald, 1986). Nevertheless, significant intra-individual correlations have been reported between urinary and plasma catecholamine measurements obtained during subjects' exposure to laboratory stressors, an association which appears to be somewhat stronger for epinephrine than for norepinephrine (Akerstedt, Gillberg, Hjemdahl, Sigurdson, Gustavsson, Daleskog, & Polare, 1983). Moreover, Forsman and Lindblad (1983) have replicated the heightened epinephrine responsivity of males, using plasma measurements and experimental procedures comparable to those employed in previous studies of urinary catecholamine excretion.

Despite the apparent consistency of findings in this literature, most studies demonstrating gender differences in catecholamine responses to stress have administered as test stimuli achievement-related challenges, such as laboratory tasks requiring mental work or skilled psychomotor performance, or school examinations. Under other psychologically "demanding" conditions, in which salient stimulus attributes do not relate to achievement, however, sex differences are less striking. For example, Lundberg, de Chateau, Winberg, and Frankenhaeuser (1981) assessed the urinary excretion of catecholamines and cortisol in parents accompanying their children to the hospital for observation and testing. In this situation, the epinephrine excretion of mothers did not differ from that of fathers, and, in fact, norepinephrine excretion was significantly greater among the mothers. The authors interpret these findings as support for the hypothesis that behaviorally elicited neuroendocrine reactions are determined largely by "psychological" factors; hence, the behavioral challenge here was viewed as one reflecting women's customary or traditional domain of concern (viz., family and child-rearing).

A second study also suggests that gender effects may depend upon the conditions under which catecholamine measurements are obtained (Johansson & Post, 1974). In this investigation, urinary catecholamine excretion was assessed in both male and female office workers and industrial employees, under two conditions: (a) during a psychological evaluation involving tests of personality and intellectual functioning; and (b) during the course of subjects' ordinary work routines. The latter measurements were obtained monthly over a period of a year. Interestingly, males excreted significantly more epinephrine than their female counterparts during the psychological test session, but did not differ in excretion rates under the more naturalistic conditions of the work environment. These findings suggest that gender differences in catecholamine reactivity, as observed in a highly controlled test situation, may not generalize to the naturally occurring events or stressors of subjects' daily lives. Because no attempt was made to assess behaviorally salient attributes of the times when work-related samples were obtained, however, it is not clear whether the failure of gender differences to generalize to the worksite indicates that females do not differ from males in their catecholamine excretion over the course of daily events, or alternatively, that neither males nor females in this study experienced significant stress during work-related activities.

That sex-role orientation may help determine catecholamine reactions to achievement-relevant tasks or stressors is suggested by results of two additional investigations. In the first of these studies, subjects' urinary catecholamine excretions were measured under control conditions and during a matriculation examination required of students seeking university admission in Sweden (Frankenhaeuser et al., 1978; Rauste-von Wright, von Wright, & Frankenhaeuser, 1981). Again, while male and female subjects performed equivalently on the test and did not differ in catecholamine excretion in the control session, males showed a higher rate of epinephrine excretion during the examination. Self-report measures obtained after the exam revealed sex differences as well: the males reported greater feelings of success and confidence, and the females reported greater discomfort, tension, and fear of failure. Further analyses indicated that girls exhibiting the least pronounced elevations in urinary epinephrine during the exam were " . . . oriented more toward a traditional 'feminine role' and less toward achievement" (Rauste-von Wright et al., 1981, p. 368). In contrast, Collins and Frankenhaeuser (1978) demonstrated that female undergraduates whose educational aspirations fell within a traditionally "masculine" field more closely resembled males in the magnitude of their urinary epinephrine excretion in an achievement-oriented task. Here, male and female engineering students drawn from classes carrying predominantly male enrollments were presented a difficult cognitive task to perform. Males still showed larger epinephrine increases over baseline measurements than females, yet the extent of the sex difference was greatly diminished when compared to earlier student studies involving female samples selected without regard to academic interests. Of course, it may be argued that the underlying psychobiological characteristics that affect epinephrine responses to cognitive stressors also influence career choice. Alternatively, female engineering students may have found the experimental task to be more meaningful than did students with traditionally "feminine" interests, and this appraisal may have accounted, in part, for their heightened catecholamine reactivity.

A sex-role interpretation of gender differences in neuroendocrine response, however, may be faulted on a number of grounds. First, none of the studies cited above involved use of a standardized and validated instrument for assessing differences in gender orientation. Rather, such differences were inferred from the nature of subjects' academic pursuits, questionnaires pertaining to personal values (e.g., the importance of marriage, parenthood, or heterosexual relationships), academic performance, or teachers' ratings of achievement. In addition, while the various indices of achievement orientation employed might reflect chronic levels of academic striving, they may not be valid predictors of subjects' motivation to perform well in a particular laboratory situation. The latter possibility is underscored by the observation that females performed either as well as or better than males on tasks presented to subjects in all of the preceding studies.

Hormonal Influences

There are as yet few investigations of hormonal influences on neuroendocrine reactivity to psychological stressors, and the studies that do exist demonstrate little relationship among these variables. One hypothesis compatible with observed gender differences in neuroendocrine response is that the estrogens and/or progesterone inhibit neuroendocrine reactivity. Results of one study are consistent with this hypothesis (Aslan, Nelson, Carruthers, & Lader, 1981). In this investigation, groups of male and female subjects in two age categories (22 to 35 and 50 to 67 years) were presented a difficult cognitive task to perform. Urinary catecholamine excretion, heart rate, and skin conductance were assessed during both baseline and stress periods. While not stated explicitly by the authors, the postmenopausal status of most of the older female group (and therefore minimal levels of reproductive hormones in these subjects) may be presumed on the basis of age. Epinephrine excretion increased during stress, relative to control values, in all but the younger group of women. The latter group showed evidence of arousal on subjective ratings, heart rate, and skin conductance, suggesting that these subjects were as engaged behaviorally in the experimental task as were members of the other three groups. To the extent that women in the two age groups differed in levels of reproductive hormones, these results support the hypothesis that such substances influence the magnitude of neuroendocrine response to stressors. However, because of the cross-sectional nature of this study, it is also possible that the reported differences in epinephrine excretion were due to some unknown age-dependent factor(s) that may exert a greater influence on females than on males.

Employing a somewhat different experimental strategy, Collins and colleagues contrasted the physiologic responses of postmenopausal women to a series of cognitive stressors presented before and following replacement therapy via a combined estrogen-progestin compound (Collins, Hanson, Eneroth, Hagenfeldt, Lundberg, & Frankenhaeuser, 1982). Results revealed no effect of the hormonal treatment on rates of urinary epinephrine, norepinephrine, or cortisol excretion, in either stress or poststress (control) periods. The authors note that the epinephrine reactions of these women were, overall, somewhat larger than those observed previously among younger females exposed to similar protocols in other investigations, but still were attenuated relative to responses typically seen in males. If it is assumed that postmenopausal women on and off replacement therapy have levels of female reproductive hormones that are, on average, intermediate between the concentrations of those substances in premenopausal and male subjects, then the similarly intermediate epinephrine responsivity of postmenopausal women appears at least to parallel the relative status of the reproductive hormones in these individuals. Nevertheless, it should be noted that reproductive hormone concentrations in such postmenopausal groups are variable, due not only to the presence or absence of an exogenously administrated estrogen-progestin compound, but also to length of time since cessation of menstruation and amount of adipose tissue (which produces the major form of estrogen present in postmenopausal women, estrone).

There is some evidence that both urinary and plasma catecholamine concentrations vary over the course of the menstrual cycle, with elevations occurring at the time of ovulation and persisting through much of the luteal phase (e.g., Collins, Eneroth, & Landgren, 1985; Goldstein, Levinson, & Keiser, 1983). A few investigators have examined whether neuroendocrine responses to behavioral challenges also differ between phases of the menstrual cycle. Wasilewska, Kobus, and Bargiel (1980) reported, for instance, that rates of urinary norepinephrine excretion increased significantly during a prolonged period of mental work among women tested during the ovulatory phase, but not when the same subjects were assessed during the premenstrual period. The authors concluded that elevated estradiol levels associated with ovulation may have potentiated norepinephrine reactivity. However, no similar effects were observed for rates of epinephrine excretion, which increased in response to the experimental stressor (relative to baseline values) during both phases. In another investigation, Marinari, Leshner, and Doyle (1976) examined plasma cortisol reactions to a stressful interpersonal challenge during the premenstrual or ovulatory phases of women taking or not taking an oral contraceptive. In this study, subjects taking oral contraceptives had higher baseline cortisol concentrations, yet cortisol reactions to the experimental stressor were most pronounced among non-pill users tested during the premenstrual phase (i.e., when estradiol and progesterone levels are declining rapidly). Together, these findings suggest that there is some variation in the reactivity of norepinephrine and cortisol, but not of epinephrine, during the course of the normal menstrual cycle.

In contrast to the foregoing studies, Collins et al. (1985) tested subjects during the follicular, ovulatory, and luteal phases of two consecutive menstrual cycles. These investigators found no appreciable or consistent effects of menstrual phase on subjects' urinary epinephrine, norepinephrine, or cortisol responses to a series of difficult cognitive and psychomotor tasks. Likewise, Abplanalp, Livingston, Rose, and Sandwisch (1977) reported no differences in plasma cortisol or growth hormone responses to public speaking among women tested during the follicular, ovulatory, early luteal, or menstrual phases. As the number of subjects assessed in each of these phases was quite small (n's = 3 to 9), however, there was likely insufficient statistical power to detect significant group differences.

In summary, there is little evidence that the reproductive hormones exert a systematic influence on neuroendocrine responsivity to laboratory stressors. One investigation suggests that postmenopausal women exhibit larger epinephrine reactivity than do younger (and, presumably, normally cycling) females. Also, in some studies the magnitude of subjects' norepinephrine and cortisol reactions appear to vary over the course of the menstrual cycle. Other investigators fail to demonstrate such effects, however. Published studies in this area are still few in number, though, and many of those reported exhibit important methodologic deficiencies, such as small sample sizes. Finally, while the effects of exogenous hormones may differ from those of endogenous estrogens and progesterone, administration of a combined estrogen-progestin compound has not been found to affect neuroendocrine reactivity.

CARDIOVASCULAR RESPONSIVITY TO STRESSORS

Studies of sex differences in cardiovascular responses to stressors comprise a larger, but more variable, literature than that reviewed in the previous section on neuroendocrine reactivity. The measurements obtained in these studies are generally limited to blood pressure and/or heart rate, and only rarely have investigators examined other cardiovascular parameters such as skeletal muscle hemodynamics, stroke volume, and cardiac output. Nevertheless, it is helpful to understand the various determinants of cardiovascular response, particularly those that give rise to changes in arterial blood pressure.

Blood pressure varies largely as a function of the volume of blood that is present in the arteries. This volume is affected both by the quantity of blood entering the arteries through the pumping action of the heart (the cardiac output) and by forces impeding the flow of blood out of the arterial system (the total peripheral resistance). An increase in either cardiac output or total peripheral resistance will produce a corresponding rise in blood pressure. Cardiac output is itself determined by two factors, the rate at which the heart beats (heart rate) and the volume of blood ejected with each cardiac cycle (stroke volume). Total peripheral resistance reflects the extent of flow restriction, or vasoconstriction, in resistance vessels (arterioles) throughout the peripheral circulation. Through the actions of the autonomic nervous system and of circulating catecholamines, psychological stimuli can affect both the cardiac output and peripheral (vascular) resistance, thereby influencing blood pressure. The relative contributions of cardiac and vascular influences on observed changes in blood pressure, however, will vary from stimulus to stimulus. Finally, it should be noted that arterial pressure varies throughout the cardiac cycle. The maximum pressure achieved, systolic blood pressure, is associated with ventricular contraction and ejection of blood into the circulation. Conversely, diastolic blood pressure is the minimum pressure of blood in the arteries and occurs at the time when the heart is at rest (i.e., during ventricular relaxation).

The pathogenetic significance of behaviorally induced cardiovascular responses is not yet clear. It is hypothesized, however, that elevations in blood pressure due to stressors may contribute to the development of a sustained hypertension; the latter may arise from a variety of intervening mechanisms, including structural changes in the arterioles (e.g., smooth muscle hypertrophy), intrinsic autoregulatory mechanisms evoked by an elevated cardiac output, or an associated disruption in the regulation of blood volume and the renal (kidney) control of blood pressure (Manuck & Krantz, 1986). In addition, large blood pressure reactions to environmental stimuli may have prognostic significance for hypertensive patients (e.g., hastening end-organ damage or vascular complications), since in these individuals such reactions are superimposed upon an already elevated basal blood pressure. Finally, acute cardiovascular reactions to stressors are also thought to promote the development of coronary artery atherosclerosis, possibly by injuring the artery wall via disturbances in intra-arterial blood flow (e.g., increased turbulence and sheer stress) (Manuck & Krantz, 1984).

Gender Differences

A small group of studies have examined gender differences in one or more aspects of cardiovascular functioning during stress. In regard to blood pressure, several investigations have demonstrated that young adult females exhibit smaller systolic blood pressure responses to behavioral challenges, such as psychomotor and cognitive tasks, relative to males of the same age (Dembroski, MacDougall, Cardozo, Ireland, & Krug-Fite, 1985; Forsman & Lindblad, 1983; Liberson and Liberson, 1975). Other investigators have failed to observe similar differences (Awaritefe & Kadiri, 1982; Lane, White, & Williams, 1984; Manuck, Craft, & Gold, 1978). In no study, however, have females shown larger systolic blood pressure reactions than their male counterparts. Findings in relation to heart rate are more consistently negative; where such differences have been observed, however, females have typically (but not always) shown larger heart rate reactions than males (Collins & Frankenhaeuser, 1978; Graham, Cohen, & Shmavonian, 1966). Studies contributing to this literature are reviewed briefly in the following paragraphs.

Forsman and Lindblad (1983) found that both plasma epinephrine levels and systolic blood pressure reactions to a difficult cognitive task were greater among males than females. Similarly, Liberson and Liberson (1975) reported that in response to electric shocks, which were administered at the limit of participants' pain tolerances, systolic blood pressure increased significantly only among male subjects. Although heart rate did not increase significantly in subjects of either sex, females showed greater respiratory changes than their male counterparts. Finally, Dembroski et al. (1985) compared female college students' cardiovascular responses to the independent and combined presentation of two stimuli—a challenging psychomotor task (video game) and cigarette smoking—with the corresponding physiologic reactions of a previously observed, comparable male sample. Both stimuli elicited significantly greater systolic blood pressure responses in males when each stimulus was administered alone, but males and females did not differ in these responses when they both smoked and played the video game.

In contrast to the foregoing investigations, several studies employing similar experimental tasks (e.g., tests of cognitive and psychomotor performance) have failed to find reliable sex differences in systolic blood pressure reactivity (Awaritefe & Kadiri, 1982; Jorgensen & Houston, 1981; Lane et al., 1984; Lorimer, Macfarlane, Provan, Duffy, & Lawrie, 1971; Manuck et al., 1978). In the study reported by Jorgensen and Houston (1981), however, males showed larger systolic elevations than females during recovery periods following subjects' performance of cognitive-conflict and mental arithmetic tasks. Interestingly, female subjects exhibited significantly higher heart rates during the same recovery periods, as well as during intervals preceding (anticipating) and following exposure to a shock avoidance task.

The heart rate findings of Jorgensen and Houston (1981) notwithstanding, most studies, as noted earlier, have shown no overall sex difference in heart rate response to behavioral stressors (e.g., Aslan et al., 1981; Dembroski et al., 1985; Forsman & Lindblad, 1983; Frankenhaeuser et al., 1980; Lane et al., 1984; Liberson & Liberson, 1975; Myrsten, Lundberg, Frankenhaeuser, Ryan, Dolphin, & Cullen, 1984). In two of these investigations, however, heart rate reactions elicited by the experimental stimuli were so small (e.g., < 5 beats per minute) as to permit little opportunity to detect reliable group differences (Frankenhaeuser et al., 1976; Liberson & Liberson, 1975), and in a third study (Aslan et al., 1981) the mean heart rate responses of both young adult and older females were substantially, if not significantly, greater than those of their age-matched male counterparts (viz., 20.3 vs. 13.3 beats per minute). Results of two other investigations suggest more strongly that females may exhibit an enhanced cardiac responsivity to behavioral stimuli. Graham et al. (1966) reported that female undergraduates showed greater heart rate acceleration during instrumental avoidance conditioning than did males, and, in a sample of male and female engineering students, Collins and Frankenhaeuser (1978) observed significantly larger increases in heart rate among females during performance of a frustrating cognitive task.

Inconsistent findings regarding sex differences in cardiovascular reactivity may be due to other sources of subject heterogeneity, including one variable that is itself associated with an increased risk for cardiovascular disease—namely, the Type A (or coronary-prone) behavior pattern. Briefly, the Type A pattern denotes a constellation of behavioral attributes including competitiveness, time urgency, and easily evoked hostility. Persons who are not characterized by these traits are said to exhibit the more placid Type B behavior pattern. Several prospective epidemiologic investigations indicate that among initially healthy individuals, Type A behavior predicts the subsequent development of clinical coronary heart disease (CHD), in both males and females (Manuck, Kaplan, & Matthews, 1986). Because the Type A–CHD association is also independent of the concomitant influences of traditional coronary disease risk factors (e.g., serum lipids, cigarette smoking, age), recent research has sought to identify other physiologic correlates of the Type A pattern that might contribute to disease pathogenesis. In turn, much of this research has focused on the psychophysiologic response characteristics of Type A and B individuals during subjects' exposure to psychological stressors.

There are now at least 50 published studies concerning the cardiovascular psychophysiology of the Type A behavior pattern, and the majority of these demonstrate that Type A individuals exhibit larger blood pressure and/or heart rate responses to common laboratory stressors than do Type Bs. It also appears, however, that the heightened cardiovascular reactivity of Type A subjects is documented more readily in male samples than among females (Manuck et al., 1978; Wright, Contrada, & Glass, 1985). There is some evidence that influences of the Type A pattern on cardiovascular reactions to stressors may be modulated, in women, by ancillary variables such as age and employment status (Lawler, Rixse, & Allen, 1983; Lawler, Schmied, Mitchell, & Rixse, 1984). In addition, aspects of the experimental stimulus may affect the cardiovascular responsivity of Type A females. MacDougall, Dembroski, and Krantz (1981) observed, for instance, that certain laboratory tasks which had previously elicited differences in the cardiovascular reactivity of Type A and B males (viz., tests of reaction time performance, cold immersion) failed to produce similar results when applied to a sample of undergraduate women. When females were required to interact verbally with a female confederate of the investigator, however, Type A women did show greater heart rate and systolic blood pressure responses than Type Bs. This finding suggests that, at least among young adult women, direct interpersonal challenge represents a more effective stimulus for the elicitation of A-B differences in psychophysiologic reactivity. A more general implication of these results is that certain attributes of the experimental stimulus, or subjects' varying appraisals of such stimuli, may serve to enhance or diminish physiologic responsivity in females (or in subsets of females, such as Type As). If so, sex differences described in some previous investigations may be due less to gender per se than to an interaction of gender and stimulus characteristics—an interaction rendering some stimuli more potent than others for female or for male subjects.

Other data indicate that stimulus attributes affect the cardiac responsivity of males, as well as females. In one study, for example, Van Egeren (1979) recorded the heart rates of male and female college students during their participation in a mixed-motive game. Each subject "played" against a male confederate, whose performance reflected use of either a competitive or cooperative strategy. Among the subjects assigned to the competitive condition, females exhibited higher peak heart rates than did males; in the cooperative condition, in contrast, males showed larger heart rate responses than females. Thus, the author concludes that heart rate reactivity was determined, in part, by an interaction of the experimental condition and subject's sex, with the most pronounced cardiac responses occurring where subjects encountered a game strategy viewed as inconsistent with gender socialization (i.e., cooperation for males, competition for females). An alternative interpretation of these data is that females were more reactive when losing to the confederate (which occurred more frequently in the competitive condition) and that males showed greater heart rate responses when winning (which characterized participation in the cooperative condition). In any case, these data indicate that, for heart rate, even the direction of observed sex differences may rest importantly on the nature of the experimental task or stimulus.

Hormonal Influences

Several researchers have explored potential hormonal influences on behaviorally elicited cardiovascular reactivity. These investigations involve the comparison of pre- and postmenopausal women, and, among ovariectomized and postmenopausal women, examination of effects associated with hormonal replacement. These studies have also examined the cardiovascular responses of women employing oral contraceptives at the time of psychophysiologic testing and of normally cycling females during different menstrual phases. The available evidence, we believe, offers preliminary, though only indirect, support for the hypothesis that female reproductive hormones are related to an attenuated cardiovascular responsivity to stressors. However, findings in this area are not well replicated and many of the published studies reveal no significant associations; a few investigations also yield clearly contradictory results despite use of quite similar experimental methodologies.

In a study reported by von Eiff, Plotz, Beck, and Czernik (1971), 28 ovariectomized women were assigned to one of three experimental conditions. These groups received intramuscular injections of either a long-acting estrogen, an estrogen-progestin combination, or a saline solution as a placebo control. Heart rate and blood pressure were then assessed during subjects' performance of a mental arithmetic task. The authors report that while resting systolic blood pressures did not differ between groups, women assigned to the two drug conditions exhibited significantly smaller systolic blood pressure responses when presented the experimental task, relative to control subjects. Diastolic blood pressure and heart rate tended also to be lower for subjects in the two drug groups than among controls, but this was primarily so during baseline recordings.

We noted earlier that in a study of postmenopausal women treated with replacement therapy, administration of a combined estrogen-progestin compound had no effect on the urinary excretion of catecholamines or cortisol during subjects' exposure to a series of cognitive stressors (Collins et al., 1985). In the same study, heart rate and blood pressure reactions to the experimental tasks were also assessed; these measures were similarly unaffected by the introduction of exogenous hormones. However, blood pressure measurements were obtained on only a portion of the participating women and were recorded following, not during, subjects' performance of the various tasks. These measurements revealed no overall effect of the experimental stimuli on subjects' blood pressures when post-task recordings were compared to control values. Since blood pressure was not significantly elevated following task periods, it is not surprising that Collins et al. (1985) found replacement therapy to have no effect on the magnitude of subjects' blood pressure responses. Thus, results of this study do not necessarily negate the positive findings reported by von Eiff et al. (1971).

In a study of gender differences in cardiovascular response (Neus & von Eiff, 1985), females recruited in a metropolitan setting showed less pronounced systolic blood pressure elevations during mental arithmetic than did males drawn from the same population. The systolic blood pressure responses of a separate group, composed of female college students, did not differ from the original male sample, suggesting that socioenvironmental variables might account for the apparent sex difference. However, the investigators noted that oral contraceptive use was much less prevalent among the student subjects. A subsequent comparison demonstrated that systolic blood pressure reactions to mental arithmetic in subjects using oral contraceptives were significantly smaller than those of women who did not. In addition, hemodynamic studies revealed that the marked rise in cardiac output typically seen during performance of a mental arithmetic task was partially offset, in the subjects taking oral contraceptives, by a concomitant and substantial fall in the total peripheral resistance. This result suggests that the oral contraceptives affected primarily subjects' vascular reactivity. To the extent that oral contraceptive use implies a more potent hormonal influence than that accompanying the normal cycling of endogenous hormones, these findings are consistent with the notion that, in women, reproductive hormones are associated with a reduced cardiovascular responsivity to stress.

Because levels of estradiol and progesterone are minimal following menopause, it is also of interest to contrast the cardiovascular reactions of pre- and postmenopausal women. In one such comparison (von Eiff et al., 1971), postmenopausal subjects did not differ significantly from normally cycling women in the magnitude of their heart rate or blood pressure responses to a mental arithmetic task. In this study, however, age differences among the comparison groups were quite large, as only 9 of 34 premenopausal subjects were over 40 years of age. In a more recent investigation by Matthews and Saab (1986), cardiovascular responses to several difficult tasks (a psychomotor challenge, mental arithmetic, and public speaking) were examined in postmenopausal women and among normally cycling controls of comparable age. Postmenopausal subjects exhibited greater increases in heart rate, relative to controls, across all task periods and showed larger systolic blood pressure responses during public speaking—the most potent of the three experimental stressors.

As in the study of neuroendocrine reactivity, several investigators have examined behaviorally induced cardiovascular responses in relation to hormonal variations occurring over the course of the menstrual cycle. For example, Ladisich (1977) required subjects to perform a memory task while receiving painful electric shocks at two laboratory sessions, which were scheduled eight days and one day prior to the expected onset of menstruation. Plasma progesterone concentrations were lower (as expected) on the latter occasion. The magnitude of heart rate acceleration seen during subjects' exposure to the experimental stressor, however, was significantly larger in the later session than when measured eight days before the predicted menses. Unfortunately, the authors' failure to present baseline heart rate data precludes a clear interpretation of these findings. In a related study, however, von Eiff et al. (1971) reported that progesterone levels during the luteal phase were inversely correlated with heart rate and diastolic blood pressure measurements recorded during mental arithmetic, but not with measurements obtained under resting conditions. Interestingly, in measurements obtained during the preovulatory phase, both the resting systolic blood pressure and systolic reactions to mental arithmetic correlated negatively with estimates of concurrent estrogenic activity. The latter relationship was observed, however, only among women 31 to 40 years of age.

In the preceding study, statistical comparison of subjects' physiologic responses in the pre- and postovulatory intervals was not reported, although the authors note that cardiovascular reactions to the experimental stressor were less pronounced during the luteal phase than in measurements obtained prior to ovulation. In our own laboratory, we observed that young adult females in the follicular phase of their menstrual cycles (days 7 to 11 of a prototypic 28-day cycle) exhibited significantly larger systolic pressure responses to two cognitive stressors (mental arithmetic and a difficult test of concept-forming abilities), relative to women examined during the luteal phase (days 17 to 22) (Polefrone & Manuck, 1984). While mean diastolic blood pressure responses were also somewhat greater among women tested in the follicular phase, subjects' heart rate reactions showed no phase-related differences. In addition to the blood pressure and heart rate measurements, we also assessed subjects' affective responses to the two experimental stimuli, in each of the two menstrual conditions. Analysis of these measures revealed no differences in the report of anxiety or anger (i.e., affects typically elicited by these laboratory tasks) between women tested in the follicular and luteal phases. Thus, the enhanced blood pressure responsivity observed during the follicular phase (when concentrations of the reproduction hormones are typically low) did not appear to be mediated by concomitant variability in subjects' emotional responses to the laboratory stimuli.

The foregoing data encourage speculation that the midluteal elevations of estradiol and progesterone are associated with attenuated vascular responses to behavioral stimuli. Largely contradictory results have been reported by Hastrup and Light (1984), however, and other investigators have observed no appreciable differences in cardiovascular responsivity as a function of menstrual phase (Carroll, Turner, Lee, & Stephenson, 1984; Collins et al., 1985; Strauss, Schultheiss, & Cohen, 1983). In the study reported by Hastrup and Light (1984), heart rate and blood pressure responses of young adult women, examined in the follicular or luteal phases of their menstrual cycles, were compared to those of age-matched males. During performance of a shock avoidance task, the "luteal" females showed elevations in heart rate and systolic blood pressure that were significantly greater than those of women tested in the follicular phase and about equal in magnitude to the responses of males. These findings are difficult to reconcile with our own, as the phase boundaries (estimated days for inclusion in each phase) were the same in both studies. About the only difference is that the elevated responses of luteal-phase subjects in the study of Hastrup and Light seem to reflect a heightened sympathetic influence on cardiac performance, as evidenced by the concomitant rises in heart rate and systolic blood pressure. These investigators also demonstrated previously that shock avoidance procedures exert a strong sympathetic effect on cardiac performance. In contrast, our results seem to favor a "vascular" interpretation, insofar as alterations in systolic and diastolic blood pressure, but not heart rate, discriminated women tested in the follicular and luteal phases. That the same hormonal events might be related inversely to two axes of hemodynamic function, however, is highly speculative, and certainly no conclusions are warranted on the basis of only these two studies.

There also exist a number of other, mostly negative findings in the literature. For instance, Collins et al. (1985) reported many differences in mood or affect across the menstrual cycle, but no variability in subjects' cardiovascular reactions to a series of cognitive and psychomotor challenges. Similar results are reported by Carroll et al. (1984) among women examined during the follicular and luteal phases. Although Strauss et al. (1983) also found no phase differences in subjects' cardiovascular responses to mental arithmetic and cold immersion, subjects here were seen only in the immediate pre- and postmenstrual intervals, when it would be expected that hormonal differences were minimal. In a recent investigation by Plante and Denney (1984), women tested during the menstrual period showed larger vasomotor responses (measured as changes in finger pulse volume) than subjects seen in either the midfollicular or luteal phases. In contrast to Collins et al. (1985), however, Plante and Denney (1984) observed no phase-associated changes in affective states such as anxiety, depression, or hostility. (As discussed above, Polefrone and Manuck, 1984, also found no differences in report of affective states.) Finally, Little and Zahn (1974) observed that the anticipatory heart rate deceleration typically seen during performance of a simple reaction time task (measured at ten intervals during the menstrual cycle) was greatest just prior to ovulation, but only among women under 25 years of age.

A number of methodologic points are relevant to the above studies. In the majority of investigations, menstrual phase was estimated by count of days alone and the occurrence of ovulation was assumed, but not established. The latter consideration is particularly important, since estimates of the frequency of anovulatory cycles range from 2 to 25 percent, depending upon sample characteristics (e.g., Friedman & Meares, 1979; Marshall, 1963). Also, no attempt has been made to correlate directly the magnitude of subjects' cardiovascular responses with concomitant measures of estradiol or progesterone concentrations. Study samples have also been quite small in many investigations, so it is likely that many of the studies cited possess, at best, marginal statistical power. Usually, too, women have been tested at a single point in time and during a single menstrual cycle. Important procedural details are lacking in many of the published reports, including the reliability of measurement instruments and the conditions under which baseline assessments were obtained. It is perhaps not surprising, then, that studies of the influence of menstrual phase on cardiovascular reactions to stress are inconsistent, or, more generally, without significant effects. Insofar as more potent manipulations (e.g., hormone replacement, oral contraceptives) and naturally occurring menopause have been found to be related to women's cardiovascular responsivity, however, continued study of the psychophysiologic correlates of hormonal variations occurring during the normal menstrual cycle is clearly warranted.

In this chapter we have reviewed recent literature concerning influences of gender and the female reproductive hormones on the magnitude of individuals' neuroendocrine and cardiovascular responsivity to psychological stimuli. The findings summarized here indicate that, relative to females, males show exaggerated reactions to stress in some, but not all of the variables measured. It has been observed consistently that both the plasma and urinary excretions of epinephrine rise more appreciably in males than in females during subjects' exposure to achievement-oriented laboratory tasks or stressors. Other neuroendocrine reactions either do not differ between males and females (e.g., norepinephrine), or show no consistent pattern related to gender (e.g., cortisol). Also, the few studies of influences of the reproductive hormones on catecholamine or cortisol responses to laboratory stressors reveal no consistent effects of menstrual phase, or, in postmenopausal women, of replacement therapy via an estrogen-progestin compound. Hence, only gender per se has yet been associated with variations in neuroendocrine reactivity, and even here on only one parameter of neuroendocrine response, epinephrine.

In regard to cardiovascular reactivity, there is some evidence that men exhibit larger systolic blood pressure responses and smaller heart rate reactions to psychological stressors than do women. These differences are inconsistently replicated across studies, however, and in at least one instance, males have shown larger heart rate responses than females. In contrast to the studies of neuroendocrine reactivity, investigations concerning the effects of female reproductive hormones on behaviorally elicited cardiovascular reactions reveal some significant associations. For example, it has been reported that among ovariectomized women, systolic blood pressure responses to laboratory stressors are reduced following administration of an estrogen or estrogen-progestin compound. An attenuated systolic blood pressure response to stressors has also been found to accompany the use of oral contraceptives. These findings, as well as a recent observation that heart rate and systolic blood pressure responses of postmenopausal women were greater than among premenopausal controls, suggest that the female reproductive hormones are associated with a reduced cardiovascular responsivity. On the other hand, studies conducted on women tested during different phases of the menstrual cycle have produced largely inconsistent results; in some investigations, female subjects' cardiovascular reactions appear to be greatest during the midfollicular phase, in other studies during the luteal phase, and in still others at the time of ovulation. There also exist several failures to demonstrate phase-dependent differences in heart rate or blood pressure responses to laboratory tasks, and almost all available studies suffer from a variety of methodologic deficiencies. Thus, the varying concentrations of endogenous reproductive hormones that occur across the normal menstrual cycle have yet shown no clear association with the patterning or magnitude of women's cardiovascular responses to stressors.

Where response differences among relevant subject groups have been observed, the role that characteristics of subjects other than gender may have played in the elicitation of such differences remains unclear. For example, there is one demonstration that gender differences in epinephrine excretion during subjects' performance of an achievement-oriented task are attenuated when female participants possess professional aspirations within a traditionally "masculine" field. Similarly, the cardiovascular reactions of men and women (as well as the presence or absence of a gender difference in cardiovascular response) are influenced significantly by such stimulus attributes as the interpersonal nature of the experimental stressor, and situational demands for competitiveness or cooperation. On the other hand, there are instances in which men and women do show significant differences on a specific response measure (e.g., epinephrine), yet exhibit equivalent arousal on other physiologic indices and appear to be equally engaged in the experimental task. With respect to cardiovascular reactivity, moreover, reported gender differences tend to be in opposite directions for systolic blood pressure and heart rate, a relationship that is difficult to attribute to concomitant behavioral differences between male and female participants. Overall, then, the present literature provides mixed evidence regarding a possible psychological origin of observed gender and hormonal influences on cardiovascular and neuroendocrine reactivity. It should be noted also that few investigators have attempted to assess the psychological attributes of subjects—be it sex-role orientation or subjective states at the time of testing—using measurement instruments commensurate in sensitivity with the indices of subjects' physiologic responsivity.

Finally, we introduced this chapter by noting the relative protection against cardiovascular disease experienced by premenopausal women, compared to males of comparable age, and the failure of traditional risk factors to account for this well-established gender difference. We suggested that insofar as individuals' physiologic responsivity to stress may contribute to cardiovascular disease, any corresponding sex difference in psychophysiologic reactivity (or covariation of such reactivity with reproductive hormone variations in women) might help to explain the phenomenon of "female protection." While the pathogenetic significance of psychophysiologic reactivity itself reflects a relatively new area of investigation, there is some evidence that heightened cardiovascular responses to stressors are associated, in an animal model, with the development of coronary artery atherosclerosis (Clarkson et al., 1986; Manuck, Kaplan, & Clarkson, 1985). These findings are based on studies of cynomolgus monkeys, which exhibit atherosclerotic lesions that are similar to those seen in human beings; likewise, females of this species show less extensive coronary atherosclerosis than do their male counterparts. Among female cynomolgus monkeys, moreover, animals that exhibit ovarian endocrine deficiencies (or low luteal-phase progesterone concentrations) also experience the largest cardiac responses to stress and develop the most severe coronary artery atherosclerosis. Interestingly, the relationship between low progesterone and enhanced cardiovascular reactivity in this animal model is consistent with studies cited previously regarding effects of the female reproductive hormones on cardiovascular responsivity in human beings. Whether influences of ovarian function and gender on the incidence of *human* coronary heart disease are mediated, in part, by concomitant differences in individuals' physiologic responsivity to stress will of course ultimately be determined only by prospective clinical investigation.

NOTES

1. Some investigators have suggested that males' elevated cardiovascular risk is due less to the absence of a protective variable common to women than to a potentiating factor in men, such as androgens. However, there is yet little evidence that male reproductive hormones play a significant role in the development of cardiovascular disease (Stout, 1982), nor is there an established literature regarding the influence of androgens on psychophysiologic reactivity.

2. Hormonal events occurring during the normal menstrual cycle may be summarized briefly. The principal hormones of interest, estradiol and progesterone, as well as follicle stimulating hormone (FSH) and luteinizing hormone (LH), remain at relatively low levels through much of the follicular, or preovulatory interval. At around the tenth follicular day (of a prototypic 28-day cycle), there is an upward surge of estradiol, FSH, and LH, with the production of these hormones peaking at ovulation (about day 14). Although FSH and LH fall again to low levels after ovulation, estradiol concentrations drop only moderately and remain elevated through most of the luteal, or postovulatory menstrual phase. With formation of the corpus luteum at ovulation, there is also a surge in the production of progesterone; indeed, the absence of a sharp rise in progesterone concentration during the luteal phase is an indicator of the failure of ovulation. Finally, estradiol and progesterone levels both fall quickly in the premenstrual interval, which begins at about day 24.

REFERENCES

Abplanalp, J. M., Livingston, L., Rose, R. M., & Sandwisch, D. (1977). Cortisol and growth hormone responses to psychological stress during the menstrual cycle. *Psychosomatic Medicine, 39,* 158–177.

Akerstedt, T., Gillberg, M., Hjemdahl, P., Sigurdson, K., Gustavsson, I., Daleskog, M., & Polare, T. (1983). Comparison of urinary and plasma catecholamine responses to mental stress. *Acta Physiologica Scandinavica, 117,* 119–126.

Aslan, S., Nelson, L., Carruthers, M., & Lader, M. (1981). Stress and age effects on catecholamines in normal subjects. *The Journal of Psychosomatic Research, 25,* 33–41.

Asterita, M. F. (1985). *The physiology of stress.* New York: Human Sciences Press.

Awaritefe, A., & Kadiri, A. U. (1982). The state-trait anxiety inventory and sex. *Physiology and Behavior, 29,* 211–213.

Berne, R. M., & Levy, M. N. (1977). *Cardiovascular physiology.* St. Louis: C. V. Mosby.

Carroll, D., Turner, J. R., Lee, H. J., & Stephenson, J. (1984). Temporal consistency of individual differences in cardiac response to a video game. *Biological Psychology, 19,* 81–93.

Clarkson, T. B., Manuck, S. B., & Kaplan, J. R. (1986). Potential role of cardiovascular reactivity in the pathogenesis of atherosclerosis. In K. D. Matthews, S. M. Weiss, T. Detre, T. M. Dembroski, B. Falkner, S. B. Manuck, & R. B. Williams (Eds.), *Handbook of stress, reactivity and cardiovascular disease.* New York: Wiley-Interscience.

Collins, A., Eneroth, P., & Landgren, B. (1985). Psychoneuroendocrine stress responses and mood as related to the menstrual cycle. *Psychosomatic Medicine, 47,* 512–527.

Collins, A., & Frankenhaeuser, M. (1978). Stress responses in male and female engineering students. *Journal of Human Stress, 4,* 43–48.

Collins, A., Hanson, U., Eneroth, P., Hagenfeldt, K., Lundberg, U., & Frankenhaeuser, M. (1982). Psychophysiological stress responses in postmenopausal women before and after hormonal replacement therapy. *Human Neurobiology, 1,* 153–159.

Dembroski, T. M., MacDougall, J. M., Cardozo, S. R., Ireland, S. K., & KrugFite, J. (1985). Selective cardiovascular effects of stress and cigarette smoking in young women. *Health Psychology, 4,* 153–167.

Dimsdale, J. E., & Moss, J. (1980). Plasma catecholamines in stress and exercise. *Journal of the American Medical Association, 243,* 340–342.

Forsman, L., & Lindblad, L. E. (1983). Effect of mental stress on baroreceptor-mediated changes in blood pressure and heart rate and on plasma catecholamines and subjective responses in healthy men and women. *Psychosomatic Medicine, 45,* 435–455.

Frankenhaeuser, M., Dunne, E., & Lundberg, U. (1976). Sex differences in sympathetic-adrenal medullary reactions induced by different stressors. *Psychopharmacology, 47,* 1–5.

Frankenhaeuser, M., Lundberg, U., & Forsman, L. (1980). Dissociation between sympathetic-adrenal and pituitary-adrenal responses to an achievement situation characterized by high controllability: Comparison between Type A and Type B males and females. *Biological Psychology, 10,* 79–91.

Frankenhaeuser, M., Rauste-von Wright, M., Collins, A., von Wright, J., Sedvall, G., & Swahn, C. (1978). Sex differences in psychoneuroendocrine reactions to examination stress. *Psychosomatic Medicine, 40,* 334–343.

Friedman, J., & Meares, R. A. (1979). The menstrual cycle and habituation. *Psychosomatic Medicine, 41,* 369–381.

Goldstein, D. S., Levinson, P., & Keiser, H. R. (1983). Plasma and urinary catecholamines during the human ovulatory cycle. *American Journal of Obstetrics and Gynecology, 146,* 824–829.

Goldstein, D. S., & McDonald, R. H. (1986). Biochemical indices of cardiovascular reactivity. In K. A. Matthews, S. M. Weiss, T. Detre, T. M. Dembroski, B. Falkner, S. B. Manuck, & R. B. Williams (Eds.), *Handbook of stress, reactivity and cardiovascular disease.* New York: Wiley-Interscience.

Graham, L. A., Cohen, S. I., & Schmavonian, B. M. (1966). Sex differences in autonomic responses during instrumental conditioning. *Psychosomatic Medicine, 28,* 264–270.

Hastrup, J. L., & Light, K. C. (1984). Sex differences in cardiovascular stress responses: Modulation as a function of menstrual cycle phases. *Journal of Psychosomatic Research, 28,* 475–483.

Herd, J. A. (1983). Physiological basis for behavioral influences in atherosclerosis. In T. M. Dembroski, T. H. Schmidt, & G. Blumchen (Eds.), *Biobehavioral bases of coronary heart disease.* Basel, Switzerland: Karger.

Johansson, G. (1972). Sex differences in the catecholamine output of children. *Acta Physiologica Scandinavica, 85,* 569–572.

Johansson, G., & Post, B. (1974). Catecholamine output of males and females over a one-year period. *Acta Physiologica Scandinavica, 92,* 557–565.

Jorgenson, R. S., & Houston, B. K. (1981). The Type A behavior pattern, sex differences and cardiovascular response to and recovery from stress. *Motivation and Emotion, 5,* 201–214.

Kannel, W. B. (1982). Incidence, prevalence, and mortality of cardiovascular disease. In J. W. Hurst (Ed.), *The heart* (5th ed.). New York: McGraw-Hill.

Kannel, W. B., Hjortland, M., McNamara, P., & Gordon, T. (1976). Menopause and risk of cardiovascular disease. The Framingham Heart Study. *Annals of Internal Medicine, 85,* 447–452.

Krantz, D. S., & Manuck, S. B. (1984). Acute psychophysiologic reactivity and risk of cardiovascular disease: A review and methodologic critique. *Psychological Bulletin, 96,* 435–464.

Ladisich, W. (1977). Influence of progesterone on serotonin metabolism: A possible causal factor for mood changes. *Psychoneuroendocrinology, 2,* 257–266.

Lane, J. D., White, A. D., & Williams, R. B. (1984). Cardiovascular effects of mental arithmetic in Type A and Type B females. *Psychophysiology, 21,* 39–46.

Lawler, K. A., Rixse, A., & Allen, M. T. (1983). Type A behavior and psychophysiological responses in adult women. *Psychophysiology, 20,* 343–350.

Lawler, K. A., Schmied, L., Mitchell, V. P., & Rixse, A. (1984). Type A behavior and physiological responsivity in young women. *Journal of Psychosomatic Research, 28,* 197–204.

Liberson, C. W., & Liberson, W. T. (1975). Sex differences in autonomic responses to electric shock. *Psychophysiology, 12,* 182–186.

Little, B. C., & Zahn, T. P. (1974). Changes in mood and autonomic functioning during the menstrual cycle. *Psychophysiology, 11,* 579–590.

Lorimer, A. R., Macfarlane, P. W., Provan, G., Duffy, T., & Lawrie, T. D. V. (1971). Blood pressure and catecholamine responses to stress in normotensive and hypertensive subjects. *Cardiovascular Research, 5,* 169–173.

Lundberg, U. (1983). Sex differences in behaviour pattern and catecholamine and cortisol excretion in 3–6 year old day-care children. *Biological Psychology, 16,* 109–117.

Lundberg, U., Chateau, P. de, Winberg, J., & Frankenhaeuser, M. (1981). Catecholamine and cortisol excretion patterns in three-year-old children and their parents. *Journal of Human Stress, 7,* 3–11.

Lundberg, U., & Forsman, L. (1979a). Consistency in catecholamine and cortisol excretion patterns over experimental conditions. *Pharmacology, Biochemistry & Behavior, 12*, 449–452.

———. (1979b). Adrenal-medullary and adrenal-cortical responses to understimulation and overstimulation: Comparison between Type A and Type B persons. *Biological Psychology, 9*, 79–89.

MacDougall, J. M., Dembroski, T. M., & Krantz, D. S. (1981). Effects of types of challenge on pressor and heart rate responses in Type A and B women. *Psychophysiology, 18*, 1–9.

Manuck, S. B., Craft, S., & Gold, K. J. (1978). Coronary-prone behavior pattern and cardiovascular response. *Psychophysiology, 15*, 403–411.

Manuck, S. B., Kaplan, J. R., & Clarkson, T. B. (1985). Stress-induced heart rate reactivity and atherosclerosis in female macaques. *Psychosomatic Medicine, 47*, 90 (Abstract).

Manuck, S. B., Kaplan, J. R., & Matthews, K. A. (1986). Behavioral antecedents of coronary heart disease and atherosclerosis. *Arteriosclerosis, 6*, 2–14.

Manuck, S. B., & Krantz, D. S. (1984). Psychophysiologic reactivity in coronary heart disease. *Behavioral Medicine Update, 6*, 11–15.

———. (1986). Psychophysiologic reactivity in coronary heart disease and hypertension. In K. A. Matthews, S. M. Weiss, T. Detre, T. M. Dembroski, B. Falkner, S. B. Manuck, & R. B. Williams, Jr. (Eds.), *Handbook of stress, reactivity, and cardiovascular disease*. New York: Wiley-Interscience.

Marinari, K. T., Leshner, A. I., & Doyle, M. P. (1976). Menstrual cycle status and adrenocortical reactivity to psychological stress. *Psychoneuroendocrinology, 1*, 213–218.

Marshall, J. (1963). Thermal changes in the normal menstrual cycle. *British Medical Journal, 1*, 102–104.

Matthews, K. A., & Saab, P. (1986). Personal communication.

Myrsten, A., Lundberg, U., Frankenhaeuser, M., Ryan, G., Dolphin, C., & Cullen, J. (1984). Sex-role orientation as related to psychological and physiological responses during achievement and orthostatic stress. *Motivation and Emotion, 8*, 243–258.

Neus, H., & von Eiff, A. W. (1985). Selected topics in the methodology of stress testing: Time course, gender and adaptation. In A. Steptoe, H. Ruddel, & H. Neus (Eds.), *Clinical and methodological issues in cardiovascular psychophysiology*. Berlin: Springer.

Obrist, P. (1981). *Cardiovascular psychophysiology*. New York: Plenum.

Plante, T. G., & Denney, D. R. (1984). Stress responsivity among dysmenorrheic women at different phases of their menstrual cycle: More ado about nothing. *Behavior Research & Therapy, 22*, 2491–258.

Polefrone, J. M., & Manuck, S. B. (1984). Parental hypertension, menstrual phase and cardiovascular response to cognitive challenge. Paper presented at the Fifth Annual Meeting of the Society of Behavioral Medicine, Philadelphia.

Rauste-von Wright, M., von Wright, J., & Frankenhaeuser, M. (1981). Relationships between sex-related psychological characteristics during adolescence and catecholamine excretion during achievement stress. *Psychophysiology, 18,* 362–370.

Rowland, M., & Roberts, J. (1980). *Blood pressure levels and hypertension in persons ages 6–74 years: United States, 1976–1980* (Vital and Health Statistics Report No. 84). Washington, DC: National Center for Health Statistics.

Schneiderman, N. (1983). Behavior, autonomic function and animal models of cardiovascular pathology. In T. M. Dembroski, T. H. Schmidt, & G. Blumchen (Eds.), *Biobehavioral bases of coronary heart disease.* Basel, Switzerland: Karger.

Stout, R. W. (1982). *Hormones and atherosclerosis.* Boston: MTP Press.

Strauss, B., Schultheiss, M., & Cohen, R. (1983). Autonomic reactivity in the premenstrual phase. *British Journal of Clinical Psychology, 22,* 1–9.

Troxler, R. G., Sprague, E. A., Albanese, R. A., Fuchs, R., & Thompson, A. J. (1977). The association of elevated plasma cortisol and early atherosclerosis as demonstrated by coronary angiography. *Atherosclerosis, 26,* 151–162.

Van Egeren, L. F. (1979). Cardiovascular changes during social competition in a mixed-motive game. *Journal of Personality and Social Psychology, 37,* 858–864.

von Eiff, A. W., Plotz, E. J., Beck, K. J., & Czernik, A. (1971). The effect of estrogens and progestins on blood pressure regulation of normotensive women. *American Journal of Obstetrics and Gynecology, 109,* 887–892.

Ward, M. M., Mefford, I. N., Parker, S. D., Chesney, M. A., Taylor, B. B., Keegan, D. L., & Barchas, J. D. (1983). Epinephrine and norepinephrine responses in continuously collected human plasma to a series of stressors. *Psychosomatic Medicine, 45,* 471–486.

Wasilewska, E., Kobus, E., & Bargiel, Z. (1980). Urinary catecholamine excretion and plasma dopamine-beta-hydroxylase activity in mental work performed in two periods of menstrual cycle in women. In E. Usdine, R. Kvetnansky, & I. J. Kaplan (Eds.), *Catecholamines and stress: Recent advances.* New York: Elsevier.

Wright, R. A., Contrada, R. J., & Glass, D. C. (1985). Psychophysiologic correlates of Type A behavior. In E. S. Katkin & S. B. Manuck (Eds.), *Advances in behavioral medicine.* Greenwich, CT: JAI Press.

2

Gender Differences
in Stress-Related Disorders

Paul D. Cleary

Exposure to stressors can affect people in innumerable ways. These effects can be physical, psychological, and social, they may be subtle or dramatic, and they may occur immediately or manifest themselves over the course of a lifetime. A thorough analysis of gender differences in stress-related outcomes ideally would (1) discuss how stressors are related to gender as a result of biological, psychological, and social factors; (2) review the data on the association between different types of gender-related stressors and various types of morbidity and mortality; and (3) present data on gender differences in morbidity and mortality that are known to be related to gender-specific stressors. Furthermore, the importance of these associations would be evaluated, in part, in terms of how commonly morbidity or mortality is associated with various forms of gender-related stressors.

Because of the diversity and complexity of stress-related outcomes and the difficulty of studying the relationships between stressors and various outcomes, it is not possible to provide definitive data concerning any of the specific topics listed above except for the relative frequency with which different types of outcomes occur. However, there is a tremendous amount of evidence that indirectly addresses these issues. We know a great deal about sex differences in morbidity and mortality, we now know that some of those outcomes are almost certainly caused, at least in part, by stressors and there is an accumulating body of evidence about the way that social roles are related to psychological distress.

Work on this chapter was supported by NIMH grant MH15783.

The outcomes most clearly related to stressors are psychiatric illness and psychological distress. The first part of this chapter reviews gender differences in the occurrence of psychiatric disorders and examines some of the research investigating whether these differences are due to gender-related roles. The second part of the chapter reviews gender differences in physical morbidity and mortality and examines the data on the linkages between gender roles and these outcomes. For each of these areas, there is a review of the basic findings, a summary of how these relationships have changed over time, and a brief discussion of some of the more plausible mechanisms that help explain gender differences.

GENDER DIFFERENCES IN MENTAL HEALTH

Several authors have advanced the argument that women are more likely than men to experience mental illness and that women's social roles are primarily responsible for the difference (Bernard, 1972; Gove & Tudor, 1973). For example, Gove and Tudor (Gove, 1978; Gove & Tudor, 1973, 1977) have asserted that women are more likely to view themselves as having emotional problems, to seek help for such problems from general practitioners and psychiatrists, to receive psychiatric treatment in outpatient clinics, and to receive more psychotropic medications. However, many of these conclusions are a function of the types of data used and the way psychiatric illness is defined (Dohrenwend & Dohrenwend, 1976; Mechanic, 1980). For example, Gove and colleagues base their conclusions primarily on treatment data and exclude treatment for certain conditions. Other researchers agree that more women than men are depressed (Hammen, 1982; Silverman, 1968; Weissman & Klerman, 1977). However, when overall prevalence rates for mental illness based on community data are examined, there are no sex differences. The results from the most recent community studies indicate that about 17 to 23 percent of adults have at least one disorder. When antisocial personality and alcohol and drug abuse are included, men and women have similar rates of disorders.

Limitations of Available Data

All epidemiologic findings are a function of the definitions, measures, and estimation techniques used. However, these issues are especially problematic in psychiatric epidemiology (see, e.g., Hammen, 1982). Therefore, in this section substantial attention will be devoted to the concerns that some researchers have expressed about nosological and methodological issues.

The earliest data used to assess gender differences were treatment data

(Belle & Goldman, 1980; Kramer, Pollack, Redick, & Locke, 1972; Vischi, Jones, Shank, & Lima, 1980). Making unambiguous interpretations from these data is especially problematic. Limitations include unrepresentative samples, unreliable diagnostic data, and the fact that cases in treatment may seriously underestimate true prevalence rates. If recognition, labeling, help seeking, and provider response are different for men and women (as we think they may well be), then treatment rates are seriously confounded indicators of prevalence differences.

A second type of social-epidemiologic study typically selects a representative sample of the community and administers a brief symptom checklist or rating scale to respondents (Cleary & Mechanic, 1983; Frerichs, Aneshensel, & Clark, 1981; Goldman & Ravid, 1980; Sayetta & Johnson, 1980). Once again, virtually all these surveys find that women report more symptoms of distress than men. One of the few early community studies that attempted a more valid assessment—using an interview that indicated whether respondents met diagnostic criteria—did not find statistically significant differences (Weissman & Myers, 1978). However, the lack of significant differences may have been due to the small sample size; the rates of disorder in that study were similar to rates in other studies.

Problems with symptom scales include the fact that they often have limited content validity (Craig & Van Natta, 1979; Newmann; 1984). For example, responses to certain scales are sometimes difficult to interpret because of the inclusion of physical symptoms (Thoits, 1981). Other methodological problems in these types of surveys include unknown refusal rates, small sample sizes, and inappropriate statistical techniques (Hammen, 1982). In fact, Parker has concluded, after a critical review of numerous studies that " . . . depression was not measured in some studies, that it can only be inferred in others, that sex differences were not examined in some studies, and not found in others" (Parker, p. 128, cited in Hammen, 1982).

Recently, several studies collectively referred to as the Epidemiologic Catchment Area (ECA) Studies have been conducted in the United States. The studies involve structured interviews with about 20,000 community residents in Baltimore, New Haven, Piedmont (North Carolina), St. Louis, and Los Angeles (Eaton, Regier, Locke, & Taube, 1981; Regier, Myers, Kramer, Robins, Blazer, Hough, Eaton, & Locke, 1984). Each of the ECA sites sampled more than 3000 community residents and 500 residents of institutions. The three ECA sites for which results are available have interviewed 10,000 respondents in the general population, plus a sample of 2000 elderly respondents in New Haven.

One of the most important features of the ECA studies is that they incorporated new assessment techniques. The three principal diagnostic instruments used currently in the United States are the Schedule for Affective Disorders and Schizophrenia (SADS), the Renard Diagnostic Interview, and the Present State Examination (Myers, Weissman, Tischler, Holzer, Leaf, Orvaschel, Anthony, Boyd, Burke, Kramer, & Stoltzman, 1984). Unfortunately, the use of these instruments requires clinically trained interviewers. Therefore, the National Institute of Mental Health funded the development of an instrument that can be used in large studies of general populations, the Diagnostic Interview Schedule (DIS). The DIS is a structured interview that asks about symptoms—their severity, frequency, time of occurrence—and whether reported symptoms are due to physical illness, drugs, alcohol, or other psychiatric conditions. A computer program can determine two-week, one-month, six-month, one-year, and lifetime prevalence rates. There has been criticism of this instrument, some of which will be reviewed in a subsequent section. However, community data collected using the DIS currently represent our best information about the prevalence of psychiatric disorders in the population.

DIS diagnoses are based on criteria from the third edition of the *Diagnostic and Statistical Manual of Mental Disorders* (DSM-III), but not all DSM-III diagnoses are covered. The diagnoses covered were selected on the basis of expected prevalence, severity and clinical importance, research interest, and validity as indicated from other research (Myers et al., 1984). The results discussed below from the ECA studies are limited to agoraphobia, alcohol abuse/dependence, antisocial personality, drug abuse/dependence, dysthymia (chronic depressed mood), major depression, manic disorder, obsessive-compulsive disorder, panic disorder, schizophrenia or schizophreniform disorder, phobia, and somatization disorder. Preliminary estimates of six-month and lifetime prevalence rates are available from the first wave of adult household interviews at three sites. The data on the six-month prevalence of psychiatric disorders are from Myers et al. (1984), and the data on lifetime prevalence rates are from a paper by Robins and colleagues (Robins, Helzer, Weissman, Orvaschel, Gruenberg, Burke, & Reiger, 1984). Data on affective disorders are presented for all five sites (Weissman, Leaf, Tischler, Blazer, Karno, Bruce, & Florio, in press).

In the following sections I review the data for different types of psychiatric disorder. Summaries are presented of treatment data, as well as the more current results from the ECA studies. A summary of the six-month prevalence rates from three of the ECA sites is presented in Table 1 and a summary of the lifetime prevalence rates is presented in Table 2.

Affective disorders. Weissman and Klerman (1977) reviewed 40 studies from 30 countries conducted prior to the ECA studies and found that, with few exceptions, women were two to three times as likely as men to be depressed. Boyd and Weissman (1981) reassessed studies of depression and

Table 1. Six-Month Prevalence of DIS/DSM-III Disorders by Sex: Range of Prevalence Rates (%) Across Three Sites

Disorder	Men	Women
Major depressive episode without bereavement	1.3–2.2	2.2–3.5
Depression due to bereavement	0.0–0.2	0.1–0.3
Manic episode	0.4–0.8	0.4–0.8
Dysthymia	1.2–2.6	2.1–3.8
Panic	0.3–0.8	0.6–1.0
Obsessive-compulsive disorder	0.9–1.9	1.3–2.0
Alcohol abuse/dependence	8.2–10.4	4.5–5.7
Drug abuse/dependence	2.5–3.0	1.8–2.2
Somatization disorder	0.0–0.0	0.1–0.1
Antisocial personality	0.8–2.1	0.6–1.3
Cognitive impairment		
Mild	4.0–6.2	4.0–5.9
Severe	1.1–1.4	1.0–1.3
Schizophrenia or schizophreniform disorder	0.7–0.9	0.6–1.2
Total phobia	2.8–8.6	5.4–13.4

SOURCE: Adapted from Myers et al. (1984).

Table 2. Lifetime Prevalence of DIS/DSM-III Psychiatric Disorders by Sex:[1] Range of Prevalence Rates (%) Across Three Sites

Disorder	Men	Women
Major depressive episode	2.3–4.4	4.9–8.7
Manic episode	0.8–1.1	0.5–1.3
Dysthymia	1.2–2.6	2.9–5.4
Schizophrenia	1.0–1.2	1.1–2.6
Simple phobia	3.8–14.5	8.5–25.9
Agoraphobia	1.5–5.2	5.3–12.5
Panic disorder	0.6–1.2	1.6–2.1
Obsessive-compulsive disorder	1.1–2.6	2.6–6.3
Somatization disorder	0.0–0.0	0.2–0.3
Alcohol abuse/dependence	19.1–28.9	4.2–4.8
Drug abuse/dependence	6.5–7.4	3.8–5.1
Antisocial personality	3.9–4.9	0.5–1.2
Cognitive impairment	1.0–1.4	1.1–1.4
Any of the covered diagnoses	30.6–39.6	25.7–36.7

[1]Rates for anorexia and schizophreniform disorder too infrequent to be reported by sex.

SOURCE: Adapted from Robins et al. (1984).

applied the DSM-III criteria of affective disorder. They concluded that the rates of bipolar disorder were approximately equal in men and women, but women were more likely than men to be depressives who were not bipolar.

Most of the studies reviewed by Weissman and her colleagues used symptom scales to assess depressive symptoms (cf. Weissman & Myers, 1978), but the ECA studies permit an examination of rates of specific DSM-III disorders as determined by a standardized interview. The main forms of affective disorder are major depression, bipolar disorder (major depression plus mania occurring at some time in the person's life), and dysthymia.

The one-year prevalence rates for major depression in the five ECA sites range from 1.7 percent in Piedmont to 3.4 percent in New Haven (Weissman, Leaf, Holzer, Myers, & Tischler, 1984; Weissman et al., in press). The ratios of the female to male rates of major depression range from 1.9 to 5.0, with the ratio in the combined sample being 2.7. The lifetime rate of dysthymia in the five samples was 3.1 percent, with the sex ratios ranging between 1.5 in New Haven and 3.0 in Piedmont. In the combined samples, women are 1.9 times as likely to have experienced dysthymia as men.

Bipolar disorder is less common, in general, and is not more prevalent among women. The one-year prevalence rates of bipolar disorder in the five ECA sites range from 0.6 percent in Piedmont and Los Angeles to 1.4 percent in St. Louis. The sex ratio of one-year prevalence rates for bipolar disorder was 1.2 in the combined sample. Weissman et al. (in press) review these data as well as data from other studies of major depression that use either Research Diagnostic Criteria or DSM-III criteria. Whereas other published rates are generally higher than those reported here, all studies find that the rate of major depression is higher among women than among men. The results from a 1975 study in New Haven (Weissman & Myers, 1978) were consistent with the ECA studies in that there were no sex differences in prevalence of bipolar depression. The results of these studies, as well as those from three large family studies (see Weissman & Klerman, 1985) provide compelling evidence that the rates of major depression are about twice as high among women as among men and that the rates of bipolar disorder are approximately equal.

Schizophrenia. There are no sex differences in the rates of hospital admissions for schizophrenia. However, there are several interesting gender differences with respect to the experience of schizophrenia. For example, males tend to be admitted at a younger age than females; women are more likely than men to report delusions but are equally likely to report hallucinations. Schizophrenia among women is more likely to have been precipitated by environmental events, and there are more female than male chronic schizophrenics in hospitals (Al-Issa, 1982).

In the ECA studies, the six-month prevalence rates for schizophrenia varied between 0.6 and 1.2 percent. However, because of changes in the diagnostic interview, the criteria varied slightly among the sites. Women were slightly less likely to have experienced schizophrenia or schizophreniform disorder in St. Louis (0.6 percent vs. 0.9 percent), but they had higher rates in New Haven and Baltimore (1.1 vs. 0.7 percent and 1.2 vs. 0.7 percent respectively). Lifetime rates were slightly higher in all the sites, but the difference was statistically significant only in New Haven (2.6 vs. 1.2 percent).

Phobia. A phobia is a persistent and irrational fear of a specific object, activity, or situation that results in compelling feelings of avoidance (American Psychiatric Association, 1980). Fodor (1982) has reviewed the clinical, research, and theoretical literature on phobias and concluded that a disproportionately large number of women and a small number of men are treated for phobias.

In the ECA studies, the six-month prevalence of phobias ranged from 5.4 percent in St. Louis to 13.4 percent in Baltimore. The lifetime rates ranged from 7.8 percent in New Haven to 23.3 percent in Baltimore. In each of the sites both the six-month and lifetime prevalence rates for each phobia assessed (i.e., simple phobia, agoraphobia, and social phobia) were higher for women than for men.

Panic and obsessive compulsive disorder. In the ECA studies, the six-month rates of panic disorder ranged from 0.6 to 1.0 percent and the lifetime rates were between 1.4 percent and 1.5 percent. The rates for women were consistently higher, although the differences were not large, except in New Haven where the lifetime rates for men and women were 0.6 percent and 2.1 percent, respectively. Similarly, the rates of obsessive compulsive disorder were similar in the three sites and consistently higher for women.

Substance abuse. Alcohol use is more common among men than women in North America. Data compiled from a number of general population surveys by Leland (1982) indicate that about 20 percent more men than women use alcohol. Furthermore, the proportion of males increases at higher drinking levels (see also Robins & Smith, 1980).

Most data on alcohol use come from general population surveys, but there are a variety of indirect indicators of alcohol use such as alcohol-related morbidity and mortality, and alcohol-related accidents and crimes (Cleary, 1978, 1979). Leland (1982), in a review of available studies of alcohol use and abuse, concludes that the best current estimates indicate that men are about three times as likely as women to be problem drinkers and that if one examines measures more closely related to clinically defined alcoholism, the ratio is about 4 to 1. The ratio of male to female drinkers is similar for blacks and whites, whereas the ratio of male to female heavy drinkers is about twice as high for whites as blacks. The proportion of males who drink heavily is similar in different income groups, but the proportion of women who drink heavily increases slightly with income. The ratio of male to female drinkers appears to be relatively stable over time (Ferrence, 1980).

In the ECA studies, the six-month prevalence of alcohol abuse or dependence was between 4.5 percent and 10.4 percent and the rates for drug abuse and dependence were between 1.8 percent and 3.0 percent. At all sites for both alcohol and drugs, the rates of abuse and/or dependence were significantly higher for men than for women. Lifetime rates of alcohol abuse/dependence were significantly higher for men at all sites and rates of drug abuse/dependence were higher at two of the sites.

Illicit drug use is extremely difficult to measure accurately. However, data from surveys conducted by the National Institute on Drug Abuse indicate that more men than women have tried illegal drugs at least once. Men and women are equally likely to be currently using drugs, but men tend to be heavier or more frequent users (Fidell, 1982).

With respect to prescribed drugs, one of the most consistent findings is that women are more likely than men to use psychotropic drugs (Biener, this volume; Chambers & Griffey, 1975; Copperstock, 1971, 1978, 1979; Guttman, 1978; Lech, Friedman, & Ury, 1975; Shapiro & Baron, 1961; Stolley, Becker, McEvilla, Lasagna, Gainor, & Sloane, 1972; Uhlenhuth, Balter, & Lipman, 1978).

Antisocial personality. Antisocial personality disorder had a six-month prevalence of 0.6 to 2.1 percent in the three ECA sites described by Myers et al. (1984). The rates were significantly higher among men in Baltimore and St. Louis. The lifetime prevalence of antisocial personality ranged from 2.1 percent in New Haven to 3.3 percent in St. Louis. In each study, men had significantly higher rates.

Suicide. Suicide accounted for 23,480 deaths in 1970 and for 26,869 in 1980. In all, suicides were responsible for at least 287,322 deaths in the United States between 1970 and 1980. The data are very consistent in showing that more men than women commit suicide (Farberow & Schneidman, 1961; Maris, 1969, 1981; Stengel, 1969). About 72.8 percent of suicide deaths occurred among males. However, the number of attempts is much higher than the number of successful suicides, and women are much more likely to attempt suicide. The implications of the data on suicides will be discussed later in the context of how they have changed over time.

Age Differences

Since many of the results from the ECA studies have been reported for different age groups, it is possible to examine how the prevalence of different disorders varies by age. The age trends are complex, but interestingly, the rates for both sexes for all disorders except phobia and dysthymia were substantially lower for persons older than 45. Within sexes, however, the relative prevalence of different disorders varies over the lifespan. Alcohol abuse and dependence predominate for men aged 18 to 24, followed closely by drug abuse and/or dependence. For women in the same age range, phobias are the most common disorder, followed by drug abuse/dependence and major depression. Between the ages of 25 and 44, alcohol abuse/dependence continues to be the most common disorder for men, followed by phobias and drug abuse/dependence. Women in this age range are most affected by phobias and major depression. Between 45 and 64, the most common disorders for men are alcohol abuse/dependence and phobia. For women, the most common conditions are phobias and dysthymia. For respondents over 65, the most prevalent disorders for men are severe cognitive impairment, phobias, and alcohol abuse/dependence. For women over 65 the most common disorders are phobias and severe cognitive impairment.

Critique of the DIS and DSM-III

The ECA data are better than previously available data because they were collected using a standardized clinical assessment instrument, but the DIS has potential limitations. For example, Kaplan (1983) has asserted that a bias inherent in the use of DSM-III criteria for defining mental illness contributes to sex differences in recorded rates of psychiatric illness. Although her main arguments center on personality disorders, her critique is quite general. Kaplan believes women may be more likely to be labeled as impaired if they assume nontraditional roles, because to do so may be viewed as inadequate social functioning.

In response to Kaplan's critique, Williams and Spitzer (1983) present data from field trials of DSM-III and evaluate the extent to which the sex ratios of the major Axis I clinical syndromes and Axis II personality disorders are consistent with Kaplan's hypothesis. In general, their analysis of Kaplan's critique fails to support her contention that masculine-biased assumptions are codified in the criteria. Kass, Spitzer, and Williams (1983) examined the sex ratios of all of the DSM-III Axis II personality disorders among 2712 patients in the second phase of the DSM-III field trials and among 531 newly evaluated outpatients and found that female patients were no more likely to be diagnosed as having a personality disorder than male patients. Their examination of specific personality disorders in both samples revealed that only a few disorders were diagnosed more commonly in one of the sexes. In summary, there was no overall tendency for women to receive more diagnoses of a personality disorder; thus Kaplan's thesis was not supported.

Trends Over Time

To the extent that mental disorders are due to the strains inherent in social roles, one would expect that as those roles change there should be corresponding changes in the rates of disorder. Also, changes in the relative rates of disorder among men and women may provide information about the changing nature of gender roles. For example, Gove and Tudor (1973) argue that women's position in American society has undergone dramatic shifts and that after World War II, women's traditional roles became less meaningful. They suggest that with industrialization and the emergence of the small nuclear family, women's child rearing years were shortened, and domestic skills were replaced by modern conveniences. Furthermore, women were receiving more education, which led them to be less satisfied with their homemaking role. To support their position, Gove and Tudor cite studies suggesting that men were more likely than women to be admitted to mental hospitals prior to World War II, whereas this trend was reversed after the war. They point out that a review of community studies published by the Dohrenwends (Dohrenwend & Dohrenwend, 1969) is consistent with such a trend.

Subsequent to Gove and Tudor's paper, Dohrenwend and Dohrenwend (1976) updated their coverage of the epidemiological literature to include over 80 studies of psychiatric disorders in communities. Overall rates in the North American and European studies were consistently higher for men in the pre-1950 investigations and higher for women in those published in 1950 or later. They note, however, that the trends in sex-specific rates for the major subclassifications of functional psychiatric disorders do not show the same pattern over time. Specifically, rates of personality disorder are consistently higher for men, and the evidence for sex differences in rates of neurosis and psychosis is not consistent in the pre-1950 studies. They conclude that the various trends in overall rates of psychiatric disorders cannot be explained by role theories of gender-related differences in psychological distress.

On the basis of results from two national surveys of mental health conducted in the 1950s and from three surveys fielded in the 1970s, Kessler and McRae (1981) conclude that the relationship between sex and psychophysiological symptoms has decreased over the past two decades—that is, the "gender gap" is narrowing. They argue that these trends may be due partially to changes in the roles of men and women over the same period, such as greater employment among women and lower rates of childbearing. They attempted to test explicitly the effects of specific variables: shifts in marital status, having children at home, education, and employment. Only employment significantly helped explain the relationship between sex and reported psychological distress. The trend toward higher female labor-force participation explained approximately 20 percent of the change in the relationship between gender and symptoms of psychopathology over the same period of time.

Data from two cross-sectional surveys, conducted in Stirling County, Nova Scotia, in 1952 and 1970, show that women were more likely than men to experience symptoms of depression and anxiety (Murphy, Sobol, Neff, Olivier, & Leighton, 1984). Over the period studied, however, the prevalence of these symptoms rose among young women in their 30s and among men in their 40s, 50s, and 60s. The rising rate among younger women increased the sex differences for that age group. The rising rates among older men, on the other hand, brought their rate closer to women of comparable ages. For respondents between 40 and 69 the rates converged, perhaps reflecting changes in access to the labor force.

Data collected more recently in large population studies indicate increased rates of depression and earlier age of onset in birth cohorts born since 1950, particularly among women (Weissman & Klerman, 1985). Similar trends suggestive of a cohort effect have been reported for suicide, homicide among black men, violent death, and substance use (Klerman, Lavori, Rice, Reich, Endicott, Andreasen, Keller, & Hirschfield, 1985). Environmental factors, such as an increase in the age at which people enter the labor force, declining economic earnings, changes in the age of marriage, changing fertility rates, and a decreasing age at which maternal child rearing functions end, have been suggested as possible factors contributing to the increase in rates of depression in more recent cohorts (Klerman et al., 1985; Weissman & Klerman, 1985).

Although many of the causes of death showing large sex ratios are stress related, the cause of death most obviously linked to the experience of stress is suicide (Harry, 1983; Kessler & McRae, 1983). Kessler and McRae (1983) recently reviewed all published studies of suicide attempts in normal populations conducted in the United States between 1940 and 1980. Until the 1960s the proportion of suicide attempters who were women increased; after that, the proportion of attempts by women declined. The most striking trend in suicide rates has been the rise among males in the 15 to 24 and 25 to 34 age groups; among males aged 15 to 24 the rate increased by about 50 percent between 1970 and 1980. Among females in the same age group, the rate increased by less than 5 percent. Among people aged 25 to 34, the suicide rate for men increased nearly 30 percent while the female rate decreased almost 20 percent.

Kessler and McRae (1983) point out that the post World War II trends are consistent with the trends in overall psychopathology reported by Gove and Tudor (1973) and lend support to the argument that women's roles were more stressful during this period. The decrease in the sex ratio of suicides in the 1960s also is consistent with studies of self-reported psychological distress by Srole and Fisher (1978), Kessler and McRae (1981), and Murphy and colleagues (Murphy et al., 1984). Kessler and McRae indicate that the trends in suicide rates parallel the increasing tendency for women to occupy nontraditional sex roles during that period. Thus, there may have been a curvilinear trend in the role strains that women have been exposed to, with their roles becoming increasingly less attractive around the time of World War II and then becoming more fulfilling in recent years as women have gained more access to labor markets.

EXPLANATIONS OF GENDER DIFFERENCES IN MENTAL HEALTH

Examining sex differences in stress-related responses is informative and heuristic. However, such a review of statistics does not tell us about the psychological or social processes giving rise to those differences. Other chapters in this book address these issues in more detail than is possible here, but it is useful to summarize some general findings and review some data on the way certain potentially stressful situations are differentially distributed between men and women. Data are also reviewed showing that certain types of situations are not equally stressful for men and women, and suggesting possible mediating variables. First, however, it is important to consider possible biological reasons for gender differences in psychiatric disorder.

Biological Explanations

There is reasonable evidence for a genetic factor in depression (Weissman & Klerman, 1977, 1985), but the mode of transmission is unclear. Furthermore, recent studies indicate that genetic transmission cannot fully account for sex differences in rates of depression (Weissman & Klerman, 1977, 1985). Nor is it possible to draw definitive conclusions with respect to the link between depression and premenstrual tension or contraceptive use. There is evidence that women do not have higher rates of depression during menopause, but they are at higher risk for psychiatric disorders in the postpartum period (Hamilton, 1962, 1977; Pitt, 1968). It is not clear, however, whether the higher rates of distress and depression after birth are due to biological factors, social factors, or a combination of the two.

Social Explanations

Some of the most specific hypotheses advanced to explain gender differences in psychological and psychiatric distress concern the socialization process and the nature of marriage (Bernard, 1972; Radloff, 1975). Bernard, for example, has argued that marriage is distinctly beneficial for most husbands but that it is much less so, or not at all so, for most wives. Gove and Tudor (1973) have presented several specific hypotheses about why married women experience more strain than do married men. First, in the past, most married women were restricted to the role of housewife, whereas married men were more likely to have both family and work as sources of satisfaction. Second, women's main instrumental activities—raising children and keeping house—are frustrating and not in line with the educational and intellectual attainment of a large number of women in our society. Third, a lack of structure and social contact allows housewives to brood over troubles. Fourth, even when a married woman is employed, she is typically in a less satisfactory position than a married man, and because she typically performs most of the household chores, she must work more hours than her husband.

All the information on treatment rates reviewed by Gove and Tudor (1973) is consistent with the hypothesis that women are more likely to receive psychiatric treatment than men. Furthermore, gender differences in rates of treated depression tend to be largest among married persons (Bachrach, 1975; Gove, 1972). However, these types of analyses confound actual prevalence and help-seeking behavior. When rates of symptom reports from community studies are examined, women tend to report more symptoms than men within all categories of marital status (Aneshensel, Frerichs, & Clark, 1981; Cleary & Mechanic, 1983; Fox, 1980; Kessler & McRae, 1982; Warheit, Holzer, Bell, & Arey, 1976; cf. Radloff, 1975). Similarly, the data from the Epidemiologic Catchment Area studies indicate that marriage is protective against major depression for both sexes (Weissman & Klerman, 1985). In order to understand these differences, it is important to consider the variety of roles that men and women occupy and how the strains and rewards associated with different roles interact. For example, several investigators have found that the parental role is a source of strain and that strains associated with parenting appear to affect women most (Barnett & Baruch, 1985; Cleary & Mechanic, 1983; Gove & Geerken, 1977; Gurin, Veroff, & Feld, 1960; Pearlin, 1975; Pearlin & Johnson, 1977). In contrast, both marriage and employment appear, on average, to be related to lower rates of distress among women (Aneshensel et al., 1981; Cleary & Mechanic, 1983; Gore & Mangione, 1983; Gove & Geerken, 1977; Pearlin, 1980; Rosenfeld, 1980). However, the effects of different roles may interact in ways that are not fully understood. Thoits (1983) has argued that participation in multiple roles tends to be beneficial, but the number of roles is confounded with occupancy of particular roles that may explain much, if not all, of the relevant variation in distress (Barnett & Baruch, 1985). Furthermore, strains associated with different roles may interact in ways that are detrimental. For example, Cleary and Mechanic (1983) found that having minor children in the household was especially stressful for employed women with low incomes. Kandel, Davies, and Raveis (1985) found that the effects of multiple roles were beneficial for maritally induced stresses, but detrimental for work-related stresses. Unfortunately, there have been no analyses of longitudinal data that answer the question of whether women with better psychological health select themselves into particular role configurations (see Aneshensel & Pearlin, this volume, for a discussion of the difficulty of studying the impact of multiple roles).

Cafferata, Kasper, and Bernstein (1983) analyzed data from the National Medical Care Expenditure Survey and found that women were much more likely than men (15.5 vs. 8.1 percent) to have obtained psychotropic drugs. The likelihood of obtaining psychotropic drugs was higher among women regardless of family role responsibilities, social support provided by family structure, or family stressors. Among both women and men, certain role responsibilities and stressors were significantly related to drug use. However, when number of health care visits and having a regular source of care were controlled, the relationship between drug use and role variables remained for women but disappeared for men. Cafferata et al. (1983) argue that these findings support theoretical work suggesting that women may be more sensitive than men to the effects of less supportive and/or more stressful family circumstances. Alternative explanations for the findings include the possibility that men may use alcohol as a functional alternative for drugs.

The frequent use of psychotropic drugs by women is often interpreted as reflecting higher levels of distress. There are, however, several other possible explanations. One is that current sex roles make it more acceptable for women to acknowledge morbidity and to use health services. This may partially explain women's higher use of medical services and consequently make it more likely that women are prescribed psychotropic drugs. An alternative explanation is that women in certain roles typically have more flexibility, and thus are more able to adopt the sick role and to seek care from a physician (Marcus & Seeman, 1981; Woods & Hulka, 1979).

It may also be that the social environment increases the probability that women develop a "learned helplessness" (Radloff & Monroe, 1978), resulting in higher need to use drugs to cope with dysphoric feelings (see Biener, this volume, for a discussion of gender differences in the use of substances to cope with stress).

It may also be that for any given level of distress, women are more likely to have their behavior labeled as mental illness because they are viewed as weaker, more emotional, and less able to deal with stress than are men. It is well known that stereotypes affect perception, memory, and behavior (McCauley, Stitt, & Segal, 1980). Also, according to certain labeling theorists, the preservation of social dominance by certain groups may depend on certain stereotypes or, as Harris (1977) has referred to them, "type-scripts." Thus, physicians, the majority of whom are men, may help maintain the social dominance of men by reinforcing the view that women are weaker and less able to cope with events and emotions than are men. One way of doing this would be to label women, more frequently than men, as mentally ill. Thus, psychotropic drug use may reflect a diffuse set of factors that may be imperfectly related to true psychiatric morbidity.

Economic Factors

Economic deprivation, prosperity, and change can influence social pathology. Absolute economic deprivation is associated with high levels of psychological distress, some forms of psychoses, and interpersonal violence (Horwitz, 1984), but not with minor crime and neurosis. In addition, there is substantial evidence that economic loss (such as that due to unemployment) is related to psychological distress and suicide, but not to psychosis or crime. There is no consistent association between absolute economic change and social pathology.

It might be expected that economic change would result in more frequent and/or pronounced stress reactions in men than in women. Men traditionally have had more access to labor markets and have been more integrated into the economy. Horwitz (1984) found that most research confirms this expectation. For example, unemployment rates are more strongly associated with psychological distress and psychiatric hospitalization among men (Brenner, 1973; Catalano, Dooley, & Jackson, 1981; Frank, 1981; Horwitz, 1982a; Marshall & Funch, 1979; Warr & Parry, 1982). However, Linsky, Straus, and Colby (1985) found that the correlation between environmental stressors and alcohol use was higher for women than for men. The authors interpet this finding as suggesting that some environmental stressors have a greater impact on women than on men.

Income has been found to be a more important variable for explaining class differences in psychological distress among men, whereas differences in education were more important for women (Kessler, 1982). Male, but not female, suicide rates have been sensitive to economic downturns in the United States, although rates have been converging (Boor, 1980; Vigderhous & Fishman, 1978). In addition, employment status is more strongly associated with arrests for men than for women. Studies of the Great Depression in the United States by Elder and Liker indicate that it had a greater immediate impact on men than on women (Elder, 1974; Elder & Liker, 1982).

It is frequently assumed that because women have gained increased access to labor markets over the past two decades, this change has resulted in women having more financial resources. However, this is not the case. Despite major changes in the economy and major antidiscrimination legislation, the economic well-being of women relative to men did not improve between 1959 and 1983 (Fuchs, 1986). The relative wages of women improved over that period, but women had less leisure time than men, more women were dependent on their own incomes, and women's share of financial responsibility for children rose. The net effect of these trends has been that women have from 4 to 15 percent less access to goods, leisure, and services, relative to men, than they did in 1959.

GENDER DIFFERENCES IN PHYSICAL HEALTH

The major causes of death in the United States are cardiovascular diseases, cancer, accidents, violence, diabetes mellitus, cirrhosis of the liver, and lung disease (U.S. Department of Health, Education and Welfare, 1979). For males, the five most important causes of death are diseases of the heart, cancer, accidents, cerebrovascular diseases, and chronic obstructive pulmonary diseases. For women the highest death rates are for diseases of the heart, cancer, cerebrovascular diseases, and pneumonia and influenza (Verbrugge, 1982, 1985).

Excluding infant mortality, the main causes of death for all those under 24 are accidents and violence, but cancer and heart disease are also common. Accidents continue to be the leading cause of death through age 44. After 44, cardiovascular disease and cancer are the leading causes, but accidents and violence continue to be important. Major causes of death after age 65 are cirrhosis of the liver, diabetes mellitus, and respiratory disease (Hamburg, Elliott, & Parron, 1982).

Death rates are only a crude, distal measure of the total impact that diseases have in a population. It is also important to consider the prevalence of different diseases. In 1978, there were approximately 3 million cases of cancer and 23 to 60 million cases of hypertension. In addition, about 30 percent of the population suffered injuries requiring medical attention or restricting activity for at least a day (Hamburg, Elliott, & Parron, 1982).

In the United States women live about seven years longer than men, on average, and have lower death rates at most ages and for most causes of death (Verbrugge, 1985; Wingard, 1984), but the ratio of male to female deaths varies greatly with age. In the United States, infant mortality is about one-third higher for males and males continue to have $33\frac{1}{3}$ to 50 percent higher mortality rates through childhood. Between 15 and 24 years of age, men have a death rate about three times as high as women, largely because of the higher rate of violent deaths among men. This difference begins to diminish during the late 20s and continues to do so until age 40, when the death rate for men is about 75 percent higher than for women. This ratio rises again until age 60, when men have about twice the mortality rate of women, primarily due to heart disease. After age 60, the sex ratio declines (Fuchs, 1974).

Between the ages of 17 and 44, men are more likely than women to suffer injuries and to have overall higher rates of life-threatening chronic diseases such as coronary heart disease, atherosclerosis, and emphysema, as well as most types of physical impairment (e.g., hearing problems). However, women tend to experience more morbidity from acute conditions and nonfatal chronic conditions, and to have more short-term disability, medical services use, and medical drug use. Women report restricting their activities because of health problems about 25 percent more than men do, and they spend about 40 percent more days in bed per year (Verbrugge, 1985). These differences are largest during women's reproductive years (ages 17 to 44) but even when reproductive conditions are excluded, there is a residual gender difference in short-term disability. In addition, more women than men in their middle and later years report impairment of social activities due to chronic health problems. Gender differences in use of health services are also largest in the age range of 17 to 44. When sex-specific conditions are excluded, women are hospitalized at about the same rate as men, but make about 30 percent more outpatient visits (Verbrugge, 1985).

In order to understand gender differences in mortality, Waldron (1983) analyzed sex differences in the incidence and prognosis of several major chronic diseases. She concluded that there was little or no relationship between sex differences in incidence and sex differences in prognosis. Sex differences in prognosis tend to be smaller than differences in incidence and, in most cases, contributed little to sex differences in mortality rates. Waldron analyzed various risk factors for morbidity and mortality and concluded that although men take more risks of certain types, there is no consistent sex difference in overall propensity to take risks or to engage in protective behavior.

Gender differences in mortality are especially striking in the case of heart disease (Wingard, 1984). In 1980, close to 30 percent of the deaths in the United States were due to ischemic heart disease (IHD). Other diseases of the heart are important causes of death, but in the aggregate they represent only about 10 percent of total deaths (Shapiro, 1983). Although age is the most important predictor of death from IHD, sex is also an important factor, with men being at higher risk at every age. Among whites less than 55 years old, IHD mortality rates are four to five times higher among males than among females. The relative excess of death among males decreases with age, but is substantial even among people over 75. The sex-ratio of IHD mortality rates is lower among nonwhites (Shapiro, 1983).

Using published data from the Framingham Heart Study, Johnson (1977b) investigated whether sex differences in rates of coronary heart disease could be explained by sex differences in the five main risk factors (serum cholesterol, systolic and diastolic blood pressure, left-ventricular hypertrophy, smoking, and glucose intolerance). He found that among persons aged 45 to 54, the risk factors examined accounted for 100 percent of the sex difference in disease. However, for those older than 54, men have fewer risk factors and the risk associated with those factors is less than it is for women, yet men still have higher rates of disease than women. Johnson speculates that the sex ratio at older ages may be due to differences in the risk factors at younger ages. However, it may also be due to unmeasured stress factors or biological differences that are not reflected in the commonly measured risk factors.

In 1980 about 21 percent of all deaths in the United States were due to cancer, and it appears that there has been a steadily increasing trend in cancer deaths. Furthermore, almost one third of the population will have a diagnosis of cancer at some time during their lifetime. Cancer mortality is greater among men than among women for most types of cancer, and the sex difference is substantially larger among nonwhites. However, by far the largest difference is for cancers of the respiratory system; men are more than three and a half times as likely as women to die from such cancers (Shapiro, 1983). Lung cancer is caused by cigarette smoking and in the past there have been large gender differences in rates of cigarette smoking. Changes over time in the sex-ratio of lung cancer will be discussed in the next section.

Trends Over Time

Any data about sex differences in outcomes are time and culture specific. Over time, the relative distribution of stressors may change, the resources and skills men and women have for coping with stressors may change, and the ways in which men and women manifest psychological distress may change. Interpreting trends in stress-related outcomes is extremely problematic, but it is useful at least to be aware of how the distribution of outcomes has changed over the past few decades.

Since 1920 American men have experienced higher levels of mortality than American women for virtually all causes of death and at every age (Johnson, 1977a). In order to evaluate the claim made by some authors that these differences are being reduced by increases in female mortality, Johnson (1977a) analyzed age-adjusted death rates for the period of 1960 through 1974. He found that most female death rates are either stable or falling, and that the sex mortality differential for all causes except lung cancer is either stable or increasing.

The female advantage was also noted by Ueshima and colleagues, who reviewed trends in age-sex-specific mortality rates for the U.S. population for all causes of death from 1960 to 1980 (Ueshima, Cooper, Stamler, Yu, Tatara, & Asakura, 1984). They found that the ratio of male to female deaths for white teenagers and young adults (aged 15 to 34) increased over both decades, even though the mortality rate for white women between the ages of 15 and 24 increased during the 1960s. Over the period studied, the mortality ratios of males to females among nonwhites also increased steadily for all age groups. The causes of death that were responsible for the unfavorable mortality trends among males were: (1) accidents, suicide, and homicide for both whites and nonwhites between 15 and 44 years of age; (2) suicide and homicide for nonwhite men aged 45 to 54; (3) cirrhosis of the liver for white men aged 35 to 44 and for nonwhite men between the ages of 25 and 54; and (4) malignant neoplasms for white men aged 35 to 44 and for nonwhites aged 45 to 54.

Wingard (1984) also has observed that the sex differential in mortality has been increasing since the early 1900s. However, since 1970, the trend has slowed for persons between 45 and 74 years of age, and in 1980, the sex differential for persons aged 55 to 64 was lower than it was in 1970. Changes over time in coronary deaths, for example, have been dramatic. In the period between 1968 and 1978 the age-adjusted rate dropped by almost 25 percent from 241.6 to 180.9 per 100,000 (Shapiro, 1983). The drop has been most pronounced for people under 45; women, especially nonwhite women, showed the largest decline, although there has also been a decline for white men and women over the age of 40 (Patrick, Palesch, Feinleib, & Brody, 1982). Interestingly, since 1968, when ischemic heart disease was divided into the categories of acute myocardial infarction (MI) and chronic IHD, the rate of acute MI has fallen, whereas chronic IHD has shown no consistent decline. Stallones (1980) has suggested that the decrease in the risk of acute MI among women is inconsistent with the notion that recent changes in women's roles are inherently stressful. However, later data showing that the difference between male and female cardiovascular death rates has been getting smaller no longer support his argument. The sex differential for heart disease has recently stabilized, and the lung cancer death rate is increasing faster for women than for men (Wingard, 1984). In 1950 the male and female rates of lung cancer were 174 and 145 per 100,000 people, respectively. However, by the late 1970s these rates had risen to 215 per 100,000 people for men and dropped to 135 for women (Marshall & Graham, 1986). A small part of the male increase may have been due to better detection, but much of the increase was real and probably due primarily to cigarette smoking. For example, age-adjusted rates of cancer of the colon and rectum, stomach, uterus, and liver were constant or dropped during this period. However, cancers related to smoking, such as pancreatic cancer and cancers of the larynx, bladder, and lungs, increased. The annual rate of deaths from lung cancer increased from 26 to 70 per 100,000 people among men and from 5 to 18 per 100,000 people among women. More recently, the increase in lung cancer mortality has been concentrated among women, and it is believed that this increase is related to smoking (American Cancer Society, 1984). It has been suggested that if current trends continue, within a few years more women will die each year of lung cancer than of breast cancer (American Cancer Society, 1984; Marshall & Graham, 1986).

Verbrugge (1980a) has also commented on the changing trend in mortality sex differentials. She focuses on the mortality experience of men and women between 1970 and 1977 and compares these data with data from the periods 1920 to 1950 and 1950 to 1970. In prior decades, females' longevity advantage over males increased. This continuing increase appeared for virtually all ages and leading causes of death. However, in the 1970s the increase slowed. Females' situation relative to males worsened for infants and for persons between the ages of 55 and 64, and for conditions of early infancy, bronchitis, emphysema and asthma, homicide, and peptic ulcer. Furthermore, the rate of women's improvement in rates of heart disease and cancer slowed and the relative gains stopped for cerebrovascular diseases and accidents.

Evidence of this reversed trend in the relative mortality of men and women has also been found by Wingard, Suarey, and Barrett-Connor (1983). In a seven-year, longitudinal community study in Southern California, they examined the sex differential in mortality from all causes (as well as IHD) among upper middle-class whites. Using sophisticated statistical techniques to adjust for numerous risk factors, they found that the sex differential in mortality was decreased for all causes as well as for IHD. When analyses were limited to healthy men and women, the adjusted sex ratio was 1.2 for all causes and 2.0 for IHD. Although women's health advantage has been lessening, the results from this study and three other population-based studies still demonstrate a substantial sex differential in mortality, even after adjustment for biologic and behavioral risk factors.

In summary, American women have had a substantial longevity advantage over men throughout this century. From the early 1900s, mortality rates have been dropping for both sexes, but they have been falling more rapidly for women. That is, over time women had been increasing their advantage. But over the past decade or so, the gender difference in mortality has been relatively stable. Verbrugge (1985) has described these trends in detail and speculated that the American population may be shifting towards greater equality in mortality for men and women. Although trends in mortality rates suggest a general improvement in health for both men and women, other indicators point in the opposite direction. The increase in the number of detected health problems suggests men's health worsened more than did women's in the 1950s and 1960s, but that in the 1970s health began to worsen faster for women. One difficulty in interpreting these trends is that they may reflect real changes in health or may be a result of earlier diagnosis and an increased propensity to adopt the sick role (Verbrugge, 1985).

EXPLANATIONS OF GENDER DIFFERENCES

Morbidity and mortality rates are influenced by genetic factors, the environment, the availability and efficacy of health care, as well as social and psychological factors. It is virtually impossible to determine what proportion of the sex differences in morbidity and mortality are due to sex differences in the presence and/or impact of stressors. However, the health statistics reviewed are suggestive in certain cases.

An outstanding review of the plausible hypotheses for gender differences in health has recently been compiled by Verbrugge (1985), who argues that there are sex differentials with respect to biological risks. Women have greater resistance to infectious diseases; until menopause they appear to be protected against cardiovascular disease by hormones; and they are at greater risk of sex-specific conditions than are men. Reviewing the hypotheses that women are more sensitive to bodily discomforts than men, are more likely to label symptoms as illness, tend to rate symptoms as more serious than men, and are more likely than men to seek care for comparable symptoms, Verbrugge (1985) concludes that whether women are more sensitive to symptoms is unknown and that there is almost no evidence about how men and women assess the severity of physical symptoms. Similarly, although numerous authors have hypothesized that sex differences in measured morbidity are due to differences in health reporting, there is no convincing evidence to support this claim (Verbrugge, 1980b, 1985). While most of the hypotheses about the ways in which health care affects gender differences in morbidity and mortality have not been tested empirically, there is some evidence that physicians perceive men and women differently and may behave differently towards them. There is little evidence, however, that different diagnoses and treatments result from differential care (Verbrugge, 1985).

Acquired Risks

Other potential causes of gender differences are the risks men and women are exposed to as a consequence of their different social roles. Explicating the role of behavioral and social factors as determinants of sex differences in morbidity and mortality is complicated and difficult. However, it is possible to identify a few central factors.

For ischemic heart disease, the main modifiable risk factors are high blood pressure, elevated serum cholesterol levels, and cigarette smoking (Dawber, 1980; Shapiro, 1983). There is also suggestive evidence that Type A behavior may be an independent risk factor for heart disease (Rosenman, Brand, Jenkins, Friedman, Straus, & Wurm, 1975). With respect to cancer, a substantial amount of work has been conducted investigating the role of behavior and psychological distress in its etiology, course, and recovery. However, smoking is by far the most important acquired risk factor for cancer.

The Surgeon General of the United States has identified cigarette smoking as "the single most important environmental factor contributing to premature mortality in the United States" (U.S. Department of Health, Education and Welfare, 1979). Although there is some evidence that mortality ratios for smokers are somewhat higher among men, smoking is also clearly an important factor among women. In addition, there is an accumulating body of evidence that smoking acts synergistically with other risk factors (Hamburg, Elliott, & Parron, 1982). For example, smoking may amplify the associations between alcohol and oral cavity cancer (McCoy & Wynder, 1979), oral contraceptives and stroke (Petitti, Wingerd, Pellegrin, & Ramcharan, 1979), and between asbestos and lung cancer (Hammond, Selikoff, & Seidman, 1979).

As indicated earlier, there has been a striking increase in female rates of lung cancer in recent years and that increase is probably due to increases in smoking among women. Fortunately, rates of smoking among both men and women appear to be decreasing again. Harris (1983) has recently reanalyzed data from the Health Interview Survey conducted by the U.S. National Center for Health Statistics. These analyses provide useful insights into gender differences in smoking. For men, the peak prevalence of smoking increased for each subsequent cohort born between 1881 and 1920, but began to decline for later cohorts. Moreover, with each successive cohort, smoking rates began to decline at progressively younger ages (Harris, 1983). For women, smoking rates continued to climb for all cohorts up to those born in 1940. Among women born after 1940, peak smoking rates declined for each successive cohort. However, rates of smoking among women began to decline later than among men and appear to be declining at a slower rate, resulting in converging rates of smoking for men and women. These trends may be partly responsible for the recently narrowing gap in rates of death from lung cancer and the overall reduction in the gender difference in mortality.

An acquired risk factor for heart disease that has received considerable attention is the Type A behavior pattern, which is characterized by extreme interpersonal competitiveness, aggression, time-urgency, and chronically hostile behavior (Friedman & Rosenman, 1974). Type A individuals are aggressively involved in a chronic, incessant struggle to achieve more and more in less time. It is difficult at this point to specify the extent to which sex differences in Type A behavior account for the observed differences in rates of heart disease. Waldron (1978) has examined the relationship between Type A behavior, socioeconomic status, and social mobility. Type A behavior was more common among women employed full-time than among housewives and women employed part-time. For the 40- to 59-year-old women in Waldron's study, Type A behavior was associated with high occupational status. In contrast, it was not associated with a greater likelihood of being married or of having a high-status husband. Waldron concludes that Type A behavior may be related to the traditional male occupational role, but not to "success" in a sphere which has traditionally been considered important for women, that of "marrying well."

Risks Related to Social Roles

To assess the impact of social roles on health, Verbrugge (1983) analyzed data from health interviews and health diaries for a sample of Detroit adults (The Health in Detroit Study). She concluded that being employed, married, or a parent is associated with good self-rated health status, low morbidity, little restricted activity, infrequent use of medical care, and low drug use for both men and women. Employment had the strongest association with health, and parenthood the weakest. Verbrugge also found that multiple roles have additive positive effects for both men and women. She found no evidence that the combination of employment, marriage, and motherhood is detrimental to women's health. Verbrugge concluded that health risks are lower for people actively involved in roles than for people without them, and that involved people may have health attitudes that reduce both their sensitivity to symptoms and their tendency to take health actions. She also noted, however, that healthy people may be more apt to engage in multiple, active roles. That is, these associations may not be due to the fact that certain roles cause the observed outcomes; rather, particular types of people may self-select for certain roles. For example, a person who is seriously ill would find it difficult to seek and maintain employment.

Marriage. The social role most frequently examined with respect to health is marriage. Disease morbidity and mortality tend to be lower among married and higher among separated or divorced persons; married persons have the lowest mortality rates and, compared to separated or divorced persons, have lower rates of contact with physicians, hospital stays, and visits to psychiatric hospitals and outpatient clinics (see Riessman & Gerstel, 1985 for a review of this literature). Investigators have tended to assume that these relationships are due to the fact that marriage is protective; however, some researchers (e.g., Bernard, 1972, 1975; Gove, 1972, 1973; Gove & Hughes, 1979) have argued that marriage is more beneficial for men than it is for women.

If men benefit more from marriage, one would expect that men would experience a greater health decrement when their marriages ended. Riessman and Gerstel (1985) examined whether marriage is more protective of men's or women's health by examining the special case of the separated and divorced. They used several data sets on physical health, mortality, and mental health, including the Health Interview Survey, the Health and Nutritional Examination Survey (a survey of the mental health among residents of Los Angeles County), and mental health treatment statistics for the U.S. population. They did not find consistent support for the prediction that marital dissolution has the greatest impact on men. Men have more of the severe health problems including mortality and hospitalization of all types; women have more of the less severe physical and mental health problems. They conclude that any discussion of the impact of marital dissolution on women's and men's health should specify the type of health risk, as well as the particular stage in the dissolution process.

Paid work. The literature indicates that men have more risks than women from their jobs, household tasks, and life styles. There is increasing evidence that many aspects of a person's work environment can have an important impact on health (House & Cottington, 1986). It has frequently been asserted that men's work environments pose greater health risks, but this has not been well documented.

Social ties. With respect to social ties beyond marriage, women tend to have larger informal social networks than do men and they tend to have more intimate and active ties to others (Verbrugge, 1985). Thus, it may be that women derive more health benefits from social support. However, several researchers have recently shown that women may be exposed to more strains related to their helping roles in social networks (Belle, this volume; Wethington, McLeod, & Kessler, this volume).

Socioeconomic factors. As mentioned earlier, some gender differences may be mediated by socioeconomic factors. It is well known that socioeconomic status is positively related to physical health. Albino and Tedesco (1984) have pointed out that the number of one-parent families headed by women is at an all-time high and that women appear to be at high risk for health problems related to socioeconomic factors. The lack of appropriate health resources, for example, appears to be related to the disproportionate number of deaths from anemias, complications of pregnancy, and abortions among black women. However, Weissman, Leaf, and Bruce (1987) analyzed the psychiatric status as well as economic and social functioning of mothers aged 18 to 44 who participated in the Epidemiologic Catchment Area Project and found that there were no appreciable differences between married and single women in social contacts, use of health services, or in six-month prevalence rates of psychiatric disorders, including major depression, alcohol, or drug abuse.

In summary, excellent data from representative samples of community populations indicate that the lifetime prevalence of the psychiatric disorders covered was similar for men and women in all three sites. However, there were important gender differences in the types of disorders experienced. Antisocial personality and alcohol abuse/dependence were more prevalent among men in all three sites and drug abuse/dependence was higher among men in two of the sites. In contrast, major depression, agoraphobia, and simple phobia were higher among women in all sites and dysthymia, somatization disorder, panic disorder, obsessive-compulsive disorder, and schizophrenia were all significantly higher for women in at least one site.

There may be a genetic component to some of the disorders, especially schizophrenia and major depression. However, the largest gender differences are for depression and recent studies indicate that genetic or biological explanations cannot explain those differences. There have been a number of hypotheses about the relationship between gender roles and affective disorders, but the empirical work in this area has not been able to demonstrate convincingly the exact nature of the relationship. There is, however, provocative evidence that recent birth cohorts, especially women, are experiencing higher rates of depression.

Women have lower death rates than men at most ages and for every cause of death, but experience more morbidity from disabling conditions, and use more medical services and drugs. The differences in mortality are probably attributable, in part, to biological and genetic factors, and the fact that men are more likely to acquire behaviors, such as Type A behavior and smoking, that increase the risk of heart disease and cancer. A substantial body of work has examined the relationship between social roles and physical health, but the results have been inconsistent. There are a number of characteristics of women's roles that are less desirable than men's, but the relationship between these characteristics and physical health has not been clearly demonstrated.

Most researchers agree that psychological and social factors have important influences on health. However, there is still little consensus about the mechanisms linking social factors and health outcomes, or the extent to which social factors explain observed differences in health. If we are to advance knowledge in this area it is incumbent upon us to move beyond descriptive studies to investigations that look in detail at the biological, psychological, and social processes that influence health. Only by continuing to test explicit hypotheses about the ways specific role constellations are linked to health will we better understand the extent to which, and the way in which, our health is determined by our social world.

It is important to keep in mind the inherent limitations in our ability to identify generalizable principles. In order to understand the meaning of sex differences in stress-related states, we must also take into account the culture in which behaviors or outcomes occur. Among the many functions culture serves, it acts as a context for the psychological development of individuals leading to effective group participation and membership, provides the context within which behavior is expressed according to social norms, and provides a basis for interpretation of what is socially approved (Maretyki, 1981). There is now an accumulation of compelling evidence that the labels people apply to behavior syndromes are a function of historical and cultural context (Engelhardt, 1974; Kleinman, 1977, 1981; Rosen, 1975; Wartofsky, 1974). In addition, culture has a range of potential effects on the biological and psychological processes underlying psychiatric disorder, illness behavior, and the way society responds (Horwitz, 1982b; Kleinman, 1981).

Fuller discussion of many of these issues is found in later chapters in this volume. However, it is important to remember that much of our research is culture and period specific. For example, Murphy (1978) has examined shifts over time in the sex ratios for peptic ulcer, diabetes, lung cancer, and coronary heart disease. His examination of these diseases is instructive. For each of the shifts examined, there is no verifiable and agreed upon explanation. However, Murphy posits explanations for the shifts and concludes that period-specific ideal types or stereotyped self-images may be more useful in explaining sex differentials in morbidity and mortality than objectively defined roles. For example, he speculates that factors that may have been responsible for sex differences in different periods include the use of tight corsets by women in the late nineteenth and early twentieth centuries, differences in child-rearing patterns, sex differences in the use of drugs linked to ulcers, specialized diets, and sex differences in acceptance of and adherence to treatment regimens for diabetes.

Murphy's observations are speculative and most of his conclusions are arguable. However, they are also quite plausible. The point, however, is not whether he is correct or incorrect. The important lesson to draw from his observations is that overly general arguments about the relationships between roles and illness are not likely to advance our knowledge of gender differences in stress-related processes. We should strive to differentiate the distribution and impact of stressors, taking into account the symbolic meaning of different physical and social environments and events.

REFERENCES

Albino, J. E., & Tedesco, L. A. (1984). Women's health issues. In A. U. Rickel, M. Gerrard, & I. Iscoe (Eds.), *Social and psychological problems of women.* New York: Hemisphere.

Al-Issa, I. (Ed.) (1982) *Gender and psychopathology.* New York: Academic Press.

American Cancer Society (1984). *Cancer facts and figures.* New York: American Cancer Society.

American Psychiatric Association (1980). *Diagnostic and statistical manual of mental disorders* (3rd ed.). Washington, DC: APA.

Aneshensel, C. S., Frerichs, R. R., & Clark, V. A. (1981). Family roles and sex differences in depression. *Journal of Health and Social Behavior, 22,* 379–393.

Bachrach, L. L. (1975). *Marital status and mental disorder: An analytical review.* DHEW Pub. No. (ADM) 75–217. Washington, DC: U.S. Government Printing Office.

Barnett, R. C., & Baruch, G. K. (1985). Women's involvement in multiple roles, role strain, and psychological distress. *Journal of Personality and Social Psychology, 49,* 135–145.

Belle, D., & Goldman, N. (1980). Patterns of diagnoses received by men and women. In M. Guttentag, S. Salasin, & D. Belle (Eds.), *The mental health of women.* New York: Academic Press.

Bernard, J. (1972). *The future of marriage.* New York: Bantam Books.

———. (1975). *Women, wives, and mothers: Values and options.* Chicago: Aldine.

Boor, M. (1980). Relationships between unemployment rates and suicide rates in eight countries, 1962–1976. *Psychological Reports, 47,* 1095–1101.

Boyd, J. H., & Weissman, M. M. (1981). Epidemiology of affective disorders: A reexamination and future directions. *Archives of General Psychiatry, 28,* 1039–1046.

Brenner, M. H. (1973). *Mental illness and the economy.* Cambridge, MA: Harvard University Press.

Cafferata, G. L., Kasper, J., & Bernstein, A. (1983). Family roles, structure, and stressors in relation to sex differences in obtaining psychotropic drugs. *Journal of Health and Social Behavior, 24,* 132–143.

Catalano, R., Dooley, D., & Jackson, R. L. (1981). Economic predictors of admissions to mental health facilities in a nonmetropolitan community. *Journal of Health and Social Behavior, 22,* 284–297.

Chambers, C. D., & Griffey, M. S. (1975). Use of legal substances within the general population: The sex and age variables. *Addictive diseases: An International Journal, 2,* 7–19.

Cleary, P. D. (1978). Some considerations in using cirrhosis mortality rates as an indicator of the prevalence of alcoholism. *Journal of Studies of Alcohol, 38,* 1639–1642.

——. (1979). A standardized estimator of the prevalence of alcoholism based on mortality data. *Journal of Studies on Alcohol, 40,* 408–418.

Cleary, P. D., & Mechanic, D. (1983). Sex differences in psychological distress among married people. *Journal of Health and Social Behavior, 24,*111–121.

Cooperstock, R. (1971). Sex differences in the use of mood modifying drugs: An explanatory model. *Journal of Health and Social Behavior, 12,* 238–244.

——. (1978). Sex differences in psychotropic drug use. *Social Science and Medicine, 12*B, 179–186.

——. (1979). A review of women's psychotropic drug use. *Canadian Journal of Psychiatry, 24,* 29–33.

Craig, T., & Van Natta, P. (1979). Influence of demographic characteristics on two measures of depressive symptoms. *Archives of General Psychiatry, 36,* 149–154.

Dawber, T. R. (1980). *The Framingham Study: The epidemiology of atherosclerotic disease.* Cambridge, MA: Commonwealth Fund.

Dohrenwend, B., & Dohrenwend, B. S. (1969). *Social status and psychological disorder.* New York: Wiley.

——. (1976). Sex differences and psychiatric disorders. *American Journal of Sociology, 81,* 1447–1472.

Eaton, W. W., Regier, D. A., Locke, B. Z., & Taube, C. A. (1981). The epidemiologic catchment area program of the National Institute of Mental Health. *Public Health Reports, 96,* 319–325.

Elder, G. H., Jr. (1974). *Children of the great depression: Social change in life experience.* Chicago: University of Chicago Press.

Elder, G. H., Jr., & Liker, J. K. (1982). Hard times in women's lives: Historical influences across forty years. *American Journal of Sociology, 88,* 241–269.

Engelhardt, H. T. (1974). The disease of masturbation: Values and concepts of the disease. *Bulletin of the History of Medicine, 48,* 234–248.

Farberow, N., & Shneidman, F. (1961). *The cry for help.* New York: McGraw-Hill.

Ferrence, R. G. (1980). Sex differences in the prevalence of problem drinking. In O. J. Kalant (Ed.), *Alcohol and drug problems in women*. New York: Plenum.

Fidell, L. S. (1982). Gender and drug use and abuse. In I. Al-Issa (Ed.), *Gender and psychopathology*. New York: Academic Press.

Fodor, I. G. (1982). Gender and phobia. In I. Al-Issa (Ed.), *Gender and psychopathology*. New York: Academic Press.

Fox, J. W. (1980). Gove's specific sex-role theory of mental illness: A research note. *Journal of Health and Social Behavior, 21,* 260–267.

Frank, J. A. (1981). Economic change and mental health in an uncontaminated setting. *American Journal of Community Psychology, 9,* 395–410.

Frerichs, R., Aneshensel, C., & Clark, V. (1981). Prevalence of depression in Los Angeles County. *American Journal of Epidemiology, 113,* 691–699.

Friedman, M., & Rosenman, R. (1974). *Type A behavior and your heart*. New York: Knopf.

Fuchs, V. R. (1974). *Who shall live?* New York: Basic Books.

——. (1986). Sex differences in economic well-being. *Science, 232,* 459–464.

Goldman, N., & Ravid, R. (1980). Community surveys: Sex differences in mental illness. In M. Guttentag, S. Salasin, & D. Belle (Eds.), *The mental health of women*. New York: Academic Press.

Gore, S., & Mangione, T. M. (1983). Social roles, sex roles and psychological distress: Additive and interactive models of sex-differences. *Journal of Health and Social Behavior, 24,* 300–312.

Gove, W. R. (1972). The relationship between sex roles, marital status, and mental health. *Social Forces, 51,* 34–44.

——. (1973). Sex, marital status, and mortality. *American Journal of Sociology, 79,* 45–53.

——. (1978). Sex differences in mental illness among adult men and women: An evaluation of four questions raised regarding the evidence on the higher rates of women. *Social Science and Medicine, 12*B, 187–198.

Gove, W. R., & Geerken, M. R. (1977). The effect of children and employment on the mental health of married men and women. *Social Forces, 56,* 66–76.

Gove, W. R., & Hughes, H. (1979). Possible causes of the apparent sex-differences in physical health: An empirical investigation. *American Sociological Review, 44,* 126–139.

Gove, W. R., & Tudor, J. F. (1973). Adult sex roles and mental illness. *American Journal of Sociology, 78,* 812–835.

——. (1977). Sex differences in mental illness: A comment on Dohrenwend and Dohrenwend. *American Journal of Sociology, 82,* 1327–1336.

Gurin, G., Veroff, J. V., & Feld, S. (1960). *Americans view their mental health*. New York: Basic Books.

Guttman, D. (1978). Patterns of legal drug use by Americans. *Addictive Diseases, 3,* 337–356.

Hamburg, D. A., Elliott, G. R., & Parron, D. L. (Eds.) (1982). *Health and behavior: Frontiers of research in the biobehavioral sciences*. Washington, DC: National Academy Press.

Hamilton, J. A. (1962). *Postpartum psychiatric problems.* St. Louis: C. V. Mosby.

———. (1977). Puerperal psychoses. In J. J. Sciarra (Ed.), *Gynecology and obstetrics.* Hagerstown, MD: Harper & Row.

Hammen, C. L. (1982). Gender and depression. In I. Al-Issa (Ed.), *Gender and psychopathology.* New York: Academic Press.

Hammond, E. C., Selikoff, I. J., & Seidman, H. (1979). Asbestos exposure, cigarette smoking, and death rates. *Annals of the New York Academy of Science, 330,* 473–490.

Harris, A. R. (1977). Sex and theories of deviance: Toward a functional theory of deviant type-scripts. *American Sociological Review, 42,* 3–16.

Harris, J. E. (1983). Cigarette smoking among successive birth cohorts of men and women in the United States during 1900–80. *Journal of the National Cancer Institute, 71,* 473–479.

Harry, J. (1983). Parasuicide, gender, and gender deviance. *Journal of Health and Social Behavior, 24,* 350–361.

Horwitz, A. V. (1982a). Sex-role expectations, power, and psychological distress. *Sex Roles, 8,* 607–623.

———. (1982b). *The social control of mental illness.* New York: Academic Press.

———. (1984). The economy and social pathology. *Annual Review of Sociology, 10,* 95–119.

House, J. S., & Cottington, E. M. (1986). Health and the workplace. In L. H. Aiken & D. Mechanic (Eds.), *Applications of social science to clinical medicine and health policy.* New Brunswick, NJ: Rutgers University Press.

Johnson, A. (1977a). Recent trends in sex mortality differentials in the United States. *Journal of Human Stress, 3,* 22–32.

———. (1977b). Sex differentials in coronary heart disease: The explanatory role of primary risk factors. *Journal of Health and Social Behavior, 18,* 46–54.

Kandel, D. B., Davies, M., & Raveis, V. H. (1985). The stressfulness of daily social roles for women: Marital, occupational and household roles. *Journal of Health and Social Behavior, 26,* 64–78.

Kaplan, M. (1983). A woman's view of DSM-III. *American Psychologist, 38,* 786–792.

Kass, F., Spitzer, R. L., & Williams, J. B. (1983). An empirical study of the issue of sex bias in the diagnostic criteria of DSM-III Axis II personality disorders. *American Psychologist, 38,* 799–801.

Kessler, R. C., & McRae, J. A., Jr. (1981). Trends in the relationship between sex and psychological distress. *American Sociological Review, 46,* 443–452.

———. (1982). The effect of wives' employment on the mental health of married men and women. *American Sociological Review, 47,* 216–227.

———. (1983). Trends in the relationship between sex and attempted suicide. *Journal of Health and Social Behavior, 24,* 98–110.

Kleinman, A. (1977). Rethinking the social and cultural context of psychopathology and psychiatric care. In T. Manschreck & A. Kleinman (Eds.), *Renewal in psychiatry: A critical rational perspective.* Washington, DC: Hemisphere.

———. (1981). Critique of the cultural paradigm. In C. Eisdorfer, D. Cohen, A. Kleinman, & P. Maxim (Eds.), *Models for clinical psychopathology.* New York: SP Medical and Scientific Books.

Klerman, G. L., Lavori, P. W., Rice, J., Reich, T., Endicott, J., Andreasen, N. C., Keller, M. B., & Hirschfield, R. M. A. (1985). Birth-cohort trends in rates of major depressive disorder among relatives of patients with affective disorder. *Archives of General Psychiatry, 42,* 689–693.

Kramer, M., Pollack, E. S., Redick, R. W., & Locke, B. Z. (1972). *Mental Disorders/suicide.* Cambridge, MA: Harvard University Press.

Lech, S. V., Friedman, G. D., & Ury, H. K. (1975). Characteristics of heavy users of outpatient prescription drugs. *Clinical Toxicology, 8,* 599–610.

Leland, J. (1982). Gender, drinking, and alcohol abuse. In I. Al-Issa (Ed.), *Gender and psychopathology.* New York: Academic Press.

Linsky, A., Straus, M., & Colby, J. (1985). Stressful events, stressful conditions and alcohol problems in the United States: A partial test of Bales's theory. *Journal of Studies on Alcohol, 46,* 72–80.

Marcus, A. C., & Seeman, T. E. (1981). Sex differences in reports of illness and disability: A preliminary test of the fixed obligations hypothesis. *Journal of Health and Social Behavior, 22,* 174–182.

Maretyki, T. W. (1981). The cultural paradigm. In C. Eisdorfer, D. Cohen, A. Kleinman, & P. Maxim (Eds.), *Models for clinical psychopathology.* New York: SP Medical and Scientific Books.

Maris, R. W. (1969). *Social forces in urban suicide.* Homewood, IL: Dorsey.

———. (1981). *Pathways to suicide: A survey of self-destructive behaviors.* Baltimore: Johns Hopkins University Press.

Marshall, J. R., & Funch, D. P. (1979). Mental illness and the economy: A critique and partial replication. *Journal of Health and Social Behavior, 29,* 282–289.

Marshall, J., & Graham, S. (1986). Cancer. In L. H. Aiken & D. Mechanic (Eds.), *Applications of social science to clinical medicine and health policy.* New Brunswick, NJ: Rutgers University Press.

McCauley, C., Stitt, C. L., & Segal, M. (1980). Stereotyping: From prejudice to prediction. *Psychological Bulletin, 87,* 195–208.

McCoy, G. D., & Wynder, E. L. (1979). Etiologic and preventive implications in alcohol carcinogenesis. *Cancer Research, 39,* 2844–2850.

Mechanic, D. (1980). Comment on Gove and Hughes. *American Sociological Review, 45,* 513–514.

Murphy, H. B. M. (1978). Historic changes in the sex ratios for different disorders. *Social Science and Medicine, 12*B, 143–149.

Murphy, J. M., Sobol, A. M., Neff, R. K., Olivier, D. C., & Leighton, A. H. (1984). Stability of prevalence: Depression and anxiety disorders. *Archives of General Psychiatry, 41,* 990–997.

Myers, J. K., Weissman, M. M., Tischler, G. L., Holzer, C. E., III, Leaf, P. J., Orvaschel, H., Anthony, J., Boyd, J. H., Burke, J. D., Kramer, M., & Stoltzman, R. (1984). Six month prevalence of psychiatric disorders in three communities, 1980 to 1982. *Archives of General Psychiatry, 41*,959-967.

Newmann, J. P. (1984). Sex differences in symptoms of depression: Clinical disorder or normal distress? *Journal of Health and Social Behavior, 25*, 136-159.

Patrick, C. H., Palesch, Y. Y., Feinleib, M., & Brody, J. A. (1982). Sex differences in declining cohort death rates from heart disease. *American Journal of Public Health, 72*, 161-166.

Pearlin, L. I. (1975). Sex roles and depression. In N. Datan & L. H. Ginsberg (Eds.), *Life-span developmental psychology: Normative life crises.* New York: Academic Press.

———. (1980). Life-strains and psychological distress among adults: A conceptual overview. In N. J. Smelser & E. H. Erikson (Eds.), *Themes of love and work in adulthood.* Cambridge, MA: Harvard University Press.

Pearlin, L. I., & Johnson, J. (1977). Marital status, life strains and depression. *American Sociological Review, 42*, 704-715.

Petitti, D. B., Wingerd, J., Pellegrin, F., & Ramcharan, S. (1979). Risk of vascular disease in women: Smoking, oral contraceptives, noncontraceptive estrogens, and other factors. *Journal of the American Medical Association, 242*, 1150-1154.

Pitt, B. (1968). A typical depression following childbirth. *British Journal of Psychiatry, 114*, 1325-1335.

Radloff, L. S. (1975). Sex differences in depression: The effects of occupation and marital status. *Sex Roles, 1*, 249-265.

Radloff, L. S., & Monroe, M. K. (1978). Sex differences in helplessness—with implications for depression. In L. S. Hansen & R. S. Rapoza (Eds.), *Career development and counselling of women.* Springfield, IL: Charles Thomas, 1978.

Regier, D. A., Myers, J. K., Kramer, M., Robins, L. N., Blazer, D. G., Hough, R. L., Eaton, W. W., & Locke, B. Z. (1984). The NIMH Epidemiologic Catchment Area Program. *Archives of General Psychiatry, 41*, 934-941.

Riessman, C. K., & Gerstel N. (1985). Marital dissolution and health: Do males or females have greater risk? *Social Science and Medicine, 20*, 627-635.

Robins, L. N., Helzer, J. E., Weissman, M. M., Orvaschel, H., Gruenberg, E., Burke, J. D., & Regier, D. A. (1984). Lifetime prevalence of specific psychiatric disorders in three sites. *Archives of General Psychiatry, 41*, 949-958.

Robins, L. N., & Smith, E. M. (1980). Longitudinal studies of alcohol and drug problems: Sex differences. In O. J. Kalant (Ed.), *Alcohol and drug problems in women.* New York: Plenum.

Rosen, G. (1975). Nostalgia: A 'forgotten' psychological disorder. *Psychological Medicine, 5*, 340-354.

Rosenfeld, S. (1980). Sex differences in depression: Do women always have higher rates? *Journal of Health and Social Behavior, 21*, 33-42.

Rosenman, R. H., Brand, R. J., Jenkins, C. D., Friedman, M., Straus, R., & Wurm, M. (1975). Coronary heart disease in the Western Collaborative Group Study: Final follow up experience of 8½ years. *Journal of the American Medical Association, 233*, 872-877.

Sayetta, R., & Johnson, D. (1980). *Basic data on depressive symptomatology: United States 1974–1975*, National Health Survey, Series 11, No. 216 (U.S. Health Service Publication Number 80–1666). Hyattsville, MD: National Center for Health Statistics.

Shapiro, S. (1983). Epidemiology of ischemic heart disease and cancer. In D. Mechanic (Ed.), *Handbook of health, health care, and the health professions*. New York: Free Press.

Shapiro, S., & Baron, S. H. (1961). Prescriptions for psychotropic drugs in a non-institutionalized population. *Public Health Reports, 76*, 481–488.

Silverman, C. (1968). *The epidemiology of depression*. Baltimore: Johns Hopkins University Press.

Srole, L., & Fisher, A. K. (Eds.). (1978). *Mental health in the metropolis: The Midtown Manhattan Study*. New York: Harper & Row.

Stallones, R. A. (1980). The rise and fall of ischemic heart disease. *Scientific American, 243*, 53–59.

Stengel, E. (1969). *Suicide and attempted suicide*. Baltimore: Penguin.

Stolley, P. D., Becker, M., McEvilla, J. D., Lasagna, L., Gainor, M., & Sloane, L. (1972). Drug prescribing and use in an American community. *Annals of Internal Medicine, 76*, 537–540.

Thoits, P. A. (1981). Undesirable life events and psychophysiological distress: A problem of operational confounding. *American Sociological Review, 46*, 96–109.

Ueshima, H., Cooper, R., Stamler, J., Yu, C., Tatara, K., & Asakura, S. (1984). Age specific mortality trends in the U.S.A. from 1960 to 1980: Divergent age-sex-color patterns. *Journal of Chronic Diseases, 37*, 425–439.

Uhlenhuth, E. H., Balter, M. B., & Lipman, R. (1978). Minor tranquilizers: Clinical correlates of use in an urban population. *Archives of General Psychiatry, 35*, 650–655.

U.S. Department of Health, Education and Welfare. (1979). *Healthy people*. DHEW Publ. No. (PHS) 79–55071. Washington, DC: U.S. Government Printing Office.

Verbrugge, L. M. (1980a). Recent trends in sex mortality differentials in the United States. *Women's Health, 5*, 7–37.

———. (1980b). Sex differences in complaints and diagnoses. *Journal of Behavioral Medicine, 3*, 327–355.

———. (1982). Sex differentials in health. *Public Health Reports, 97*, 417–437.

———. (1983). Multiple roles and physical health of men and women. *Journal of Health and Social Behavior, 24*, 16–30.

———. (1985). Gender and health: An update on hypotheses and evidence. *Journal of Health and Social Behavior, 26*, 156–182.

Vischi, T., Jones, K., Shank, E., & Lima, L. (1980). *The alcohol, drug abuse, and mental health national data book*. Rockville, MD: Alcohol, Drug Abuse and Mental Health Administration.

Vigderhous, G., & Fishman, G. (1978). The impact of unemployment and familial integration on changing suicide rates in the U.S.A., 1920–1969. *Social Psychiatry, 13*, 239–248.

Waldron, I. (1978). The coronary-prone behavior pattern, blood pressure, employment and socio-economic status in women. *Journal of Psychosomatic Research, 22*, 79–87.

———. (1983). Sex differences in illness incidence, prognosis, and mortality: Issues and evidence. *Social Science and Medicine, 17*, 1107–1129.

Warheit, G. J., Holzer, C. E., III, Bell, R. A., & Arey, S. A. (1976). Sex, marital status, and mental health: A reappraisal. *Social Forces, 55*, 459–470.

Warr, P., & Parry, G. (1982). Paid employment and women's psychological well-being. *Psychological Bulletin, 91*, 498–516.

Wartofsky, M. W. (1974). Organs, organisms and disease: Human ontology and medical practice. In H. T. Engelhardt & S. F. Spicker (Eds.), *Evaluation and explanation in the biomedical sciences*. Dordrecht, Holland: Reidel.

Weissman, M., & Klerman, G. L. (1977). Sex differences and the epidemiology of depression. *Archives of General Psychiatry, 34*, 98–111.

———. (1985). Gender and depression. *Trends in Neurosciences, 9*,416–420.

Weissman, M. M., Leaf, P. J., & Bruce, M. L. (1987). *Single parent women: A community study*. Unpublished manuscript.

Weissman, M. M., Leaf, P. J., Holzer, C. E., III, Myers, J. K., & Tischler, G. L. (1984). The epidemiology of depression. An update on sex differences in rates. *Journal of Affective Disorders, 7*, 179–188.

Weissman, M. M., Leaf, P. J., Tischler, G. L., Blazer, D. G., Karno, M., Bruce, M. L., & Florio, L. P. (In press). Affective disorders in five United States communities. *Psychological Medicine*.

Weissman, M., & Myers, J. (1978). Affective disorders in a U.S. urban community. *Archives of General Psychiatry, 35*, 1304–1311.

Williams, J. B. W., & Spitzer, R. L. (1983). The issue of sex bias in DSM-III. *American Psychologist, 38*, 793–798.

Wingard, D. L. (1984). The sex differential in morbidity, mortality, and lifestyle. *Annual Review of Public Health, 5*, 433–458.

Wingard, D. L., Suarey, L., & Barrett-Connor, E. (1983). The sex differential in mortality from all causes and ischemic heart disease. *American Journal of Epidemiology, 117*, 165–172.

Woods, N., & Hulka, B. (1979). Symptom reports and illness behavior among employed women and homemakers. *Journal of Community Health, 5*, 36–45.

SOCIAL
ROLES

3

Structural Contexts of Sex Differences in Stress

Carol S. Aneshensel
Leonard I. Pearlin

Research on gender and stress has evolved largely from attempts to account for differences between women and men in psychological distress. With consistency that is quite extraordinary in social and behavioral research, women have been shown to be more likely than men to manifest certain psychological disorders, particularly depression and anxiety (Belle, 1980; Comstock & Helsing, 1976; Frerichs, Aneshensel, & Clark, 1981; Myers, Weissman, Tischler, Orvaschel, Gruenberg, Burke, & Regier, 1984; Robins, Helzer, Weissman, Orvaschel, Gruenberg, Burke, & Regier, 1984; Weissman & Klerman, 1977). Since stress has a prominent place in the conceptual frameworks of research into psychological distress, it is not surprising that it should emerge as a central explanatory construct in theories seeking to account for sex differences. The rationale here is deceptively simple. If both gender and stress-provoking life conditions are related to psychological distress, then women and men should also differ with regard to the magnitude and/or impact of such stressors in their lives (e.g., Kessler, 1979; Kessler & McLeod, 1984; Radloff & Rae, 1981).

In many ways, the investigation of the stress process among women

This work was supported by research grants from the National Institute of Mental Health to Carol S. Aneshensel (MH32267) and to Leonard I. Pearlin (MH38830) and benefited from the participation of the authors in the Consortium for Research Involving Stress Processes funded by a grant from the W. T. Grant Foundation.

has been entered into through the back door. Starting with the presumed outcome—gender differences in psychological distress—stress researchers have sought to identify differences in the stress-producing circumstances of men's and women's lives that might account for the differences in their levels of distress. This concern with explaining gender differences in psychological distress has deflected attention from a logically prior question; namely, how stressors come to arise differentially in the lives of women as compared to men. Thus, the preempting concern with accounting for distress has been at the expense of efforts to account for the presence of stressors. The result has been a failure to ask about the broadly based, socially rooted processes and mechanisms that bring about stress-provoking conditions among women (or men) in the first place. Because such conditions have been exclusively treated as explanations of sex differences, they have been largely ignored as phenomena that need to be explained in and of themselves. For many problematic life circumstances, particularly eventful life changes, we therefore seem to know more about whether they are associated with distress than about how they come to be features of people's lives (Pearlin, 1982). Correspondingly, we seem to know better the extent to which they are differentially distressing than the way in which they arise in the lives of women and men.

At a very basic level we need to understand why certain stressors occur with differential frequency in the lives of women and men. Stressors that regularly occur only or more often to one sex or the other, or to certain subgroups of men or women, are not random occurrences. Instead, the sources of these difficulties are likely to be tied to the group's position in the organization of the society at large. One critically important feature of this organization lies in the particular constellations of social roles occupied by women and men, constellations that change over the life course and that may differ among cohorts as well as between the sexes. Gender differences in social role occupancy and in experiences within similar social roles affect the types of stressors typically encountered by women and men. Moreover, these structured differences have their origins not in the psyches of individual women and men, we submit, but in the sex stratification of the social system. This chapter describes how such stratification orders the occurrence and impact of certain types of stress-provoking circumstances in women's lives by shaping the roles they occupy, their experiences within and across these roles, and the histories they bring to current experience.

Our orientation, therefore, is based on the assumption that to understand gender differences in stressors and associated psychological distress, we must ultimately direct our attention to fundamental aspects of social organization and the places of women and men in it. In this regard, the system of social stratification—the distribution of resources, status, and power—is of great importance, for the system of sex stratification in institutionalized roles reflects and parallels this larger system. Thus, it is insufficient to compare employed men and women, for example, even when they appear to be in similar occupations. The expectations that guide work and careers, the opportunity structures to which people have had and will have access, and the ordering of interpersonal and authority relations may be vastly different for men and women who seem to share the same occupational placement.

The primary goal of this chapter, then, is to identify some of the structural forces that need to be taken into account in attempting to explain how potentially stressful experiences arise around the roles occupied by women, particularly in work and the family. We shall address three issues: how social roles determine the range of potentially stressful experiences that may be encountered; the conditions under which stressors arise among those occupying these roles; and how stressors occur at the junctures of multiple roles. A final section traces the implications of these issues for directions of future research into the origins and impact of stress among women. To examine these issues, we shall draw largely on our own research endeavors, particularly on a pair of longitudinal studies of social stressors and psychological distress.

Before we take up the substantive issues of the chapter, it is useful to define several terms whose boundaries can be quite blurred. When we speak of *stressors*, we refer to any set of conditions that threaten the well-being of people. *Stress* is a generic term that pertains to the psychological, physical, physiological, or biochemical impact of the stressor on the organism. *Distress* is thus a particular form of stress reaction involving a disordered affective state such as depression or anxiety. When we speak of the *stress process*, finally, we refer to the evolving connections between stressors and their stress manifestations and to the mediating effects of coping, social supports, and personal resources (Pearlin, Lieberman, Menaghan & Mullan, 1981).

One aspect of the stress process merits additional comment. Individuals are frequently confronted not with isolated stressors, but with constellations of interrelated stressors. In many instances these clusters reflect the diffusion of problems throughout a person's life. For example, a serious chronic illness may create additional stressors in the person's family, work, or economic life, or the individual's adaptation to such illness may create problems involving family, co-workers, or friends (Pearlin & Aneshensel, 1986). The multiplicity of problematic life circumstances and their functional interrelatedness need to be borne in mind when considering the sources of stress and distress in women's lives.

SOCIAL ROLES AND THE OCCURRENCE
OF STRESSFUL EXPERIENCES

Since social roles are central to our discussion, it would be useful to describe what we mean by this construct. By social roles we refer to the rights, responsibilities, and normatively prescribed behaviors that adhere to occupants of a given status or position. Much of social interaction occurs within the context of roles. In essence, roles specify how individuals occupying a particular status *should* act towards others with whom they typically interact—i.e., members of the role set. As convergence points between the sociocultural system and the individual, roles are the translation of abstract cultural values into specific prescribed ways of acting. Individuals enact social roles—particularly major ones within central social institutions such as family, work, and the economy—because roles provide the opportunity and means to achieve important internalized life goals. Problems arising within and around roles, then, pose a threat both to the functioning of the social system and to the well-being of the individual. Because of the pivotal importance of roles, problems arising within them are not likely to be sloughed off as trivial. And because social roles function to provide form and structure to social relationships among individuals, they are critical to the study of the social sources of stress.

The notion that social roles figure prominently in the stressful life experiences of women and men is certainly not a novel idea. Indeed, much of what concerns us in this chapter represents an extension and elaboration of issues that have a presence in the research literature. Thus, our attention will first be directed to role occupancy, a perspective that has guided much of past research efforts to explain gender differences in psychological distress (Aneshensel, Frerichs, & Clark, 1981; Cleary & Mechanic, 1983; Gore & Mangione, 1983; Gove, 1972, 1979; Gove & Tudor, 1973). Like others, we also see the occupancy and stratification of social roles as critical elements structuring the stressful experiences of men and women.

But, as we shall elaborate, we believe that role occupancy is important primarily because it determines ranges of potentially stressful experiences. That is, it is not role occupancy per se that is critical to the stress process. It is, rather, that role occupancy increases the chances of exposure to some stressors and precludes the presence of others. For example, one can certainly face a range of stressors as a full-time homemaker, but homemakers cannot be exposed directly to those stressors that reside in the workplace. A second perspective that we shall also elaborate regards differential stress as a consequence of the conditions people face once they occupy a role. Thus, to use the example above, two homemakers may have very different experiences within the same role. Third and finally, we shall consider the junctures between roles as a source of stressful conditions associated with gender. Where a person's multiple roles intersect, competition and conflict can be found and can help us to understand differences in stressful experiences between women and men.

STUDY BACKGROUND

Much of our discussion of role-related stressors is based on our own research, specifically on a pair of longitudinal studies examining stress and psychological distress in community-based populations. Because we shall draw heavily on these studies, a brief description of them is useful.

The Chicago study. The first study was conducted between 1972 and 1976–77 in the urbanized area of Chicago. It had three major foci: the assessment of a wide range of problems people experience in major social roles; the identification of the social and personal resources and the coping responses they bring to bear in dealing with these life stressors; and the examination of how these stressors and coping responses relate to emotional distress and psychological disturbance. A representative sample of 2300 individuals between the ages of 18 and 65 was first interviewed in 1972. Of these respondents, 1106 were reinterviewed four years later. Data that describe the types of stressful experiences encountered by women and men within marital, parental, and occupational roles are summarized in the following sections. The methods used to conduct this inquiry can be found in greater detail elsewhere (Pearlin & Lieberman, 1979; Pearlin & Schooler, 1978).

The Los Angeles study. The second study was designed to examine the antecedents and consequences of depressive symptoms, with a particular focus on stressors and help-seeking behavior. The subjects for this investigation were 1003 adults selected to be representative of the adult population of Los Angeles County (Frerichs et al., 1981). These respondents were interviewed four times at four-month intervals in 1979 and 1980, and one additional time four years after the initial interview in 1983. A total of 674 respondents were interviewed at the final interview; 602 were interviewed on all five occasions. Details of the longitudinal portion of this study are provided elsewhere (Aneshensel, 1985). Findings from this study on the nature and impact of family and work-related stressors are summarized in the following section.

ROLE OCCUPANCY AND STRESSORS

The first critical point concerning role-bound sources of stress appears rather obvious: the occurrence of the stressor within a particular role is contingent upon the occupancy of the role, for nonoccupancy of the role places the stressor outside of the realm of possible direct experience. Thus, for example, only the married may encounter problems with their husbands or wives; only the employed may experience problems with supervisors, co-workers, and subordinates at the workplace. Conversely, only the unmarried may be exposed to problems associated with being single, widowed, or divorced; those who are retired, unemployed, or homemakers encounter role-related stressors that differ from those who are employed. Thus, the constellation of social roles an individual occupies differentially exposes him or her to specific types of stressors while shielding him or her from others.

This contingency, unfortunately, is frequently not recognized in comparisons of intergroup differences in the occurrence of stressful events or circumstances. The problem is particularly salient for comparisons based on composite scores on life events measures, since many of the events assess role transitions which are inherently conditional on role occupancy, such as job loss or death of a spouse. To the extent that women and men differ in their rates of holding relevant roles, this introduces a systematic source of bias when comparable events are not included for those not holding these roles. Makosky (1980) cites the inclusion of events most relevant to men (e.g., employment-related events) and the exclusion of items most relevant to women (e.g., rape, abortion, events occurring to significant others) as a systematic source of bias in estimating sex differences in exposure to stress.

Because many social roles are differentially allocated by gender, men and women differ in their potential for exposure to role-bound stressors. At the extreme are roles occupied only by women or only by men; stressors associated with these roles are necessarily unique to one gender or the other. For example, difficulties in enacting the homemaker role are largely unique to women, not because they are women but because this is a role almost exclusively assigned to women. More typically, men and women occupy particular roles at differential rates, with the result that larger or smaller subgroups of women than men have the potential for encountering the associated stressors.

The complexity of this seemingly straightforward dependency of certain stressors on role occupancy can be illustrated quite clearly for employment-related stressors. Due to overall gender differences in employment rates, a greater proportion of men than women can encounter stressors whose occurrence is contingent upon being employed. This does not necessarily mean, however, that more men *do* encounter employment-related stressors than women, for those who hold jobs may or may not encounter stressors associated with the role. Take as an example the involuntary loss of a job, a stressor that can be experienced only by those who hold a job in the first place. Because more men than women are employed, it would seem that men are more likely as a group to be exposed to job loss. However, if a greater proportion of *employed* women than employed men do actually encounter this stressor, this could lead to an overall female excess of stress reactions resulting from job loss.

Results from the Los Angeles study illustrate these issues with respect to the stress engendered by transitions into and out of occupational roles. When the total sample of women and men was considered, irrespective of employment status, only a few gender differences were found in the occurrence of events signaling changes in employment. Over the four years of the study, men were more likely than women to report changing a job for a similar one (15.4 vs. 8.5 percent, $p < .05$), but were less likely to report starting a first job or returning to the labor force (5.7 vs. 11.5 percent, $p < .05$). However, there were no substantial or consistent sex differences for employment-related loss events (fired, laid off, quit, retired, or changed jobs for a worse one) or for changing a job for a better one. Thus, men did not evidence a greater rate of loss events than women, even though proportionately more men than women were employed and eligible to suffer job loss.

On the contrary, women appear to be more caught up in the loss and acquisition of jobs than men. The Chicago study, for example, found that over a four-year period women were more likely to be entering or reentering the labor market or giving up outside employment for homemaking (Pearlin & Lieberman, 1979). In the Los Angeles data, substantially more men than women were consistently employed over time, whereas almost twice as many women as men reported patterns of being both employed and not employed at different times over the course of the study. Based on reports of employment status at time 1, time 4, and time 5, the following percentages were found to be significantly different ($p < .001$) between women and men, respectively: 44.7 versus 73.6 percent employed on all three occasions; 25.4 versus 11.2 percent not employed on all three occasions; 29.9 versus 15.2 percent employed on at least one occasion and not employed on at least one occasion.

Important gender differences are found when the occurrence of events is assessed among only those eligible to encounter the event, thus providing a critical linkage between gender, employment status, and stressors attendant upon the occupancy of job roles. Only the employed can lose their jobs or change them for better, similar, or worse jobs; only those who are not working can start working or return to work. However, workers who lose their jobs become, at least temporarily, ineligible for further job loss;

they instead become candidates for reentry events. This means that the pool of individuals to whom certain events can possibly occur shifts over time as a result of other events having occurred.

Men and women were found to differ significantly from one another in the pattern of events they are eligible to encounter over time ($p < .001$). Because men are most likely to be consistently employed, they are most likely to be at risk for only job loss or change (52.2 percent) and less likely to risk exposure to both types of events (36.8 percent) or to only entry-reentry events (11.1 percent). By contrast, women tend to be at risk for both types of events (46.9 percent) more often than they are at risk for only loss or change events (29.1 percent) or for only entry-reentry events (24.0 percent). Over time, therefore, women more than men are eligible to be exposed to both sets of events—loss events and entry events.

Moreover, women who are at risk for employment-related losses during the course of the study experience such losses to a greater extent than men. Women who have been employed at some point during this time are more likely than comparable men to experience any employment loss event, including, specifically, being fired, laid off, or quitting. When only those who are out of the labor force at some point in time are considered, on the other hand, there is no sex difference in the occurrence of entry or reentry events.

In summary, considering the total sample, irrespective of employment status, the frequency of employment loss among women is no greater than among men. However, women who have been employed during the study are disproportionately likely to lose or relinquish their jobs. Overall, women are also more likely than men to enter or reenter the labor force. Women who have been out of the labor force during the study, however, do not enter the labor force in significantly greater proportions than similar men, at least over the length of time studied here.

We detail these findings because these patterns of instability and change partially characterize the nature of women's employment roles and have several implications for research into the sources and impact of stress. Since women in general experience employment-related loss no more often than men, the overall female excess of psychological distress would not appear attributable merely to differential exposure to these loss events. By contrast, those women who are labor force participants typically encounter loss events more often than comparable males, which may help to explain why women do not seem to accrue the same level of psychological and emotional benefits from working as do men (cf. Aneshensel et al., 1981; Gore & Mangione, 1983). Comparisons of employed men and women or of the impact on men and women of being employed implicitly assume that the employment role is the same for the two sexes. What we have seen here, however, is that employment status, by itself, masks important contextual differences shaped by the career trajectories of women and men.

We submit, therefore, that the history of one's role occupancy shapes both current experience within that role and the meaning of such experience. Furthermore, the role histories of men and women are likely to differ in ways that influence the stress-provoking nature of current experience. For example, shorter, discontinuous employment patterns are typically associated with little occupational advancement, low financial compensation, and limited employment security. These are precisely the areas in which female workers experience more difficulties than male workers—difficulties with depressive consequences (Pearlin, 1975). Thus, occupational role transitions over a period of time generate an employment history that functions as a context in shaping the meaning of current role transitions and, more importantly, that impacts on the conditions encountered in current work roles. The present cannot be understood when separated from the past. Otherwise, we shall mistakenly believe that people who are really different by virtue of past experience are the same because of the similarity of current positions and statuses. We turn now from current and past role occupancy as forces that distinguish women and men to a consideration of gender differences within roles.

STRESSFUL CONDITIONS WITHIN ROLES: OCCUPATION AND FAMILY

The second major point concerning role-bound sources of stress appears as obvious as the first, namely that exposure to role stressors cannot be predicted solely on the basis of role occupancy. The potential for stressful experience resides in the conditions and demands of the role, as does the potential for achievement and gratification. Stress results from the quality of experiences within and across roles, not from the mere occupancy of roles. This is illustrated in a recent study by Barnett and Baruch (1985) which found that the quality of experience within a woman's social roles—the balance between rewarding and distressing role attributes—was more important in explaining role conflict, role overload and anxiety among midlife women than either the sheer number of roles occupied or role occupancy per se.

As obvious as intrarole variability appears, it is often overlooked, particularly when interrole comparisons are made. This is perhaps most clearly evident when comparisons are drawn between homemakers and employed women. As described by Gove (Gove & Geerken, 1977; Gove & Tudor, 1973), the homemaker role is unstructured and invisible, involves women in boring, repetitive, and unskilled tasks, affords little prestige, and is enacted in a context of isolation from adult interaction. Such conditions may evoke a perceived lack of control over one's environment, time, and future—circumstances likely to be conducive to the development of psychological distress. Employed wives and mothers, on the other hand, are seen as being denied the full psychological benefits of work because they presumably experience stress resulting from role overload and conflict with family roles (Gove & Geerken, 1977). Married women, therefore, are seen as facing two unattractive alternatives, being a homemaker or being employed, both of which are viewed as inherently stressful. From this perspective, merely occupying these roles exposes women to stressful conditions, regardless of the particular circumstances that women confront within their roles.

A different perspective, supported by data from the Chicago study, is that while the limitations and demands of the homemaker role are stressful for some women, others value the role highly and do not find it onerous (Pearlin, 1975; Pearlin & Lieberman, 1979). Overall, there was no difference in the level of depression between full-time homemakers and employed women in this study. *Within* each of these groups, however, the level of role strain that women experienced was associated with their level of depression. The types of persistent life strains reported by homemakers include feeling unappreciated for work done in the home, being uninterested or bored with household chores, experiencing fatigue due to housework, and being lonely for the company of adults. These strains, then, are similar to the conditions typically attributed to the role. However, rewards associated with this role include enjoying work done in the home, satisfaction from using talents and abilities, and having free time to oneself. The intensity of the strains varies considerably among women, with most falling between the extremes of finding the homemaker role excessively burdensome or fully rewarding.

It is not the homemaker role per se that is stressful, then, as there is considerable variability among these women in the degree to which they experience problems as homemakers. This variability is related to the substance and intensity of the demands imposed on them within the role. Moreover, the intensity of homemaking strains does not vary with women's status aspirations, their formal training, previous occupational experience, or social class. These strains emerge because of the demands encountered within the home rather than because of unfulfilled dreams outside the home. The household demands, in turn, are related to the location of families in the life course, being less severe in advanced stages where there are fewer and older children in the home, and being more severe where the mother is the sole parent. To the extent that a homemaker is isolated from social networks, she is likely both to have greater difficulty in managing problems encountered in the role and to rely exclusively on the immediate family to fulfill emotional and affiliative needs.

Moreover, how a woman copes with the demands of the role alters its impact on her. Women under the same strain who evaluate themselves as better off than others and who see these problems as temporary tend to be less distressed than those who make less favorable evaluations of themselves and who see their present burdens as continuing far into the future.

For roles occupied by both women and men (e.g., occupational roles), an additional issue that arises is whether men or women are more likely to encounter stressful circumstances in enacting them. Answering this question is a complex matter because the nature or types of difficulties encountered may be qualitatively different for women and men. Hence, quantitative comparisons between the sexes can be misleading. This point can be illustrated quite clearly for the case of persistent strains emerging in the workplace.

First, it must be recognized that one consequence of sex stratification of the occupational system is that women and men typically hold different types of jobs. Despite the influx of women into the work force and their entry into many male-dominated fields, the majority of women are still clustered in those clerical and service occupations traditionally assigned to their sex (U.S. Bureau of the Census, 1985). This sex stratification of occupations can be traced, in part, to the types of gender differences in labor force participation discussed in the preceding section. That is, women who have interrupted their employment or who have worked part-time find themselves at a disadvantage in occupations where full-time, continuous employment is normative. Such women may have difficulty obtaining employment or may be channeled into traditional female occupations where variable labor force participation is more acceptable but where salaries are low and advancement unlikely (Zellman, 1976). Thus, the characteristics of the current occupational system, including overt sex discrimination, serve to channel women into occupations that differ from those held by men. Because men and women typically occupy different jobs, the demands, opportunities, and rewards associated with employment differ as well. Moreover, men and women in the same jobs frequently experience different conditions, most notably with respect to power relationships, peer relationships, and benefits to self and others (Long & Porter, 1984).

Consequently, men and women are likely to differ in the nature of problems typically encountered in the workplace. The types of persistent life strains associated with occupational roles were one of the main foci of the Chicago study (Pearlin & Lieberman, 1979). For only one of four general types of role strain examined in this research did women and men have similar experiences: encountering noxious environmental conditions in the work setting, such as the presence of dust and dirt, or exposure to injury or illness. Two of the remaining types of strain were more commonly experienced by men, while one was more common among women. Men were more likely than women to encounter strain from job pressures and the time demands of the work task. Problems of this type include having too much work to do, working too many hours, and doing tasks that no one else wants to do. Men were also more likely than women to report having depersonalizing experiences; that is, being treated by others as a person without feelings or sensitivities, or being treated unfairly or in an unfriendly way. In contrast, women were more likely than men to experience difficulties related to receiving inadequate rewards for their work, such as earning insufficient income, lack of job security, inadequate fringe benefits, and limited opportunities for future job advancement.

None of these areas of role strain is the sole province of either men or women. Instead, these conditions impinge on both sexes, although they do so with somewhat different frequency or intensity. To simply combine strain across these areas of functioning would erroneously assume that each type is equivalent in its capacity to arouse stress. Receiving inadequate compensation may or may not have the same stress potential as encountering depersonalizing situations with one's co-workers, for example.

Problems and frustrations encountered on the job and at home, however, are differentially distressing to women and men, as evidenced by data from the Chicago study (Pearlin, 1975). Men were found to be more depressed than women by strains encountered at work, while women were more depressed than men by marital problems. This does not mean that the strains encountered are more severe; rather, similar types and intensities of strain have greater depressive consequences for one gender than the other.

Difficulties in each of these two major areas of adult functioning are, of course, distressing to both sexes, as most individuals place a high value on the family and on work (see Barnett & Baruch, this volume). The differential impact of these strains, however, may reflect the importance attached to these domains within the traditional sociocultural milieu. To the extent that work is defined as centrally important to men and the family to women, then, problems in these areas may take on an added potential to evoke distress. Because the sociocultural system values and supports the employment and occupational attainment of men, it is not surprising that difficulties within the work role are more consequential for men (Pearlin, 1975). Although the family is highly valued for women, the homemaker role is currently devalued by many, and there is no clear consensus concerning the roles that *are* desirable for women. Both a family and a career are presented as attractive paths to follow. Those opting for one or the other often feel that something valuable may have been lost along the way. Yet women combining marriage and motherhood with a career must contend with a lack of institutionalized means for achieving integration of the two. At many crossroads they must choose between one or the other. We turn now to a consideration of how stress arises for women at the junctures between occupational and family roles.

STRESS BETWEEN OCCUPATIONAL AND FAMILY ROLES

Individuals do not enact roles in isolation but in constellations, and strain is as likely to occur at the juncture of roles as within a role. Thus, a given role may be experienced as stressful not because of anything inherent in the role itself, but because it is incompatible with other important social roles. Alternately, the tasks of one role may become excessively demanding only when added to those from other roles. To illustrate, a woman may experience stress from working not because of the conditions of work, but because working results in conflict with her husband, or because she is taxed by an overload of household tasks. On the other hand, participation in certain roles may mitigate the stressful effects of other roles. As described by Kandel, Davies, and Raveis (1985), for example, marital stressors among mothers had greater depressive consequences among those not employed outside of the home than among the employed. Ideally, then, to study the stressors that a person experiences, it is desirable to incorporate the entire constellation of major roles the person occupies and the interconnections that exist among these roles.

Considerable research attention has been paid to stressors arising at the junctures of social roles, particularly family and work roles among women. Early theoretical formulations in this area were based on attempts to explain sex differences in psychological distress. Gove and his colleagues, for example, attribute the overall sex difference to differences among the married (even though the unmarried have higher rates of distress), contending that the social roles of men and women differ more among the married (Gove, 1972, 1979; Gove & Tudor, 1973). According to this perspective, married women more than married men experience extensive family role demands. Due to different normative expectations for appropriate behavior, the roles of wife and mother are likely to be more time consuming and expansive, to invoke more areas of responsibility, and to be more disruptive of other social roles than the roles of husband and father. One consequence of familial role demands, the one of immediate concern here, is the potential for interrole conflict due to excessive or incompatible demands associated with work and family obligations.

Occupancy of both work and family roles is frequently implicitly equated with role conflict or overload, as when comparisons are made between women who work outside of the home and those who do not. Such strain, however, is not the inevitable consequence of dual role occupancy. Instead, as data from the Chicago study indicate, it is the problematic integration of roles that is the source of tension, rather than the duality of roles in and of itself (Pearlin, 1975). For employed mothers, whether the occupancy of both work and family roles produced interrole conflict depended, first, upon the demands experienced within each role, and, second, upon the commitment to or investment in each role.

Three distinct dimensions of interrole conflict for employed women were examined in the Chicago study. One concerned the extent to which working contributed directly to problems in the management of the household, resulting in more housework than could be handled, too little time to do household tasks, or no free time for oneself. The second dimension concerned the consequences of having a job for strain in the marital relationship. Problems of this type included having the husband object to his wife's employment, having work interfere with joint leisure activities, or having working lead to conflict over finances, household chores, or disagreement over who was the head of the household. The third dimension of interrole conflict pertained directly to maternal roles. This dimension encompassed concern about the adequacy of child care, concern that children were not getting proper attention or were getting into trouble, and feelings that maternal pleasures were being missed. As with the other types of strain we have been considering, there was considerable diversity among these women in the extent to which family and work roles actually came into conflict with one another. Moreover, when such conflicts did occur, they stemmed from the interplay of several social factors including the degree of involvement in each role, the structure of the family, and the position of the woman in the larger class structure.

The results of the Chicago study, which are given in greater detail elsewhere (Pearlin, 1975), indicate that interrole conflict is generally more likely to occur when family role demands are extreme and inflexible or when commitment to work is strong. For working-class women, having young children is particularly associated with interrole strain. The relatively inflexible job demands these women typically encounter may contribute to excessive interrole conflict, especially when familial demands are great, that is, when there are young children at home. For middle-class women, involvement in the work role seems a more important determinant of maternal role conflict than the demands directly associated with the maternal role. Among these women, employment and maternal roles run the greatest risk of coming into conflict when the mother is highly invested in both roles. The woman most exposed to dilemmas and cross pressures is the one who is committed to her maternal role while deeply absorbed in her work, valuing work for itself rather than for what it instrumentally provides. These conflicts and their depressive consequences arise and abate as women move through various stages of the life course, largely because the associated demands of family roles change.

Data from the Los Angeles study similarly indicate that it is not dual role occupancy in and of itself that is consequential, but rather the experiences women have within work and family roles (Aneshensel, 1986). Married women not employed outside of the home and unmarried women were compared to employed married women and to employed women who experienced either little or considerable strain in each of the roles. Dual role women who experienced little strain in either the workplace or the marriage were found to have the lowest risk of being depressed. Married employed women experiencing high levels of strain within each role ran a rather high risk of being depressed, but this risk was exceeded by women with comparable strain in their marriages who were not employed outside of the home. Thus, dual role occupancy need not necessarily generate strain within each of the roles, and when it does not, women appear to accrue substantial psychological benefits.

Overall, then, a presumed inherent conflict between work and family roles is very limited in its ability to explain women's distress either as it compares to that of men or by itself. Although such conflict does exist and is of obvious importance, it is apparent that it is the *quality* of experiences within the roles more than their occupancy alone that mainly matters to the well-being of women. While no single strategy is likely to answer all questions about distress and the conditions contributing to it, it does appear necessary to look more closely at the internal circumstances of roles and the contexts in which these roles are enacted.

Moreover, we must emphasize that the stressful role conflicts experienced by employed married women and by those having young children at home are irrelevant to full-time homemakers, to the unmarried, and to those without young children in the household. Although it is clearly useful to look at work and family role conflict as a source of women's stress, there are large numbers whose statuses place them outside the reach of such conflict. Thus in the Los Angeles sample, only about 50 percent of the men and 40 percent of the women between the ages of 25 and 45 are partners in marriages with children in the household; fewer than 20 percent of women younger than 25 or older than 45 fit this profile (Aneshensel et al., 1981). Women who are free of the potential for work and family role conflicts, however, are certainly not free of stress. While they do not experience these conflicts, they may nonetheless be subject to other severe stressors. We know, for example, that the unmarried are both more exposed and more vulnerable than the married to persistent life strains, particularly economic strains and social isolation, hardships with depressive consequences (Pearlin & Johnson, 1977). In looking for sources of women's distress, it is clear that we must tailor our search to the specific circumstances of subgroups of women.

PERSPECTIVES FOR FUTURE WORK

Our intent in this chapter has been to delineate some of the ways in which gender shapes the life experiences of women so as to create stress. Specifically, we have been concerned with aspects of sex stratification that lead to problematic experiences within and across social roles, particularly employment and family roles. This approach is highly selective, addressing only a limited portion of the spectrum of problematic conditions potentially arising in the lives of women. More importantly, sex stratification is but one specific way in which social stratification generally leads to the occurrence of stressors. Nevertheless, this approach has identified some of the strengths and limitations of current strategies for the study of stressors in women's lives. We turn now to a consideration of promising directions for future work.

Understanding stressors and their consequences requires first that the full range of problematic circumstances encountered by women be studied. This is difficult to accomplish when comparisons between women and men are emphasized. The focus of prior work has tended to be limited either to those areas of functioning where women and men are thought to have the most similar experiences (life event change) or to those where they are thought to have the most dissimilar experiences (conflict between family and occupational roles). Identification of the limitations of these research strategies, rooted in the research tradition of explaining sex differences in psychological distress, helps point toward areas for future research.

Two can be outlined. The first is to identify more completely those sources of stress uniquely impinging on the lives of women. Because the very organization of societies limits the areas of comparability across genders, reliance on shared stressors necessarily limits our understanding of how the structure of men's and women's lives around fundamentally different social roles gives rise to and shapes the experience of stress. Thus, as long as we confine our efforts to explaining gender differences, we can at best achieve only limited success in identifying those circumstances influencing women qua women, not as they compare to men. We suggest, therefore, that it would be productive to devote more attention to the stressful conditions that impinge on women but that might lie outside the lives of men (and vice versa). For example, we know little about the impact on the psychological well-being of women of overt and covert sex discrimination in education, employment, or finances. Comparisons with men can help to identify that which is and is not shared, but intensifed investigation of women is necessary to uncover those areas of functioning that are uniquely problematic for women.

The second direction is to specify more thoroughly how gender orders the occurrence and impact of stressors that arise in the lives of women and men alike. Typically, this issue has been addressed by asking whether gender *directly* affects either exposure or vulnerability to stressors (see Wethington, McLeod, & Kessler, this volume). The effects associated with gender are often *indirect* however, involving basic elements of social organization and stratification. As discussed above, occupying certain roles creates the opportunity for some events and circumstances to occur and precludes others, as in the case of employment-dependent stressors. To the extent that men and women occupy relevant roles at varying rates, differentially sized subgroups are at risk for the possible occurrence of role-bound stressors. Differential role occupancy is tied to other status characteristics ascribed to and achieved by individuals as well as to their gender, such as age, race, social class, marital status, and so on. The linkages between social characteristics, position in the social system, and exposure to problematic conditions of life need to be investigated more thoroughly than has been the case to date. An added complexity is that these linkages change as people traverse the life course. Problematic conditions can differ from one life to stage to another and the ways they differ may further vary with people's social and economic characteristics.

More generally, we have not yet adequately incorporated into our theoretical and analytical paradigms the contingency of stressors on social role occupancy, with the result that the meaning of intergroup comparisons remains unclear. Intergroup comparisons of exposure to and the impact of particular stressors typically fail to distinguish those eligible and ineligible to encounter the stressor. When such contingency exists, those to whom the event or circumstance did not occur comprise two distinct types of individuals: those for whom the stressor is irrelevant and those for whom it is relevant but absent. Combining these two types for analysis is problematic, especially when the groups being compared differ widely in the rate at which they occupy the relevant role, as was the case for gender differences in employment and employment-related losses. To assess intergroup differences adequately, then, requires a specification of those within each group who are eligible to encounter the stressor.

We propose several specific directions for future work that we think will be productive. To begin with, we espouse a general maxim: the study of stressful conditions and their consequences demands a longitudinal, developmental perspective. The nature of the stressors that people experience and, perhaps, the nature of their emotional responses to these stressors are in a state of flux along the life course. It can be very misleading to speak of "women's stress" without specifying the life stages at which individual women are located. We can think of virtually no stressful conditions that are likely to impinge with equal probability or equal force on women at all life stages. This is particularly important because the impact of at least some role transitions appears to depend upon when they occur; those that occur at normatively scheduled times of the life course seem to be generally less distressing than those which occur at other times (Neugarten, 1965; Pearlin, 1980). While the need for a longitudinal, developmental perspective seems self-evident, it is not often used as a systematic approach to research.

Life course linkages can be extremely complex and difficult to establish. For example, our analysis of employment-related life events documented that a substantial subgroup of women experience a disproportionate number of life event stressors comprising labor market entries and exits. Unstable career trajectories, often set during early adulthood, may leave a legacy of more enduring problems later in life, in addition to their immediate effect on the individual. Such a possibility is suggested by the employment strains that are more common among women than men; compensation-related strains are precisely the types of problems that one would expect to find associated with discontinuous or part-time labor force participation. In this regard, Long and Porter (1984) observe that the most notable feature of midlife for women is an economic vulnerability that derives directly from the combination of work and family histories. Thus, how a woman manages the competing demands of family and work roles at one stage of the life course may in part determine the types of stressors encountered later in life. Because the biographical histories of individuals shape the nature and the meaning of current conditions that people face, it is imperative that we start to bring this type of life course perspective to bear on our investigations of stressors and stress reactions. The past can be a crucial context for the present.

There are, of course, other contextual factors that shape the types of stressors arising in the lives of women. Given the issues we have been discussing, one seems to be particularly pertinent—the manner in which the collective experiences of women influence those of the individual. For example, the fact that many women have discontinuous employment histories impacts on women who follow a pattern similar to the modal pattern followed by men as well as on those who do leave the labor force to care for families. The societal stereotype is that all women will do so and that their work will take second place to the family. This expectation is, for example, commonly used as a rationale for tracking females into sex-segregated occupations which, in turn, appears to generate stressors in occcupational life that are qualitatively different from those typically encountered by males. Thus, Long and Porter (1984) observe that familial priority is imputed even when it does not apply, contributing to low earnings for women relative to men among those with comparable, nonintermittent employment histories. The individual's own experience in the work realm is shaped not only by her own personal history but by societal expectations concerning women's work and family roles.

The importance of the sociocultural context is evidenced in a recent study in which Gore and Mangione (1983) found, first, only a small female excess of depression relative to men and, second, a beneficial effect of employment on psychological well-being among women that was comparable to the effect found among men. This urban sample was characterized by an unusually high employment rate among women. They suggest that having a "critical mass" of working wives may operate as an aggregate contextual factor enhancing the effect of employment on the psychological well-being of women. Societal changes over time in the roles occupied by women and men and in the values attaching to sex roles may alter the interrelationships among social roles, stress, and gender (see Barnett & Baruch, this volume).

Finally, it is our position that to comprehend the stressful conditions people experience and the social underpinnings of these conditions, it is desirable to address ourselves to entire constellations of major social roles, not one or two. We state this in full recognition of the difficulties in fulfilling such a desideratum. Nevertheless, it should be recognized that the problems a person confronts while enacting one role may well create problems in other roles. We know that people do seek to inhibit the changes and strains in one area of functioning from permeating others. Regardless of these efforts, the threats and transformations that people experience in different roles tend to become functionally interrelated (Pearlin et al., 1981). It is especially useful to keep this in mind when searching for the sources of women's distress. Their more frequent transitions into and out of the labor market and their broader range of responsibilities for family and household affairs may be reflected in areas of life seemingly remote from these immediate domains. Stressors beget stressors, and we need to know more about their diffusion through constellations of roles.

In this chapter, we have attempted to identify some of the dimensions of role-bound experience that structure the occurrence of stress. In doing so, we have sought to go beyond single roles to explore how the organization of lives around multiple roles might contribute to the experience of stress. This consideration has demonstrated the need to consider both the areas in which the life experiences of women overlap with those of men and the areas in which they do not. Finally, it is important to recognize that we can neither understand women's psychological functioning nor, it follows, differences between women and men, if we fail to encompass in our observations the full range of significant experiences that challenge both women and men.

REFERENCES

Aneshensel, C. S. (1985). The natural history of depressive symptoms: Implications for psychiatric epidemiology. In J. R. Greenley (Ed.), *Research in community and mental health* (Vol. 5). Greenwich CT: JAI Press.

———. (1986). Marital and employment role-strain, social support, and depression among adult women. In S. E. Hobfoll (Ed.), *Stress, social support, and women*. Washington, DC: Hemisphere.

Aneshensel, C. S., Frerichs, R. R., & Clark, V. A. (1981). Family roles and sex differences in depression. *Journal of Health and Social Behavior, 22,* 379–393.

Barnett, R. C., & Baruch, G. K. (1985). Women's involvement in multiple roles and psychological distress. *Journal of Personality and Social Psychology, 49,* 135–145.

Belle, D. (1980). Who uses mental health facilities? In M. Guttentag, S. Salasin, & D. Belle (Eds.), *The mental health of women*. New York: Academic Press.

Cleary, P. D., & Mechanic, D. (1983). Sex differences in psychological distress among married people. *Journal of Health and Social Behavior, 24,* 111–121.

Comstock, G. W., & Helsing, K. J. (1976). Symptoms of depression in two communities. *Psychological Medicine, 6,* 551–563.

Frerichs, R. R., Aneshensel, C. S., & Clark, V. A. (1981). Prevalence of depression in Los Angeles County. *American Journal of Epidemiology, 113.* 691–699.

Gore, S., & Mangione, T. W. (1983). Social roles, sex roles and psychological distress: Additive and interactive models of sex differences. *Journal of Health and Social Behavior, 24,* 300–312.

Gove, W. R. (1972). The relationship between sex roles, marital status, and mental illness. *Social Forces, 51,* 34–44.

––––––. (1979). Sex differences in the epidemiology of mental disorder: Evidence and explanations. In E. S. Gomberg & V. Franks (Eds.), *Gender and disordered behavior: Sex differences in psychopathology.* New York: Brunner/Mazel.

Gove, W. R., & Geerken, M. R. (1977). The effect of children and employment on the mental health of married men and women. *Social Forces, 56,* 66–76.

Gove, W. R., & Tudor, J. F. (1973). Adult sex roles and mental illness. *American Journal of Sociology, 78,* 812–835.

Kandel, D. B., Davies, M., & Raveis, V. H. (1985). The stressfulness of daily social roles for women: Marital, occupational and household roles. *Journal of Health and Social Behavior, 26,* 64–78.

Kessler, R. C. (1979). Stress, social status, and psychological distress. *Journal of Health and Social Behavior, 20,* 259–272.

Kessler, R. C., & McLeod, J. D. (1984). Sex differences in vulnerability to undesirable life events. *American Sociological Review, 49,* 620–631.

Long, J., & Porter, K. L. (1984). Multiple roles of midlife women: A case for new directions in theory, research, and policy. In G. Baruch & J. Brooks-Gunn (Eds.), *Women in midlife.* New York: Plenum.

Makosky, V. P. (1980). Stress and the mental health of women: A discussion of research and issues. In M. Guttentag, S. Salasin, & D. Belle (Eds.). *The mental health of women.* New York: Academic Press.

Myers, J. K., Weissman, M. M., Tischler, G. L., Orvaschel, H., Gruenberg, E., Burke, J. D., & Regier, D. A. (1984). Six-month prevalence of psychiatric disorders in three communities. *Archives of General Psychiatry, 41,* 959–967.

Neugarten, B. L., Moore, J., & Lowe, J. C. (1965). Age norms, age constraints, and adult socialization. *American Journal of Sociology, 70,* 710–717.

Pearlin, L. I. (1975). Sex roles and depression. In N. Datan & L. H. Ginsberg (Eds.), *Life-span developmental psychology: Normative life crises.* New York: Academic Press.

––––––. (1980). The life cycle and life strains. In H. M. Blalock, Jr. (Ed.), *Sociological theory and research: A critical approach.* New York: Free Press.

––––––. (1982). The social contexts of stress. In L. Goldberger & S. Breznitz (Eds.), *Handbook of stress: Theoretical and clinical aspects.* New York: Free Press.

Pearlin, L. I., & Aneshensel, C. S. (1986). Coping and social supports: Their functions and applications. In L. Aiken & D. Mechanic (Eds.), *Applications of social science to clinical medicine and health policy.* New Brunswick, NJ: Rutgers University Press.

Pearlin, L. I., & Johnson, J. (1977). Marital status, life-strains and depression. *American Sociological Review, 42,* 704–715.

Pearlin, L. I., & Lieberman, M. A. (1979). Social sources of emotional distress. In R. G. Simmons (Ed.), *Research in community and mental health* (Vol.1). Greenwich, CT: JAI Press.

Pearlin, L. I., Lieberman, M. A., Menaghan, E. G., & Mullan, J. T. (1981). The stress process. *Journal of Health and Social Behavior, 22,* 337–356.

Pearlin, L. I., & Schooler, C. (1978). The structure of coping. *Journal of Health and Social Behavior, 19,* 2–21.

Radloff, L. S., & Rae, D. S. (1981). Components of the sex difference in depression. In R. G. Simmons (Ed.), *Research in Community and Mental Health* (Vol. 2). Greenwich, CT: JAI Press.

Robins, L. N., Helzer, J. E., Weissman, M. M., Orvaschel, H., Gruenburg, E., Burke, J. D., & Regier, D. A. (1984). Lifetime prevalence of specific psychiatric disorders in three sites. *Archives of General Psychiatry, 41,* 949–958.

U.S. Bureau of the Census. (1985). *Statistical abstract of the United States 1986* (106th Ed.). Washington, DC: U.S. Government Printing Office.

Weissman, M. M., & Klerman, G. L. (1977). Sex differences and the epidemiology of depression. *Archives of General Psychiatry, 34,* 98–111.

Zellman, G. L. (1976). The role of structural factors in limiting women's institutional participation. *Journal of Social Issues, 32,* 33–46.

4

Gender Differences in the Health Effects of Workplace Roles

Andrea Z. LaCroix
Suzanne G. Haynes

More women hold jobs outside the home today than ever before. Like men, the majority of women now participate in paid employment. Though our knowledge of how work affects the well-being of men and women is far from complete, there is little doubt that occupational environments— physical, chemical, and psychosocial—do play a role in altering health risks.

As increasing numbers of women entered the labor force, studies of gender and employment began with such basic questions as: Are employed women at greater risk for illness compared to those working in the home? Further, the multiplicity of roles (worker, spouse, parent) engaged in by men and women was suspected as a potential health risk. Most recently, the focus of research has turned to the quality of workplace roles and the identification of particular stressors that pose health risks. Examining these issues is made more challenging by differences in occupational sources of stress and strain for men and women and by the possibility that men and women differ in many other ways—in their expectations of work, perceptions of work environment qualities, role burdens outside the domain of work, and abilities to adapt and cope with stressful job situations.

Moving from the simplest of these questions to the most complex, we begin this chapter by examining the movement of American women into the labor force and asking what has been learned in the last decade about employment status and health among women. We next discuss potential causal pathways through which work could affect the health of men and women, emphasizing possible gender differences in these relationships. Finally, selected research is reviewed concerning the identification of specific occupational stressors, their potential impact on health risks for men and women, and our (limited) knowledge of gender differences in the health effects of workplace stress.

EMPLOYMENT TRENDS OF WOMEN
ENTERING THE LABOR FORCE

Roles and responsibilities associated with paid employment are incorporated into the daily experience of unprecedented numbers of American women today. At present, there are nearly 50 million employed women, constituting 44 percent of all workers (U.S. Dept. of Labor, 1984). Historically, the movement of women into the paid labor force has been gradual but persistent. Whereas only one in five women was employed at the turn of the century, today the majority of women occupy working roles. By 1990, it is projected that about 55 percent of all working-age females, or 52 million American women, will be employed, representing a threefold increase from the 18 percent who were working in 1890 (Bureau of Economic Statistics, 1981; Smith, 1979).

Furthermore, the majority of women with family responsibilities (60 percent) are choosing to work today. In 1984 nearly 20 million employed women had children under the age of 18. In contrast, in 1970, 60 percent of such women chose not to work outside the home (Hayghe, 1984). This trend is no doubt fueled in part by the growing proportion of working mothers who are single and head their households—one in four in 1984. For these women in particular, the decision to work is likely to be made foremost in the context of economic necessity, and second, in pursuit of other aspirations. In fact, paid employment is sought out of economic necessity for the majority of working women today, many of whom are single (26 percent), divorced (11 percent), widowed (5 percent), separated (4 percent), or have spouses with annual earnings under $15,000 (19 percent; U.S. Dept. of Labor, 1984). In sum, an expanding population of American women has joined men in the paid labor force and in the responsibilities of assuming multiple roles.

Women have yet to join men equally, however, in the types of occupations in which they are employed. Indeed, gender differences in the distribution of occupations have persisted over the past 20 years despite consistent growth in women's participation in paid work. Women were no more likely to be employed in jobs traditionally held by men in 1980 than in 1960, nor have men moved into traditionally female dominated occupations (Rytina & Bianchi, 1984). Employed women are concentrated in fewer occupations than men, and are particularly concentrated in the clerical category. There has been little change in the past 14 years with respect to women's movement into executive or blue-collar jobs traditionally held by men. Further, it is apparent from examination of detailed job categories that occupational segregation continues to divide working roles along gender lines, with the 25 largest predominantly male occupations accounting for 42 percent of men's work in 1980 and the 25 largest predominantly female occupations accounting for 57 percent of women's work (Rytina & Bianchi, 1984). Nevertheless, a decline in occupational segregation has been observed between 1970 and 1980 that is largely attributable to an increase of employment for both sexes in "sex-neutral" occupations. Overall, progress for women has been greatest in entering a limited group of white-collar occupations, including bookkeepers, managers, sales workers, supervisors, accountants, and auditors.

These data suggest that occupational segregation continues to differentiate the work experience of a large proportion of men and the majority of women. To the extent that access to various working roles is unequal for men and women, so too are the qualities of physical and psychosocial work environments which may affect perceptions of stress and be related to alterations in health status. Jobs traditionally held by women are often characterized by tedious and repetitive tasks, low authority and autonomy, limited upward mobility, rewards for vicarious rather than direct achievements, and underutilization of skills and talents. In a national survey of the U.S. labor force, women constituted a greater percentage of the "working class" than men (Wright, Costello, Hachen, & Sprague, 1982). In this investigation, "working class" referred to employment in occupations that were removed from decision making, had no supervisory responsibilities and little or no authority and autonomy. Furthermore, clerical occupations, which account for more than one-third of women's jobs, often had more "working class" attributes than skilled and semi-skilled manual labor occupations (Wright et al., 1982).

Even within the same occupational category, there is evidence that the allocation of power and authority to men and women is unequal (Wolf & Fligstein, 1979; Wright et al., 1982). Women have been found to have less control over the work of other people than men, even in positions of similar educational and occupational status (Wolf & Fligstein, 1979). In addition, the tasks allocated to men and women in the same job (e.g., computer programmer) have been found to differ systematically, with women performing more supplementary and support activities and fewer delegating and decision-making functions (Kraft, 1984). Earnings, perhaps the most objective and quantifiable of all job characteristics, also show a sex difference within narrow categories of occupations which has persisted over time. Women's earnings were less than two-thirds of their male counterparts in 1982, and this gap can be only partially explained by differences in age, education, and uninterrupted years of labor force participation (Mellor, 1984; Shack-Marquez, 1984). Where gender-specific disparities in job characteristics within similar occupations exist, the effects of work in generating or alleviating stress may also differ greatly for men and women.

Currently, tremendous redistributions in work are taking place for both men and women as the U.S. economy shifts from an industrial base to one based upon high technology and service industries. In the past few years, 3 million manufacturing jobs have been lost, contributing to the 10 percent unemployment rate in 1983 (Kuttner, 1983). It is projected that new technology will displace 3 million more manufacturing jobs by 1990 (Alcalay & Pasick, 1983).

However, the jobs created by the emerging service economy and high technology will not necessarily be characterized by more favorable working conditions or more pay than mass production manufacturing jobs. The Bureau of Labor Statistics estimates that the economy will generate 7 million new jobs by 1990 for low-wage service and clerical workers as compared to only 3.5 million jobs for professional and technical employees (Kuttner, 1983). Eventually, initial gains in the number of clerical jobs may be offset by the increased efficiency of high technology. For example, the need for data-entry workers will decrease as the technology for automatic data entry (e.g., through optical scanners) becomes available. Therefore, one effect of new technology in the future may be a loss of clerical jobs, which is likely to result in greater unemployment for women, especially minority women (U.S. Congress, 1985).

Another concern resulting from current labor force trends is the effect of office automation on the health and well-being of white-collar and clerical workers. By 1990, one in three of all such workers will use a video display terminal (VDT). For many workers, especially professionals, computer technologies will enhance efficiency and decrease or eliminate time-consuming and repetitive tasks. The introduction of computer-mediated work systems into clerical jobs will undoubtedly change, and perhaps improve, the nature of work for millions of clerical workers, 85 percent of whom are women. However, early studies have shown that clerical jobs characterized by prolonged and intense use of VDTs result in perceptions of higher job strain and more frequent reports of musculoskeletal problems, eye strain, and fatigue (Haynes, LaCroix, & Lippin, 1987; Smith, Cohen, & Stammerjohn, 1981). The long-term health effects of VDT exposure are currently unknown and a topic of high priority for future investigation.

In sum, the work environments of men and women differ substantially, because they tend to hold different kinds of jobs and because even in the same job they are assigned different kinds of tasks. Furthermore,

the nature of work is changing due to shifts toward a service-based economy and the impact of high technology. Men and women may also differ
in their responses to the demands of the worker role. All of these factors
influence and distinguish the work experience of men and women and
therefore require consideration if we are to understand the worker-job interaction.

PAID EMPLOYMENT AND WOMEN'S HEALTH:
THE ANSWERS TO BASIC QUESTIONS

The influx of women into the labor force initially generated concern that
paid employment might increase health risks for working women as compared to housewives. Such concerns arise in the context of women's greater
longevity and lower mortality from most major causes since the turn of
the century (Wingard, Suarez, & Barrett-Connor, 1983). It was hypothesized that men's higher rates of employment and exposure to occupational
hazards might explain some proportion of their higher mortality rates and
shorter life expectancy. If so, then women's increasing participation in paid
employment might be accompanied by declines in these health parameters. Neither postulation has found support in empirical research.

Table 1 summarizes the results of several recent studies comparing risk
factors for chronic diseases and health status indicators among employed
women and housewives. Working women appear to be healthier than nonemployed women in several respects. Compared to housewives, working
women have been found to have fewer sick days, fewer limitations in activity as a result of chronic conditions, fewer acute conditions, fewer hospital days, better self-reported health status, and better psychological well-
being (Hibbard & Pope, 1985; Wheeler, Lee, & Loe, 1983). (See Warr &
Parry, 1982, for a systematic and comprehensive review of studies examining employment status in relation to several measures of psychological
well-being.) In addition, employed women have not been found to experience greater risk of developing coronary heart disease than housewives
(Haynes & Feinleib, 1980) or elevations in standard coronary risk factors
(Haynes & Feinleib, 1980; Hazuda, Haffner, Stern, Knapp, Eifler, & Rosenthal, 1986; Slaby, 1982). In fact, limited evidence suggests that working
women may be at lesser risk for coronary heart disease by virtue of more
favorable levels of serum cholesterol (Slaby, 1982) or lipoproteins (Hazuda
et al., 1986). The evidence showing similar or more favorable health profiles among employed women is strengthened by the consistency of the
results in Table 1 and the use of both nationally representative and geo-
graphically circumscribed community populations.

The fact that increasing numbers of employed women are engaged in
meeting the demands of multiple roles such as worker, parent, and spouse
has also been suspected as a contributor to physical health risks among

Table 1. Employment Status[1] and Physical Health Among Women: A Review of Selected Studies

Author/Year	Study Population	Physical Health Outcome(s)	Comparison of Housewives (HW) and Working Women (WW)[2]
Hauenstein, Kasl, & Harburg, 1977	508 married women aged 25–60; Detroit, 1968–1969	Blood pressure	No difference
Haynes & Feinleib, 1980	737 women aged 45–64; Framingham Heart Study; 1965–1967, 10-year followup	Incidence of coronary heart disease (CHD), CHD risk factors	No difference in CHD incidence or risk factors
Waldron, 1980	Nationwide sample of women aged 17 and over; Two National Health Interview Surveys in years 1965–1966 and 1974	Self-reported chronic conditions and activity—limiting chronic conditions	WW reported fewer conditions than HW
Slaby, 1982	Nationwide sample of women; First National Health and Nutrition Examination Survey; 1971–1975	Cigarette smoking, hypertension, serum cholesterol	WW had lower serum cholesterol than HW
Verbrugge, 1983	412 women aged 18 and over; Health in Detroit Study; 1978	Self-rated health status, morbidity (symptoms and conditions), restricted activity, chronic limitations, medical drug use	WW reported better health than HW

(continued)

Table 1. Employment Status[1] and Physical Health Among Women: A Review of Selected Studies (*Cont.*)

Author/Year	Study Population	Physical Health Outcome(s)	Comparison of Housewives (HW) and Working Women (WW)[2]
Hibbard & Pope, 1985	1140 women aged 18–64; Portland, Oregon; 1970–1971	Self-reported health status, non-obstetrical hospital days	No difference for women < 40 years; Among women ≥ 40 years, WW reported better health than HW
Verbrugge & Madans, 1985	Nationwide samples of women aged 17–64; National Health Interview Surveys; 1964–65, 1977–1978	Disability days, activity limitations due to chronic conditions, acute conditions, self-rated health status	WW reported better health than HW
Hazuda et al., 1986	1041 women aged 25–64 years; San Antonio Heart Study; 1972–1982	CHD risk factors	WW had more favorable high density lipoprotein levels/ratios than HW. No differences in other risk factors
House et al., 1986	1318 women aged 35–69; Tecumseh (Michigan) Community Health Study; 1967–1969	Prevalence of CHD, hypertension, bronchitis, cigarette smoking, alcohol consumption, obesity	No differences in CHD, hypertension, or bronchitis. Few differences in risk factors among subgroups of WW compared to HW

[1]Employment status refers to paid employment outside the home.
[2]Definitions of working women and housewives differ in the various studies.

working women. Several investigations that have examined multiple roles in relation to perceived and objective health status measures have shown just the opposite (Verbrugge, 1983; Verbrugge & Madans, 1985). That is, the more roles a women occupies, the healthier she is likely to be. In addition, much of this evidence suggests that the employment role is the strongest correlate of good health for women. For example, in a recent investigation of several health indicators, including disability days, restrictions in activity due to chronic conditions, acute conditions, and perceived health, Verbrugge and Madans (1985) rank ordered various role configurations and found that women who were employed and married, with or without children, had the most favorable health status. Nonemployed, nonmarried women with no children reported the worst health profiles.

With the exception of Haynes and Feinleib (1980), the studies summarized in Table 1 are cross-sectional, making the direction of causality in the relationships just described difficult to establish firmly. Employed populations are known to exhibit more favorable health profiles and lower disease rates than the general population (which includes both employed and nonemployed persons) due to selection processes that recruit and retain healthier persons in active employment. Thus, employment may be health promoting and risk reducing for women, or women in poor health may be unable to obtain and/or to keep jobs. Both pathways are likely to exist in community populations and to be difficult to distinguish in research. However, when it has been possible to examine relationships between risk factor levels and employment status, excluding women with histories of medically diagnosed chronic conditions, the health advantage of employed women persists (Hazuda et al., 1986). Nevertheless, the movement of women into and out of the labor force occurs in response to health, social, and economic factors that are not fixed. The influence of such factors must be considered when interpreting studies such as those in Table 1.

In sum, the experience of paid employment does not appear to put women at greater health risk, nor do working roles taken as a whole appear to explain the sex differential in mortality and life expectancy. We have little data with which to explain the possible health enhancing effect of paid employment which might account for the observed trends. Current hypotheses point to an increase in available social support from co-workers or supervisors, the socioeconomic benefits of working outside the home, and greater access to and use of health services.

PROPOSED LINKS BETWEEN THE WORK ENVIRONMENT, PERCEIVED STRESS, AND HEALTH RESPONSES

We can conclude that employment status per se does not appear to explain sex differences in mortality, nor does employment appear to impact negatively on health among women in general. However, for employed persons of either sex, there may be particular qualities of different jobs that are stress-producing and thus affect well-being.

Gender differences arising from occupational segregation and sex-specific patterns of perception, expectations, and coping become central issues when examining what is stress-producing about jobs. The specification of potential causal pathways that consider gender differences at several junctures is a prerequisite to understanding the stressful attributes of jobs and how aspects of work can affect health.

Various frameworks have evolved over the past decade to describe the mechanisms by which occupational roles could be related to health outcomes. Figure 1 depicts a paradigm for occupational stress research originally developed by House (1974) that includes five basic elements. The first component of the model (Box 1) contains objective characteristics of the job or work environment that are potentially stress-producing. Operationally, these characteristics have included occupational status, income, self-employment, hours worked, machine-paced work, responsibility for and/or authority over the work of others, and job complexity. The main distinction between objective conditions of jobs and other elements in this model is that these dimensions of work are "environmental," in the sense of being situational, structural, or determined by the organization of employment. Objective conditions exist outside of, rather than within, the persons exposed to them.

The individual person is, however, a key modulator between objective

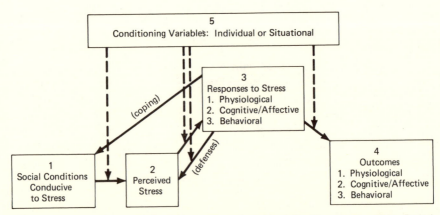

Note: Solid arrows between boxes indicate presumed causal relationships among variables. Dotted arrows from the box labeled "conditioning variables" intersect solid arrows, indicating an interaction between the conditioning variables and the variables in the box at the beginning of the solid arrow in predicting variables in the box at the head of the solid arrow.

Figure 1. A Paradigm of Stress Research. (Source: House, 1974. Reprinted with permission of the American Sociological Association.)

job conditions, stress, and health responses, since all objective conditions are filtered through the cognitive processes of the individual (Box 2). Thus a particular challenging job structure may or may not be perceived as stressful, depending on how it is appraised by the individual. Operationally, many researchers rely heavily on perceived job characteristics alone to determine exposure to stress-producing work environments. Perceived aspects of work measured in previous research have included job demands, tension, pressure, status, opportunities, rewards, and satisfactions.

When stress is perceived by an individual, multiple levels of response may subsequently occur (Box 3). Individual responses include physiologic (e.g., elevations in blood pressure or cholesterol), behavioral (e.g., risk-producing lifestyle habits, such as drinking, smoking, or being over-weight), cognitive (e.g., use of defense mechanisms, such as denial and suppressed hostility), and affective (e.g., development of depression, anxiety, or anger) (Haw, 1982). Relationships among the first three components of the framework (Boxes 1-3) are mediated and may be modified by active or passive coping mechanisms, the former directed at changing the objective environment (e.g., by exerting control) and the latter directed at making the organism more resistant to stress by changing or reevaluating one's perceptions of the objective conditions (e.g., defenses). Thus, according to this paradigm, coping can include two approaches (Kahn, 1981): environmental mastery (changing the aspects of jobs) and adaptation (changing people).

The fourth component specifies the alterations in health status, usually chronic or long-lasting, that result from exposure over time to stress-producing occupational conditions when coping strategies and adaptation are unsuccessful or the individual's capacities are exceeded. As with the acute responses to stress, health outcomes may be physiologic, behavioral, cognitive, or affective in nature.

Examples of health outcomes linked to occupational stress include coronary heart disease, hypertension, chronic bronchitis, depression, psychosomatic symptomatology, disability days, and hospitalizations. This list illustrates the multiplicity of effects which have been postulated to result from extended exposure to work situations that are overwhelmingly demanding. However, little is known about the extent to which stress-producing occupational exposures increase risks for specific diseases, or exert effects on health in general which can be manifested in a variety of ways, depending on parameters of individual susceptibility.

Finally, an array of individual and situational conditioning variables (Box 5) can influence the relationship of objective conditions to perceived stress, to acute responses, and to chronic outcomes. Individual characteristics of major importance in this process include age, race, sex, education, the availability of social supports, and the occurrence of major life events and everyday hassles outside of work. For example, we have already argued that gender influences occupation both through socialization, which affects choices, and/or through unequal access to all types of work. Situational conditioning variables provide the broader life context of work experiences for men and women. For example, the presence of children, the need to care for elderly parents, the absence of spouse or significant other, the quality of relationship with spouse or significant other, and the employment status and occupation of spouse or significant other can each add to working role burdens. Indeed, gender can often influence such relationships. Gender can also affect every element of the stress paradigm, as will be illustrated with research findings in a later section.

In addition, conditioning variables on the organizational level can also affect the specified relationships, through policies, practices, and the authority structure of the work setting. Moreover, organizational parameters can determine the range of acceptable coping mechanisms and response behaviors on the job. This is especially important since it is likely to be difficult to intervene in the stress process by changing enduring personal characteristics or circumstances, whereas it could be very efficient and beneficial to alter aspects of the organization in health-promoting ways.

House's paradigm serves as a description of the cognitive processes that translate environmental working conditions into health outcomes and can provide a structure for understanding possible causal mechanisms and deriving a priori hypotheses. However, House's paradigm is only a general framework for stress research. The model does not specify key environmental attributes of work that either promote or alleviate stress.

Recently, Karasek and colleagues (Karasek, Baker, Marxer, Ahlbom, & Theorell, 1981; Karasek, Theorell, Schwartz, Schnall, Pieper, & Michela, 1987) have proposed a two-dimensional model of occupational stress, focused on describing the objective conditions conducive to stress (Figure 2). The two key operating forces are: (1) job demands—the psychological (or physical) costs necessary to accomplish work tasks, and (2) job decision latitude—control over the use of one's abilities (skill discretion) and the way in which work is accomplished (decision authority). The Job Strain Model asserts that job challenges can either be health-damaging or health-promoting, depending on the level of job control afforded by the work environment. That is, jobs with similar environmental demands may differ substantially in the degree of strain and health risks created, by virtue of the degree of individual control over the job situation. A job characterized by a high level of demand produces job strain only when accompanied by constraints placed on the worker in terms of the possible mechanisms for coping with the demands. The job with high demand that also affords the worker resources for meeting and coping with the demands may develop the worker's ability to meet future challenges and therefore be health-enhancing (Karasek, Russell, & Theorell, 1982). Thus, job strain is postulated to result from a specific stress-producing imbalance in the objective work environment—high demands in combination with low

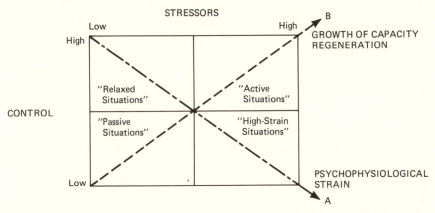

Figure 2. The Job Strain Model. (Source: Reprinted from "Job Demands, Job Decision Latitude and Mental Strain: Implications for Job Redesign" by Robert A. Karasek, Jr. published in *Administration Science Quarterly*, *24*(2), by permission of *Administrative Science Quarterly*. Copyright © 1979 by *Administrative Science Quarterly*.)

control over work. Although measurement of job demands and control in empirical research may be accomplished by either objective ratings or perceptions of individuals, Karasek et al. (1982) emphasize that the concept of "job strain" is an attribute of the job environment and not the individual.

Karasek et al. (1987) have operationally defined "psychological workload" (job demands) as having components of time pressure, deadline stress, excessive workloads, and conflicting demands which result in psychological arousal, consistent with measures of overload used by several occupational stress researchers (Caplan, Cobb, French, Van Harrison, & Pinneau, 1975; House, Wells, Landerman, McMichael, & Kaplan, 1979). Measures of job control in previous studies have consistently centered around a continuum of four basic job characteristics: (1) the routinization versus variety of job content, (2) control over decision making, (3) control over the content (e.g., skill utilization) and pace of work, and (4) clarity of working roles versus role ambiguity (LaCroix, 1984). The first three of these elements are encompassed in Karasek's measure of decision latitude.

Although occupational stress research specifically motivated by the job strain model is in its early development, several studies examining the effect of job strain on risk of cardiovascular disease (CVD) or coronary heart disease (CHD) have been reported by Karasek and others (see Table 2 for a summary). The results of these studies suggest consistently that job strain is an independent risk factor for CVD morbidity and mortality and may also be indirectly related to CVD through increased levels of blood pres-

Table 2. Job Strain[1] and Risk of Coronary Heart Disease

Investigator/Year	Country	Study Design	Study Population	Source of Job Characteristic Data	Variable(s) Studied	CHD Related Findings
Frankenhaeuser, 1979	Sweden	Cross-sectional field study	Males employed in sawmill	Type of job held in sawmill	High strain (machine controlled, noisy) conditions	Higher excretion of catecholamines
Karasek et al., 1981	Sweden	Prospective case-control	1461 randomly sampled employed males	Questionnaire responses	Job demands, decision latitude (high strain)	Increased risk of CHD signs and symptoms, and CVD mortality
Karasek et al., 1987	United States	Cross-sectional	2409 male participants in HES[2]; 2432 participants in NHANES I[2]	Job titles[3]	Job demands, decision latitude (high strain)	Increased prevalence of prior myocardial infarction
Alfredsson et al., 1982	Sweden	Case-control	334 males with new cases of myocardial infarction; 882 randomly selected males matched for age and residence	Job titles[3]	Hectic work, low control over work tempo/skill variety	Increased risk of myocardial infarction
Karasek & Gardell, 1984	Sweden	Cross-sectional	2500 men and women who had undergone forced job changes in previous 2 years	Job titles[3]	Changes in job demands and job control	Lower prevalence of CHD signs and symptoms among those changing to jobs with greater control

Haan, 1985	Finland	Prospective	600 men, 292 women employed in metal fabrication company	Questionnaire responses	Low job control and variety, high physical demands	Increased risk of incident CVD events and mortality
Pieper et al., 1985	USA	Cross-sectional and prospective	Male participants in four large U.S. studies[4]	Job titles[3]	Job demands, decision latitude (high strain)	Increased levels of systolic and diastolic blood pressure, serum cholesterol, and smoking
Alfredsson et al., 1985	Sweden	Cross-sectional	958,096 census-registered currently employed men and women	Job titles[3]	Hectic work, possibilities to learn new things at work, monotonous work, little influence over work tempo	Higher rates of hospitalization for myocardial infarction among men and women employed in hectic, monotonous occupations. Higher rates of hospitalization for myocardial infarction among men employed in hectic jobs with few possibilities to learn new things

[1] Job strain refers to the combination of high demand and low control work environment characteristics, according to Karasek's job strain model.
[2] HES refers to the Health Examination Survey 1960–1962; NHANES I refers to the First National Health and Nutrition Examination Survey, 1971–1975.
[3] Job titles merged with occupation-level job dimension scores using the job characteristics scoring system developed by the authors, using data bases from the country of the study population.
[4] The four studies include the HES, NHANES I, Western Collaborative Group Study, and Exercise Heart Study.

109

sure, serum cholesterol, and cigarette smoking. The studies reported are diverse in methodology, ranging from field studies that utilized laboratory measurements of neuroendocrine response patterns to observational prospective studies with medically diagnosed CVD endpoints.

For example, Frankenhaeuser (1979) identified high-strain sawmill workers by the restricting content of their work and compared these workers to others sampled from low-strain operations at the same sawmill. High-strain sawmill workers were exposed to jobs characterized by prolonged machine pacing and high levels of noise. The high-risk workers reported a higher frequency of psychosomatic symptoms and greater absenteeism than sawmill workers with greater control. Moreover, in response to stressors, high-strain workers had higher excretions of catecholamines, a hormone related to activation of the sympathetic nervous system, which increased during the workday. In contrast, workers in jobs with greater control had lower levels of catecholamine excretion that actually decreased toward the end of the workday.

Karasek and colleagues (Alfredsson, Karasek, & Theorell, 1982; Alfredsson, Spetz, & Theorell, 1985; Karasek et al., 1987; Pieper, Karasek, & Schwartz, 1985) have tested the job strain hypothesis in several populations where no direct measures of job characteristics were available, by applying a job characteristics scoring system. In studies of American workers, job scores were derived from interview response data collected over three U.S. Quality of Employment Surveys in 1969, 1972, and 1977. Mean values of job demands and job control were computed for subjects with the same job title, and these scores were found to be capable of differentiating occupations according to the aggregate measures of demands and control. The job characteristic scores were then imputed by job title to subjects in health surveys to predict CVD outcomes. Persons employed in occupations falling into the high demand/low control quadrant of the job strain model were found to have a higher prevalence of myocardial infarction (Karasek et al., 1987) after controlling for several standard coronary risk factors, higher rates of hospitalization for myocardial infarction (Alfredsson et al., 1985), and increased levels of systolic and diastolic blood pressure, serum cholesterol, and cigarette smoking (Pieper et al., 1985). Similarly, Alfredsson et al. (1982) conducted a case-control study using incident myocardial infarction cases in Stockholm, Sweden, and found that men under the age of 55 employed in occupations characterized by the combination of hectic work and low control over work tempo and skill variety had higher risk of myocardial infarction.

The job strain model has also been predictive of CVD signs, symptoms, and mortality in the Swedish male working population, based on stratification by measures of perceived demands and control, using both prospective and case-control designs (Karasek et al., 1981). In the six-year prospective analysis, men who had jobs characterized by lower intellectual discretion (control) had 1.4 times the risk (logistic odds ratio) of CHD morbidity, determined by a self-reported indicator of chest pain, dyspnea, hypertension, and heart weakness. Men with highly demanding jobs had 1.3 times the risk of reporting these symptoms during the study period. The case-control study was based on CVD and CHD deaths and revealed findings consistent with the prospective analysis. Measures of perceived job strain (low control and variety, high physical demands) were also significantly related to development of CHD during a ten-year follow-up period in a metal fabrication plant in Finland (Haan, 1985).

Karasek and Gardell (1984) have recently reported a study of CHD risk in relation to forced job changes among 2500 men and women white-collar workers in Sweden. In the two years prior to the study's inception, some workers had taken new jobs characterized by more or less job control than their former jobs. Among men of all ages and women over age 40, Swedish workers who underwent job changes into situations of greater control had fewer coronary symptoms than those who changed into jobs having less control and those undergoing no job changes. However, since no information was available on symptoms or health status before the onset of job changes, this study is purely observational and cannot be considered as having a prospective, or "intervention," design.

It is noteworthy that little is known about the effects of job strain on the health of employed women, although women are frequently exposed to work environments characterized by high demands and low control, as shown by the summary of studies investigating the influence of job strain on CHD (Table 2). Only three studies reported thus far have included employed women subjects (Alfredsson et al., 1985; Haan, 1985; Karasek & Gardell, 1984) and none has focused on explaining similarities or differences in the effects of job strain according to gender. Preliminary findings from studies of working women in the United States have shown that high-strain employment is associated with several health complaints, e.g., chest pain, among office workers in the communications industry in North Carolina (Haynes, LaCroix, & Lippin, 1987) and with a higher prevalence of cigarette smoking among women employed in hospitals (Biener, Abrams, Follick, & Hitti, 1986). However, the job strain hypothesis has yet to be tested in larger studies of working women employed in a spectrum of occupations, using validated measures of job demands and control and medically (or otherwise) verified determinations of health outcomes.

In sum, the Karasek job strain model identifies specific qualities of the work environment of special significance and suggests that particular conditions—high demands and low control—interact to produce stress reactions and ultimately cardiovascular disease. The data available to test the model currently have several limitations, but taken together show consistent support for the hypothesis. Nevertheless there are tremendous gaps in our knowledge of gender differences in job strain and the health effects of high demand/low control jobs.

POTENTIAL GENDER DIFFERENCES IN THE RELATIONSHIP OF WORK ENVIRONMENT TO HEALTH

We turn now to findings from the Framingham Heart Study to illustrate the issues that can arise when comparing the effects of occupational conditions among men and women. As discussed earlier, employed women in the Framingham Heart Study were found to be at no greater risk than housewives of developing CHD in a ten-year period (Haynes & Feinleib, 1984). However, women employed in clerical jobs were at almost twice the risk of developing CHD as housewives (12.0 vs. 7.1 percent respectively), white-collar workers (5.2 percent), and blue-collar workers (7.1 percent). Among clerical women, risk of CHD was greater for those who had ever married, had children, and whose spouse was employed in a blue-collar occupation. Other risk factors for CHD among clerical women were suppressed hostility, having a nonsupportive boss, fewer job changes over the past ten years, and greater family responsibilities. Subsequently, the role of work environment exposures has been explored in relation to the higher rates of CHD among clerical women in the Framingham Heart Study.

Motivated by Karasek's hypothesis that employment in jobs characterized by high demands and low control would increase risk of CHD, LaCroix (1984) examined the effects of several job characteristics on risk of coronary heart disease among 548 men and 328 women from the Framingham sample, aged 45 to 64, who were actively employed and initially free of CHD. Between 1965 and 1967 these persons completed a psychosocial questionnaire and were followed for the development of CHD over a ten-year-period as previously described (Haynes & Feinleib, 1984). Coronary heart disease events were medically diagnosed at biennial examinations, when a panel of investigators agreed that myocardial infarction, coronary insufficiency syndrome, angina pectoris, or CHD death had occurred.

A job-demands scale was developed from six items, three measuring quantitative workload (working overtime, meeting deadlines or rigid time schedules, working at night) and three measuring perceptions of job pressure (feeling pressed for time, thinking about work after working hours, and being stretched to the limits of one's energy and capacity). A scale measuring clarity of supervision from the immediate supervisor was developed as one indicator of job control. The scale is similar in concept to role ambiguity (Caplan, 1975) and was derived using two items pertaining to clarity of feedback and expectations from the respondent's boss. In order to examine the effects of high demand/low control work, the two scales were dichotomized at the median for each age-sex group, and a categorical measure of high-strain employment was created for persons reporting high job demands in combination with low supervision clarity.

Employed women who described their jobs as high in strain exhibited a threefold relative risk of CHD compared to women reporting low-strain job situations (13.7 vs. 4.7 percent). In support of Karasek's hypothesis, rates of CHD were lowest among women with low job demands and high supervision clarity (4.0 percent) and highest among women in high-strain jobs (13.7 percent) as shown in Figures 3a and 3b. These findings were most striking among clerical women; those in high-strain jobs exhibited over five times the risk of CHD as did women in low-strain jobs. The associations persisted even after controlling for standard coronary risk factors, including age, systolic blood pressure, serum cholesterol, and cigarettes smoked per day. The relationship between perceived high-strain employment and CHD incidence observed among women was confined to coronary events involving angina pectoris. In contrast, no significant associations were observed among men (LaCroix, 1984; LaCroix & Haynes, 1984). Thus, the central issue emanating from this study was the sex specificity in self-reported high-strain employment as a predictor of future CHD events.

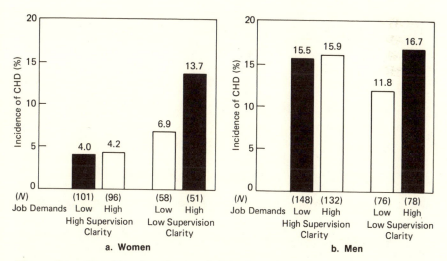

Figure 3. a. Ten-Year Incidence of CHD by Job Demands and Supervision Clarity Among Currently Working Women b. Ten-Year Incidence of CHD by Job Demands and Clarity of Supervision Among Currently Working Men

Several competing explanations have been put forth with respect to this sex specificity that illustrate important research problems. First, due to occupational segregation, objective job characteristics are not distributed equally among men and women. The nature of women's work is characteristically lower in job control than that of men. The occupational distribution in Framingham, similar to that of the nation, indicated that men typically had higher-status positions with greater control, whether they worked in white-collar, blue-collar, or clerical jobs. In addition, men had greater upward mobility, as evidenced by a higher mean number of promotions in the previous ten-year period (Haynes & Feinleib, 1980). Because Framingham men were more likely than women to have held jobs characterized by higher levels of control and a greater degree of autonomy (attributes which it was not possible to measure directly), lack of clear supervision under these favorable circumstances may have implied more freedom on the job to make independent decisions and to work in a self-directed manner. In contrast, women's work, particularly in the clerical and service sector, was probably closely tied to the expectations of their supervisors (Kanter, 1977). For all women, and clerical women in particular, insufficient information to perform work tasks, such as receiving ambiguous messages from their supervisors, could easily have been perceived as a loss of control and generated stress reactions.

In sum, the differing structure of work for men and women may influence which aspects of job control are more salient for each gender of worker. For example, Miller (1980) found that high levels of job satisfaction among men were determined primarily by the absence of close supervision in their jobs, whereas for women, high job satisfaction was more closely connected to the use of thought and independent judgment on the job. To go further, positional authority and having decision-making powers were the most important determinants of high job satisfaction for men, whereas the use of skills and abilities was more salient for women. Because there was a lower correlation between job complexity and closeness of supervision among women than men, the author concluded that "freedom from supervision in a woman's job does not necessarily imply autonomy in her work . . . [and] may not be the same source of gratification for women as for men because this freedom does not offer the same opportunities for occupational self-direction" (p. 350). Thus, in the present context, supervision clarity may have been a more relevant and important job control parameter for women than men because of the differing structure of work for each gender. Other aspects of job control not measured directly in this study, such as job complexity, decision authority, and control over work pace, may have had more impact on employed men.

A second explanation for the sex specificity of the findings is that perceptions of work environment characteristics may be determined differently for men and women, even when objective conditions conducive to stress are the same. For example, candor in reporting aspects of the work environment could be affected by gender; thus men may have more difficulty than women identifying and expressing negative aspects of their job situations. Women are known to report more illness symptoms and higher levels of depressive symptomatology than men (Gove, 1978; Nathanson, 1975; Weissman & Klerman, 1977), suggesting that women in general may more frequently respond positively to questionnaire items that inquire about their feelings of distress in social roles and mental well-being. Men may be more reluctant to do so if they tend to use defenses such as denial to cope with job stressors, or if they perceive such questions as threatening to and incongruent with their masculine self-image.

Third, gender is clearly associated with both the development of CHD (men are at greater risk than women of the same age) and the way in which CHD is manifested. Men more often than women present with manifestations of CHD not accompanied by angina. In addition, among people with angina pectoris referred for coronary catheterization, only about one-half of the women as compared to 70 to 90 percent of the men have been found to have significant coronary occlusion (Haynes, LaCroix, White, & Tyroler, 1984; Waxler, Kimbiris, & Dreifus, 1971). Thus many women reporting chest pain are found to be free of extensive coronary artery disease as an explanation for their symptoms. Because significant relationships between high-strain employment and CHD were limited to coronary events involving angina, the sex specificity of the associations may have been a function of a tendency among women who reported these occupational characteristics to also report symptoms of chest pain and be diagnosed as having angina. If this were true, it could be argued that working women who reported high-strain job situations were more emotionally expressive than men. When we examined this expectation it was not supported by the data. Reports of job demands were correlated with measures of emotional lability, symptoms of anxiety, and anger, equally among men and women. Perceptions of supervision clarity were uncorrelated with these scales for both sexes. Therefore, it is unlikely that emotional reactivity alone explains the sex specificity of the relationship between high-strain employment and CHD. These issues illustrate the problems that arise when measures of objective working conditions and health outcomes are connected, at least in part, to the perceptions of the study subject. In sum, men and women may differ in how objective exposure translates into perceptions and symptoms of disease processes.

A fourth explanation for the lack of association between employment conditions and CHD among men concerns the traditional sex roles of working men and women in the mid 1960s. At that time, men were more likely to have spouses not employed outside the home. Thus, men, as compared to working women, may have had additional buffers to occupational stressors emanating from their roles as husbands and primary providers. Among the women, in contrast, non-workplace roles may have exacerbated the effects of occupational stressors. About two-thirds of the ever-married working women in the Farmingham Study of employed women had children, according to Haynes and Feinleib (1980). Haynes and Feinleib (1980) had previously noted that the eight-year incidence of CHD among working women increased with the number of children and that excess risks observed among clerical women were concentrated among those who had ever married and had children. In secondary analysis La-Croix (1984) found that, after controlling for the added responsibilities of marriage and children, perceived job strain persisted as an important predictor of CHD among clerical workers. In sum, social supports and responsibilities from sources outside the job, such as household maintenance and child care, may be differentially available, be experienced differently, and have different effects on health for men and women.

A final possible explanation is that men and women may have different expectations of their work. In the findings presented pertaining to employed women in the Framingham Heart Study (LaCroix, 1984), men may have been more culturally or socially prepared to survive and adapt to conditions of demanding work and unclear supervision. In contrast, middle-aged women who were employed in the mid-1960s were not in the overwhelming majority of their female counterparts and were likely therefore to have been socialized to a lesser degree than men to cope effectively with these occupational stressors.

The alternative explanations for the findings concerning working men and women participating in the Framingham Heart Study illustrate the types of questions that arise when interpreting gender differences in the perception and effects of occupational stressors. Few studies have considered such questions directly.

FUTURE DIRECTIONS IN THE STUDY OF PSYCHOSOCIAL WORK ENVIRONMENT FACTORS

Currently there are major gaps in our knowledge of how men and women experience and are affected by occupational stress. At this juncture, it is important to highlight several methodologic issues in studies of workplace stressors that should be considered in the design of future investigations.

First, the majority of previous studies have been cross-sectional and have studied occupational exposures as if they were enduring and stable characteristics. Yet it is clear that employed persons change jobs frequently in a lifetime and during the course of their work histories have multiple psychological perspectives on their interactions with the job environment. In this sense, hypothesized associations between work and chronic diseases must be viewed as a lengthy process of chronic job exposures and repeated psychobiologic insults. A recent prospective investigation provides insight into the value of repeated measures of job stress by showing that risk of chronic outcomes was elevated only among men reporting high levels of job tensions at two time points during the follow-up period as compared to those reporting job tensions at only one time point or not at all (House, Strecher, Metzner, & Robbins, 1986). Thus, it is likely that the stability of occupational stressors over time is an important parameter in gauging the extent of health risk. There is clearly a need for prospective studies designed to obtain measurements of individuals' complete work histories and to make multiple assessments of job attributes and perceptions as person's jobs and cognitions change over time.

Second, it has become increasingly important for research on workplace stressors to keep pace with modern working conditions, as jobs change with the introduction of new technologies and as new jobs are created. If employment trends create similar occupational distributions for men and women in the future, gender differences in the stressfulness of workplace roles may diminish. Similarly, burdens associated with family roles may be shared more equally by men and women in the future. Further, young women entering the workplace today may be more socially prepared for a lifetime of employment than in the past, rendering them better able to adapt and cope with workplace stressors (Verbrugge, 1984). Also, the expectations that men and women have of their work may converge in the future. Thus, secular changes in workers and in workplace environments must be considered in future investigations if we are to succeed in the identification of high-risk employed populations.

Finally, the majority of previous investigations have relied solely on the use of subjective measures (perceptions) of occupational stressors. However, even the best questionnaire measures provide limited estimations of worker-environment transactions that occur as a process. Caplan (1983) cautions:

> [Do] not assume that low strain and high mental health are necessarily associated with high degrees of either self- or environmental- knowledge. A little bit of distortion of reality can sometimes help a person to face and overcome a stressor whereas an inability to distort the potential harm-producing nature of a stressor may render the person emotionally disabled (p. 37).

In sum, the tendency for people to deny stressful aspects of work or to attenuate the threat they experience in a situation of conflict or strain may protect health in some ways and be health-damaging in others. Little is known about how men and women might use such coping mechanisms differentially. Our understanding of the role that work environment stressors play in disease causation will be increased to the extent that future research can utilize both objective and subjective measures of occupational stressors and elucidate the coping processes that intervene between the two.

REFERENCES

Alcalay, R. & Pasick, R. J. (1983). Psycho-social factors and the technologies of work. *Social Science and Medicine, 17,* 1075–1084.

Alfredsson, L., Karasek, R., & Theorell, T. (1982). Myocardial infarction and psychosocial work environment: An analysis of the male Swedish working force. *Social Science and Medicine, 16,* 463–467.

Alfredsson, L., Spetz, C. L., & Theorell, T. (1985). Type of occupation and near-future hospitalization for myocardial infarction and some other diagnoses. *International Journal of Epidemiology, 14,* 378–388.

Biener, L., Abrams, D. B., Follick, M. J., & Hitti, J. R. (1986). *Gender differences in smoking and quitting.* Paper presented at the Society for Behavioral Research Meetings, San Francisco.

Bureau of Economic Statistics (1981). *The handbook of basic economic statistics* (Vol. 35). Washington, DC: Economic Statistics Bureau of Washington, DC.

Caplan, R. D. (1983). Person-environment fit: Past, present and future. In C. L. Cooper (Ed.), *Stress Research.* New York: Wiley Interscience.

Caplan, R. D., Cobb, S., French, J. R. P., Van Harrison, R., & Pinneau, S. R. (1975). *Job demands and worker health, main effects and occupational differences.* Washington, DC: U.S. Department of Health, Education and Welfare, PHS, CDC, National Institute of Occupational Safety and Health.

Frankenhaeuser, M. (1979). Psychobiological aspects of life stress. In S. Levine & H. Ursin (Eds.), *Coping and health.* New York: Plenum Press.

Gove, W. R. (1978). Sex differences in mental illness among adult men and women: An evaluation of four questions raised regarding the evidence on the higher rates of women. *Social Science and Medicine, 12B,* 187–198.

Haan, M. (1985). *Job Strain and cardiovascular disease: A ten-year prospective study.* Paper presented at the eighteenth annual meeting of the Society for Epidemiologic Research, Chapel Hill, North Carolina. *American Journal of Epidemiology, 122,* 532. (Abstract.)

Hauenstein, L. S., Kasl, S., & Harburg, E. (1977). Work status, work satisfaction and blood pressure among married black and white women. *Psychology of Women Quarterly, 1,* 334–349.

Haw, M. A. (1982). Women, work and stress: A review and agenda for the future. *Journal of Health and Social Behavior, 23,* 132–144.

Hayghe, H. (1984). Working mothers reach record number in 1984. *Monthly Labor Review,* December, 31–34.

Haynes, S. G. & Feinleib, M. (1980). Women, work and coronary heart disease: Prospective findings from the Framingham Study. *American Journal of Public Health, 70,* 133–141.

———. (1984). Clerical work and coronary heart disease in women: Prospective findings from the Framingham Study. In B.G.F. Cohen (Ed.), *Human aspects in office automation.* Amsterdam, The Netherlands: Elsevier.

Haynes, S. G., LaCroix, A. Z., & Lippin, T. (1987). The effect of high job demands and low control on the health of employed women. In J. C. Quick, Rabbi Rasbhagat, J. Dalton, & J. D. Quick (Eds.), *Work stress and health care:* New York: Praeger.

Haynes, S. G., LaCroix, A. Z., White, A., & Tyroler, H. A. (1984). *The Type A–atherosclerosis controversy.* Paper presented at the Seventeenth Annual Meeting of the Society for Epidemiologic Research, Houston, Texas. *American Journal of Epidemiology, 120,* 488. (Abstract.)

Hazuda, H. P., Haffner, S. M., Stern, M. P., Knapp, J. A., Eifler, C. W., & Rosenthal, M. (1986). Employment status and women's protection against coronary heart disease: Findings from the San Antonio Heart Study. *American Journal of Epidemiology, 123,* 623–640.

Hibbard, J. H. & Pope, C. R. (1985). Employment status, employment characteristics and women's health. *Women and Health, 10,* 59–77.

House, J. S. (1974). Occupational stress and coronary heart disease: A review and theoretical integration. *Journal of Health and Social Behavior, 15,* 12–27.

House, J. S., Strecher, V., Metzner, H. L., & Robbins, C. A. (1986). Occupational stress and health among men and women in the Tecumseh Community Health Study. *Journal of Health and Social Behavior, 27,* 62–77.

House, J. S., Wells, J. A., Landerman, L. R., McMichael, A. J., & Kaplan, B. H. (1979). Occupational stress and health among factory workers. *Journal of Health and Social Behavior, 20,* 139–160.

Kahn, R. L. (1981). *Work and health.* New York: Wiley.

Kanter, R. M. (1977). *Men and women of the corporation.* New York: Basic Books.

Karasek, R., Baker, D., Marxer, F., Ahlbom, A., & Theorell, T. (1981). Job decision latitude, job demands, and cardiovascular disease: A prospective study of Swedish men. *American Journal of Public Health, 71,* 694–705.

Karasek, R. A. & Gardell, B. (1984). *Managing job stress.* Unpublished manuscript. New York: Columbia University, Department of Industrial Engineering and Operations Research.

Karasek, R. A., Russell, R. S., & Theorell, T. (1982). Physiology of stress and regeneration in job related cardiovascular illness. *Journal of Human Stress,* March, 29–42.

Karasek, R. A., Theorell, T., Schwartz, J. E., Schnall, P. L., Pieper, C., & Michela, J. L. (1987). Job characteristics in relation to the prevalence of myocardial infarction in the U.S. Health Examination Survey and the First National Health and Nutrition Examination Survey. Unpuplished manuscript.

Kraft, P. (1984). *Computer programming: Do males and females do the same work?* Paper presented at the Office of Technology Assessment Symposium on the Impacts of Office Automation and Computer Mediated Work on the Quality of Worklife, Washington, DC.

Kuttner, B. (1983). The declining middle. *The Atlantic Monthly,* July, 60–72.

LaCroix, A.Z. (1984). *High demand/low control work and coronary heart disease incidence in the Framingham cohort.* Unpublished doctoral dissertation, Department of Epidemiology, School of Public Health, University of North Carolina at Chapel Hill.

LaCroix, A. Z. & Haynes, S. G. (1984). *Occupational exposure to high demand/ low control work and coronary heart disease incidence in the Framingham cohort.* Paper presented at the Seventeenth Annual Meeting of the Society for Epidemiologic Research, Houston, Texas. *American Journal of Epidemiology, 120,* 481. (Abstract.)

Mellor, E. F. (1984). Investigating the differences in weekly earnings of women and men. *Monthly Labor Review,* June, 17–28.

Miller, J. (1980). Individual and occupational determinants of job satisfaction, a focus on gender differences. *Sociology of Work and Occupations, 7,* 337–366.

Nathanson, C. A. (1975). Illness and the feminine role: A theoretical review. *Social Science and Medicine, 9,* 57–62.

Pieper, C., Karasek, R., & Schwartz, J. (1985). *The relationship of job dimensions to coronary heart disease risk factors.* Paper presented at the eighteenth annual meeting of the Society for Epidemiologic Research, Chapel Hill, North Carolina. *American Journal of Epidemiology, 122,* 540. (Abstract.)

Rytina, N. F. & Bianchi, S. M. (1984). Occupational reclassification and changes in distribution by gender. *Monthly Labor Review,* March, 11–17.

Shack-Marquez, J. (1984). Earnings differences between men and women: An introductory note. *Monthly Labor Review,* June, 15–16.

Slaby, A. R. (1982). *Cardiovascular risk factors in women by their working status.* Paper presented at the 22nd Conference on Cardiovascular Disease Epidemiology, San Antonio, Texas.

Smith, M., Cohen, B., & Stammerjohn, L. (1981). An investigation of health complaints and job stress in video display operations. *Human Factors, 23,* 387–400.

Smith, R. E. (1979). The movement of women into the labor force. In R. E. Smith (Ed.), *The subtle revolution.* Washington, DC: The Urban Institute.

U.S. Congress, Office of Technology Assessment (1985). *Automation of America's offices.* (OTA-CIT-287.) Washington, DC: U.S. Government Printing Office.

U.S. Department of Labor, Bureau of Labor Statistics, Women's Bureau (1984). *Facts on women workers.* (909–710.) Washington, DC: U.S. Government Printing Office.

Verbrugge, L. M. (1983). Multiple roles and physical health of women and men. *Journal of Health and Social Behavior, 24,* 16–30.

―――. (1984). Physical health of clerical workers in the U.S., Framingham, and Detroit. *Women and Health, 9,* 17–41.

Verbrugge, L. M. & Madans, J. H. (1985). Social roles and health trends of American women. *Milbank Memorial Fund Quarterly/Health and Society, 63,* 691–735.

Waldron, I. (1980). Employment and women's health: An analysis of causal relationships. *International Journal of Health Services, 10,* 435–454.

Warr, P. & Parry, G. (1982). Paid employment and women's psychological well-being. *Psychological Bulletin, 91,* 498–516.

Waxler, E. B., Kimbiris, D., & Dreifus, L. (1971). The fate of women with normal coronary arteriograms and chest pain resembling angina pectoris. *American Journal of Cardiology, 28,* 25–31.

Weissman, M. M. & Klerman, G. L. (1977). Sex differences in the epidemiology of depression. *Archives of General Psychiatry, 34,* 98–111.

Wheeler, A. P., Lee, E. S., & Loe, H. D. (1983). Employment, sense of well-being, and use of professional services among women. *American Journal of Public Health, 73,* 908–911.

Wingard, D. L., Suarez, L., & Barrett-Connor, E. (1983). The sex differential in mortality from all causes and ischemic heart disease. *American Journal of Epidemiology, 117,* 165–172.

Wolf, W. C. & Fligstein, N. D. (1979). Sexual stratification: Differences in power in the work setting. *Social Forces, 58,* 94–107.

Wright, E. O., Costello, C., Hachen, D., & Sprague, J. (1982). The American class structure. *American Sociological Review, 47,* 709–726.

5

Social Roles, Gender, and Psychological Distress

Rosalind C. Barnett
Grace K. Baruch

Research into the relationship between multiple role involvement and stress is taking new directions in the wake of numerous studies showing positive effects of multiple role involvement on women's and men's physical and mental well-being (Barnett & Baruch, 1985; Crosby, 1984; Thoits, 1983; Verbrugge, 1983). Concern about the negative effects on women of involvement in multiple roles is abating because of increasing evidence that for women as well as men, the more roles one occupies, the greater the chances of being physically healthier, more satisfied with life, and less depressed. Nevertheless, echoes still resound of past warnings that multiple role involvement would take a heavy toll, especially on women. Fortunately, an initial focus in the research literature on number of roles and role occupancy is now widening to include consideration of the quality of experience in roles (e.g., see Aneshensel & Pearlin, this volume). Indeed, many studies suggest that role quality is a more significant predictor of stress and well-being than is role occupancy per se. Studies further show that some roles and role combinations may be less beneficial than others. Moreover the relationship between roles and stress may be different for men and for women (Barnett & Baruch, 1985; Baruch, Biener, & Barnett, 1987; Dytell, Pardine, & Napoli, 1985; Kandel, Davies, & Raveis, 1985; Verbrugge, 1982).

In this chapter we examine how gender influences the relation between involvement in social roles and stress-related outcomes. We first discuss the hypotheses linking multiple role involvement to stress outcomes. We then focus on specific roles, especially the major ones of spouse, parent, and paid worker, considering both role occupancy and role quality.

We also discuss the specific dimensions of roles that seem crucial to determining whether a particular role has beneficial or detrimental effects on the occupant's level of distress.

Our discussion of the effects of role-related experiences focuses both on stress indicators, such as depression and anxiety, and on well-being indicators, such as happiness, satisfaction, and self-esteem.

MULTIPLE ROLES AND STRESS

With respect to the relationship between the number of roles one occupies and the experience of stress, two questions are central to this chapter: Does role multiplicity augur well or poorly for psychological distress? Are there gender differences in the effects of multiple roles? Although many studies suggest that involvement in multiple roles may be beneficial, not all roles have equally positive effects. Further, the effects of the same role combinations may be different for men and for women; many researchers argue, for example, that the combination of paid worker and spouse roles has more beneficial effects for men than for women (Cleary & Mechanic, 1983; Gove & Tudor, 1973). In this section we will review the evidence about the effects of multiple role involvement on well-being for women and men, focusing on the well-being dimensions of self-esteem, happiness, and satisfaction, and on the stress reactions of depression and psychophysiological symptoms.

Research on multiple roles and their effects has focused largely on within-sex differences among women; men have received scant attention (Gove & Zeiss, 1987). Thus, only recently have researchers addressed the issue of gender differences in these effects.

The Scarcity Hypotheses

Many studies explore the relationship between the number of roles women occupy and particular role combinations, using such measures as self-reported happiness or depression. Underlying many of these studies is the expectation that roles drain energy; hence the more roles a woman occupies the less energy she will have, the more conflict she will experience, and the more negatively will her well-being be affected. This hypothesis, called the scarcity hypothesis, was first put forth by Goode (1960) and extended by Coser (1974), Slater (1963), and others. It rests on two premises: (a) that individuals have a limited amount of energy; and (b) that social organizations are greedy, demanding all of an individual's allegiance. According to the scarcity model, people do not have enough energy to fulfill their role obligations; thus role strain is normal and compromises are required. Therefore, the more roles one accumulates, the greater the probability of exhausting one's supply of time and energy and of confronting conflicting obligations, leading to role strain and psychological distress. This hypothesis was developed to account for men's behavior in formal workplace organizations. When applied to women, the assumption is that family roles are greedy, demanding total allegiance and energy. Accordingly, when women assume the role of paid employee, a role that exposes them to the demands of the organization, the net effect is hypothesized to be debilitating. The scarcity hypothesis assumes that women have limited resources with which to meet the demands of the workplace.

The Expansion Hypothesis

In the mid-1970s a competing hypothesis about human energy, the expansion hypothesis, emerged. It focuses on the net positive gains to be had from multiple roles. The major theorists of this revisionist position (Marks, 1977; Sieber, 1974) emphasize the privileges rather than the obligations that accrue to incumbents of multiple roles. They argue that such rewards as self-esteem, recognition, prestige, and financial renumeration more than offset the costs of adding on roles. Through role bargaining—that is, delegating or eliminating onerous role obligations—men could reduce, to a manageable and presumably attractive set, the many demands on them associated with operating in two arenas. Thus for men multiple role involvement was hypothesized to enhance well-being. Early support for this view came from the work of Gove and Tudor (1973), who suggested that men experience fewer symptoms of psychiatric dysfunction than do women because they are committed simultaneously to work and family roles.

Recent research supports the expansion hypothesis for women as well as men (Crosby, 1984; Thoits, 1983; Verbrugge, 1982). Thoits (1983) reports a positive association between the number of roles a woman or man occupies and her or his psychological well-being. In an analysis of within-sex differences in women's physical health, Verbrugge (1982) concludes that multiple role involvement is associated with better health. In sum, the expansion hypothesis is well supported; the more roles, the better (Gove & Zeiss, 1987; Thoits, 1983).

ASSUMPTIONS ABOUT CORE ROLES

Beyond the issue of number of roles per se, however, is the more intriguing question of the effect on the experience of psychological distress of particular roles, role combinations, and role quality. Furthermore, in contrast to other stress-related research areas, most literature on negative effects of multiple role involvement, such as role strain and role conflict, has centered on women. How can we account for this phenomenon? Theoretical formulations regarding men's lives assume the centrality of the paid employee role and relegate non-workplace roles to positions of minor importance. Because the roles of husband and father are viewed as subordinate to the employee role and traditionally have involved few obligations, issues of conflict and strain are rarely addressed. Theories of women's lives, in contrast, have assumed both the primacy of and major commitment to non-workplace roles. Involvement in the paid employee role, which also requires commitment, is assumed to entail strain and conflict. Therefore, with the rapid entrance into the paid labor force of women who already occupied their primary roles, that is, women who were married and had children, researchers sought to examine the presumed deleterious effects of women's multiple role involvement. Thus assumptions about core roles have generated strikingly different expectations about the effects of role occupancy for men and women.

Men's Core Roles

The centrality of paid work in theories of men's lives (Erikson, 1959; Levinson, Darrow, Klein, Levinson, & McKee, 1978; Vaillant, 1977) is reflected in the descriptors Levinson uses to identify the "Seasons of a Man's Life": "Entering the Adult World," "Settling Down," "Becoming One's Own Man" (BOOM). The markers Levinson and colleagues use to distinguish one "season" from another, and to assess "success" at each stage, are tied most strongly to events in the workplace. For example, a man's judgment regarding his relative success or failure in meeting the goals he set for himself during the BOOM stage depends on whether "he has achieved the desired position on his 'ladder'"; whether he has been "affirmed within his occupational and social world"; and whether he is "becoming a senior member of that world with all the rewards and responsibilities seniority brings" (Levinson et al., 1978, p. 191). Further, we read, failure to achieve occupational goals results in a sense of personal failure.

> When a man experiences a developmental crisis in the late thirties, it stems from the overwhelming feeling that he cannot accomplish the tasks of Becoming One's Own Man: he cannot advance sufficiently on his chosen ladder; cannot gain the affirmation, independence and seniority he wants; cannot be his own man in the terms defined by his current life structure (p. 191).

According to recent writers, this "myth of monism" (Long & Porter, 1984) presents a sorely impoverished view of men, even for the upwardly mobile, white middle-class men on whom it was based (see, e.g., Farrell

& Rosenberg, 1981; Lamb, Pleck, Charnov, & Levine, 1985). Nevertheless it has had profound impact on theory and research. Indeed, most of the landmark studies on stress that focus on men (e.g., Rosenman, Brand, Jenkins, Friedman, Straus, & Wurm, 1975) do not even report the marital or parental status of their subjects, an omission that testifies to the pervasiveness of this one-dimensional view of men. Moreover, this view has several consequences that impair the accuracy and comprehensiveness of our knowledge about the relationship between social roles and the experience of stress in men's lives: (a) an overemphasis on the sources of strain in men's workplace role; (b) a neglect of rewarding aspects of their workplace role; and (c) an absence of research on the relationship between men's non-workplace roles and their well-being or psychological distress. There is little discussion, moreover, of how men's work and family roles interact to affect men's experience of distress (see Farrell & Rosenberg, 1981, for an exception). As yet, therefore, we have no answers to such questions as: How does the quality of experience in the role of husband and/or father affect men's health? Do married or nonmarried men experience more stress at the workplace? Do men's experiences as parents influence the effects of workplace stressors on physical and mental health outcomes?

Women's Core Roles

For women, family roles have been assumed to be the core roles. Indeed, in Erikson's seminal work, *Identity: Youth and Crisis* (1968), marriage and motherhood were considered crucial to the completion of a woman's identity.

> Young women often ask whether they can "have an identity" before
> they know whom they will marry and for whom they will make a
> home. . . . Something in the young woman's identity must keep itself
> open for the peculiarities of the man to be joined and of the children
> to be brought up . . . (p. 283).

"Success" in the roles of wife and mother has been considered a prerequisite for women's psychological well-being. Indeed, the roles of "wife and mother," although in reality quite separate, and at times in conflict, are linked together as if one. Women's family roles typically have been seen as natural and as crucial for women's well-being; until recently, women who did not occupy at least one or even both of these roles were assumed to be immature, unfeminine, incomplete, selfish, unnatural, deviant (Rossi, 1984; Teicholtz, 1978). Accordingly, with few exceptions the wife and mother roles have been assumed to be less stressful than the role of paid worker (Barnett & Baruch, 1985).

This view of women is being challenged by research exploring the impact of marriage and motherhood on women's well-being. Evidence is accumulating that women who have never married as well as those who are no longer married (i.e., divorced, separated, and widowed women) are not doomed to an "identity-less" fate. Indeed, several studies suggest that unmarried women fare at least as well as their married counterparts on many indices of psychological well-being (Baruch & Barnett, 1986a; Birnbaum, 1975; Gigy, 1980; Sears & Barbee, 1977).

In the next sections we explore in more detail the question of whether research data support the "core role" assumptions. We first examine evidence on this point separately for men's roles and women's roles. We then turn to the evidence about gender differences in interactions among roles, and in the nature of social roles. Finally, we suggest ways in which changes in social roles may affect future research findings.

MEN'S ROLES

Men's Family Roles

In contrast to the almost exclusive emphasis on men's work roles as determinants of male stress and well-being, the data from several studies suggest that men's family roles are very important and have significant direct (and indirect) effects on well-being. Farrell and Rosenberg (1981), in their major study of 500 randomly selected men, report they were surprised to discover the powerful impact of family relations on the experiences of men at midlife.

> Our contact with the families demonstrated the ways in which a man's experience of midlife is very much dependent on the culture and structure of his family. The changing relationships to wife and children act as precipitants for development in men. . . . This interlocking of individual and family developmental processes is a critical element in men's experiences of midlife (p. vii).

The failure to expect such findings may be due to a middle-class bias, a bias also evident in the samples on which many of the theory-building studies were based (Levinson, 1978; Vaillant, 1977). In contrast, in an intensive interview study of two-earner working-class and lower middle-class families with preschool children (Lein, Durham, Pratt, Schudson, Thomas, & Weiss, 1974), the authors concluded that "men in contemporary industrial culture seek their primary emotional, personal, and spiritual gratification in their family setting" (p. 118). Using a national probability sample, the authors of *The Inner American* (Veroff, Douvan, & Kulka, 1981) report similar findings. Male respondents who held all three roles of spouse, parent, and paid worker rated family roles as more critical than occupational roles; there was one exception: older men who chose self-actualization or security as their critical value in life over such alternatives as sense of belonging or being well-respected.

Recently Pleck (1985) reviewed the literature on the consequences of husbands' psychological involvement in work and family roles, and conducted new analyses of data from two national surveys completed in the late 1970s. He found that husbands experience their family roles as far more psychologically significant than their paid work roles and that these non-workplace roles had greater positive impact on men's psychological well-being. Commenting on the discrepancy between the assumptions in the literature and these data, he says, "What is perhaps most surprising is that the view that most men are obsessed by their work and oblivious to their families has persisted so long in spite of the fact that the available data have almost always disconfirmed it" (p. 134).

Pleck notes, however, that there is a minority of men who are more involved with their work than with their families. These men tend to be found among those who are highly educated and/or of high occupational status. Thus studies based on samples of such men (see for example, Erikson, 1959; Vaillant, 1977) "generally find somewhat higher work involvement and somewhat lower family involvement than is found in more representative samples. Moreover, in even these highly educated samples, men who are more involved in their work than in their family are still in the minority" (Pleck, 1985, pp. 134–135). Similarly, Farrell and Rosenberg (1981) note that models such as the one proposed by Levinson et al. "apply to a subset of men—most likely a creative and intellectual elite who achieve many of our cultural ideals of success. . . . " (p. 23). These authors go on to say that Levinson's data "speak more to our cultural image of 'success' and 'self-actualization' than to either the reality of most people's lives or to universal psychological processes" (p. 23).

The marital role is central to men's mental and physical health. Several studies of psychological health indicate that men benefit more than women from being married (Gove, 1972, 1973, 1978; Cleary & Mechanic, 1983). With respect to physical health too, there are indications that men benefit more from the role of spouse than do women. Whereas disease morbidity and mortality rates tend to be lowest among the married, they are lower among married men than married women. Similarly, compared to the nonmarried, married persons have the lowest rates of contact with physicians, hospital stays, and visits to psychiatric hospitals and outpatient clinics (Cleary, this volume). Furthermore, married men have lower rates than married women. Overall, findings suggest that marriage is more protective for men than it is for women (Cleary, this volume; Belle, this volume).

Such findings suggest that loss of the marriage role will be more devastating for men than for women. Evidence supporting this view comes from studies of gender differences in the experience of both divorce and widowhood. In one longitudinal study, men were found to have a more difficult time coping with marital separation and divorce than did women (Wallerstein & Kelly, 1980). Widowers suffer more than widows, as reflected in such distress indicators as depression, psychiatric disorders, physical illness, mortality, and suicide (Stroebe & Stroebe, 1983).

Whereas the role of spouse seems to have largely beneficial, health-promoting effects for men, evidence concerning the role of father is less consistent. Many studies suggest that this role is more stressful than that of husband.

In a recent study of 160 fathers, their wives, and their children, we found that although fathers who participated more in child care and home chores felt more involved and competent as parents, they also were more likely to report having too little time for their careers and to complain that their family responsibilities were interfering with their work (Baruch & Barnett, 1986b). These fathers were also more critical of their wives' patterns of time allocation and of their performance as mothers.

In summary, the consensus appears to be that "the majority of men are more psychologicaly involved in their families than in their jobs" (Pleck, 1985, p. 135); their psychological well-being is more dependent on their family roles than on their work roles. The core role model that depicts men's lives as dominated by their workplace roles is too simplistic and overdrawn. Although it captures the essence of the Protestant Work Ethic, it fails to relate to the actual experiences and values of most men's lives and needs to be updated to reflect the complexities that are emerging from recent research.

Men's Workplace Roles

Interestingly, the role of paid employee is treated as both stressful in itself and as stress reducing or buffering when combined with family roles. Research is now directed toward specifying which aspects of that role are beneficial and which deleterious. Surprisingly little research has been done to determine which aspects of the work role contribute to men's psychological well-being. The considerable literature on job conditions has focused almost exclusively on the relationship of such conditions as autonomy and challenge to job satisfaction and to psychological distress, but not to well-being (House, Strecher, Metzner, & Robbins, 1986; Quinn, Mangione, Barnowe, Seashore, Cobb, Campbell, Fine, Herrick, Gupta, Levitin, Staines, Crowley, Bouxsein, & Bradford, 1973; Quinn, Walsh, & Hahn, 1977). Within the stress research field, attention has been paid primarily to work as a source of psychological distress. Indeed the operating assumption is that the workplace is a jungle, exposing men to such dangers as time pressure, competition, and noxious stimuli.

By inference, if conditions opposite to those associated with psychological distress are present, the job is assumed to contribute to men's sense of well-being. For example, the work of Robert Karasek and others (see below) suggests that lack of control over both resources and pacing at work contributes to stress. Thus, the presence of control over these aspects of one's job is assumed to contribute to one's sense of well-being. This formulation is an intriguing first step toward understanding more completely the impact on men—and women—of the paid employee role.

Given that the role of paid employee can have a positive effect on men's well-being (Gore & Mangione, 1983; Pleck, 1985), we can better understand the impact of this role by examining both its rewarding and its problematic aspects. Awareness that roles have these two aspects and that each can function differently with respect to well-being outcomes is not new (Blood & Wolf, 1960; Bradburn & Caplovitz, 1965). Similarly the notion that subjective experience in a role is a predictor of well-being has a long history (Aneshensel & Pearlin, this volume; Barnett & Baruch, 1985). In the later section on gender differences in interaction among roles, we discuss the relationship between rewarding and problematic role attributes.

The Interaction of Men's Family and Workplace Roles

As more and more men and women combine work and non-workplace roles, an understanding of role interaction is crucial to the study of stress and well-being. The concept of role interaction is relevant both to role occupancy and to the quality of experience in roles. The quality of a person's experience in any one role may affect the impact of other roles.

Men's family roles, at least until recently, have been less implicated than women's in role conflict and ensuing stress reactions. Central to the traditional role of husband is being a good economic provider. Historically, success in that arena has satisfied both the demands of the paid worker role and those of the husband and father roles. In theory, husbands in general, and good providers in particular, could fulfill their family role obligations without having to meet any additional demands within the home. Recent work by Weiss (1985) supports the view that men do define their work role as fulfilling their family roles: he finds that fathers define work as a means of fulfilling their family responsibilities. In short, although work and family demands may compete for men's time, they are experienced as mutually supportive. Having a job makes it possible to discharge family responsibilities; having a family makes work meaningful.

As a result, men are not often likely to experience interrole conflict when, for example, having to stay late at work cuts into their family time.

Indeed men may experience role synergy where women experience role conflict. By virtue of their status as sole economic provider, husbands traditionally have had considerable authority over their wives, their children, and their households. By employing the mechanisms of role bargaining within the home, employed men, especially those employed in prestigious, well-paying jobs, can trade off to their wives onerous aspects of the parenting role as a means of managing conflicts between the demands of the workplace and of the home. Thus, the busy executive who is called away on a business trip is forgiven by his wife for not going to the boy scout meeting; she understands and takes over for him.

It is illuminating to view the husband role as an occupation and to apply to it Karasek's model of job roles. Karasek and his colleagues (Karasek, Schwartz, Theorell, Pieper, Russell, & Michela, 1982) have been examining job conditions associated with impaired health. Although their work was based on all-male samples and was limited to the workplace, their concepts may, we believe, be applicable to males and females in their non-workplace roles. These researchers have been trying to specify the particular attributes of an occupation that arouse stress-related hormones which then set in motion various disease processes, especially those affecting the cardiovascular system and the immune system. According to their research, the most stressful set of job conditions combines having a low level of decision latitude—for example, having little control over the pacing of tasks or the allocation of resources—and having highly psychologically demanding tasks, such as those that have time pressures, deadlines, large workloads, and conflicting or heavy emotional demands. This "high-strain" combination is related to elevated risk for such negative health outcomes as coronary heart disease and ulcers. Presumably the high level of demands creates arousal and the inability to exert control leads to frustration. To illustrate, a surgeon and a nurse may face similar levels of psychological demands, but they differ greatly in their power to control how they deal with these demands and thus presumably in the stressfulness of their occupational role.

The traditional husband role typically combines low demands and high control, thus perhaps accounting for the beneficial effects of marriage on health outcomes for men. It also follows from this analysis, however, that the role of husband may be a high-strain role for men who have trouble being good economic providers, for example, minority married men. These men have relatively little control over their opportunities in the paid labor force, few opportunities for role bargaining within the paid employee role, and slim chance that role synergy will occur due to their success as breadwinners.

The role of father traditionally has been low in demands and high in control. Fathers' participation in child rearing in our culture has been quite minimal, and mothers have rarely expected or demanded much involvement. Yet, at least in principle, fathers have wielded ultimate authority; they could control their children's behavior in ways not possible for mothers. Viewing the traditional father role in Karasek's terms, we see that the combination of low demands and high control places it in the low-strain category. However, pressure for men to become more deeply involved in day-to-day parenting while maintaining their traditional provider role is likely to increase demands and reduce control. Increased psychological distress may result.

WOMEN'S ROLES

Women's Family Roles

In contrast to the belief that women's occupancy of family roles is critical to their psychological well-being, the evidence is that women's mental and physical health is not dependent on their being in the role of wife or mother (Bart, 1972; Baruch & Barnett, 1986a; Bernard, 1972). With respect to the role of wife, some studies show that wives do not have a psychological health advantage over women who are not married. In a sample of gifted women, highest life satisfaction was reported by women who were single and employed (Sears & Barbee, 1977). In our recent study, we found never-married and divorced women to be as high on some indices of well-being, such as self-esteem, as women who were married (Baruch & Barnett, 1986a). However, some studies do show well-being advantages for married women (Verbrugge, 1983). The inconsistent results from these studies are due in part to differences in the outcome variables. When psychological well-being is assessed by indices measuring happiness, marital status turns out to be predictive (Baruch & Barnett, 1986a; Campbell, Converse, & Rodgers, 1976; Depner, 1979). However, when self-esteem or life satisfaction are the measures of well-being, marital status has little impact (Baruch & Barnett, 1986a; Gigy, 1980).

Evidence about the role of mother is more consistent: being a mother is rarely associated with psychological well-being and is often associated with psychological distress. Findings from recent studies, for example, indicate that being in the role of mother did not predict any of three well-being indicators—that is, self-esteem, pleasure, or low levels of depressive symptomatology (Baruch & Barnett, 1986a). With respect to physical health, mothers compared to nonmothers have a small advantage (Verbrugge, 1984). This health advantage, however, is dependent on the ages and number of children. Having preschoolers or numerous children is associated with health problems. The "health debit" seems largest for employed nonmarried mothers (Verbrugge, 1984). Thus, whether mother-hood has a positive or negative effect on physical health depends on the children's characteristics and the mother's marital status.

Indeed, some studies suggest that the role of mother may be women's primary source of stress (Barnett & Baruch, 1985; Veroff, Douvan, & Kulka, 1981), whether alone or in combination with work and marital roles. Compared to other groups of women, those with children, partic-ularly children six years of age and younger, are at greater risk for depres-sion, and the risk increases with the number of children at home (Pearlin, 1975; Radloff, 1975). Moreover, in our recent study of women's three ma-jor social roles, only occupancy of the role of mother, not of wife or paid worker, was related to the experience of role strain, that is, role overload and role conflict (Barnett & Baruch, 1985). Gore and Mangione (1983) also found that after controlling for marital and employment status, women with children, especially minor children, reported higher levels of psychophysiological complaints, such as trouble with breathing, poor ap-petite, and difficulty with sleeping.

These findings suggest that burdensome demands are associated with women's family roles (Aneshensel & Pearlin, this volume). Focusing on role occupancy per se masks the fact that although for some women the roles of wife and of mother can be very rewarding, for others they can be very troublesome (Baruch & Barnett, 1986a).

Central to the traditional roles of wife and mother is the obligation to be available to meet the needs of the family, to be ready to respond whenever someone calls. In addition, wives and mothers are held, and hold themselves, responsible for the well-being of their role partners—their husbands and their children. In the traditional view, if a woman's husband is unhappy, it is assumed to be due to her failings; if her children have problems, she is assumed to be at fault. This assumption of responsi-bility is particularly strong for the role of mother. In spite of the reality that one has relatively little control over the welfare and happiness of another person, mothers are vulnerable to self-blame whenever their chil-dren show signs of distress. The combination of little control, relentless demands, and great responsibility exposes wives and mothers to many frustrations and failures, and, applying Karasek's model, may account in part for the stressfulness of these roles.

Compounding this picture and adding to the stressfulness of women's family roles, is the cultural expectation that women should perform them naturally and with no negative consequences. To admit to stress is tan-tamount to admitting to failure as a woman. This picture contrasts sharply with that of men, who are seen as legitimately experiencing stress in their primary role as breadwinner and as needing support, especially from their wives.

In sum, it appears that women's non-workplace roles, especially the role of mother, are both low in control and high in demands, that is, high-strain roles that are particularly problematic with respect to stress-related outcomes. Clearly the core assumption that occupying these two roles is a prerequisite for women's psychological well-being is not supported.

Women's Workplace Roles

When women's role as paid employee is considered, it is always in the context of women's non-workplace roles. Since the paid employee role is assumed to be "added on" and thus to cause conflict, burden, and strain, women who occupy both family and workplace roles are automatically thought to be stressed. Yet it appears that the role of paid employee is associated with significant physical and mental health benefits for women. In contrast to women who occupy only the roles of wife and mother, those who also occupy the paid employee role experience a significant health advantage (Thoits, 1983; Verbrugge, 1983).

Recent evidence indicates that the role of paid employee is both a direct and an indirect source of well-being (Barnett & Baruch, 1985). Using such indices as self-reports of physical symptoms (Coleman, Antonucci, & Adelmann, 1987; Verbrugge, 1983; Waldron & Herold, 1984) and psychological well-being indices (Baruch & Barnett, 1986a; Merikangas, 1985), many studies show significant mental and physical health differences that favor employed versus nonemployed women. Moreover, despite the belief that the more high-powered a woman's career, the more danger to her well-being, the advantage is greater for women in higher occupational statuses (Verbrugge, 1984). However, being employed is beneficial even to women in low-level jobs (Belle, 1982; Ferree, 1976). Despite the growing consensus that the employee role is not typically as stressful for women as it has been assumed to be, scant attention has been paid to the beneficial effects of women's workplace roles.

Considering the accumulated evidence about the core role assumptions for men and women, it seems clear that they have not been confirmed. In sum, it is ironic that the roles that appear to be most predictive for women's and men's well-being are those ignored in the core role models. For men the role of husband seems central for psychological well-being; for women, it is the role of paid employee.

The Interaction of Women's Family and Workplace Roles

In contrast to assumptions about men, there has been no assumption of a natural congruence between a woman's role as wife and mother and her role as a paid worker. Even now, little recognition exists of the many important ways in which women function as economic providers in relation to their children and husbands. This is but one reason why women traditionally have not been able to role bargain successfully with their husbands and with their children.

Because women's occupational roles are typically lower than men's in prestige, in power, and in income, opportunities for eliminating and delegating family-role tasks are fewer, making role bargaining less viable (Long & Porter, 1984). The weight of social sanctions and the low probability that women can trade off to their husbands or children onerous aspects of the wife and mother roles reduce the likelihood for successful negotiation between their workplace and non-workplace roles. It thus appears that women have fewer options than do men to achieve control over competing role demands.

The distress a woman experiences as a mother, however, may be affected by her experience as a paid worker. Dissatisfaction in the maternal role can be buffered, for example, by a positive experience in the paid employee role. Barnett and Baruch (1985) found that among married employed mothers, the more positive their experience in the worker role, the less likely role overload was to be associated with being a mother. Other studies demonstrate the buffering effect of employment on parental distress for women. Gove and his associates (Gove, 1972; Gove & Tudor, 1973) report that married nonemployed women with children report higher levels of depressive symptoms than their employed counterparts. Perhaps because of a greater sense of control, employed mothers appear less impaired by the stresses of child rearing than are housewives. However, Kandel et al. (1985) found that among married, employed women, parenthood exacerbated the effect of work stress reactions on depressive symptomatology. This inconsistency may reflect differences in the number and age of the children in these samples.

As further evidence of how the work role may buffer the stress experienced in family roles, Barnett and Baruch (1985) found that self-reports of role overload—having too many demands—and role conflict—having conflicting demands—were significantly related to self-reported symptoms of anxiety only among women who were nonemployed. In other words, nonemployed wives and mothers experience more anxiety when they are feeling stressed in their family roles than do wives and mothers who are employed. In another study (Kandel et al., 1985), the overall level of family distress reported by women was lower than their reported level of work distress; however, family distress was more strongly related to negative mental health outcomes. Finally, Dytell et al. (1985) found that although workplace stressors were more strongly related to self-reported stress symptoms than were family-role stressors, the latter more strongly predicted actual physical illness.

There are also important stress-related interactions among all three of women's major social roles. The well-known Framingham Heart Study (Haynes & Feinleib, 1982) provides evidence of the interactive effects of women's employment, marital, and parental roles on their risk for coronary heart disease (CHD). By looking at the family role occupancy of the employed women in this longitudinal study, the authors found that the only groups at high risk were clerical workers who were married to blue-collar husbands, or had more than two children, or both. Perhaps when a woman has children, being in a paid job that is high in demands and low in control in combination with being married to a traditional husband creates a particularly high risk for CHD.

GENDER DIFFERENCES

Interaction Among Roles

There is considerable evidence, as noted above, that for certain role combinations, having a positive experience in one role can offset the stressful effects associated with having a negative experience in another role. Only a few studies have addressed the question of gender differences in these effects. Spreitzer, Snyder, and Larson (1979) studied the compensatory effect on happiness of satisfaction or dissatisfaction in major social roles. For men and women, dissatisfaction in the paid employee role was compensated for by satisfaction in the marital role. However, for men but not women, satisfaction in the parental role offset dissatisfaction in the marital role. Indeed, for women, it appears that dissatisfaction in the marital role cannot be compensated for by satisfaction in any other role.

The experiences of one role partner can influence the experiences of the other. A wife's experience as a mother, for example, is affected by her husband's performance of the paternal role. The mothers in our study of fathers mentioned above, especially those who were employed, were less satisfied in their marriages when they did more child care relative to their husbands (Barnett & Baruch, 1987). In addition, wives of more participant fathers were more likely to criticize themselves, especially if employed, reporting that their work was interfering with their family responsibilities. Thus for these women the quality of their experience in one of their two family roles has direct effects on the quality of their experience in the other, and the role behavior of the spouse has an impact on that experience. Similarly, Kessler and McRae (1982), focusing on role quality, found that the health advantage to married women of being employed was negated if their husbands did not participate in child care. Apparently well-being is enhanced when mothers are employed only if they perceive their husbands to be doing their "fair share" of child care. Even so, they are vulnerable to their husbands' anger and their own feelings of guilt.

Fathers' experiences are similarly conditioned by their wives' role behavior. In our study of fathers' roles (Baruch & Barnett, 1986b), we found that when fathers acted more as solo parents—that is, interacted with the child when the mother was absent or unavailable—their feelings about their marriages suffered. Compared to men who did little of this form of child care, these men felt less benefited in their marriages and were more critical of their wives as mothers. Further, the less the employed mothers interacted with their children relative to the father, the more dissatisfied the father was with the wife's employment pattern and with the rewards he was getting in the marriage. For both married men and women, the spouse's performance of the parental role has a strong influence on their experience of the marital role. Thus, the cumulative positive effect of marriage and employment for men's well-being may be modified by the role behavior of their wives.

Theoretical Perspectives: Gender, Role Involvement, and Psychological Distress

Two hypotheses underlie the research on gender and involvement in social roles. The first, the "social-role hypothesis," asserts that there are no gender differences in the nature of social roles. According to this hypothesis, both employment and marriage confer many mental health advantages; since men more often than women occupy both roles, they therefore more often enjoy their benefits. By implication, as more and more women enter the labor force, the health advantage currently enjoyed by men will disappear. This formulation assumes that the differences between the roles of female employee and male employee as well as those between husband and wife are of negligible significance. "The benefits and liabilities of work, marriage, and other structured social experiences should be identical for all populations. Thus, sex differences in indicators of mental health would be accounted for by differences in the roles . . . that are occupied by each sex" (Gore & Mangione, 1983, p. 200). This perspective is apparent in studies indicating that employed, married women have lower rates of depression than do nonemployed, married women; such studies suggest that the mental health of men and women will resemble each other more as women assume the same set of social roles now occupied by men. This approach to the study of gender differences is exemplified by Verbrugge's (1986) work on physical health. Indeed, she found the oft reported sex differential indicating higher morbidity for women disappeared when social role occupancy was controlled. In fact, " . . . when social differences between men and women are controlled, excess morbidity for *men* emerges."

The second hypothesis, the sex-role hypothesis, posits interactive effects of gender. Specifically, it states that the nature of role demands differs for men and women, so that, for example, the effect of being a parent is conditional upon the sex of the role occupant (Gore & Mangione, 1983). The sex-role hypothesis assumes that these differences are important; that occupancy per se will not account for the gender differences in the outcome variables. More specifically, advocates of this latter position note that for men and women in the same family roles, that is, spouse and parent, the demands on women exceed those on men, putting women at greater risk for depression. Research indicating that there is an excess of psychological disorder among women and that this is due to the higher than expected rates among married women supports this hypothesis (Gore & Mangione, 1983).

With respect to gender differences in the effects of role involvement on depression, two recent analyses support the social-role hypothesis (Aneshensel, Frerichs, & Clark, 1981; Gore & Mangione, 1983). When social role membership was controlled, the frequently reported sex difference in depression, which these studies also found, failed to reach significance, and in fact disappeared. Thus the positive mental health benefits of employment and of marriage seem to accrue similarly to women as well as to men. Recent analyses indicate that these relationships hold even when race is controlled (Gore & Mangione, 1983).

However, in Gore and Mangione's study (1983), the sex-role hypothesis was supported when the indicator of distress was self-reports of physiological symptoms, such as "trouble getting your breath" and "trembling." Having children at home was unrelated to reports of psychophysiological complaints among men; among women, in contrast, regardless of employment status, having children at home was highly related to such complaints.

Despite these important studies, the task of sorting out gender differences in the effects of role involvement on stress-related outcomes is in its infancy, perhaps because issues of role quality are just beginning to be addressed. Does having a negative experience in one's parental role have different effects on the experience of stress related to the paid work role for men and for women? Does having a negative experience in one's work role exacerbate the stressful effects of the parental role for men and for women? Because family roles have been neglected in the study of stress reactions in men, gender differences in the effects on psychological distress and well-being of quality of experience in family roles are not yet well understood.

SOCIAL CHANGE: IMPLICATIONS FOR MULTIPLE ROLE INVOLVEMENT AND PSYCHOLOGICAL DISTRESS

Recent shifts in family patterns may be changing the ways women and men are defining marital and parental roles. In the wake of the women's movement, wives' expectations for sharing and cooperation from their husbands are also increasing, especially among employed women. Employment may offer married women opportunities to gain control that are not available in their non-workplace roles. Income allows women to exert influence in their marital relationship and to buy services, thereby reducing some of their household responsibilities. As wives become less dependent, their marital and parental roles may become less stressful. However, at least in the short term, some new stressors are emerging. As employed women redefine their participation in child rearing so that it is more equal to that of their husbands, marital tensions seem likely to surface. These tensions will probably be felt more acutely by women, who have historically been more vulnerable to marital dissatisfaction. In the long term one can hope that these changes will result in a greater sense of equity for both husbands and wives.

How might these changes affect men's experience of psychological distress in their family roles? There is evidence that the preponderance of dual-earner families is having an effect on the role of husband (Baruch & Barnett, 1986b; Gilbert, 1985; Rosenfield, 1980). Using wives' employment status as a measure of traditional versus nontraditional sex roles, Rosenfield compared the depression scores of more versus less traditional husbands with those of more versus less traditional wives. When the wives were not working, that is, when the division of labor was traditional, the women had much higher levels of depressive symptoms than the men. However, when the wives were employed, that is, when the sex roles were less traditional, the sex difference was reversed! This important finding qualifies the oft reported conclusion that marriage benefits men more than women, and suggests that in the future the role of husband may not be as low in stress as it has been. We can see in these results some indications that nontraditional fathers may be feeling less control and more demands than more traditional fathers. Rosenfield conjectures that the relative loss of power implied for males in less traditional sex roles "may be experienced as a loss of control" (p. 38), thereby accounting for the increase in depression. Conversely, nontraditional sex roles imply a relative gain in power for women, accounting for the lower levels of depression reported in some studies among these women. In nontraditional marriages, wives may demand more participation from their husbands and insist on sharing control. This change may cause an increase in the stress associated with the role of husband (Baruch & Barnett, 1986b; Pleck, 1985). Perhaps role synergy will be replaced by role conflict as the obligations of the role of father become differentiated from those of successful economic provider.

Marital strain appears to be the cost, at least the short-term cost, of current social redefinitions of family roles. These new strains may tax women's well-being more strenuously than men's, since women's well-being has been more closely related to the quality of their marital role. It is to be hoped that these effects are indeed short term, since difficulties are experienced whenever there are shifts in expectations. With time, the old notion of control may be replaced with a new notion of shared power, the effects of which we know very little about.

REFERENCES

Aneshensel, C. S., Frerichs, R. R., & Clark, V. A. (1981). Family roles and sex differences in depression. *Journal of Health and Social Behavior, 22*, 379–393.

Barnett, R. C., & Baruch, G. K. (1985). Women's involvement in multiple roles and psychological distress. *Journal of Personality and Social Psychology, 49*, 135–145.

——. (1987). Maternal participation in child care: Patterns and consequences. In F. Crosby (Ed.), *Spouse, parent, worker: On gender and multiple roles.* New Haven: Yale University Press.

Bart, P. (1972). Depression in middle-aged women. In J. M. Bardwick (Ed.), *Readings on the psychology of women.* New York: Harper & Row.

Baruch, G. K., & Barnett, R. C. (1986a). Role quality, multiple role involvement, and psychological well-being in midlife women. *Journal of Personality and Social Psychology, 51*, 578–585.

——. (1986b). Consequences of fathers' participation in family work: Parents' role-strain and well-being. *Journal of Personality and Social Psychology, 51*, 983–992.

Baruch, G. K., Biener, L., & Barnett, R. C. (1987). Women and gender in research on stress. *American Psychologist, 42*, 130–136.

Belle, D. (Ed.), (1982). *Lives in stress: Women and depression.* Beverly Hills, CA: Sage.

Bernard, J. (1972). *The future of marriage.* New York: World-Times.

Birnbaum, J. L. (1975). Life patterns, personality style and self-esteem in gifted family oriented and career committed women. In M. Mednick, S. Tangri, & L. W. Hoffman (Eds.), *Women and achievement: Social and motivational analysis.* New York: Hemisphere–Halstead.

Blood, R. O., & Wolfe, D. M. (1960). *Husbands and wives.* Glencoe, IL: Free Press.

Bradburn, N. M. & Caplovitz, D. (1965). *Reports on happiness.* Chicago: Aldine.

Campbell, A., Converse, P. E., & Rodgers, W. L. (1976). *The quality of American life.* New York: Sage.

Cleary, P., & Mechanic, D. (1983). Sex differences in psychological distress among married people. *Journal of Health and Social Behavior, 24,* 111–121.

Coleman, L., Antonucci, T., & Adelmann, P. (1987). In F. Crosby (Ed.), *Spouse, parent, worker: On gender and multiple roles.* New Haven: Yale University Press.

Coser, L. (with R. Coser). (1974). *Greedy institutions.* New York: Free Press.

Crosby, F. (1984). Job satisfaction and domestic life. In M. D. Lee & R. N. Kanungo (Eds.), *Management of work and personal life.* New York: Praeger.

Depner, C. (1979). *The parental role and psychological well-being.* Paper presented at the meeting of the American Psychological Association, New York.

Dytell, R. S., Pardine, P., & Napoli, A. (1985). *Importance of occupational and nonoccupational stress among professional men and women.* Paper presented at the Eastern Psychological Association, Boston.

Erikson, E. (1959). Identity and the life cycle. *Psychological Issues, 1,* 1–171.

———. (1968). *Identity: Youth and crisis.* New York: Norton.

Farrell, M. P. & Rosenberg, S. D. (1981). *Men at midlife.* Dover, MA: Auburn.

Ferree, M. (1976). The confused American housewife. *Psychology Today, 10,* 76–80.

Gigy, L. L. (1980). Self-concept of single women. *Psychology of Women Quarterly, 5,* 321–340.

Gilbert, L. A. (1985). *Men in dual-career families: Current realities and future prospects.* Hillsdale, NJ: Erlbaum.

Goode, W. (1960). A theory of strain. *American Sociological Review, 25,* 483–496.

Gore, S., & Mangione, T. W. (1983). Social roles, sex roles and psychological distress: Additive and interactive models of sex differences. *Journal of Health and Social Behavior, 24,* 300–312.

Gove, W. (1972). Sex, marital status, and mental illness. *Social Forces, 51,* 34–55.

———. (1973). Sex, marital status, and mobility. *American Journal of Sociology, 79,* 45–67.

———. (1978). Sex differences in mental illness among adult men and women: An examination of four questions raised regarding whether or not women actually have higher rates. *Social Science and Medicine, 12,* 187–198.

Gove, W. R., & Tudor, J. (1973). Adult sex roles and mental illness, *American Journal of Sociology, 78,* 812–835.

Gove, W. R., & Zeiss, C. (1987). Multiple roles and happiness. In F. Crosby (Ed.), *Spouse, parent, worker: On gender and multiple roles.* New Haven: Yale University Press.

Haynes, S. G., & Feinleib, M. (1982). Women, work, and coronary heart disease:

Results from the Framingham 10-year follow-up study. In P. Berman & E. Ramey (Eds.), *Women: A developmental perspective* (NIH Publication No. 82–2298). Washington, DC: U.S. Government Printing Office.

House, J. S., Strecher, V., Metzner, H. L., & Robbins, C. A. (1986). Occupational stress and health among men and women in the Tecumseh community health study. *Journal of Health and Social Behavior, 27,* 62–77.

Kandel, D. B., Davies, M., & Raveis, V. H. (1985). The stressfulness of daily social roles for women: Marital, occupational and household roles. *Journal of Health and Social Behavior, 26,* 64–78.

Karasek, R. A., Schwartz, J., Theorell, T., Pieper, C., Russell, B. S., & Michela, J. (1982). *Final report: Job characteristics, occupation and coronary heart disease.* New York: Columbia University, Dept. of Industrial Engineering and Operations Research.

Kessler, R. C., & McRae, J. A., Jr. (1982). The effect of wives' employment on the mental health of married men and women. *American Sociological Review, 47,* 217–227.

Lamb, M. E., Pleck, J. H., Charnov, E. L., & Levine, J. A. (1985). Paternal behavior in humans. *American Zoologist, 25,* 883–894.

Lein, L., Durham, M., Pratt, M., Schudson, M., Thomas, R., & Weiss, H. (1974). Final Report: Work and family life. Cambridge, MA: Center for the Study of Public Policy.

Levinson, D. J., Darrow, C. N., Klein, E. B., Levinson, M. H., & McKee, B. (1978). *The seasons of a man's life.* New York: Ballantine.

Long, J. & Porter, K. L. (1984). In G. K. Baruch & J. Brooks-Gunn (Eds.), *Women in midlife.* New York: Plenum.

Marks, S. R. (1977). Multiple roles and role strain: Some notes on human energy, time and commitment. *American Sociological Review, 41,* 921–936.

Merikangas, K. (1985). *Sex differences in depression.* Paper presented at Murray Center (Radcliffe College) Conference: Mental Health in Social Context, Cambridge, MA.

Pearlin, L. (1975). Sex roles and depression. In N. Datan (Ed.), *Life-span developmental psychology: Normative life crises.* New York: Academic Press.

Pleck, J. H. (1985). *Working wives/working husbands.* Beverly Hills, CA: Sage.

Quinn, R. P., Mangione, T. W., Barnowe, J. T., Seashore, S. E., Cobb, W. Jr., Campbell, D. B., Fine, B. D., Herrick, N. Q., Gupta, N., Levitin, T. E., Staines, G. L., Crowley, J. E., Bouxsein, S., & Bradford, A. J. (1973). *The 1969–1970 survey of working conditions: Chronicles of an unfinished enterprise.* Ann Arbor, MI: Survey Research Center, University of Michigan.

Quinn, R. P., Walsh, J. T., & Hahn, D. L. K. (1977). *The 1972–73 quality of employment survey: Continuing chronicles of an unfinished enterprise.* Ann Arbor, MI: Survey Research Center, University of Michigan.

Radloff, L. (1975). Sex differences in depression: The effects of occupation and marital status. *Sex Roles, 1,* 249–265.

Rosenfield, S. (1980). Sex differences in depression: Do women always have higher rates? *Journal of Health and Social Behavior, 21,* 33–42.

Rosenman, R. H., Brand, R. J., Jenkins, C. D., Friedman, M., Straus, R., & Wurm, M. (1975). Coronary heart disease in the Western Collaborative Group Study: Final follow-up experience of 8½ years. *Journal of the American Medical Association, 233,* 872–877.

Rossi, A. (1984). Gender and parenthood. *American Sociological Review, 49,* 1–19.

Sears, P. S. & Barbee, A. H. (1977). Career and life satisfaction among Terman's gifted women. In J. Stanley, W. George, & C. Solano (Eds.), *The gifted and the creative: Fifty-year perspective.* Baltimore: Johns Hopkins University Press.

Sieber, S. D. (1974). Toward a theory of role accumulation. *American Sociological Review, 39,* 567–578.

Slater, P. (1963). On social regression. *American Sociological Review, 28,* 339–364.

Spreitzer, E., Snyder, E. E., & Larson, D. L. (1979). Multiple roles and psychological well-being. *Sociological Focus, 12,* 141–148.

Stroebe, M. S., & Stroebe, W. (1983). Who suffers more? Sex differences in health risks of the widowed. *Psychological Bulletin, 93,* 279–301.

Teicholtz, J. G. (1978). *Psychological correlates of voluntary childlessness in married women.* Paper presented at the Eastern Psychological Association, Washington, DC.

Thoits, P. (1983). Multiple identities and psychological well-being. *American Sociological Review, 48,* 174–187.

Vaillant, G. E. (1977). *Adaptation to life.* Boston: Little, Brown.

Verbrugge, L. M. (1982). Women's social roles and health. In P. Berman and E. Ramey (Eds.), *Women: A developmental perspective* (Publication No. 82–2298). Washington, DC: U.S. Government Printing Office.

———. (1983). *Pressures, satisfactions, and the link to physical health of young women.* Paper presented at meeting of the American Psychological Association, Anaheim, CA.

———. (May 1984). *Role burdens and physical health of women and men.* Paper presented at conference, "Modern woman: Managing multiple roles," Yale University.

———. (1986). *Sex differences in physical health: Making good sense of empirical results.* Paper presented at Society of Behavioral Medicine, San Francisco.

Veroff, J., Douvan, E., & Kulka, R. A. (1981). *The inner American.* New York: Basic Books.

Waldron, I., & Herold, J. (1984). *Employment, attitudes toward employment and women's health.* Paper presented at Society of Behavioral Medicine, Philadelphia.

Wallerstein, J., & Kelly, J. (1980). *Surviving the breakup.* New York: Basic Books.

Weiss, R. S. (1985). Men and the family. *Family Process, 24,* 49–58.

6

The Importance of Life Events for Explaining Sex Differences in Psychological Distress

Elaine Wethington
Jane D. McLeod
Ronald C. Kessler

Women report significantly higher rates of psychological distress than men, a difference that is now widely documented (Al-Issa, 1982). Research has aimed to determine under what specific conditions the difference exists, and inferentially, why it exists.

Most prior research on this topic has focused on the day-to-day stressors of normal role functioning. It is generally believed, although difficult to document rigorously, that women suffer from more psychological distress than do men because the stressors in women's roles are more intense and persistent.

In reviewing the available evidence about sex differences in psychological distress, we have developed an interpretation that is consonant with current thinking about sex role socialization and the sexual division of labor. This interpretation takes as its starting point our finding that women are more affected emotionally than men not only by their own stressful

This research was supported by NIMH Research Scientist Development Award MH00507 to Ronald Kessler, by NIMH grants MH34479, MH16806, and MH40136, and by an NIH Biomedical Research Support Grant to the Vice President for Research at the University of Michigan.

144

experiences, but also by the stressful experiences of people they care about. Women's roles *obligate* them to respond to the needs of others.

Our emphasis on sex differences in social roles is not unique. Most writers have attributed sex differences in psychological distress to differences in the social roles and attendant stresses that men and women experience (e.g., Bernard, 1971; Gove & Tudor, 1973). Women's social roles are thought to be more stress provoking and less fulfilling than the roles occupied by men (Gove, 1978). Other writers have suggested that women's socialization experiences produce susceptibility to depression through the learning of a "helpless" style in coping with stressors (Radloff & Rae, 1979).

The role-stress argument has fostered a large body of sociological research on sex differences in chronic role-related stress reactions. Typically, this work has used indicators of role status, such as marital status, number and ages of children, and employment status (Gove, 1972; Gove & Geerken, 1977; Radloff, 1975) to substitute for more direct measures of stressors within the role, such as task demand and overload. For example, the sex-distress relationship has been shown to be more pronounced among the married than the previously or never married (Cleary & Mechanic, 1983; Fox, 1980; Gove, 1972), but the specific role stressors responsible for the relationship have not been established.

There have been several attempts to understand the specific mechanisms involved in social roles that may produce or lessen psychological distress (Kessler & McRae, 1982; Pearlin, 1975). This has proved to be a difficult task. Measures of chronic role stressors and resources tend to be perceptions of the social environment, such as the sense of "demandingness" or "overload." They are subjective, rather than objective, in content. When psychological distress and chronic stressors are measured at the same time (as they are in the typical cross-sectional study), it is impossible to establish whether the stressors or the feelings of helplessness and low morale came first (see Kessler, 1983).

In response to this difficulty, some researchers have turned to the study of acute stressors, examining sex differences in exposure and response to undesirable life events (Dohrenwend, 1973; Kessler, 1979; Radloff & Rae, 1981). Typically, exposure to life events is measured retrospectively. The analysis of acute stressors thus offers methodological advantages over the analysis of chronic stressors because the stress exposure is reported to be prior to current distress.

Research on acute stressors has discovered that although men and women do not differ much in the number of undesirable life events they experience, women are significantly more affected emotionally by life events. This greater female vulnerability accounts for a substantial part of the overall relationship between sex and psychological distress (Kessler, 1979). It is not possible to conclude from this previous research, however, whether the type and intensity of the stressors vary across sex. Nevertheless, many explanations for the sex difference have not taken into account differences in exposure to stressors.

Radloff and Monroe (1978) and Radloff and Rae (1979) suggested women are socialized so that they are more susceptible than men to reactive depression. Pearlin and Schooler (1978) examined male-female differences in strategies used to cope with stressors. They argued that the coping strategies typically used by women tend to be somewhat less effective in buffering the psychological effects of life stress than the strategies used by men. Although both Radloff and Rae and Pearlin and Schooler explicitly link the origins of the sex differences in stress response and coping response to structural disadvantages that women suffer—Radloff and Rae, for example, argue that girls are less positively reinforced than boys when they try to control their environments—they emphasize the importance of these intermediate behavioral and psychological differences for the development of distress.

Although these arguments differ in their conceptions of how female vulnerability comes about, they share the assertion that women are *pervasively* disadvantaged in their capacity to withstand the psychological distress created by life experiences. These arguments have all been influential and have guided recent attempts to elaborate the social-structural or socialized bases of female vulnerability.

The image of pervasive female vulnerability to stressors was established by results from event studies that combined many different types of life events into a single, aggregated measure of life-event exposure. Such measures have a significantly stronger relationship to psychological distress among women than among men. From this, it has been assumed that women are more vulnerable to the effects of all types of events. Yet this assumption has not been tested in the aggregated life-event analyses themselves.

Evidence inconsistent with the pervasive vulnerability assumption can be found in studies of people who have all experienced the same life event. For example, one study suggests that women adjust somewhat *better* than men to the death of a spouse (Stroebe & Stroebe, 1983). Women are also less emotionally affected than men by financial difficulties (Kessler, 1982), and cope more adequately than men with the long-term aftermath of separation and divorce (Wallerstein & Kelly, 1980).

These examples show clearly that women are not pervasively more vulnerable to acute stress than men; only that certain events may affect women more. It is not possible to determine what these events are when many different life events are aggregated. It seems likely, though, that a disaggregated analysis would show that the selective vulnerability which differentiates men and women can be traced to different roles and to the different salience of role domains to men and women.

DISAGGREGATED LIFE-EVENT ANALYSES

Studies of coping with a specific type of crisis have not been done for enough different events to allow a systematic comparison of sex differences in vulnerability. Most studies, moreover, do not use samples that are representative of the general population. Any attempt to establish that men and women differ in their vulnerability to stressors should use the same general population surveys that have previously been used to conduct aggregate life-event analyses.

It is difficult to conduct disaggregated analyses in data bases like these, however, because only a handful of people report the occurrence of any one event in a life-event survey. This is true even in very large surveys. It is consequently necessary to combine results across a number of samples to arrive at stable parameter estimates, as we were able to do by working with data from five large epidemiologic surveys (Kessler & McLeod, 1984).

Even with this large data base it was necessary to combine some events into clusters in order to obtain reliable estimates. Five types of personal life-event clusters were created: income losses, separation/divorce, death of a loved one, other love losses (such as broken engagements and friendships), and physical illnesses and injuries. In addition, a series of "network life-event" clusters was created paralleling the personal event clusters. Network life events are events that occur to people important to the respondent.

In four of the five surveys included in our analysis, network life events were assessed by presenting respondents with a life-event list twice, the first time asking them to report all events that occurred to them personally in the last year and the second time asking them to report events that occurred to people important to them. In the remaining survey we analyzed, however, respondents were not presented with a life-event list. Instead respondents were asked to describe the most recent undesirable event that occurred to them. Some respondents reported that events that happened to network members were the most distressing.

A disaggregated analysis of these event clusters yielded consistent results across the surveys. For the most part, men and women reported the same number and types of events. There were two notable exceptions to this pattern, however. Men reported considerably more income losses than women. Women reported many more network events and deaths of loved ones. As income loss in these samples was rare, the more frequent reports by men of this type of event were not major contributors to the male-female distress differences. Network events, however, were quite common.

Further analysis showed that the higher rate of network events reported by women plays a central part in their higher levels of distress as measured by standard screening scales of psychological symptoms (depression and psychophysiological symptoms). We found consistently across the different surveys that the psychological impact of network events is significantly greater among women than men. We found equally clear evidence that there are no sex differences in the effects of income loss, separation/divorce, or most other personal events, even though previous studies suggested that we would. Coupled with the earlier finding that women report the occurrence of many more network events than men, we were able to demonstrate that the psychological disadvantage of women is due, in large part, to these events. Indeed, by adjusting statistically for sex differences in the reporting of and psychological response to network events, we were able to account for one-half of the total sex difference in average distress levels (Kessler & McLeod, 1984). In other words, statistical analysis indicates that if men reported as many network events as women and responded to them as women do, their average advantage in distress would be cut in half.

INTERPRETING THE EFFECTS OF NETWORK EVENTS

It is an obvious inference from the role-domain perspective that women would report more network events than men. Responsiveness to the needs of others is the "work" of women, both at home and on the job. In the surveys we examined, women were 50 percent more likely than men to report the death of a loved one (other than a spouse) and a third more likely to report other network events.

These differences probably reflect the fact that women consider the events of a wider range of people relevant when in an interview situation that asks them to report events that happened to "someone important to you." What this means on a deeper level, though, is unclear. On one hand, women may be more aware of events that happen to the people around them because they are obligated to respond to the needs of others. On the other hand, women may be defining more people as "important" to them.

We examined first whether women are in fact more involved than men with the people in their social networks and because of this involvement become aware of more network events. Although we cannot examine this possibility explicitly using the present data, we reasoned that if it were true, we could expect to find that women more frequently than men provide help to people in crisis situations. Relevant data are available in several large surveys of help seeking. We turned to one of these, a national survey conducted by Veroff, Douvan, and Kulka (1981), in which respondents were asked to name all people who had helped them manage their most recent undesirable event and to describe what these helpers did.

These data confirm that women are more likely than men to be named as helpers in a crisis situation. For each of four types of problems—economic and work-related, interpersonal, death, and health—the proportion of female helpers exceeds that of male helpers. Women are somewhat more likely than men to seek the support of other women, but men also report more female than male helpers. Women report having more helpers than men for all four types of problems. Adjusted for sex differences in the distribution of problem types, women are between 10 and 40 percent more likely than men to have been reported as helpers. Summed across all problem types, women were 30 percent more likely than men to provide some type of support.

Despite the strength of this result, this sex difference in level of involvement does not seem to explain the sex difference in vulnerability to network events. If it did—and assuming the relationship were linear—the relationship between network events and distress would be approximately 30 percent larger among women than men, the same difference that we find in levels of involvement as helpers. But this is not what we find. The relative emotional impact of network events is far greater among women than this predicted level.

Despite their involvement as helpers in a substantial minority of cases, men are apparently somehow able to avoid the personal distress that women experience from network events. One possible explanation for this male advantage is that men are less able to empathize with the distress of other people. This explanation, however, is inconsistent with available evidence that in experimental situations when the demand for empathy is disguised (Eisenberg & Lennon, 1983) nonverbal empathic reactions can be elicited as much from men as women. Rather, we suspect that men, despite their ability to empathize, live lives that are less involved with the emotional concerns of others. Men's concern for others may show itself in particular relationships, but compared to women's concern it does not extend as far into their social networks. We turn now to some evidence consistent with this speculation.

EVENTS THAT OCCUR TO CLOSE NETWORK MEMBERS

One way to investigate the hypothesis that women have a wider field of concern than men is to see whether the effects of network events vary depending on the relationship of the respondent to the person who experienced the event. If our reasoning is correct, the sex difference in vulnerability to distress should be smaller for events that occur to very close network members and larger when we consider more distant relationships.

This analysis was possible in just one of the surveys we analyzed (Myers, Lindenthal, & Pepper, 1974). Network events were classified by whether the event occurred to a son, daughter, spouse, or "other important" person. Because of the small number of events involved, those events that occurred to children and spouses were combined into a single category that we call "immediate family" events. All others were grouped into an "other network" events category.

Statistical analyses focused on psychological distress in relation to events occurring to immediate family and other network events, separately for men and women. Men are distressed by events that occur to members of their immediate family, but not by other network events. In contrast, both types of network events have a strong and significant effect on women.

It is interesting to note that the other network events reported by men are much more serious than the immediate family events reported. Sixty-six percent of other network events involved bereavement, and almost 25 percent involved serious illnesses. The events that respondents reported as having occurred to their spouses and children were much less serious, with school-related events (among children) and minor illnesses predominating. This contrast makes it all the more striking that immediate family events affect men, while other network events evidently do not.

Among women, events occurring to others in the network have stronger effects than those occurring to immediate family members; however, women, like men, reported mostly serious events for other network members. When we adjusted for differences in the average severity of the events in these two event groups, immediate family events have greater emotional effects on women.

The more interesting comparison is between men and women. Here we find that other network events have a much greater effect on women than men. As predicted, the sex difference in vulnerability to events is considerably more pronounced at the edges of caring networks than at their centers. Women seem to cast a wider net of concern and so are affected emotionally not only by the well-being of their immediate family but also by lives of those to whom they may be less intimately related. Men, by comparison, are less affected emotionally by events occurring to people outside their immediate family.

CONCRETE AND EMOTIONAL INVOLVEMENT IN NETWORK EVENTS

Our reasoning up to this point has led us to consider the greater involvement of women in their social networks as a likely determinant of their vulnerability to network events. Yet much of this reasoning has been speculative. None of the surveys considered in our secondary analysis contains explicit information about what respondents did or felt about the network events that occurred to people important to them. In a later section we discuss our efforts to go beyond this line of speculation and to collect new data that can answer the central questions that have emerged from our secondary analysis. Before doing so, we will clarify the reasoning guiding us by elaborating our interpretations of the results already presented.

Our secondary analysis, as noted earlier, showed that women provide more support than men and that women become more distressed by crises that occur in their networks. It is important to recognize, however, that we have not directly implicated the provision of support itself in this relationship. Men are reported by recipients of support to have been important helpers in a sizable minority of cases. Male helpers, furthermore, are reported as providing the same types of emotional support as female helpers and as being "very helpful" as often as female helpers (Kessler, McLeod, & Wethington, 1984). Yet men are not distressed by network events other than those that occur to their immediate families. Providing support is apparently not sufficient in itself to explain why network events are more related to distress among women than men.

Other circumstances may modify the relationship between providing support and distress. One possibility is that providing support leads to distress only when the provider is overloaded with so many other demands that his or her capacities to endure the emotional effects of caregiving break down. Women may experience more social demands for support than men. This is congruent with what is known about the day-to-day social burdens that women face in their roles as spouses, parents, children, and friends (Brody, 1981).

A second possibility is that the distressing effects of providing support may vary with the degree of emotional involvement. Women may be socialized to feel and express a greater concern for their loved ones; women may be more likely to place the needs of others before their own (Gilligan, 1982). Men, in contrast, may be more able to provide concrete assistance while maintaining emotional distance.

It is also possible, however, that providing support can play a part in creating emotional involvement. If the person in crisis is one about whom the supporter would not normally care (a neighbor whom the supporter knows only casually), the act of providing support may be a vehicle for creating more caring and, potentially, more distress. If the person in crisis is someone with whom the supporter is already emotionally involved, support may not have the same effect. (Indeed, it is easy to imagine a situation in which the opportunity to provide support to a very close loved one is less stress provoking than a situation in which one is helpless.) Since women's traditional roles involve them in helping, more numerous and deeper emotional involvements may be a consequence of the social expectation that women "help."

We believe that each of these possibilities has some validity. The time and energy demands placed on a supporter can themselves lead to distress, particularly when they are added to an already demanding set of role responsibilities. This overload can be exacerbated by social expectations or a socialized style that promotes both commitment to the needs of others and emotional involvement. Personal concern for the well-being of others can lead to distress even when no support is being provided. The precise way in which support and emotional involvement combine to determine the effect of network crisis events will vary depending on characteristics of the situation and the helper.

These same processes could account for the higher rates with which women report network events. We have already suggested that some part of this difference—as, for example, the 50 percent higher rate among women than men of reporting that someone "important to you" died recently—reflects the wider field of concern of women. Yet part of the difference may also be real: women are actually exposed to more network life crises than men.

One way in which this could be true, obviously, is that people in crisis might confide more in women than men. (Our analysis confirms that women are more likely than men to be named as supporters.) Perhaps those social networks in which women bear the emotional burdens of being confidantes may be those in which male network members are least burdened by demands for support. The differentiation of "caring" in a social network may be as sharp as the traditional household division of labor. Thus, the emotional costs paid by women may create a context in which men are able to avoid exposure to distressing network events. For example, a wife may conceal from her husband her own health worries or her concern about their children's sexual activity.

THE REWARDS AND COSTS OF NETWORK MAINTENANCE

Up to this point we have emphasized the negative consequences of caring for others. This aspect of the support transaction is important to bear in mind because it has been neglected in most studies of social support (Jung, 1984; Rook, 1984). As Belle (1982) has noted, the assumption implicit in most discussions is that social support takes place within networks of mutual obligation. This view gives the impression that social networks have health-promoting effects for all their members, overlooking the fact that women are overrepresented among providers of support. Thus, conventional views fail to appreciate that women may be unfairly burdened by their responsibility for the most distressing aspects of the work that maintains social networks.

We do not suggest that women do not reap emotional benefits from network involvement. Caring has emotional rewards as well as costs. In one national survey, for example, there was a *negative* relationship between personal distress and the amount of time one reported "doing things to help or please other people" (Veroff et al., 1981). Involvement in large social networks is associated with good mental health (Fischer, 1982), even though people in large networks complain that their loved ones make too many demands on them. We do suggest, however, that the ratio of costs to benefits from involvement with others may be more unfavorable for women than for men. Women are more likely than men, for example, to report that their networks are too demanding (Fischer, 1982).

Other evidence suggests, moreover, that women are more emotionally responsive than men to the quality of interpersonal ties. Marital quality, for example, seems to be more strongly related to emotional well-being among women than men (Williams, 1985). The stress-buffering effect of social support may be somewhat stronger among women than men (Wethington & Kessler, 1986). This greater sensitivity to emotional support can be advantageous, but the absence of high-quality emotional support can also lead to distress among women that men do not experience.

It is not surprising, then, that many researchers have observed that men profit more than women from social ties. The most telling observation, perhaps, is that the health-promoting effects of marriage are considerably greater among men than women (Gove, 1972). We have found, moreover, that sex differences in network event exposure and vulnerability are most pronounced among the married. Addressing ourselves to these differences between married men and women in primary data collection that we recently carried out, we interviewed a general population sample of 778 couples. Husbands and wives were interviewed separately. The interviews emphasized daily social burdens, social support, socioeconomic resources, exposure to acute personal stress, and the respondent's involvement in network events.

By interviewing couples it is of course possible to discover the occurrence of a network event even when one spouse fails to report it. Our new analyses have focused on determining what types of events both spouses report, and what types of events wives are more likely to report than husbands are. We found that wives are significantly better reporters of most types of network events, most especially the major illnesses of their children and their relatives (Kessler & Wethington, 1986). (Women report on the average 2.31 network events, while the men report 1.97.)

If respondents reported network health events and difficulties, we asked whether the respondent had been involved in giving care to the person affected. Here also the sex difference was marked. Wives are much more likely to report being involved during a network acute health crisis. Wives who helped, moreover, devoted significantly more hours per week during the crisis than husbands who helped (9.7 hours vs. 5.5 hours). This sex difference held regardless of whether or not the wife was employed. Although there was no difference in the number of husbands and wives who reported being involved in the care of a loved one who had a chronic health problem or serious disability, women reported, on the average, spending twice as much time helping.

More striking was the difference in the proportion of caregiving husbands and wives who helped a loved one more than 20 hours a week; 5.5 percent of the husbands did so, compared to 15 percent of the wives. For chronic, intense health care, homemakers reported spending more time than women employed outside the home.

Whenever a respondent reported that a network member had experienced a serious personal crisis unrelated to health, we asked how much he or she had been involved in either helping the person or talking over the problem. Here too, employed wives and homemakers were significantly more likely to spend time than husbands.

Such information about caregiving is useful in examining the part played by support in mediating the impact of network events on emotional functioning; it is also useful for investigating whether the impact of network events on men is lessened when their wives are the primary supporters. Our analyses to this point show that this is likely to be true: women's involvement in family crises shields men from the burdens of caring for others in need. The differences between the burdens of wives and husbands are difficult to quantify, but the picture that emerges from our data shows women engaged in the troubles of others, providing hands-on assistance in times of crisis.

The analysis of life events per se certainly will not provide a full explanation of the higher distress levels found among women than men. As we have argued above, however, vulnerability to network events does account for a substantial part of this pattern. Our empirical research relying on intensive interviewing of couples provides a means of studying the processes which underlie subtle and ongoing interactions of daily living that create more emotional distress for women than men in our society.

REFERENCES

Al-Issa, I. (1982). Gender and adult psychopathology. In I. Al-Issa (Ed.), *Gender and psychopathology*. New York: Academic Press.

Belle, D. (1982). The stress of caring: Women as providers of social support. In L. Goldberger & S. Breznitz (Eds.), *Handbook of stress: Theoretical and clinical aspects*. New York: Free Press.

Bernard, J. (1971). *Women and the public interest*. Chicago: Aldine-Atherton.

Brody, E. M. (1981). Women in the middle and family help to older people. *The Gerontologist, 21,* 471–480.

Cleary, P., & Mechanic, D. (1983). Sex differences in psychological distress among married people. *Journal of Health and Social Behavior, 24,* 111–121.

Dohrenwend, B. S. (1973). Social status and stressful life events. *Journal of Personality and Social Psychology, 9,* 203–214.

Eisenberg, N., & Lennon, R. (1983). Sex differences in empathy and related capacities. *Psychological Bulletin, 94,* 100–131.

Fischer, C. S. (1982). *To dwell among friends: Personal networks in town and city.* Chicago: University of Chicago Press.

Fox, J. W. (1980). Gove's specific sex-role theory of mental illness: A research note. *Journal of Health and Social Behavior, 21,* 260–267.

Gilligan, C. (1982). *In a different voice: Psychological theory and women's development.* Cambridge, MA: Harvard University Press.

Gove, W. R. (1972). The relationship between sex roles, marital status and mental illness. *Social Forces, 51,* 34–44.

———. (1978). Sex differences in mental illness among adult men and women: An evaluation of four questions raised regarding the evidence of higher rates of women. *Social Science and Medicine, 12,* 187–198.

Gove, W. R., & Geerken, M. R. (1977). The effect of children and employment on the mental health of married men and women. *Social Forces, 56,* 66–76.

Gove, W. R., & Tudor, J. (1973). Adult sex roles and mental illness. *American Journal of Sociology, 78,* 812–835.

Jung, J. (1984). Social support and its relation to health: A critical evaluation. *Basic and Applied Social Psychology, 5,* 143–169.

Kessler, R. C. (1979). Stress, social status and psychological distress. *Journal of Health and Social Behavior, 20,* 259–272.

———. (1982). A disaggregation of the relationship between socioeconomic status and psychological distress. *American Sociological Research, 47,* 752–764.

———. (1983). Methodological issues in the study of psychosocial stress. In H. B. Kaplan (Ed.). *Psychosocial stress: Trends in theory and research.* New York: Academic Press.

Kessler, R. C., & McLeod, J. D. (1984). Sex differences in vulnerability to undesirable life events. *American Sociological Review, 49,* 620–631.

Kessler, R. C., McLeod, J. D., & Wethington, E. (1984). The costs of caring: A perspective on the relationship between sex and psychological distress. In I. G. Sarason & B.R. Sarason (Eds.). *Social support: Theory, research and applications.* Dordrecht, Netherlands: Martinus Nijhoff.

Kessler, R. C., & McRae, J. A., Jr. (1982). The effect of wives' employment on the mental health of married men and women. *American Sociological Review, 47,* 217–227.

Kessler, R. C., & Wethington, E. (1986). Some strategies for improving recall of life events in a general population survey. Manuscript in preparation. Institute for Social Research, The University of Michigan.

Myers, J. K., Lindenthal, J. J., & Pepper, M. P. (1974). Social class, life events and psychiatric symptoms: A longitudinal study. In B. P. Dohrenwend &

B. S. Dohrenwend (Eds.), *Stressful life events: Their nature and effects*. New York: Wiley.

Pearlin, L. I. (1975). Sex roles and depression. In N. Datan & L. H. Ginsberg (Eds.), *Proceedings of fourth life-span developmental psychology conference: Normative life crises*. New York: Academic Press.

Pearlin, L. I., & Schooler, C. (1978). The structure of coping. *Journal of Health and Social Behavior, 19*, 2–21.

Radloff, L. S. (1975). Sex differences in depression: The effects of occupational and marital status. *Sex Roles, 1*, 249–265.

Radloff, L. S., & Monroe, M. K. (1978). Sex differences in helplessness—with implications for depression. In L. S. Hansen & R. S. Rapoza (Eds.), *Career development and counseling of women*. Springfield, IL: Charles Thomas.

Radloff, L. S., & Rae, D. S. (1979). Susceptibility and precipitating factors in depression: Sex differences and similarities. *Journal of Abnormal Psychology, 88*, 174–181.

———. (1981). Components of the sex difference in depression. In R. G. Simmons (Ed.), *Research in community and mental health*. Greenwich, CT:JAI Press.

Rook, K. (1984). The negative side of social interaction: Impact on psychological well-being. *Journal of Personality and Social Psychology, 46*, 1097–1108.

Stroebe, M. S., & Stroebe, W. (1983). Who suffers more? Sex differences in health risks of the widowed. *Psychological Bulletin, 93*, 279–301.

Veroff, J., Douvan, E., & Kulka, R. (1981). *The inner American: A self-portrait from 1957–1976*. New York: Basic Books.

Wallerstein, J., & Kelly, J. (1980). *Surviving the breakup*. New York: Basic Books.

Wethington, E., & Kessler, R. C. (1986). Perceived support, received support, and adjustment to stressful life events. *Journal of Health and Social Behavior, 27*, 78–89.

Williams. D. G. (1985). Gender differences in interpersonal relationships and well-being. In A. Kerckhoff (Ed.), *Research in sociology of education and socialization*. Greenwich, CT: JAI Press.

SPECIFIC
STRESSORS

7

The Role of Gender
in Reactions
to Criminal Victimization

Ronnie Janoff-Bulman
Irene Hanson Frieze

Every day in our society people experience psychological distress as a result of being victimized by interpersonal violence or other crimes. Even if not victims themselves, individuals may nevertheless feel stressed by the fear that is aroused when others around them are victimized. How do crime victims react to their misfortune and the resulting stress? How can we better understand the variations in intensity of victims' responses? In this chapter we will provide a framework for considering the reactions of victims and, within this framework, will explore the significance of gender in understanding victims' responses.

There is a good deal of direct and indirect evidence that being a victim is associated with stereotypical feminine characteristics (Howard, 1984; Schur, 1984). Victims are regarded as passive, trusting, and helpless, traits also associated with being a female in our society. At the same time that the victim role is associated with being female, the assailant role is considered masculine, especially if the victimization involves violence, aggression, or daring (Schur, 1984). The ideas we hold about victims and victimizers are embedded within our basic theories and beliefs about the roles and characteristics of males and females in our society.

A GENERAL FRAMEWORK FOR UNDERSTANDING VICTIMS' REACTIONS

The Victim's Assumptions

The tremendous toll exacted by victimization can be understood in light of people's deeply embedded basic assumptions about the world. Each of us maintains a coherent set of assumptions or schemas about ourselves and our environment that enables us to understand and organize our experiences. This conceptual system has been variously labeled our "assumptive world" (Parkes, 1971, 1975), "theory of reality" (Epstein, 1973, 1979, 1980), "world models" (Bowlby, 1969), and "structures of meaning" (Marris, 1975), and in all cases refers to personal theories we have built over years of experience that provide a framework within which we can live from day to day (also see Kuhn's, 1962, notion of "paradigm"). According to Epstein (1980), our theory of reality is organized hierarchically into major and minor postulates. The minor postulates are narrow generalizations that are derived directly from experience; these, in turn, are organized into increasingly more major postulates. Thus, "I am a worthy person" would represent a major postulate, whereas "I am a good ping-pong player" would represent a minor postulate, with "I am a good athlete" falling somewhere between the two (Epstein, 1980). Our most basic assumptions about the world or our most generalized theories about the nature of ourselves and our world are essentially our highest-order postulates (Janoff-Bulman & Timko, in press), including beliefs about the benevolence and meaningfulness of the world as well as beliefs about our own self-worth and efficacy (Janoff-Bulman & Frieze, 1983).

Our personal theory of reality provides us with expectations about ourselves and our world. We interpret and understand events in light of already existing assumptions. This orientation echoes recent work by psychologists on "schemas." A schema is a "cognitive structure that represents organized knowledge about a given concept or type of stimulus" (Fiske & Taylor, 1984, p. 140). Although the most basic kind of schema is that which represents common categories such as dog, hat, or table, psychologists have used the schema concept to explain our judgments of others (Cantor, 1980), our perceptions of ourselves (Markus, 1977), our understanding of event sequences ("scripts"; Abelson, 1981), and our perceptions of appropriate roles and norms for social groups (Fiske & Taylor, 1984). In positing these schemas, psychologists present people as actively constructing their reality. Our schemas function as preexisting theories that guide what we notice and remember, as well as how we interpret new information. Research on schemas has demonstrated quite clearly that people strive for schema-consistent information. Not only are we biased toward perceiving schema-consistent information, but we even misremember and reinterpret stimuli so as to render them consistent with our schemas (e.g., Crocker, Hannah, & Weber, 1983; Kulik, 1983). There is evidence demonstrating that we persevere in maintaining our schemas and that such perseverance occurs even in the face of clearly falsifying evidence (e.g., Anderson, Lepper, & Ross, 1980; Ross, Lepper, & Hubbard, 1975). From research on schemas, one can conclude that people seek to maintain their personal theories of the world and thereby are able to maintain stability in their conceptual system.

Challenging the Assumptive Framework

It is clear that victims experience more than the debilitating physical or material consequences of the victimizing event. Being a victim challenges people's deeply embedded basic assumptions (Janoff-Bulman & Frieze, 1983). Their personal theories, or schemas, which generally serve people well and are solidified over their lifetime, are suddenly challenged by the traumatic experience of victimization; their perceptions of themselves and the world are now marked by threat, danger, insecurity, and self-questioning. The higher-order the postulate, the more difficult and traumatic becomes the adjustment to one's personal theory (see Epstein, 1980). The experience of victimization is so powerful that victims are threatened with a complete breakdown in their conceptual system, the very same system that has previously provided them with stability in interacting with their world.

When the victimization does not seem to make sense (i.e., it does not follow theories we use to explain and understand events in our lives), the victim's world begins to seem inexplicable, random, and meaningless. Assumptions related to the benevolence of people may be badly shaken, particularly in the case of interpersonal violence and criminal victimization involving an assailant (Janoff-Bulman, 1985). In such instances, victims are dramatically confronted by the malevolence of another human being, and prior generalized assumptions about the benevolence and basic goodness of others are severely challenged. People generally operate on the basis of an assumption of invulnerability which derives from beliefs in the goodness of others and the fairness of the world, as well as one's own efficacy and sense of self-worth (Janoff-Bulman & Frieze, 1983; Janoff-Bulman & Lang-Gunn, in press; Perloff, 1983). Although we realize that victimizations are relatively common, we generally believe these misfortunes will strike others rather than ourselves. As Weinstein (1980; Weinstein & Lachendro, 1982) has demonstrated, people overestimate the likelihood that they will experience positive events and underestimate the likelihood that they will experience negative events. Victimization shatters this assumption of invulnerability (Janoff-Bulman & Frieze, 1983; Perloff, 1983). Victims can no longer say, "It can't happen to me"; the world is no longer safe and benign (Bard & Sangrey, 1979; Lifton & Olson, 1976; Notman & Nadelson, 1976; Weisman, 1979; Wolfenstein, 1957; Wortman & Dunkel-Schetter, 1979).

Although women report feeling more vulnerable to victimization than do men (e.g., Riger & Gordon, 1981), they nevertheless develop protective strategies or rules that enable them to maintain an "illusion of invulnerability" (Janoff-Bulman & Lang-Gunn, in press; Perloff, 1983). Thus, women may avoid walking in certain neighborhoods, may not walk alone at night, and may avoid hitchhiking (Scheppele & Bart, 1983). Strong fears of rape may lead many women greatly to restrict their activities, especially at night (Bowker, 1979; Riger, Gordon, & Le Bailly, 1978). Nevertheless, women feel safe as long as they abide by their protective strategies. All of this may backfire, however, if, as may well happen, these rules do not protect against victimization. Women rape victims have often become victims in spite of following all of their rules (e.g., women are raped while sleeping in the comfort and protection of their own home). Research has shown that fear reactions were greatest and general psychological functioning lowest in those rape victims attacked while in a situation they had perceived as safe (i.e., they had been following their own rules of personal safety; Scheppele & Bart, 1983). These women felt particularly vulnerable, for the rules that had assumed would work did not protect them. Rape victims who could instead attribute the rape to their violation of personal safety rules had fewer psychological difficulties following the rape. For them, it was still possible to feel at least potentially invulnerable to future rapes (Scheppele & Bart, 1983).

A primary assumption that is also challenged by the experience of victimization involves one's self-theory or assumptions about the self (Janoff-Bulman & Frieze, 1983). We generally operate on the basis of positive beliefs about ourselves and maintain relatively high levels of esteem (Epstein, 1973). Following victimization, there is a great deal of self-questioning and self-doubt. Victims see themselves as weak, frightened, out of control, lacking autonomy, and powerless (Bard & Sangrey, 1979; Horowitz, Wilner, Marmar, & Krupnick, 1980; Krupnick, 1980). Victims feel singled out for misfortune and are also apt to perceive themselves as deviant, thereby reinforcing negative images of themselves (Coates & Winston, 1983). In a study of college students, it was found that those who had experienced an extreme negative event in their past (death of a parent, death of a sibling, rape, incest, fire that destroyed a home, or accident resulting in physical disability) had significantly lower perceptions of their own self-worth than those who had not experienced such events (Janoff-Bulman, 1986). This decreased self-esteem was found even when the victimization had occurred 10 to 12 years prior to the completion of the survey instrument. Further, of the many assumptions and personal theories tapped by the instrument (e.g., benevolence of people, benevolence of the impersonal world, the extent to which randomness operates in the world), perceived self-worth emerged as the variable that best discriminated between victims and nonvictims for both male and female respondents. Apparently, the effects of victimization on assumptions about the self are powerful and long lasting.

COPING WITH VICTIMIZATION

It would be difficult to overestimate the coping task confronting the victim. Personal theories and assumptions that have served the person well and have gone unquestioned are suddenly shaken by the experience of victimization. The victim's task is to rebuild and reestablish a conceptual system that can account for and incorporate the victimization. The more severely an assumption is challenged and the more basic and primary the assumption, the more difficult the coping process.

Redefinition of the Self as a Victim

Once one is victimized, one of the first issues that arises for the "victim" is an assessment of what happened (Folkman, 1984; Lazarus & Launier, 1978). To the extent that one can redefine oneself as a nonvictim or can interpret the events within the framework of one's already existing assumptions, the negative impact of the experience should be minimized. Thus, in a survey of college students, Frieze (1985) found that most students did not define themselves as ever having been victims, in spite of having been robbed, raped, assaulted, or in automobile accidents. Redefining the event as not being serious or as a result of carelessness allows "victims" to return to their previctimization functioning. If individuals are not able to deny that a victimization has occurred, they are forced to see themselves as victims, with all the negative connotations associated with this concept.

Even if people have defined themselves as victims, they may be able to convince themselves that they have not been *severely* victimized. The initial assessment of the "victimizing event" may be that it is not so bad. Taylor, Wood, and Lichtman (1983) have identified a number of the processes by which female cancer victims have redefined their victimization. First, victims have been found to make downward social comparisons. In general, when people are feeling threatened, they are most likely to compare their own situation to that of persons who are less fortunate (Gruder, 1977). Burgess and Holmstrom (1979) found that rape victims often make downward comparisons. By comparing herself with another victim who suffered even more than she did, the rape victim is able to build her own self-esteem. In fact, Taylor (1983) reports that people experiencing serious illness may assume without objective evidence that they are coping better than others.

Bart and Scheppele (1980) provide a concrete example of some of these processes in their study of rape victims and rape "avoiders." Although all of the women in their sample were victims of acts legally classified as rape, those who had been forced to perform sexual acts other than sexual intercourse defined themselves as having "escaped" rape. Conversely, most of those who had been penetrated vaginally, orally, or anally did define the crime as rape. Those who defined themselves as rape victims rather than rape avoiders had the most negative reactions to the crime and were most likely to report to the police.

Additionally, stress resulting from the victimization can be minimized by reconstructing the event as leading to personal growth or some other benefit (Taylor, 1983). Taylor et al. (1983) cite an example of this process in a woman who had been severely beaten, shot in the head, and left to die, but did survive and was able to describe in a newspaper interview how the assault had led to a "joyful reconciliation with her mother." Gaining a sense of "mystical consciousness" has also been reported by some victims (Noyes & Slymen, 1978).

Situational or other external factors may affect the ability of the victim to redefine the event as being less traumatic than it appeared to be. Some of Bart and Scheppele's (1980) victims appeared to be unable readily to redefine the event. Certain groups of people appear to be more susceptible than others to stress associated with victimization. Older and poorer and black victims react more strongly than other rape victims a year after the event (Atkeson, Calhoun, Resick, & Ellis, 1982; Sales, Baum, & Shore, 1984). Women burglary victims who had been separated from their husbands by death or divorce were especially likely to experience acute distress as a result of burglary of their homes (Maguire, 1980). In general, people with a history of prior stressors have been found to be more vulnerable to maladaptive stress reactions (Atkeson et al., 1982; Burgess & Holmstrom, 1976, 1979; Symonds, 1980). Personality also enters into this process. Those with "hardy" personalities react better to stress of any type (Ganellen & Blaney, 1984; Kobasa, 1979).

Self-Blame in Victims

When a person is victimized and labels himself or herself as a victim, he or she begins to ask a variety of attributional questions: "Why me?" "What could I have done differently?" "What can I do about this now?" In answering such questions, victims may make any of a number of types of attributions. Attributions can be about the original cause of the victimization or about future coping with the stress of the victimization (Brickman, Rabinowitz, Karuza, Coates, Cohn, & Kidder, 1982). Victims can see themselves or others as blameworthy, and they can make an attribution to stable or unstable (i.e., changeable or unchangeable) factors.

Reviews of research dealing with the reactions of all types of victims have indicated a general tendency for victims to take some responsibility for their victimization (e.g., Coates, Wortman, & Abbey, 1979; Frieze, 1979; Wortman, 1976). Such attributions are often associated with self-blame (Shaver & Drown, 1986). It is not uncommon, for example, for victims of unprovoked sexual assaults or of battering to engage in some self-blame following the crime (Frieze, 1979; Janoff-Bulman, 1979; Medea & Thompson, 1974). Thus, a battered woman may say to herself, "If only I had gotten dinner ready on time." A rape victim may focus on the clothing she was wearing or on not being viligant enough in observing others around her.

Attribution theory makes certain predictions about emotional and behavioral consequences depending on the type of attribution made. Particular attributions may serve to reinforce perceptions of vulnerability or reestablish perceptions of invulnerability. Thus, attributing the victimization to enduring and pervasive factors within oneself should lead to hopelessness about the future (Abramson, Seligman, & Teasdale, 1978; Frieze, 1979) and to a tendency to see oneself as a chronic victim. On the basis of attribution theory and common sense, blaming oneself would appear to be very maladaptive. However, such attributions can be quite functional for the victim; this is especially true if the self-blame is behavioral rather than characterological in nature (Janoff-Bulman, 1979; also see Tennen, Affleck, & Gershmann, 1986; Timko & Janoff-Bulman, 1985; cf. Meyer & Taylor, 1986). Characterological attributions are made to aspects of one's personality, a relatively nonmodifiable cause. It is this type of self-blame that is associated with depression (Janoff-Bulman, 1979). Such attributions give one little confidence that future victimization can be avoided and can lead to feelings of helplessness and vulnerability. Rape victims who make characterological attributions may see the rape as deserved. Thus, not only do these women see themselves as the type of woman who gets raped, but also as the type of person who should be raped.

Compared with women who blame themselves characterologically, rape victims who attribute their rapes to behavioral factors are more confident about avoiding future rapes (Janoff-Bulman, 1979). By seeing particular actions or behaviors they engaged in as responsible for the event, they are able psychologically to take control over it. To avoid future victimization it is necessary only to act in a different way. Consistent with this reasoning, Janoff-Bulman (1982) found that behavioral self-blame was associated with high self-esteem and the perception of the avoidability of subsequent victimization. Similarly, Friedman, Bischoff, Davis, and Person (1982) found that crime victims who took responsibility for not preventing the crime reported having fewer psychological problems both two weeks and four months after the crime as compared to those who did not see themselves as responsible.

SOCIETAL REACTIONS TO VICTIMS

Our society does not take a very positive view of victims, and social support for them is often lacking (Frieze, Hymer, & Greenberg, 1984; Taylor et al., 1983). People look for evidence in the behavior or character of victims that could account for their victimization, often leading to blaming them for their plight. Victims become stigmatized individuals whom others would rather avoid (Coates & Winston, 1983; Coates, Wortman, & Abbey, 1979); they may be ignored (Reiff, 1979) because they are seen as losers (Bard & Sangrey, 1979) or because of fear of guilt by association (Frederick, 1980; Weis & Weis, 1975). Even the closest relationships may be threatened by negative reactions of others to the victim (Frieze, 1983; Russell, 1974; Silverman, 1978). Miller, Williams, and Bernstein (1982) found, for example, that a husband or boyfriend of the rape victim often had very negative reactions, frequently expressing feelings of anger and resentment toward her. For the female rape victim, feelings of shame, guilt, and fear of negative consequences are often reinforced by negative feedback in the form of a sizeable number of disrupted relationships or divorces initiated by husbands who were unable "to adjust"(Mazelon, 1980; Weis & Weis, 1975).

There are strong motivational reasons that account in part for the generally negative attitudes people have toward victims of crime or other traumatic events. People appear to have a need to believe in a just world where people get what they deserve. Such beliefs provide psychic protection; after all, if the world is a place in which bad things happen only to bad people, good people will not be victimized (Lerner, 1980). People want to defend themselves against the belief that they too could be victims of misfortune (Burger, 1981; Shaver, 1970). In addition to motivational explanations, there are cognitive biases that help to account for the blame attached to the victim. Janoff-Bulman, Timko, and Carli (1985) found that the hindsight effect—a cognitive bias that leads people to overestimate the prior probability of an outcome once that outcome is known (Fischhoff, 1975)—leads people to overestimate the likelihood of a victimization (e.g., rape) having occurred, and thereby results in greater blame being attributed to the victim (who, it is believed, should have foreseen the outcome).

Gender Schemas and Reactions to Victims

A review of the literature on victimization provides clear evidence of a gender bias. Women are overrepresented in research on victimization, a finding that contrasts sharply with the underrepresentation of research on women in many other areas of psychological inquiry. Research on the psychological responses of male victims is virtually absent. This focus on women is far out of proportion to the percentages of women actually victimized by crime. For example, men are nearly twice as likely as women to be the victims of violent crimes. Men are also more often victims of theft. As adults, the only crimes women experience more than men are rape and sexual harassment, and these account for a relatively low proportion of all crimes (Zawitz, 1983). Thus, it is only sexual victimization that is experienced more by females.

Interestingly, rape victims have received more research attention than any other victims of crime. Certainly, this focus on rape reflects concerns of the women's movement in its attempt to demonstrate and alleviate the relative powerlessness of women in our society. Nevertheless, the choice of victimizations studied and the overemphasis on women as victims seems to represent far more than a positive political motive. Rather, in our society women are viewed as "natural victims," and rape is the prototypical form of victimization (Schur, 1984). In fact, as will be discussed below, the research on rape and child sexual abuse has largely ignored the male victim; maleness is not consistent with these victimizations, and we have largely underestimated the representation of males in these victimizations.

One way of understanding differences in societal reactions to male and female victims is through the concept of gender schema. Within our society, the distinction between male and female is central to our understanding and interpretation of social behavior. Bem (1981) has popularized the notion of gender schema to describe our cognitive structures for the particular attributes and behaviors that are associated with males versus females. Our gender schemas include conceptions of physical differences, reproductive functions, division of labor, and personality attributes that are culturally defined as male or female. The content of our gender schema includes our cultural stereotypes for males versus females. Thus, men are typically viewed as aggressive, competitive, and independent, whereas women are typically regarded as passive, emotional, dependent, and understanding (e.g., Deaux & Lewis, 1984; Eagly & Steffen, 1984). In light of these beliefs, one might expect differences in societal reactions to male and female victims.

Given that victimization is associated with femaleness in our society (Howard, 1984; Schur, 1984), people may have an easier time accepting women as victims since they are not uncomfortable with the notion that women are weak and helpless. They find it harder to accept male victims, given the inconsistency between our gender schemas for masculinity and the experience of victimization. Some have argued that we lack any "cultural sensitivity" to male victims (Farber, Showers, Johnson, Joseph, & Oshins, 1984). If we have a societal belief that the victim should have defended himself or herself better against the assailant (i.e., didn't do enough to prevent the victimization), this response is likely to be engendered more in the case of the male victim than the female victim and result in greater blame of the male.

Evidence for these ideas is seen in a number of empirical studies. Hammen and Peters (1977) found that males were rejected significantly more by college students than were females when they were labeled as depressed. Nasjleti (1980), in her study of male incest victims, found that the boys who disclosed their incest experiences reported a great deal of blame and disbelief on the part of family members. Rogers and Terry (1984), on the basis of their work with sexual assault victims, claim that many of the reactions of parents and family were the same for male and female victims—anger, guilt, even support and concern. However, when the victims were male and the assailant was male, as is typically the case, parents and friends were more likely to attempt to deny or minimize the event, to blame the victim, and to have unrealistic fears about the event's impact in terms of their child's sexual identification. In particular, parents and family often have strong feelings of disgust and revulsion about the homosexual nature of male-male sexual victimization and find it very difficult to accept the fact that their son was victimized by another male. Further, Rogers and Terry (1984) state that although sexually victimized girls are frequently blamed for their victimization, blaming is an even greater problem for boys, who are expected to "fight back."

The more negative societal reactions to male victims should not lead to an underestimation of the problems of female victims who, in the end, may depend on social support more than males, yet find it difficult to obtain. There is considerable evidence that women, more than men, seek help from others when experiencing difficulties (e.g., Butler, Giordano, & Neren, 1985; Shinn, Rosario, Morch, & Chestnut, 1984). Padesky and Hammen (1981) found that male college students are significantly less likely than women to report they would seek help when depressed. In looking more closely at the rape literature, it is clear that social support is an important factor in facilitating the victim's postrape adjustment (Atkeson, et al., 1982; Burgess & Holmstrom, 1978; Norris & Feldman-Summers, 1981; Ruch & Leon, 1983).

THE ROLE OF GENDER SCHEMA IN VICTIMS' REACTIONS

Do men and women differ in their responses to criminal victimization? Given the role of people's basic theories and assumptions in understanding victims' reactions to their misfortune, we might predict that gender would affect victims' responses to these extreme, negative events.

Recent work in social psychology has demonstrated the importance of self-schemas in people's interpretations and evaluations of their behavior. As Markus and her colleagues have written (Markus, Crane, Bernstein, & Siladi, 1982), "With social experience we gain a diversity of self-relevant information that becomes organized into cognitive structures. It is by means of these structures that we categorize, explain, and evaluate our behavior in various focal domains. . . . We will refer to these cognitive structures as *self-schemas* and to the union of these particular schemas in the various domains as the *self-concept*" (p. 38).

People are assumed to vary a great deal in terms of their self-schemas; the content is believed to differ with regard to personal traits, such as independence, honesty, intelligence, or social sensitivity. Nevertheless, "there are some aspects of behavior that are so prominent and central that virtually everyone develops at least rudimentary schemas for them. These universal schemas, which everyone has to one degree or another, develop with respect to those aspects of the self that are particularly salient and available for social evaluation and comment. One's sex, for example, becomes a point of focus and a salient distinguishing trait early in life, and it remains a significant parameter of the person's social interactions" (Markus et al., 1982, p. 39).

For most people, gender schemas make up an important part of the self-concept. Gender is typically a salient dimension we use to evaluate our own and others' behavior, and it therefore functions as a part of the self-schema. Although people differ in terms of the primacy of this gender self-schema (Bem, 1981; Markus et al., 1982), most people are likely to maintain gender as an important dimension of their self-concept. As Bem (1981) has written, the child "learns to evaluate his or her adequacy as a person in terms of the gender schema, to match his or her preferences, attitudes, behaviors, and personal attributes against the prototypes stored within it. The gender schema becomes a prescriptive standard or guide, and self-esteem becomes hostage" (p. 355).

In evaluating ourselves, then, the appropriateness of our behaviors is considered in light of our personal theory, or schema, regarding maleness and femaleness. Our gender schemas are simultaneously part of the larger cultural belief system as well as of our own self-concept; they are cultural and personal theories of gender appropriateness. Given that gender schemas contribute to our larger self-concept, our positive versus negative feelings about ourselves will in part be determined by the extent to which particular behaviors or outcomes are consistent with or are contrary to our gender expectations. In other words, our gender schemas represent deeply embedded assumptions that we hold about maleness and femaleness in our society, and that we use to evaluate ourselves as well as others.

The stress of victimization may be attributable in part to the challenging or shattering of the basic gender-related assumptions that we hold.

Given that gender is an important component of self-concept, to the extent that self-relevant assumptions related to gender are challenged, one might expect decreased self-esteem. The victim is an individual who has been forced into a helpless, passive, powerless role. Because men in our society are expected to be strong, active, and powerful, the experience of victimization is likely to challenge seriously a male victim's assumptions about himself. The experience of victimization is less apt to challenge gender-relevant schemas or assumptions held by women regarding "femaleness," for societal expectations for women are more consistent with the helplessness and passivity experienced by victims. Certainly, many women do perceive themselves as powerful and strong, although these self-perceptions probably do not derive from considerations of themselves as women per se. The fact that these attributes are defined as part of the male role, however, suggests that in general, men are more likely than women to regard the victim role as inconsistent with self-perceptions.

Gender Differences in Reactions to Victimization

There is very little research that looks at the reactions of male victims. Much of our detailed knowledge of victims' reactions derives from research conducted with rape victims (see, e.g., Burgess & Holmstrom, 1974a, 1974b, 1979; Ellis, Atkeson, & Calhoun, 1981; Kilpatrick, Resick, & Veronen, 1981; Nadelson, Notman, Zackson, & Gornick, 1982; Sutherland & Scherl, 1970), and this research has focused almost exclusively on female victims. Recently, a few studies focusing on male victims have appeared; these have dealt primarily with male victims of rape and child sexual assault (e.g., Ellerstein & Canavan, 1980; Farber et al., 1984; Groth & Burgess, 1980; Kaufman, Divasto, Jackson, Voorhees, & Christy, 1980; Nasjleti, 1980). This work suggests that males, like females, experience shock, confusion, fear, shame, and depression following victimization. However, male and female victims appear to differ in terms of three behaviors that reflect different psychological responses to the trauma of victimization. First, it appears that men are far less likely to report or disclose their victimizations. Second, women are more likely to engage in social withdrawal, and third, men are far more likely than women to engage in aggressive behaviors. What is known about these differences, and what do they tell us about the role of gender in understanding reactions to victimization?

Reporting behaviors. Many crimes against people are not reported (e.g., Ruback, Greenberg, & Westcott, 1984), and the two most frequently cited reasons for this nonreporting are the expectations that police can do nothing about the matter and the belief that the crime is really a personal, not a criminal matter (e.g., Ennis, 1967). In the case of sexual assaults, nonreporting seems particularly common (Finkelhor, 1979).

Female rape victims fear courtroom procedures and publicity, as well as retaliation by the rapist; some say that they are too ashamed or embarrassed to report the rape, and others simply want to forget it and not prolong the agony (Katz & Mazur, 1979). The figures on nonreporting by women suggest that as few as one in ten rapes are reported to the police (Katz & Mazur, 1979), although other data suggest much higher rates of reporting (Zawitz, 1983). For those who do report the crime, primary considerations that appear to account for the reporting are the need for help and comfort and the desire to help other women (Peters, Meyer, & Carroll, 1976). Certainly, there exists a tremendous problem of underreporting by female rape victims; the degree of the problem is difficult to ascertain in light of our actual lack of knowledge regarding the true incidence of rape.

There is increasing evidence suggesting that the problem of underreporting may be even greater for male than for female victims (Zawitz, 1983). In virtually all cases of male sexual assault, the perpetrator is also male. Apart from rape in prison environments, we generally do not think of rape of males when considering sexual assaults. In the general population, male victims constitute a very small percentage—generally 4 or 5 percent—of victims reporting rape (e.g., Hayman, Lanza, Fuentes, & Algor, 1972; Hursch & Selkin, 1974; Massey, Garcia, & Emich, 1971). Nevertheless, male rape may be more common than we suppose. Several recent studies discuss nonreporting by male victims of sexual assault. Kaufman and his colleagues (Kaufman et al., 1980) argue that "if only 10%–20% of female rape victims report their assault," as maintained by the 1970 Uniform Crime Reports of the FBI, "a far smaller proportion of male victims report theirs. If male victims do seek medical attention, they are more likely than female victims to seek help for secondary physical and emotional trauma without reporting the sex assault" (p. 223). In one study involving a small sample of respondents, approximately 30 percent (6 of 20) of college-age men (19 to 24 years old) admitted anonymously in a confidential questionnaire that they had been victims of "at least one act of criminally forced sodomy" (20 percent) or "violent attempted sodomy" (10 percent); none of these had ever been reported to authorities (Schultz & DeSavage, 1975).

For boys, sexual abuse also appears to pose particular problems of reporting and disclosure. Child sexual abuse is frequently not disclosed by either sex, for children themselves rarely report the abuse to authorities (Katz & Mazur, 1979). The question of disclosure of the victimization to others is therefore of particular interest. Studies of child sexual assault victims have found that males account for approximately 15 percent of reported sexual abuse cases (DeFrancis, 1969; Showers, Farber, Joseph, Oshins, & Johnson, 1983); the National Incidence Study conducted by the National Center on Child Abuse and Neglect (1981) places the number at 17 percent. Yet Landis (1956), in an early survey of college students, found that male children were almost as vulnerable to an "adult sexual deviate" as female children (30 vs. 35 percent), although not a single incidence of male sexual assault in this sample had been reported to authorities. More importantly, of those assaulted, 43 percent of the sexually assaulted girls reported the assault to their parents, whereas only 17 percent of the boys did so. Farber et al. (1984) claim that studies of offender behavior (including the gender of their victims) indicate that male victims report less than do female victims; that is, offenders' preferences for male victims is considerably higher than would be expected on the basis of males' reporting behavior. Groth (1979), for example, found that of the 500 convicted male offenders he studied, 51 percent chose girls as victims, 28 percent chose boys as victims, and 21 percent chose both boys and girls. Nasjleti (1980) also found tremendous resistance to disclosure in her sample of male incest victims and argues that such resistance is greater in male victims than female victims. Swift (1977) maintains that the sexual victimization of boys approaches or is equal to that of girls. Rogers and Terry (1984) found that 25 percent of their sample of sexual abuse victims (based on cases seen at Children's Hospital Medical Center in Washington, D.C.) were boys. They conclude that the "true incidence is probably substantially higher in that boys are substantially less likely to report their victimization" (p. 93).

Social withdrawal. A common response of female victims is to withdraw from others. Female victims frequently engage in a series of defensive behaviors following rape; many move to a new residence or change phone numbers (Binder, 1981; Burgess & Holmstrom, 1974a,b). Although such actions may make the victim less accessible to the assailant, they may also be the first step in a larger process of social withdrawal. It is not uncommon for female rape victims to avoid social contacts and simply not to leave home (Scheppele & Bart, 1983; Waller, 1976). Elderly crime victims (who are usually women) are also especially likely to be afraid to leave their homes afterwards (Friedman et al., 1982).

Other forms of withdrawal involve relationships with men, particularly close relationships. There is considerable evidence that following rape by a man, women report a great deal of distrust of men in general and frequently engage in avoidance or hesitation in their interactions with them (e.g., Nadelson & Notman, 1984). It is not uncommon for close relationships between men and women, particularly marriages, to be seriously disturbed following a woman's rape (Miller, Williams, & Bernstein, 1982). Withdrawal from sexual contact is often cited as a primary reason for this marital disruption. Many female victims of sexual assault report problems in sexual functioning which may persist for years. Retrospective studies of female rape victims, conducted up to several years post-rape, have found a high incidence of sexual dysfunction and dissatisfaction with sex (Becker, Skinner, Abel, & Treacy, 1982; Nadelson et al., 1982; Norris & Feldman-Summers, 1981; Silver, Boon, & Stones, 1983). The sexual/aggressive nature of the victimization itself, coupled with the woman's increased distrust of men, in part explain these effects.

The impact of sexual assault on the sexual functioning of male victims is not addressed in the scant literature on male victims. One might speculate that increased sexuality (rather than decreased sexual impulses, as is found with women) would be likely to occur, in light of the male's efforts to reassert his male identity following victimization, as discussed below. Given differences between men and women in the meaning and role of sex (Frieze, Parsons, Johnson, Ruble, & Zellman, 1978), sexual dysfunction is more apt to be tied to disturbances in relationships and to reflect social withdrawal for women than for men.

Aggressive behaviors. Increased aggression following victimization appears to be primarily a male phenomenon. In reviews of female rape victims' responses to their victimization, aggression is not even mentioned as an aftereffect (e.g., Katz & Mazur, 1979). Although some turn to self-defense techniques, they do so in a deliberate attempt to increase self-confidence and decrease their self-perceptions of weakness and vulnerability (Kidder, Boell, & Moyer, 1983; Kidder & Cohn, 1979). All of these women are apparently responding to the fears and self-perceptions of helplessness brought on by the victimization.

For men, newfound self-perceptions of oneself as a victim appear to result in increased aggressiveness. In a study of psychiatric patients whose life experiences were reconstructed through hospital records, Carmen, Rieker, and Mills (1984) concluded, "Perhaps the most important characteristic that distinguished the behavior of abused males and females was that the males had become more aggressive while the females had become more passive" (p. 382). Abused individuals in this sample included victims of child abuse, incest, marital violence, and assault or rape outside of the family. At the time of hospitalization, abused females did not differ from nonabused female patients in terms of suicidal or depressive symptoms. Abused males, however, differed from nonabused male patients in that they were less likely to be depressed and suicidal and more likely to be aggressive and to engage in disordered conduct. In terms of their prehospitalization behaviors, abused males in this psychiatric sample were much more likely than abused females and nonabused males to have abused others; 60 percent of abused males had been violent toward others, whereas only 17 percent of abused females had been violent (Carmen et al., 1984).

Based on their extensive work with child victims of sexual assault and abuse, Rogers and Terry (1984) describe the common emotional reactions of these victims, irrespective of the child's gender: guilt, shame, depression, fear, anger, and anxiety. Common behavioral reactions of both male and female victims of child sexual assault include a preoccupation with sexuality (reflected in increased masturbation, increased sex play, or, in older children, promiscuous behavior), disturbed eating or sleeping patterns, changes in interpersonal behaviors (ranging from withdrawal from peers and family to—in younger children—increased dependency). The most common behavioral reaction of boys is aggressive behavior, and this is a reaction unique to male victims (Rogers & Terry, 1984). Forms of aggression include picking fights and bullying others, destruction of property, confrontational behaviors to parents and teachers, and reenactments of their own victimization in which the victim is now the offender using force in assaulting others. Rogers and Terry (1984) claim that many adolescent and adult male sexual offenders were molested as children. Several other researchers have similarly argued that there is a link between being a young male victim of sexual assault and becoming an abuser (e.g., Groth, 1979). Swift (1977), for example, maintains that it is important to establish empirically the incidence of sexual abuse of young males, because there is a strong possibility "that it is this group that constitutes a high risk for community sexual offenses later in life" (p. 324).

These findings are consistent with research on male-female patterns of coping with depression. Kleinke, Staneski, and Mason (1982), for example, found that male and female college students reported using different strategies for coping with depression, with women more likely to report crying, eating, smoking cigarettes, becoming irritable, and confronting their feelings, and men more likely to report becoming aggressive and engaging in sexual behavior when depressed. Further, it is interesting to note that Miller and Williams (1979) found that the female rape victims in their sample typically reacted to their victimization with fear, guilt, or anger and hostility toward men, whereas their male partners were more likely to feel rage. Indeed, the male partners frequently engaged in recurrent fantasies of killing and maiming the rapist, clearly reflections of aggressive impulses.

Explaining Behavioral Differences

Although the reactions of male and female victims are marked by many of the same emotional responses (e.g., fear, anxiety, shame, depression, confusion), there do appear to be, as noted, at least three behaviors that differ for male and female victims. Whereas nonreporting is common in the case of female victims, there is evidence that it may be even more frequent in the case of male victims. Social withdrawal appears to be a far greater problem for women than for men. Further, increased aggression following victimization appears to be a relatively common response of male victims, whereas it is generally absent in the case of female victims.

These differences can be understood within the framework of the victims' gender assumptions. The experience of victimization does not violate or challenge women's gender-relevant assumptions about themselves, but rather their assumptions regarding other people. Powerlessness, weakness, and not fighting back are consistent with female gender schemas. Certainly, prior assumptions regarding invulnerability, meaningfulness of the world, and other aspects of self-worth may be utterly shattered by victimization and thereby lead to tremendous stress, anxiety, and depression. Nevertheless, female victims are not apt to question the legitimacy and stability of their identity as women.

Male victims, however, are likely to question their male identity. Men are not expected to be helpless, powerless, and vulnerable in our culture. "From early childhood boys learn that masculinity means not depending on anyone, not being weak, not being passive, not being a loser in confrontation, in short, not being a victim" (Nasjleti, 1980, p. 271). Men are ashamed about not being the dominant person in the situation, about not being strong or powerful enough to resist assault successfully. It is generally believed that men are powerful enough to defend themselves; yet they are susceptible to the very same techniques used to gain control over female victims—a combination of entrapment, intimidation, and brute strength (Groth & Burgess, 1980). In forcing a victim to experience utter helplessness, victimization challenges a very basic component of male identity.

It is not just the assumption of power/strength that is challenged in men, however. Given that sexual assault of male victims almost always involves male perpetrators as well, the homosexual nature of the assault produces special problems for male victims (Kaufman, 1984). The experience of homosexuality is confusing for heterosexual boys and men, and raises concerns about sexual identity. Many male victims question whether they are effeminate or in fact homosexual, and whether their feminine attributes contributed to the assault. Their self-perceived failure to resist successfully reinforces these questions about sexual identity. Thus, victimization challenges core assumptions of the male victim's self-concept, for his very identity as a male is questioned.

Given the male victim's concerns about helplessness and his confusion about sexual identity, nonreporting and aggressive behavior become comprehensible aftereffects of victimization. Male victims are ashamed, and they believe others will question their masculinity if they report or disclose the victimization (Groth & Burgess, 1980). They have been forced to question their own masculinity; they certainly don't want others to question it as well. Aggression becomes a means of reasserting masculinity for the victim himself and in the eyes of others (Rogers & Terry, 1984). In trying to be "super-masculine," the victim attempts to prove his power and dominance—and by implication, his "nonhomosexuality"—to himself and others.

As noted, several researchers claim that the trauma of sexual assault may be more psychologically devastating for males than for females (Cotton & Groth, 1980; Ellerstein & Canavan, 1980). Whether or not this is a valid conclusion, it is certainly the case that at the level of gender-relevant aspects of the self-concept, victimization threatens males more than females. It is probable, however, that other basic assumptions—not necessarily related to the self-concept—are more severely challenged in women than in men and create particular difficulties for female victims.

Social and sexual withdrawal may be especially common for women because the idea of violation by another person is particularly distressing. As a result of early childhood experiences in the family, in which mothers tend to be the primary caretakers, and of subsequent socialization, women come to value highly interpersonal relationships. As Chodorow (1978) argues, femaleness itself is defined "relationally," whereas maleness is defined in terms of separation. In her discussion of male versus female moral reasoning and decision making, Gilligan (1982) maintains that women make moral decisions based on judgments of contextual caring, whereas men make moral decisions based on judgments of abstract rights. Again, women are perceived as more interpersonally oriented. Given this orientation, it is likely that women are more positively disposed toward people and that they regard people more positively. In fact, in a survey of people's basic assumptions about the world, Janoff-Bulman (1986) found that women assume people are more benevolent than do men. It seems very likely, therefore, that the experience of victimization that involves an assailant (rather than, for example, a natural disaster or disease) will have a more devastating effect on women's assumptions about the benevolence of people than men's assumptions. The victimization involves coming face to face with human evil and ill intent and becomes a dramatic demonstration of malevolence. Given women's positive expectations of others as well as the significance of other people in women's lives, violation of the assumption of people's benevolence is likely to be quite traumatic. The shattering of such a basic belief for women is apt to produce considerable stress and anxiety, and their positive perceptions of others are likely to be seriously undermined.

We have seen several ways in which victimization affects women and men differently; further analyses of victimization in the context of gender beliefs will no doubt uncover other differences between male and female victims in our society. Women's tendency to withdraw socially and sexually following victimization may reflect a dramatic loss of trust. It follows that social support may play a more central role in the coping process of female victims than in the coping process of male victims. Women may seek not only help from others, but also reassurances that they can still trust other people. For men, victimization severely threatens the masculine self-concept. The inconsistency between our schema for maleness and our victim schema no doubt accounts for the vast underreporting of sexual victimization by male victims. On the basis of gender schema, we would expect male victims to seek to restore a sense of potent masculinity. The increased aggression found among victimized men represents one means of accomplishing this end. Valuable topics for future research include how to restore an appropriate sense of trust in female victims and how to encourage male victims to seek restoration of their sense of masculinity in more socially useful ways.

REFERENCES

Abelson, R. P. (1981). The psychological status of the script concept. *American Psychologist, 36,* 715–729.

Abramson, L. Y., Seligman, M. E. P., & Teasdale, J. (1978). Learned helplessness in humans: Critique and reformulation. *Journal of Abnormal Psychology, 87,* 49–74.

Anderson, C. A., Lepper, M. R., & Ross, L. (1980). Perseverance of social theories: The role of explanation in the persistence of discredited information. *Journal of Personality and Social Psychology, 39,* 1037–1049.

Atkeson, B. M., Calhoun, K. S., Resick, P. A., & Ellis, E. M. (1982). Victims of rape: Repeated assessment of depressive symptoms. *Journal of Consulting and Clinical Psychology, 50,* 96–102.

Bard, M., & Sangrey, D. (1979). *The crime victim's book.* New York: Basic Books.

Bart, P. B., & Scheppele, K. L. (1980). *There ought to be a law: Women's definitions and legal definitions of sexual assault.* Paper presented at the Annual Meeting of the American Sociological Association, New York.

Becker, J. V., Skinner, L. J., Abel, G. G., & Treacy, F. (1982). Incidence and types of sexual dysfunctions in rape and incest victims. *Journal of Sex and Marital Therapy, 8,* 65–74.

Bem, S. L. (1981). Gender schema theory: A cognitive account of sex-typing. *Psychological Review, 88,* 354–364.

Binder, R. L. (1981). Difficulties in follow-up of rape victims. *American Journal of Psychotherapy, 35,* 534–541.

Bowker, L. H. (1979). The criminal victimization of women. *Victimology, 4,* 371–384.

Bowlby, J. (1969). *Attachment and loss* (Vol. 1, *Attachment*). London: Hogarth.

Brickman, P., Rabinowitz, V. C., Karuza, J., Coates, D., Cohn, E., & Kidder,

L. (1982). Models of helping and coping. *American Psychologist, 37,* 368–384.

Burger, J. M. (1981). Motivation biases in the attribution of responsibility for an accident: A meta-analysis of the defensive attribution hypothesis. *Psychological Bulletin, 90,* 496–512.

Burgess, A. W., & Holmstrom, L. L. (1974a). Rape trauma syndrome. *American Journal of Psychiatry, 131,* 981–985.

———. (1974b). *Rape: Victims of crisis.* Bowie, MD: R. J. Brady.

———. (1976). Coping behavior of the rape victim. *American Journal of Psychiatry, 13,* 413–417.

———. (1978). Recovery from rape and prior life stress. *Research in Nursing and Health, 1,* 165–174.

———. (1979). Adaptive strategies and recovery from rape. *American Journal of Psychiatry, 136,* 1278–1282.

Butler, T. M., Giordano, S., & Neren, S. (1985). Gender and sex-role attitudes as predictors of utilization of natural support systems during personal stress events. *Sex Roles, 9/10,* 515–524.

Cantor, N. (1980). Perceptions of situations: Situation prototypes and person-situation prototypes. In D. Magnusson (Ed.), *The situation: An interactional perspective.* Hillsdale, NJ: Erlbaum.

Carmen, E. H., Rieker, P. P., & Mills, T. M. (1984). Victims of violence and psychiatric illness. *American Journal of Psychiatry, 141,* 378–383.

Chodorow, N. (1978). *The reproduction of mothering.* Berkeley: University of California Press.

Coates, D., & Winston, T. (1983). Counteracting the deviance of depression: Peer support groups for victims. *Journal of Social Issues, 39,* 169–194.

Coates, D., Wortman, C. B., & Abbey, A. (1979). Reactions to victims. In I. H. Frieze, D. Bar-Tal, & J. S. Caroll (Eds.), *New approaches to social problems: Applications of attribution theory.* San Francisco: Jossey-Bass.

Cotton, D. J., & Groth, A. N. (1984). Sexual assault in correctional institutions: Prevention and intervention. In I. R. Stuart & J. G. Greer (Eds.), *Victims of sexual aggression: Treatment of children, women, and men.* New York: Van Nostrand Reinhold.

Crocker, J., Hannah, D. B., & Weber, R. (1983). Person memory and causal attributions. *Journal of Personality and Social Psychology, 44,* 55–66.

Deaux, K., & Lewis, L. L. (1984). Structure of gender stereotypes: Interrelationships among components and gender label. *Journal of Personality and Social Psychology, 46,* 991–1004.

DeFrancis, V. (1969). *Protecting the child victim of sex crimes committed by adults.* Denver, CO: American Humane Association.

Eagly, A. H., & Steffen, V. J. (1984). Gender stereotypes stem from the distribution of women and men into social roles. *Journal of Personality and Social Psychology, 46,* 735–754.

Ellerstein, N., & Canavan, J. (1980). Sexual abuse of boys. *American Journal of Diseases of Children, 134,* 255–257.

Ellis, E., Atkeson, B., & Calhoun, K. (1981). An assessment of long-term reaction to rape. *Journal of Abnormal Psychology, 90*, 263–266.

Ennis, P. H. (1967). Criminal victimization in the United States: A report of a national survey. *National Opinion*. Washington, DC: U.S. Government Printing Office.

Epstein, S. (1973). The self-concept revisited, or a theory of a theory. *American Psychologist, 28*, 404–416.

――――. (1979). The ecological study of emotions in humans. In P. Pliner, K. R. Blanstein, & I. M. Spigel (Eds.), *Advances in the study of communication and affect: Vol. 5: Perception of emotions in self and others*. New York: Plenum.

――――. (1980). The self-concept: A review and the proposal of an integrated theory of personality. In E. Staub (Ed.), *Personality: Basic issues and current research*. Englewood Cliffs, NJ: Prentice-Hall.

Farber, E. D., Showers, J., Johnson, C. F., Joseph, J. A., Oshins, L. (1984). The sexual abuse of children: A comparison of male and female victims. *Journal of Clinical Child Psychology, 13*, 294–297.

Finkelhor, D. (1979). *Sexually victimized children*. New York: Free Press.

Fischhoff, B. (1975). Hindsight ≠ foresight: The effect of outcome knowledge on judgment under uncertainty. *Journal of Experimental Psychology: Human Perception and Performance, 1*, 288–299.

Fiske, S. T., & Taylor, S. E. (1984). *Social cognition*. Reading, MA: Addison-Wesley.

Folkman, S. (1984). Personal control and stress and coping processes: A theoretical analysis. *Journal of Personality and Social Psychology, 46*, 839–852.

Frederick, C. (1980). Effects of natural vs. human-induced violence. *Evaluation and Change*, Special issue on services for survivors, 71–75.

Friedman, K., Bischoff, H., Davis, R., & Person, A. (1982). Samaritan blues. *Psychology Today*, July, 26–28.

Frieze, I. H. (1979). Perceptions of battered wives. In I. H. Frieze, D. Bar-Tal, & J. S. Carroll (Eds.), *New approaches to social problems: Applications of attribution theory*. San Francisco: Jossey-Bass.

――――. (1983). Investigating the causes and consequences of marital rape. *Signs, 8*, 532–553.

――――. (1985). *Female and male reactions to potentially victimizing events*. Invited address, 10th National Conference of the Association for Women in Psychology, New York.

Frieze, I. H., Hymer, S., & Greenberg, M. S. (1984). Describing the crime victim. In A. S. Kahn (Ed.), *Victims of crime and violence: Final report of the APA task force on victims of crime and violence*. Washington, DC: APA.

Frieze, I. H., Parsons, J. E., Johnson, P. B., Ruble, D. N., & Zellman, G. (1978). *Women and sex roles: A social-psychological perspective*. New York: Norton.

Ganellen, R. J., & Blaney, P. H. (1984). Hardiness and social support as moderators of the effects of life stress. *Journal of Personality and Social Psychology, 47*, 156–163.

Gilligan, C. (1982). *In a different voice.* Cambridge, MA: Harvard University Press.

Groth, A. (1979). *Men who rape: The psychology of the offender.* New York: Plenum.

Groth, A., & Burgess, A. (1980). Male rape: Offenders and victims. *American Journal of Psychiatry, 137,* 806–810.

Gruder, C. L. (1977). Choice of comparison persons in evaluating oneself. In J. M. Suls & R. L. Miller (Eds.), *Social comparison processes: Theoretical and empirical perspectives.* New York: Hemisphere.

Hammen, C. L., & Peters, S. D. (1977). Differential responses to male and female depressive reactions. *Journal of Consulting and Clinical Psychology, 45,* 994–1001.

Haymen, C. R., Lanza, C., Fuentes, R., & Algor, K. (1972). Rape in the District of Columbia. *American Journal of Obstetrics and Gynecology, 113,* 91–97.

Horowitz, M. J., Wilner, N., Marmar, C., & Krupnick, J. (1980). Pathological grief and the activation of latent self-images. *American Journal of Psychiatry, 137,* 1137–1162.

Howard, J. A. (1984). Societal influences on attribution: Blaming some victims more than others. *Journal of Personality and Social Psychology, 47,* 494–505.

Hursch, C. J., & Selkin, J. (1974). *Rape prevention research project.* Denver, CO: Annual report of the Violence Research Unit, Division of Psychiatric Service, Department of Health and Hospitals.

Janoff-Bulman, R. (1979). Characterological versus behavioral self-blame: Inquiries into depression and rape. *Journal of Personality and Social Psychology, 37,* 1798–1809.

———. (1982). Esteem and control bases of blame: "Adaptive" strategies for victims versus observers. *Journal of Personality, 50,* 180–192.

———. (1985). Criminal vs. non-criminal victimization: Victims' reactions. *Victimology: An International Journal, 10,* 498–511.

———. (1986). Exploring people's assumptive worlds. Manuscript submitted for publication.

Janoff-Bulman, R., & Frieze, I. H. (1983). A theoretical perspective for understanding reactions to victimization. *Journal of Social Issues, 39,* 1–17.

Janoff-Bulman, R., & Lang-Gunn, L. (in press). Coping with disease and accidents: The role of self-blame attributions. In L. Y. Abramson (Ed.), *Social-personal inference in clinical psychology.* New York: Guilford.

Janoff-Bulman, R., & Timko, C. (in press). Coping with traumatic life events: The role of denial in light of people's assumptive worlds. In C. R. Snyder & C. Ford (Eds.), *Coping with negative life events: Clinical and social psychological perspectives.* New York: Plenum.

Janoff-Bulman, R., Timko, C., & Carli, L. (1985). Cognitive biases in blaming the victim. *Journal of Experimental Social Psychology, 21,* 161–177.

Katz, S., & Mazur, M. (1979). *Understanding the rape victim: A synthesis of research findings.* New York: Wiley.

Kaufman, A. (1984). Rape of men in the community. In I. R. Stuart & J. G. Greer (Eds.), *Victims of sexual aggression: Treatment of children, women, and men.* New York: Van Nostrand Reinhold.

Kaufman, A., Divasto, P., Jackson, R., Voorhees, D., & Christy, J. (1980). Male rape victims: Non-institutionalized assault. *American Journal of Psychiatry, 137,* 221–223.

Kidder, L. H., Boell, J. L., & Moyer, M. (1983). Rights consciousness and victimization prevention: Personal defense and assertiveness training. *Journal of Social Issues, 39,* 153–168.

Kidder, L. H., & Cohn, E. (1979). Public views of crime and crime prevention. In I. H. Frieze, D. Bar-Tal, & J. S. Carroll (Eds.), *New approaches to social problems: Applications of attribution theory.* San Francisco: Jossey-Bass.

Kilpatrick, D. G., Resick, P. A., & Veronen, L. J. (1981). Effects of a rape experience: A longitudinal study. *Journal of Social Issues, 37,* 105–122.

Kleinke, C. L., Staneski, R. A., Mason, J. K. (1982). Sex differences in coping with depression. *Sex Roles, 8,* 877–889.

Kobasa, S. C. (1979). Stressful life events, personality and health: An inquiry into hardiness. *Journal of Personality and Social Psychology, 37,* 1–11.

Krupnick, J. (1980). Brief psychotherapy with victims of violent crime. *Victimology, 5,* 347–354.

Kuhn, T. S. (1962). *The structure of scientific revolutions.* Chicago: University of Chicago Press.

Kulik, J. A. (1983). Confirmatory attribution and the perpetuation of social beliefs. *Journal of Personality and Social Psychology, 44,* 1171–1181.

Landis, J. (1956). Experience of 500 children with adult sexual deviation. *Psychiatric Quarterly, 30,* 91–109.

Lazarus, R., & Launier, R. (1978). Stress-related transactions between person and environment. In L. Pervin & M. Lewis (Eds.), *Internal and external determinants of behavior.* New York: Plenum.

Lerner, M. J. (1980). *The belief in a just world.* New York: Plenum.

Lifton, R. J., & Olson, E. (1976). Death imprint in Buffalo Creek syndrome: Symptoms and character change after a major disaster. In H. J. Parad, H. L. P. Resnik & L. G. Parad (Eds.), *Emergency and disaster management.* Bowie, MD: Charles Press.

Maguire, M. (1980). Impact of burglary upon victims. *British Journal of Criminology, 20,* 261–275.

Markus, H. (1977). Self-schemata and processing information about the self. *Journal of Personality and Social Psychology, 35,* 63–78.

Markus, H., Crane, M., Bernstein, S., & Siladi, M. (1982). Self-schemas and gender. *Journal of Personality and Social Psychology, 42,* 38–50.

Marris, P. (1975). *Loss and change.* Garden City, NY: Anchor/Doubleday.

Massey, J. B., Garcia, C. R., & Emich, J. P. (1971). Management of sexually assaulted females. *Obstetrics and Gynecology, 38,* 29–36.

Mazelon, P. (1980). Stereotypes and perceptions of the victims of rape. *Victimology, 5,* 121–132.

Medea, A., & Thompson, K. (1974). *Against rape.* New York: Farrar, Straus & Giroux.

Meyer, C. B., & Taylor, S. E. (1986). Adjustment to rape. *Journal of Personality and Social Psychology, 50,* 1226–1234.

Miller, W. R., & Williams, A. M. (1979). The impact of rape on marital and sexual adjustment. Symposium on women as victims of physical abuse, presented at the meeting of the Eastern Psychological Association, Philadelphia.

Miller, W. R., Williams, M., & Bernstein, M. H. (1982). The effects of rape on marital and sexual adjustment. *American Journal of Family Therapy, 10,* 51–58.

Nadelson, C. C., & Notman, M. T. (1984). Psychodynamics of sexual assault experiences. In I. R. Stuart & J. G. Greer (Eds.), *Victims of sexual aggression: Treatment of children, women, and men.* New York: Van Nostrand Reinhold.

Nadelson, C. C., Notman, M. T., Zackson, H., & Gornick, J. (1982). A follow-up study of rape victims. *American Journal of Psychiatry, 139,* 1266–1270.

Nasjleti, M. (1980). Suffering in silence: The male incest victim. *Child Welfare, 59,* 269–275.

National Center on Child Abuse and Neglect (1981). *Study findings: National study of the severity of child abuse and neglect* (DHHS Pub. No. OHDS 81-30325). Washington, DC: U.S. Government Printing Office.

Norris, J., & Feldman-Summers, S. (1981). Factors related to the psychological impacts of rape on the victim. *Journal of Abnormal Psychology, 90,* 562–567.

Notman, M., & Nadelson, C. (1976). The rape victim: Psychodynamic consideration. *American Journal of Psychiatry, 133,* 408–412.

Noyes, R., & Slymen, D. J. (1978). The subjective response to life-threatening danger. *Journal of Death & Dying, 9,* 313–321.

Padesky, C. A., & Hammen, C. L. (1981). Sex differences in depressive symptom expression and help-seeking among college students. *Sex Roles, 7,* 309–320.

Parkes, C. M. (1971). Psycho-social transitions: A field of study. *Social Science and Medicine, 5,* 101–115.

———. (1975). What becomes of redundant world models? A contribution to the study of adaptation to change. *British Journal of Medical Psychology, 48,* 131–137.

Perloff, L. S. (1983). Perceptions of vulnerability to victimization. *Journal of Social Issues, 39,* 41–62.

Peters, J. J., Meyer, L. C., & Carroll, N. E. (1976). *The Philadelphia assault victim.* Washington, DC: National Institute of Mental Health.

Reiff, R. (1979). *The invisible victim: The criminal justice system's forgotten responsibility.* New York: Basic Books.

Riger, S., & Gordon, M. T. (1981). The fear of rape: A study in social control. *Journal of Social Issues, 37,* 71–92.

Riger, S., Gordon, M. T., & Le Bailly, R. (1978). Women's fear of crime: From blaming to restricting the victim. *Victimology, 3,* 274–284.

Rogers, C. M., & Terry, T. (1984). Clinical intervention with boy victims of sexual abuse. In I. R. Stuart & J. G. Greer (Eds.), *Victims of sexual aggression: Treatment of children, women, and men.* New York: Van Nostrand Reinhold.

Ross, L., Lepper, M. R., & Hubbard, M. (1975). Perseverance in self-perception and social perception: Biased attribution processes in the debriefing paradigm. *Journal of Personality and Social Psychology, 32,* 880–892.

Ruback, R. B., Greenberg, M. S., & Westcott, D. R. (1984). Social influence and crime-victim decision making. *Journal of Social Issues, 40,* 51–76.

Ruch, L. O., & Leon, J. J. (1983). Sexual assault trauma and trauma change. *Women and Health, 8,* 5–21.

Russell, D. E. H. (1974). *The politics of rape: The victim's perspective.* New York: Stein & Day.

Sales, E., Baum, M., & Shore, B. (1984). Victim readjustment following assault. *Journal of Social Issues, 40,* 117–136.

Scheppele, K. L., & Bart, P. B. (1983). Through women's eyes: Defining danger in the wake of sexual assault. *Journal of Social Issues, 39,* 63–80.

Schultz, L. G., & DeSavage, J. (1975). Rape and rape attitudes on a college campus. In L. G. Schultz (Ed.), *Rape victimology.* Springfield, IL: Charles Thomas.

Schur, E. M. (1984). *Labeling women deviant: Gender, stigma, and social control.* New York: Random House.

Shaver, K. (1970). Defensive attribution: Effects of severity and relevance on the responsibility assigned for an accident. *Journal of Personality and Social Psychology, 14,* 101–113.

Shaver, K. G., & Drown, D. (1986). On causality, responsibility and self-blame: A theoretical note. *Journal of Personality and Social Psychology, 50,* 697–702.

Shinn, M., Rosario, M., Morch, H., & Chestnut, D. E. (1984). Coping with job stress and burnout in the human services. *Journal of Personality and Social Psychology, 46,* 864–876.

Showers, J., Farber, E., Joseph, J., Oshins, L., & Johnson, C. (1983). The sexual victimization of gays: A three-year survey. *Health Values, 7,* 15–18.

Silver, R. L., Boon, C., & Stones, M. L. (1983). Searching for meaning in misfortune: Making sense of incest. *Journal of Social Issues, 39,* 81–101.

Silverman, D. C. (1978). Sharing the crisis of rape: Counseling the mates and families of victims. *American Journal of Orthopsychiatry, 48,* 166–173.

Sutherland, S., & Scherl, D. (1970). Patterns of response among victims of rape. *American Journal of Orthopsychiatry, 40,* 503–511.

Swift, C. (1977). Sexual victimization of children: An urban mental health center survey. *Victimology, 2,* 322–326.

Symonds, M. (1980). The "second injury" to victims. *Evaluation and Change,* Special issue on services for survivors, 36–38.

Taylor, S. E. (1983). Adjustment to threatening events: A theory of cognitive adaptation. *American Psychologist, 38,* 1161–1173.

Taylor, S. E., Wood, J. V., & Lichtman, R. R. (1983). It could be worse: Selective evaluation as a response to victimization. *Journal of Social Issues, 39,* 19–40.

Tennen, H., Affleck, G., & Gershmann, K. (1986). Self-blame among parents of infants with perinatal complications: The role of self-protective motives. *Journal of Personality and Social Psychology, 50,* 690–696.

Timko, C., & Janoff-Bulman, R. (1985). Attributions, vulnerability, and psychological adjustment: The case of breast cancer. *Health Psychology, 4,* 521–544.

Waller, E. (1976). Victim research, public policy and criminal justice. *Victimology, 1,* 242–252.

Weinstein, N. D. (1980). Unrealistic optimism about future life events. *Journal of Personality and Social Psychology, 39,* 806–820.

Weinstein, N. D., & Lachendro, E. (1982). Egocentrism as a source of unrealistic optimism. *Personality and Social Psychology Bulletin, 8,* 195–200.

Weis, K., & Weis, S. (1975). Victimology and the justification of rape. In I. Drapkin & E. Viano (Eds.), *Victimology: A new focus* (Vol. 3). Lexington, MA: Lexington Books.

Weisman, A. D. (1979). *Coping with cancer.* New York: McGraw-Hill.

Wolfenstein, M. (1957). *Disaster: A psychological essay.* Glencoe, IL: Free Press.

Wortman, C. B. (1976). Causal attributions and personal control. In J. H. Harvey, W. J. Ickes, & R. F. Kidd (Eds.), *New directions in attributions research* (Vol. 1). Hillsdale, NJ: Erlbaum.

Wortman, C. B., & Dunkel-Schetter, C. (1979). Interpersonal relationships and cancer: A theoretical analysis. *Journal of Social Issues, 3,* 120–155.

Zawitz, M. W. (Ed.). (1983). *Report to the nation on crime and justice: The data.* Washington, DC: U.S. Department of Justice.

8

Gender and Coping with the Entry into Early Adolescence

Diane Mitsch Bush
Roberta G. Simmons

Many investigators have characterized adolescence as a far more stressful period than childhood or early adulthood. G. Stanley Hall's (1904) major book on adolescence began a long line of both scholarly and lay work which argued that adolescence was intrinsically stressful. In contrast, Margaret Mead (1928) and others have contended that adolescence has been defined differently, and has varied in its stressfulness, within various societies and within the United States during different historical periods (Bakan, 1971; Douvan & Adelson, 1966; Elder, 1975; Kagan, 1971; Kagan & Coles, 1971; Offer, Ostrov, & Howard, 1981; Stinchcombe, 1964; Westley & Elkin, 1957).

We begin with an overview of conceptions of adolescence and gender. We next focus upon the intersection of gender and cohort effects on the individual's experience of adolescence, emphasizing observed gender differences in self-esteem and aspirations in adolescence. We then draw on secondary evidence to link our findings to a broader framework of gender, class, and race in society.

THE SOCIAL CONSTRUCTION AND SOCIAL ORGANIZATION OF ADOLESCENCE AS A TRANSITION IN THE LIFE COURSE

Recent research on adolescence as a life transition shows that the inevitability of "storm and stress" in adolescence has been greatly overrated

(Bakan, 1971; Offer et al., 1981; Simmons, Blyth, VanCleave, & Bush, 1979). Popular culture, worried parents, and clinicians all paint a picture of adolescence as fraught with stress, yet empirical research on samples of normal adolescents (i.e., not clinical samples) finds that large proportions of people between 12 and 18 in the United States are coping quite well with the physiological, psychological, and social changes they encounter. Offer et al. (1981, p. 126) found that mental health professionals describe the "normal" adolescent as "significantly more disturbed than the normal adolescent viewed himself or herself." This kind of discrepancy between the images of adolescence held by adult professionals and those held by adolescents themselves points to a potential source of bias in theorizing and research on adolescence.

The Social Construction of Age and Sex in Adolescence

Much research begins with the assumption that adolescence is stressful rather than the assumption that there is variation in the extent of stress encountered and/or in the coping resources available to the individual. Moreover, until quite recently research focused on clinical populations and generalized to normal populations of adolescents. Research that uses representative samples finds significant variation in the extent to which adolescence is experienced as stressful (Offer et al., 1981; Simmons et al., 1979).

Such findings suggest that the social construction and social organization of biological age into a period of life called adolescence may make this life transition more or less difficult for individuals. Social construction of one's environment is the process whereby individuals, groups, and/or societies create a socially agreed upon definition of an object, trait, situation, individual, or group of people (Marx (1848), 1972; G. H. Mead, 1934; Stone & Farberman, 1970; Thomas & Thomas, 1928). This construction then becomes "reality" in that it shapes social behaviors.

Adolescence is socially constructed in contemporary American culture in at least two ways. First, adolescence has become defined as a unique period in the life course. As recently as the late nineteenth century "adolescence" did not exist (Aries, 1962). There were children, and children became adults. Now, as noted above, it is widely assumed that this period in life is particularly and uniformly difficult for all individuals, even though research findings cast doubt on this assumption. Such social constructions of reality may or may not "fit the facts." Nevertheless, what is most important about them is that they have an enormous impact upon behavior and upon conceptions of self (G. H. Mead, 1934; Rosaldo, 1974; Schur, 1985; Stone & Farberman, 1970; Thomas & Thomas, 1928). The social construction of two "biological facts," age and sex, into adolescence and gender is a primary focus of this chapter.

The Social Organization of Adolescence and Gender

A central theme of our chapter concerns the social organization of adolescence. Social organization is created by and simultaneously creates social interactions. It is both a process and a structure comprising values, norms, roles, organizations, institutions, the links between them, and the networks of individuals who create, enact, and are socially created by them. The social organization of adolescence consists of social constructions of the teen-age years, roles of parents and teens, roles of teens and their peers, as well as roles of teachers and parents. Families and schools take on special significance for the social organization of adolescence, as does awareness of the future world of work.

Neither the social construction nor the broader social organization of adolescence can be comprehended without an understanding of the social organization of gender during adolescence. The "social organization of gender" (Chodorow, 1978) and the "sex-gender system" (Rubin, 1975) are largely interchangeable concepts which describe how sex, as a biological trait, becomes socially constructed as an ascribed basis for differential status by gender (Rosaldo, 1974).

We emphasize two concepts in our discussion of gender and coping during adolescence: the public/domestic dichotomy and gender intensification. Rosaldo (1974) argued that ideology and division of labor in virtually all societies "interpret" biological sex differences so as to define women's primary responsibility and identity as lying in the domestic sphere. This public/domestic (public/private) separation is a basis for social inequality for women in that "feminine traits," however defined in a specific culture, are deemed inferior in the public sphere of economy and polity. In Western society, subsequent to the industrial revolution, the domestic sphere has been culturally linked to expressivity, nurturing, and emotion while the public sphere has been characterized as instrumental, competitive, and rational (Chodorow, 1978; Mead, 1928; Parsons & Bales, 1955; Rosaldo, 1974; Rubin, 1975; Weber, 1947). Chodorow (1978) elaborated on the ways in which the social division of labor in the family (child care and nurturing vs. breadwinning) reproduces the domestic/public split, thus recreating gender inequality. The fact that women are primarily responsible for nurturing and rearing children in the nuclear family means that each generation of women develops the capacity and need for close interpersonal connection and men develop the capacity and need for separation and instrumentality. According to Chodorow, the female need for connection leads women to emphasize husband, children, and close friendship (i.e., interaction in the private sphere), while the need for separation leads men to the public sphere of the bureaucratically organized workplace.

While Rosaldo's and Chodorow's theoretical frameworks provide a basis for exploring the ways in which the social organization of gender may create different stressors and resources for coping in adolescence, they are not explicitly aimed at explaining adolescence as a key period in the life course. Most importantly, they do not focus on school as the central arena of adolescent life. These general conceptualizations of the social organization of gender provide a starting point for our specific analysis of variation in coping with the transition of early adolescence (for a more complete review and synthesis of gender and cohort effects, see Bush, 1985; for a review and analysis of the interaction of school and family on gender socialization and the reproduction of sex segregation of occupations, see Bush, 1986a).

The "gender intensification hypothesis" (Hill & Lynch, 1983) suggests that the public/domestic separation becomes especially salient for girls and boys during early adolescence (Block, 1984; Bush, 1985), when expectations become more gender specific. Traditional sex-typed expectations of peers, parents, and teachers become more pronounced in early adolescence (Hall & Sandler, 1982; Hill & Lynch, 1983; Huston-Stein & Higgins-Trenk, 1978; Weitzman, 1984). At the same time, girls' school achievement drops in comparison to boys, especially in mathematics (Hall & Sandler, 1982; Maccoby & Jacklin, 1974; Weitzman, 1984), and their occupational aspirations contract into a narrow range of "traditional female" occupations (Best, 1983; Herzog, Bachman, & Johnston, 1983; Huston-Stein & Higgins-Trenk, 1978; Macke & Morgan, 1978; Rosen & Aneshensel, 1978). Girls' values become significantly different from boys during early adolescence (Bakan, 1971; Bush, Simmons, Hutchinson, & Blyth, 1978; Gilligan, 1982); they focus much more on expressive values, while boys in contrast emphasize instrumental values.

Since expressivity is the underlying theme of the domestic sphere, and instrumentality is the predominant focus in the public sphere, these findings suggest that early adolescence may be the key period for the reproduction of the domestic/public split as the basis for the social organization of gender and, therefore, for gender inequality. Research indicates that girls have greater difficulty in coping with this life transition than do boys: adolescent girls are more likely to attempt suicide than are boys (Deykin, 1986; Deykin, Perlow, & McNamara, 1985). Research reveals that some girls at this age have more problems with self-image than do boys (Offer et al., 1981; Simmons & Rosenberg, 1975; Simmons et al., 1979), perhaps in part because the major roles that girls prepare for during adolescence are valued less than the major roles toward which boys are aiming (Bush,

1985; Huston-Stein & Higgins-Trenk, 1978; Macke & Morgan, 1978; Rosaldo, 1974). It is also possible that future conflicts between the domestic and public spheres become more evident to girls at this age (Bush, 1985, 1986a; Herzog et al., 1983), thus producing gender-specific stressors.

The key research issue here is the identification of social and individual factors that lead to more or less difficulty in coping with adolescence and may make the transition to adolescence more difficult for girls than for boys. We will focus on the domestic/public separation and gender intensification in our discussion.

EMPIRICAL AND THEORETICAL FRAMEWORK

The question of how biology, individual experience, and social structure interact to affect the reaction to adolescent life transitions has guided our research on the impact of coping with life transitions in early adolescence. A major variable is self-image; we treat a favorable picture of the self as an indicator of positive coping. Throughout this chapter, we will integrate findings from our own longitudinal study with other literature to show how the social organization of gender shapes both stressors and available coping mechanisms. Our findings reveal that girls experience more difficulty in coping during early adolescence than boys. The study, described below, was done in Milwaukee, Wisconsin, between 1974 and 1979.[1] Our sampling design enabled us to compare children who moved into a junior high (K–6 to junior high) at the beginning of early adolescence with those who remained in a kindergarten through eighth grade (K–8) school. Within the public school system, some schools were structured as K–6 to junior high while others were K–8.[2]

This "natural experiment" allows us to examine the relative importance of biological age—especially at the onset of puberty—socially constructed age, and social organization, especially school structures, for gender-specific coping with the transition to adolescence. In contrast to a simple conceptualization that equates adolescence and puberty, adolescence can be viewed as an age-graded sequence in the life course. In the United States ages 12 to 13 are viewed as the lower boundary and ages 18 to 21 are seen as the upper boundary of adolescence (Elder, 1975; Erikson, 1950; Kagan & Coles, 1971; Offer et al., 1981). For girls in the United States, the onset of pubertal change may occur at any point from ages 9 to 16; for boys, pubertal development begins an average of two years later than it does for girls (Brooks-Gunn & Peterson, 1983). (Most physiological measures of puberty reflect the processual nature of puberty; it is a series of biological changes, not simply one event—see Tanner, 1961; Tobin-Richards, Boxer, & Petersen, 1983. However, historically and currently menarche is often viewed as the key event for girls.) Our design allows us to examine the joint effects of gender and onset of puberty, timing of puberty, school structure, and peer relations upon several indicators of coping.

The chapter will draw on our own research as well as that of other investigators to build a general model of the effects of gender upon the ways in which individuals cope with adolescent transitions. Briefly, we will argue that the social construction of biology is a key process which creates gender-specific stressors and coping mechanisms. Class, race, and cohort moderate both the creation of stressors and the availability of coping mechanisms. Age and gender are conceptualized as key elements of social organization which interact so that for female adolescents there are more stressors and fewer resources for coping. For early adolescents the social structure of school affects both the stressors experienced and available coping mechanisms. Self-esteem and body image, as components of global self-image, will be emphasized as indicators of coping. Variables and processes which make it difficult for the individual to construct and maintain a positive self-image will be discussed as stressors.

Self-Image, Self-Esteem, Body Image, and Identity in Adolescence

Self-image (self-concept) refers to the way in which the individual sees herself or himself; it includes both self-definitional and self-evaluative elements. Self-esteem is the primary, global evaluative component of self-concept; it consists of the individual's global positive or negative attitude toward herself or himself. Theory and research suggest that high self-esteem may be an indicator of effective coping as well as a potential resource in dealing with stress (see Rosenberg, 1981, for summary).

One element of the self-concept that takes on increased salience in adolescence is body image, reflecting self-evaluation of one's physical appearance. Self-esteem and body image are correlated, but change in one does not necessarily *cause* change in the other. Because body image becomes so important to adolescents, it has often been investigated as the sole indicator of self-image. This approach to self-image leaves out the more global evaluation of self by the individual, that is, self-esteem. Both components of self-image are crucial for an understanding of the self and, especially, for comprehending changes in self-image.

Identity is a component of the self that becomes more complex during early adolescence. The concept refers to meanings attached to the self by the individual which correspond to the social placement of that individual by others (Rosenberg, 1981; Stryker, 1981). The creation of identities involves others' reactions to the individual, primarily on the bases of status and role. However, it also includes the individual's appropriations of others' definitions and evaluations of her or him.

Regardless of the theoretical perspective taken, there is general agreement that creation of a coherent identity first becomes possible with the entry into early adolescence. Erikson (1950, 1968) points out how the construction of identity may be problematic for adolescents and how the process of identity formation is dependent on individual characteristics, interpersonal interactions, and larger sociohistorical forces, especially ideology. He suggests that identity formation may be more stressful for adolescent girls because the future roles to which they aspire are devalued by boys and by the culture generally (Erikson, 1950, 1968, 1975). In his original formulation of life-cycle stages, creation of an identity was envisioned as the essence of adolescence, whereas developing the capacity for intimacy (primarily in the sense of a monogamous, lasting, sexual partnership with a primary other) was seen as the focal point of early adulthood. Identity had to be formed prior to developing intimate relations.

This life-cycle sequence, though called "human," appeared to apply primarily to men. Erikson (1950, 1975) acknowledged that this discrete sequence might be blurred for girls and women so that developing identity and intimacy were two inextricable elements of one process for women. Because of the narrow range of primarily expressive, socioemotional roles traditionally available to women, the formation of female identity focuses upon interpersonal intimacy first with a mate, then with children (Erikson, 1975).

More recently, Chodorow (1978), Gilligan (1982), and Rossi (1980) have provided key reformulations of female development that expand upon Erikson's insight. Such feminist conceptions of the ideological separation of domestic/public spheres as a primary basis for a social organization of gender in which women are deemed socially inferior to men also focus upon lack of choice and the instrumental/expressive dichotomy (Chodorow, 1978; Rosaldo, 1974; Rubin, 1975) as discussed above. The instrumental/expressive, public/domestic dichotomy suggests that for early adolescent girls both stressors and coping mechanisms may arise from connection with others and may depend more on factors outside the individual than they do for boys. External assessments of the more expressive component of self, such as popularity with peers, become more important for girls in adolescence (Bush et al., 1978). In contrast, instrumental components of the self such as academic achievement and athletic prowess appear to be relatively more important for boys.

Individuals may find that they have less control over who likes them than over attributes where practice and individual initiative influence success. We discuss later observed gender differences in the relative importance of expressive versus instrumental traits and values and the effect these values have on coping. Throughout, we will emphasize how the social construction of age into adolescence differs for boys and girls due to the intersection of social organization of adolescence and the social organization of gender. We will show how the domestic/public separation, as the primary basis for the social organization of gender, becomes enmeshed in the social organization of adolescence to make the adolescent transition more difficult for girls than for boys. We argue that the interaction of the social organization of adolescence and gender result in more stressors and fewer coping resources for girls than for boys, but that there is also variation *within* gender in coping with adolescence.

THE TIMING OF PUBERTY: GENDER DIFFERENCES IN THE SOCIAL CONSTRUCTION OF ADOLESCENCE

Having shown that there are age differences in the onset of puberty, the key biological event that defines the physical transition to adolescence, we next consider how such "biological facts" become socially constructed. It is the social construction of biological age that creates variation in potential stressors during adolescence.

Research that links pubertal development to social and psychological constructs finds that variation in timing of the onset of puberty may make the adolescent transition more or less smooth in the United States (Brooks-Gunn & Petersen, 1983). Data from a variety of studies show that early-pubertal boys have a more positive body image than later-developing boys, whereas early-developing girls have a more negative body image than "on-time" girls[3] (Tobin-Richards, Boxer, & Petersen, 1983). More generally our own and others' findings show that early-pubertal boys may have some social advantages over late-developing boys; for girls, early development may be disadvantageous (Simmons, Rosenberg, & Rosenberg, 1973; Tobin-Richards et al., 1983). This interaction between gender and timing may be due to the cultural value placed on masculine traits; the sooner boys "become men," the closer they are to a valued status. In contrast, menarche is viewed ambivalently at best in contemporary American culture, as well as many other cultures (Brooks-Gunn & Petersen, 1983; Rosaldo, 1974). Indeed, both ritual and slang construct the onset of menses as negative or "unclean." However, although this explanation may account for the gender difference, it does not offer an adequate account of variation among girls, for whom being "early" or "on-time" may be related to distinctive sets of expectations from self and others.

Given that puberty as a biological process occurs at different ages for different individuals of both sexes, part of the observed variation in coping with these dramatic biological changes may be due to being socially off-time or on-time. Much of the impact of being on-time or off-time in pubertal change comes from social construction by the adolescent and the larger society of the "appropriate" body for one's age. This social definition of the physical self is an integral part of the social organization of adolescence. As such, it is closely connected with the social organization of gender. Not only are there obvious sex differences in the features of the "ideal body," but ideal female and male bodies and related elements of gender role expectations are valued differently in the adult world. Since female characteristics (physical, psychological, and social) are linked ideologically in most societies to the domestic sphere of nurturant interactions rather than the public sphere of "important" political and economic interactions, they have been deemed as inferior both by lay people and by traditional theorists of human development (for comment and review, see Bem, 1983; Broverman, Vogel, Broverman, Clarkson, & Rosenkrantz, 1972; Chodorow, 1978; Gilligan, 1982; Rosaldo, 1974). When coupled with the possible effects of gender intensification, these findings on body image point to greater difficulty for girls at early adolescence.

When we examined how timing of puberty affects coping, we found that being on- or off-time in pubertal development (i.e., being an early, middle, or late developer) had less impact than we expected on coping for either sex; onset of menarche and time of peak rate of height growth were used as indicators of onset for girls and boys, respectively (Simmons et al., 1979; Simmons & Blyth, 1987). (It is possible that hormonal measures might indicate more of an impact.) Early pubertal development does affect body image as measured by satisfaction with various aspects of looks. We asked, for example, "How satisfied are you with your figure/physique?" Being early led to a more positive body image for boys and a more negative one for girls. However, pubertal timing alone had no significant effect on self-esteem. Thus, although one element of self-image—that is, body image—was affected by timing, as found in earlier research, the primary evaluative component of self-image—that is, self-esteem—was not affected by timing for girls or boys. It is possible that timing of puberty alone does not affect the more global component of self-image (self-esteem) because a variety of social factors intervene, whereas both the individual and significant others see a more direct link between body image and timing of puberty. We explore this issue more fully below when we discuss our overall findings on self-esteem.

It is also possible that the presence or absence of menstrual periods alone, rather than timing, may be a better predictor of difficulty in coping, as reflected in self-image. Evidence suggests that the onset of menstruation is viewed with great ambivalence by girls and significant others (Faust, 1983). However, our data, based on a representative sample, show no impact of presence or absence of menstrual period on self-esteem.

Given other research that shows gender differences in self-image in adolescence (Offer et al., 1981; Simmons & Rosenberg, 1975), it would be tempting to conclude that the onset of puberty is the cause of a lower self-image for girls. Our data dispel such notions. Because of the complexity of the social organization of adolescence and gender, we must examine changes in self-image at this age by looking more closely at such important variables as self-esteem and satisfaction with looks for girls and boys, and at another key component of self and identity in adolescence, one's set of values.

GENDER DIFFERENCES IN SELF-IMAGE AND VALUES: SOURCES OF STRESS AND RESOURCES FOR COPING IN JUNIOR HIGH

In our late 1970s sample there are significant differences in self-esteem, satisfaction with looks, and value of popularity between boys and girls in all grades. Although there are a variety of other indicators of self-image on which there are no differences (see Simmons & Blyth, 1987), self-esteem, satisfaction with looks, and popularity are often cited in the literature on gender socialization as keys to adolescent well-being. In every grade, boys have significantly higher self-esteem than girls; the gender difference increases by 30 percent from sixth to seventh grade, by 20 percent from seventh to ninth grade, and by less than 1 percent from ninth to tenth grade. The gender difference in satisfaction with looks remains relatively stable from sixth grade through tenth grade; boys are consistently more satisfied with their looks than are girls. Gender differences in the value placed on popularity over competence and independence more than triple in magnitude from sixth grade to seventh grade; girls are far more concerned with popularity than are boys. This difference drops almost to zero in ninth and tenth grades. Gender differences in concern with same-sex popularity increase two and a half times from sixth to seventh grade. From seventh to ninth grade these differences remain stable, then drop in tenth grade.

In short, gender differences increase for self-esteem and valuing popularity during early adolescence, while they remain stable for satisfaction with looks. Girls appear to have lower self-esteem when compared to boys, and this disadvantage increases during early adolescence. Moreover, as they enter adolescence girls attach more significance than do boys to popularity.

The Social Organization of the Junior High School

In the United States, early adolescence coincides with the move to junior high school for many children.[4] With the relatively new move to middle schools (grades six through eight) this structure is changing. Nonetheless, the seventh-to-ninth-grade junior high is still common in many areas of the country. Observers have pointed to size and the "impersonal" nature of interactions in the junior high as problematic for early adolescents (see Blyth, Simmons, & Bush, 1977, for review).

Size and impersonal relations, however, may not be the only, nor even the major, factors which affect adolescent coping for either sex in the junior high. The social organization of the junior high school corresponds closely to that of the bureaucracy (Weber, 1947): there is task specialization in that each classroom corresponds to a particular subject matter and is taught by a different teacher; children occupy multiple roles (student, student government, team athlete, etc.); there is a distinct hierarchy of authority, including an age-graded authority structure among students; there are written rules and formal procedures governing behavior; relationships among teachers and students may be based less on particularistic, affective ties; the scholarly sphere of competence is defined very clearly and may be related to task specialization via tracking or ability grouping. A long tradition in the social sciences focuses on the way in which such secondary group interaction poses difficulties for the individual (Cooley, 1922). Recent research emphasizes how bureaucratic structures (the quintessence of the secondary group) lead to problems in coping at work (Kanter, 1977; Rothschild-Whitt, 1979). Similarly, the bureaucratic features of the junior high may pose problems for early adolescents. Such difficulties may be exacerbated by the coincidence of the onset of puberty and entry into junior high. Our research shows evidence of such an interaction effect (Blyth et al., 1977; Simmons et al., 1973; Simmons et al., 1979; Simmons & Blyth, 1987).

There appear to be gender differences in children's and adolescents' preference for and capacity to cope with bureaucratic organizations. Chodorow (1978) contends that the sexual division of labor in parenting and the domestic/public split produce gender-specific experiences in childhood. Because of these gender-specific processes, adolescent boys (and later, men) have the need and capacity to compete and achieve in the bureaucratically organized public world of capitalist societies. In contrast, girls' needs and capacities are oriented toward interpersonal intimacy and social relationships. Lever's (1978) research shows that 11-year-old boys play games that approximate bureaucratic interaction while girls' free play revolves more around smaller interpersonal, less task-differentiated activity. Girls' play does not involve the abstract rules entailed in boys' games. Rather, girls emphasize social relationships that are personalized. Within the bureaucracy, such capacities are devalued, if not proscribed.

Gilligan (1982) expands on Chodorow's themes of connection versus separation in female and male experience and maintains that women's moral decisions are based on connection and personal responsibility to other individuals. Men's moral decisions are grounded in separation from others and concern with rights of the abstract "other." Gilligan's female respondents, both adults and adolescents, have difficulty in reconciling their personal concerns about concrete people with the universalistic requirements of bureaucracies. They attempt to spin webs of caring within the context of hierarchical structures characteristic of a bureaucratized society.[5]

Given Chodorow's and Gilligan's theories and given the social organization of gender, we expect early adolescent girls to find the bureaucratic structure of junior high (compared to grade school) more stressful than do boys. Furthermore, we predict that girls in the junior high will find it more difficult to cope, in part because of the formal structure. On the other hand, junior high would present the early adolescent boy with fewer stressors because he is already more comfortable with the greater emphasis on independence and separation inherent in the structure of the junior high. Since the adolescent boy would tend to value formal rules and hierarchy, the new school might appear less foreboding and less stressful for him than for the early adolescent girl. The consequences of gender intensification should appear most clearly within the junior high context.

Our findings tend to confirm these predictions. Figure 1 reveals that

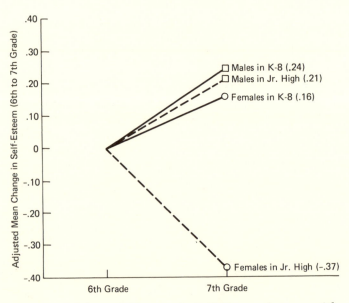

Figure 1. Adjusted Changes in Self-Esteem between 6th and 7th Grade by Sex and School Type.

girls who enter junior high in the seventh grade experience a marked drop in self-esteem. This deficit does not diminish as they move through tenth grade. Girls who remain in a K–8 school experience a steady increase in their self-esteem from sixth through tenth grade. When they do enter into a bureaucratic school structure, they appear to cope far better than the K–6 girls did during their transition to such a school structure. Boys start in sixth grade with higher self-esteem, and their scores increase steadily, regardless of the type of or change in school structure.

It is not simply moving into a bureaucratic structure that is difficult for girls; rather the problems seem to stem from the *timing* of the transition to a bureaucratic structure. The K–8 girls appear to be protected from multiple stressors at a time of change in definition of self by the intimacy of the grade school. In many ways, grade school classes with their predominance of female teachers (U.S. Bureau of the Census, 1983) resemble the organization of the family. A "mother figure" who interacts on an affective level with children as individuals and the close relationships between the children themselves may intersect to provide the supportive resources the early adolescent girl appears to need to cope with the changes of early adolescence. Such resources become especially important as pressures mount for her to take on roles which correspond to more adult female roles.

Gender Differences in the Experience of Dating

Dating is one measure of the assumption of adolescent gender roles. Given the importance often placed on heterosexual developmental tasks, we might imagine that dating would be a mark of high status for early adolescent girls. On the other hand, the dating-rating game includes a variety of possible stressors. The data in Figure 2 reveal that the situation is far more complex in seventh grade. Overall, girls in the K–8 schools show an increase in self-esteem with the exception of pubertal dating girls. Girls in the junior high who date and who have begun to menstruate show the largest drop in self-esteem. These results appear to support a "developmental readiness" hypothesis for girls: it is more difficult to assume a number of new, discontinuous, *and* inconsistent roles at an earlier than a later age (see Simmons & Blyth, 1987). The reason that many girls have a more negative experience at early adolescence within the junior high is not simply that they are "too young." Rather, the social organization of junior high is built around a confluence of new, inconsistent roles, and girls enter this structure at a stage in the life course marked by redefinitions of the self.

The K–8 school appears to cushion girls, to some extent, from the stressors of early adolescence, while the junior high seems to exacerbate the

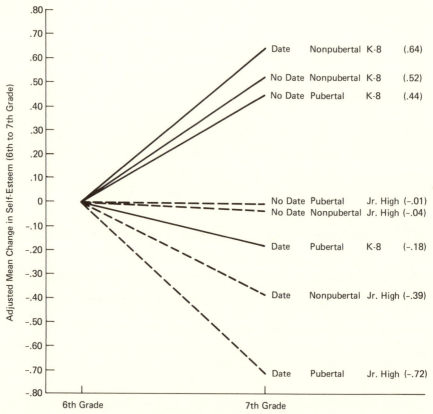

Figure 2. White Girls in Comparable Schools: Adjusted Change in Self-Esteem between 6th and 7th Grade by Dating Behavior, Puberty, and School Type.

impact of stressors. Why should girls who date in the junior high have such a difficult time? Moreover, why is it that girls who are pubertal, who date, and who attend junior high demonstrate such problems in adjusting? Each of these changes can be interpreted as a move toward adulthood; each represents potential mastery of a developmental task. This paradox is even more puzzling when we examine how boys' self-images are affected by this same set of variables.

As a group, boys appear to cope well with dating, entry into puberty, and entry into junior high. For boys, becoming an adolescent means moving closer to a set of valued adult roles; for girls the change is ambivalent and discontinuous. The meaning of "becoming a woman" is not necessarily positive. The contradictory nature of adult female roles is pointed out more clearly in the junior high. Expectations regarding careers[6] and expectations regarding socioemotional, intimate relationships are much more consistent for boys than for girls. For example, several studies show that boys expect future wives to "take care" of them so that they may achieve in the work world, whereas contemporary adolescent girls expect to work for pay and be mothers and wives (Bush, 1985, 1986a; Corder & Stephan, 1984; Herzog et al., 1983; Keith & Brubaker, 1980).

An important element of the stressors for the junior high girl appears to be boys' attempts to be dominant in a dating relationship. We conducted in-depth interviews with five ninth-grade girls who had been identified in seventh grade as dating, being pubertal, and having low self-esteem. Since these girls had been rated by nurses as being more developed, including breast development, there were external signs of their quasi-adult status. These girls reported sexual pressures from boys in seventh grade: "Well, I don't like a guy trying to touch me and that's what they tried to do." Furthermore, one girl cited boys' general demands on her as a source of stress.

> GIRL: "Yeah, I was meeting guys, and then going out roller skating and stuff. . . . I'd always go with a group. I find that I do feel more comfortable when I'm with a group. . . . My main reason is because, the reason I don't want to be with just one boy is because like I said, I don't know what to talk about. And I'm not the kind who likes to hold hands all the time. I've got to be free, you know? And there's some guy the other night that was wanting me to sit down and I wouldn't. I mean, not me, I mean I'm a happy person, I guess. I feel happy, and the only way I can keep feeling happy that way is if the guy doesn't want to hold my hand, and I don't really like to be kissed, you know."
>
> INTERVIEWER: "You feel that's not where the boys are? They do want to hold hands and kiss you?"
>
> GIRL: "Yeah. That's what happened when, like I told you, [I went out with] my brother and his girlfriend [and a guy] and, well, they were kissing up in front, and he wanted to; I didn't. So I faked sleeping which I shouldn't of did cause he caught me."

These stressors reported by adolescent girls are analogous to those cited in recent research on adult couples. Rubin (1983) and Philipson (1982) both point to the gender asymmetry in perceptions of intimate relations. From their descriptions of the relationship, male and female partners appear to be in two entirely distinct relationships. Their definitions of the intimate elements of their lives together appear to have little correspondence. This same asymmetry can be seen, in a much simpler way, in these responses of the girls in our study. While they like companionship and closeness, they find sexual pressure stressful and they perceive that boys seem to want something very different out of the dating relationship from what they want. Girls want closeness and connection which does not necessarily include sexual attention, whereas boys appear more concerned with sexual aspects of the relationship.

The establishment of intimate relationships can be conceived of as a coping mechanism which renders the individual better equipped to deal with the stressors of school or workplace. However, we should note that having an intimate partner, either lover, fiancee, or spouse, has a positive effect on adult male attainment, but either no effect or a negative one on adult female attainment (see Bush, 1986a, for review of this literature). This finding suggests that experiences that serve as coping resources for young men may be sources of stress for young women.

Gender asymmetry in the potential stress embedded in heterosexual relationships and in coping resources may be due in part to gender intensification (Hill & Lynch, 1983). Our data reveal that girls begin to value popularity over competence and independence in seventh grade (Bush et al., 1978; Simmons & Rosenberg, 1975), and in some contexts they exhibit a drop in self-image between sixth and seventh grade (Simmons et al., 1979). Other research shows a drop in academic performance (Eccles & Hoffman, 1984; Weitzman, 1984), especially in mathematics (Parsons, Adler, & Kaczala, 1982; Parsons, Kaczala, & Meese, 1982; Parsons, Meese, Adler, & Kaczala, 1982; Sherman, 1980). Rosen and Aneshensel (1978) found that the proportion of girls who want executive-professional occupations drops when comparing seventh–eighth graders to eleventh–twelfth graders. Gender intensification suggests that parents, peers, teachers, and the girl herself begin to see the primary goal of adolescence as finding a suitable husband (Huston-Stein & Higgins-Trenk, 1978; Stericker & Kurdek, 1982).

As a life transition for girls, adolescence appears to be characterized by discontinuity and inconsistency. Expectations by significant others seem to change greatly from grade school to junior high (Best, 1983; Eccles & Hoffman, 1984; Parsons et al., 1982a,b,c). Just as they are expected to become more concerned with boys, some data suggest that girls discover that boys expect them to act dependent and not to compete (Best, 1983; Braito & Klundt, 1984; Herzog et al., 1983). At the same time, girls realize that these "feminine" behaviors are devalued, not only in their public world of school, but in the adult public world as well (Broverman et al., 1972; Siltanen & Stanworth, 1984; Thorne, 1983).

Gender Differences in Attributions for Success and Failure

Since girls depend more on others than do boys for assessments of ability, achievement, appropriateness of future family aspirations, and morality

(Corder & Stephan, 1984; Gilligan, 1982; Saltiel, 1985), conflicting or contradictory messages may be key sources of stress for adolescent girls. Much evidence shows that parents and teachers are less supportive of girls' attempts at mastering achievement tasks than of boys (Bush, 1986a; Parsons, 1982; Sadker & Sadker, 1985). Possible consequences for stress and coping strategies can best be understood when contrasted with boys' general experience at adolescence. Data on school achievement and self-assessment of intellectual ability, for example, attest to the inconsistency of the adolescent girl's world. It is interesting to note that girls in our Milwaukee sample have consistently higher grade point averages than boys in all four years, and that girls' scores on standardized tests of verbal achievement remain consistently higher than boys'. Results for math achievement are mixed; in grade six girls do worse, in grade seven they do better, and in grade ten there is no gender difference. In spite of girls' achievement, they rate themselves as less "smart" than boys. This finding is consistent with data from attribution studies showing that girls are less likely than boys to attribute success at a task to ability. Our findings on perceived intellectual ability and self-esteem suggest that girls not only have a more negative self-image than boys, but that they tend not to have a stable set of internal standards for judging task performance. When confronted with the necessity to evaluate the self, they may well turn to others as yardsticks. As noted above, this pattern may reduce a girl's ability to cope.

From childhood on, cross-sex behaviors and attributes are strongly discouraged in boys (Eccles & Hoffman, 1984; Weitzman, 1984). In this sense, expectations at adolescence are not discontinuous for boys. Moreover, there is a high valuation of the masculine in our culture. The value placed on being masculine seems to be translated into messages given by parents and teachers to boys that they are expected to, and can, achieve (Eccles & Hoffman, 1984; Parsons et al., 1982a,b). Such messages may place a great deal of stress on the boy to achieve, yet at the same time both parents and teachers appear to be more supportive of boys, even if they make mistakes (Parsons et al., 1982a,b: Sadker & Sadker, 1985; see Bush, 1986b, for a review of parent and teacher expectations). These factors may influence boys to attribute success to ability and failure to either lack of effort or luck (see Frieze, Whitley, Hansuy, & McHugh, 1982, for review; also see Bush, 1986a; Dusek & Joseph, 1983; Kaufman & Richardson, 1982).

In contrast, girls either fail to attribute success to ability or make unstable internal attributions for success and more stable internal attributions for failure (Gitelson, Petersen, & Tobin-Richards, 1982; Kaufman & Richardson, 1982; Parsons et al., 1982a,b,c). Since girls attribute failure to lack of ability and success to luck, effort, or ease of task, they are more likely to expect to fail again (Stipek, 1984). Research carried out in the 1970s and early 1980s indicates that actual failure has a more lasting impact on early adolescent girls' expectations than on boys of the same age.

Early adolescent boys expect to do better on future tasks regardless of past performance than do girls (Gitelson et al., 1982; Stipek, 1984; Stipek & Hoffman, 1980).

It appears that the social organization of gender in early adolescence provides girls with conflicting messages and demands while simultaneously leading them to look to others for validation. In contrast, boys at early adolescence encounter a more consistent set of demands that push them toward an internalized set of standards. Thus, adolescence provides more potential problems and fewer coping resources for girls than for boys in part because girls are so oriented to others' expectations.

The research reviewed above dispels the notion that the same constellation of factors that describe and explain male experience also account for female experience. It also points to ways in which real life interactions with peers and with adults continue to define adolescent girls in ways that a girl may perceive as inconsistent with the adult social world as well as with the future she sees for herself. This may lead to a constantly shifting sense of self, largely dependent on others' assessment. Thus a key resource for coping—for maintaining a firm internal self-image—may be missing or overshadowed by an identity largely dependent on the reactions and evaluations of others. This problem appears to be mirrored in girls' tendency to attribute success to external elements and failure to internal traits.

COHORT EFFECTS AND GENDER EFFECTS ON COPING IN ADOLESCENCE

The issues we have raised need to be placed within the context of specific historical and social realities. A variety of research, especially Elder's work (Elder, 1975, 1980), shows that adolescence is experienced in distinct ways by different cohorts. The variety and intensity of potential stressors depends on the historical context of adolescence. Researchers have distinguished between both stressors and resources for coping prevalent in the 1960s and those available to the 1970s cohort of adolescents. Offer et al. (1981) report that the 1970s adolescents "feel worse about themselves than did teenagers of the 1960s"; this difference is said to be due to the "enthusiasm and optimism of the 1960s in contrast with the more negative zeitgeist of the 1970s" (Offer et al., pp. 102, 104–5). In addition, the increases in divorce rates and in households headed by a single parent are cited as possible explanations for this cohort difference. In fact, evidence regarding the impact of family structure and context on self-esteem is contradictory (Offer et al., 1981). Regardless of the explanation, however, the Offer study fits with other research that finds a significant cohort effect in self-image, values, and expectations for adolescents (American Council on Education, 1984).

Much speculation has focused on how 1970s and 1980s cohorts of adolescents might be different from 1960s cohorts along various dimensions of gender-specific expectations. The assumption underlying expectations of fewer gender differences and more "nontraditional" orientations for girls today is that there has been a change in the social organization of gender since the early 1960s. Such change, it is argued, leads parents, peers, and teachers to have similar future occupational and familial expectations for girls and for boys. Thus, the gender-specific stressors associated with adolescence for earlier cohorts of girls are said to have diminished.

Gender and Adolescence: Is There Significant Cohort Change?

Studies comparing current and prior cohorts of adolescents reveal unchanged expectations about the future with respect to some areas and changed attitudes in other areas (see Bush, 1986a, for a review). Our research and that of others shows that adolescent girls in the late 1970s and early 1980s are somewhat more likely than 1960s girls to report that they intend to work full time outside the home (Bush et al., 1978; Lueptow, 1980). Moreover, the 1970s girls are less likely to value interpersonal orientations over instrumental orientations than were 1960s girls (Bush et al., 1978). Among current adolescents there are sex differences in role expectations; there is a decided tendency for boys to be more conservative than girls. Boys are more likely to expect future wives to quit work after children are born, whereas girls are more likely to expect to combine work, marriage, and children (Corder & Stephen, 1984; Herzog et al., 1983). This difference between boys and girls in family aspirations and expectations may be a source of tension between young men and women as they move into young adulthood. Indeed, a wide variety of research suggests that relationships with the opposite sex are more problematic for girls than for boys (Best, 1983; Burke & Weir, 1978; Huston-Stein & Higgins-Trenk, 1978; Simmons et al., 1979; Thorne, 1983).

All of these findings point to the persistence of gender-specific stressors for current cohorts of girls. However, prior studies have not explicitly compared boys and girls from more than one cohort as they move through adolescence. Our longitudinal data set (Bush et al., 1978; Simmons & Blyth, 1987; Simmons et al., 1979) allows us to examine gender differences and changes in those differences from sixth through tenth grades in the late 1970s (1974–1979). Furthermore, our data from comparable or identical items from a 1968 sample in Baltimore (Bush et al., 1978; Simmons & Blyth, 1987; Simmons et al., 1973) enable us to make cohort comparisons.

Gender and Future Aspirations in Adolescence for the 1970s Cohort

In our 1974–1979 Milwaukee sample, there are few gender differences in educational and occupational aspirations. One difference is that in grades nine and ten, girls are significantly more likely than boys to plan to go to college. The meaning of gender-specific occupational aspirations is difficult to assess because of problems with the usual measures of occupational status. Jobs such as nurse or elementary school teacher receive a higher ranking in occupational status scales than skilled blue-collar jobs that pay more (Bush, Simmons, & Blyth, 1985).[7] Boys in our sample are highly likely to aspire to blue-collar jobs while girls' aspirations vary among clerical and semi-professional categories. Thus, boys obtain a lower mean score on occupational aspirations while the jobs they aspire to pay more on the average than those aspired to by girls.

Our data on work orientation are difficult to compare to those of Herzog et al. (1983) and Corder and Stephan (1984) because boys were not asked what they wanted or expected of their future wives regarding work and family roles. Among the tenth-grade white girls, 17 percent expected to work "all the time, even if I have children" and 54 percent chose the response "all the time except when I have young children." The remaining 29 percent chose "just until I get married" or "just until I have children." The corresponding proportions for sixth grade were 25, 37, and 38 percent; for seventh grade 24, 41, and 35 percent; and for ninth grade 18, 57, and 25 percent.

Thus large proportions of these adolescent girls in the late 1970s expected to be in the paid labor force for the majority of their adult lives. Changes from sixth grade to tenth grade in the proportion of girls who expected to be in the labor force suggest that the older adolescents may have more realistic further work expectations than the younger girls. In 1950, 24 percent of married women were in the paid labor force; by 1970 the rate was 44 percent, and by 1980 it was 51 percent (U.S. Bureau of the Census, 1974). Among all women aged 24 to 45 in 1982, 70 percent were in the labor force, and 50 percent of women with children aged 5 to 16 were working for pay.

At first glance, it is difficult to reconcile these girls' nontraditional work expectations with their more sex-typed concerns with popularity and dissatisfaction with looks. One relevant factor is attitude toward one's own gender role. In all but tenth grade, girls are significantly less likely to say that "it's great to be a girl" than boys are to say "it's great to be a boy." The gender difference narrows considerably from sixth through tenth grade, but the proportion of girls who say "it's great to be a girl" does not change significantly over time.

There are many reasons why females may be dissatisfied with gender roles in a society that more highly values males and the masculine (Chodorow, 1978; Rosaldo, 1974). In the current era, contradictions between girls' values and life expectations may cause dissatisfaction. These girls are concerned with looks and popularity, yet they expect to work for a substantial portion of their lives. As they enter adolescence the contradictory demands of being popular with boys so as to attract an appropriate husband while training for an occupation become clearer to the adolescent girl. In contrast, for the adolescent boy the future role of provider, while burdensome in terms of the heavy financial responsibilities involved, is relatively consistent.

Cohort Differences in Stressors and Coping by Gender

How do our findings from a 1970s cohort compare to those from a 1960s cohort? As noted above, although there has been much discussion of possible cohort changes in male and female adolescents' expectations and selves, there is little evidence for substantial change in the social organization of gender. Our data suggest that gender differences in stressors, coping, and consequences in adolescence have not narrowed from the 1960s to the 1970s (Bush et al., 1978; Simmons & Blyth, 1987). Indeed, the gender differences in self-esteem in the Milwaukee (1974–1979) sample are significantly larger than those found in the 1968 Baltimore sample in all grades. Gender differences in body image, satisfaction with looks, value of popularity, and attitude toward gender in some grades in the 1970s are either larger or about the same.

Part of the persistence of gender-related anxieties among girls may be due to the greater complexity and inconsistency of expectations about the sexual division of labor today. The "superwoman" concept seems to contain the message that to "have it all" she has to "do it all" without his help. One interpretation of the gender difference in girls' and boys' future family expectations (Corder & Stephan, 1984; Herzog et al., 1983; Keith & Brubaker, 1980; Tittle, 1981) is that girls do "want it all" but they wouldn't mind some help from their future partners. Yet the males in their pool of future partners seem to want an "independent career woman" who will take care of them and their children.

THE EFFECTS OF CLASS AND RACE ON THE SOCIAL CONSTRUCTION OF ADOLESCENCE

Our discussion thus far has not addressed the interaction of class and race in relation to the social organization of adolescence and gender. Much of the research on normal adolescents has sampled middle-class, white children; only a few studies have focused on class and race-related variations in stress and coping during adolescence.

Class

Stinchcombe's (1964) research suggests that social class may affect adolescent experience in ways analogous to the gender effects suggested above. He found that high school students in the early 1960s who did not perceive a bright future in the labor market were more likely to be alienated from school and to act rebelliously in school. These attitudes and behaviors were more likely to be found among children of lower-status parents. Because they perceived little connection between current performance at school and future possibilities for high-status employment, these students did not attach much value to conforming to high school expectations. Stinchcombe's work alerts us to the possibility that "adolescent turmoil" varies by class because of class-specific experiences rooted in social organization.

Kohn's (1969) findings similarly suggest class differences in both stressors and coping mechanisms at adolescence. Although his research is not concerned with adolescent stress, his finding that middle-class (whitecollar) parents emphasize children's self-direction while working-class (blue-collar) parents emphasize conformity in their children implies that class-specific experience may prepare middle-class children to cope more easily with some adolescent issues. If these children are more internally controlled, their coping strategies may entail constructing a coherent set of values and norms in response to a changing social environment. On the other hand, externally controlled children may have more difficulty with the conflicting demands of adolescence—the netherworld of not-child and not-quite-adult may be more likely to look negative. This issue is especially problematic if, as Stinchcombe (1964) argued, the working-class youngster sees fewer adult opportunities open.

Both Stinchcombe (1964) and Kohn (1969) contend that the social organization of work and the economy generally results in different experiences by class. Stinchcombe further argues that these experiences lead adolescent students to react to school in class-specific ways. Bowles and Gintis (1976) show that education as an institution is, itself, structured by class relations in the larger society. Thus opportunities in school depend in part on class background rather than solely on ability, motivation, or achievement. Recent critiques of tracking or ability grouping (Persell, 1977; Rosenbaum, 1976) have shown similar effects, although there is debate on whether tracking decisions are affected by the child's class background.[8]

Race

Race has been discussed as a significant feature of social organization which shapes the adolescent transition in ways analogous to class. Stinchcombe

(1964) argued that higher rates of delinquency among black teenagers could be interpreted as a response to the reality of discrimination, especially the knowledge that one's future opportunities were narrowed by race. There is relatively little work on normal black adolescents; however, several studies show that black adolescents have relatively high self-esteem (Powell & Fuller, 1973; Rosenberg & Simmons, 1972) and are resourceful and adaptable in coping strategies (Ladnor, 1971). Data from our study show that black adolescent girls have higher self-esteem than do white girls (Simmons, Brown, Bush, & Blyth, 1978). This research is consistent with work on the black family that shows the resilience of woman-centered black family structures (Stack, 1974).

Such findings may reflect differences in coping with stress rather than differences in the number or intensity of stressors encountered by minority group adolescents. Evidence suggests, however, that black youths face more severe stressors than whites. In 1983, adult black men who were employed full time, year-round earned, on the average, 64 percent of what adult white men employed full time, year-round earned. The unemployment rate for blacks was more than twice that for whites in 1983, and 58 percent of black female-headed households fell at or below the poverty level, compared to 11 percent of all family households (U.S. Bureau of the Census, 1984). These data suggest that economic stressors for black adolescents are more intense and extensive than for whites.

Race and gender may intersect to produce different patterns of stressors for black and white girls. As a group, black adolescent girls exhibit secondary sex characteristics earlier than do white girls (Brooks-Gunn & Petersen, 1983). These data are fragmentary, yet if black girls develop visible signs of puberty (especially breast development) early, it is possible that such early development relative to other children may be disadvantageous if these girls perceive themselves to be off-time and if their opposite-sex peers view them in more sexual terms. (Whether these girls perceive themselves as off-time depends on peer group norms. Since data on black children are sparse, it is difficult to determine what is perceived as "off-time.")

GENDER INTENSIFICATION, THE SOCIAL ORGANIZATION OF GENDER, AND COPING WITH THE ENTRY INTO ADOLESCENCE

The world of adolescence is a world of both genders. As Lever (1978) and Thorne (1983) have shown, even when boys and girls interact in same-sex groups, they do so with reference to the other sex. According to Thorne's (1983) research, to be a boy is to not be a girl; she found that the worst epithet an early adolescent boy can toss at another boy is "you girl." To be a girl in adolescence is to be attractive, to be well-liked by both boys and girls; in short, to conceive of self in terms of concrete, personal others.

If we are to understand the origins, extent, and consequences of stress for both boys and girls, we must comprehend the social organization of gender. In adolescence, heterosexual meanings become more important to both genders, but relationships with the opposite sex appear to be perceived in very different ways by girls and boys. Likewise, academic achievement and aspirations mean different things to boys and girls, and these meanings are rooted in the social organization of gender. Boys' tendencies to make strong internal attributions for success, for example, grow out of gender-specific socialization at home and at school. Attributing success to ability and failure to bad luck may help boys to cope with anxiety over a bad performance. In contrast, girls' attributions for success at instrumental tasks are external, just as are their evaluations of self. While dependence on others may provide a coping resource (Burke & Weir, 1978), it can also give the girl a much less stable sense of self.

What appear at first glance to be individual resources, individual perceptions, and individual interpretations are, in fact, shaped by interactions embedded in the social organization of gender. As research on schools shows, both teacher expectations[9] and actual teacher-student interactions vary by gender of student (Parsons et al., 1982a,b,c; Sadker & Sadker, 1982, 1985; see Bush, 1986a, for review). Moreover, as organizations, schools are structured, formally and informally, into a gender dichotomy that corresponds to the public/domestic separation (Bem, 1983; Thorne, 1983). Our findings on the negative impact of entry into junior high for pubertal dating girls suggest that organizational structure and gender-specific needs and capacities interact to produce very different stressors and mechanisms for coping among girls and boys.

We contend that the growing inconsistencies and contradictions of female adolescence provide greater stress and fewer coping resources for girls. The dominant social organization of gender, which remains focused on women's responsibilities in the domestic sphere, results in expressive, other-oriented attributes, capacities, and cognitions as definitive of the female self. Because of gender intensification, early adolescence is a period in which these expressive elements of self and social organization come into direct conflict with the instrumental elements valued in the public sphere of school (which presages the world of work). Our data show these contradictions most clearly in our interviews with pubertal dating girls who attended junior high.

It appears that current cohorts of girls experience stress because of conflicting demands to achieve in the public sphere and be successful in interpersonal relations, especially dating. Yet it is possible that they reconcile these contradictions by achieving at instrumental tasks, yet not incorporating their success into a general self-concept, or by choosing to be successful in either the domestic *or* public sphere but not both. Research on adult attainment fits with the latter contention; as noted above, marriage or the presence of a sexual intimate has a positive effect on male occupational attainment, but either no effect or a negative one on female attainment. Perhaps adolescent girls see that for boys the combination of marriage and work will be relatively easy, while for girls some difficult choices lie ahead.

Clearly we need further research following current cohorts into adulthood. It is possible that encountering the contradictions of the female adolescent transition may equip these girls to handle the work/family conflict better than previous cohorts have. Obviously a complete examination of this question requires investigation of both family and work organization.

Much of our discussion on the impact of class and race on adolescent gender differences was speculative because data are so sparse. We need research on the interaction of age, gender, class, and race on coping. Although research on the feminization of poverty shows that gender, class, and race intersect to reproduce a cycle of poverty for single-parent, female-headed households (Stallard, Ehrenreich, & Sklar, 1983), we know very little about these processes during adolescence. Given recent attention to increases in teenage pregnancy, especially among poor minority teenagers, class, race, and gender as interconnected elements of social organization take on added significance.

It is impossible to understand the complexities of the domestic/public, expressive/instrumental splits unless we are able to see both the overlap and the separation between the two spheres. Prior work has tended to focus on family *or* school when studying adolescent transitions. Studies that have attempted to examine the relative impacts of each have used closed-ended, survey techniques. Yet some of the most provocative findings on school have come from participant observation, for example, Thorne's (1983) research on boys and girls "together and apart." More participant observation and in-depth interviewing in schools and families is highly desirable.

Prior work on adolescence as a period in the life course has assumed that the processes of development are the same for girls and boys, with gender differences due simply to different attributes of the sexes or to the gender-specific content of socialization (Bush, 1985; 1986a, 1986b). This chapter suggests that gender cannot simply be included as a variable in models of the stress process. Rather, the social organization of gender creates experiences and interactions for women and men that may overlap, conflict, or be entirely distinct. We contend that what may constitute coping resources for boys may be stressors for girls.

In summary, present evidence indicates that the organization of schools interacts with gender and age to produce a constellation of stressors and reduce effective coping for girls. The discontinuity and complexity of female adolescent socialization appear to increase girls' difficulties. We hypothesized that the process originates in the social organization of gender, particularly in the ideological separation of public and domestic spheres, and in the persistence of sex-typed division of labor in these spheres.

NOTES

1. The original data collection (1974–1979) was funded by a grant from the William T. Grant Foundation to Roberta G. Simmons and by NIMH MH-30739 and NIMH Research Development Award MH-41688.

2. The data for our longitudinal study were gathered in a five-year period from 1974 to 1979 in Milwaukee. Eighteen elementary schools were randomly sampled from all public schools using a randomized, stratified design. Within the schools sampled, all sixth-grade students were invited to participate, and parental consent was secured from 82 percent of the sample or 924 students, 621 of whom were white. Survey instruments were administered to these students once a year from grades six through ten (with the exception of grade eight) if they remained in the Milwaukee public school system. Physical measurements to determine pubertal timing were collected more frequently. Time of onset of menarche for girls and time of peak rate of height growth for boys were the indicators used. All schools sampled reflected the school population from which they were drawn (see Blyth et al., 1977; Bush et al., 1978; Simmons et al., 1979; Simmons & Blyth, 1987). We sampled all K–8 schools and drew a sample of K–6 schools that were comparable to the K–8 schools along a number of demographic dimensions (e.g., achievement test scores, median family income, and racial composition).

3. The conception of being "on-time" or "off-time" in making major life transitions was introduced by Neugarten and Datan (1973). Riley, Johnson, and Foner (1972) elaborate on the concept by emphasizing age-graded norms. Both theory and research have focused on age-grading, social perceptions of "off-time" transitions, the extent of discontinuity in transitions, and the effect of ritual on smoothing discontinuous life transitions (see Bush & Simmons, 1981, for a re-review; see especially Benedict, 1938, & Kett, 1977, for discussions of discontinuity and ritual).

4. The majority (over 70 percent) of public secondary schools are either separate or combined junior-senior high schools (see Blyth et al., 1977).

5. By "bureaucratized society" we mean a society in which the public sphere (including economy, politics, and religion) consists primarily of bureaucracies as Weber (1947) originally defined them. We do not use the term "bureaucratized" as synonymous with "dehumanized," nor do we suggest that bureaucratic modes of decision making are necessarily "more rational." Rather we are referring to formal organizations characterized by task specialization, hierarchy of authority, written rules, a sphere of competence, ostensibly governed by impartiality—in short, an organization in which positions and the rules that

define them are the key to organizational structure (see Weber, 1947; contrast with Kanter, 1977).

6. Research on status attainment shows that variance in male attainment is reasonably accounted for by training, formal education, parental encouragement, and earlier aspirations, while these variables have much less effect on women's attainment (in some cases none) (Rosenfeld, 1980; Saltiel, 1985; Sewell et al., 1980; see Bush, 1986a, for review).

7. See Bush et al., 1985, for further discussion of problems in using occupational status scores to assess sex-typing of occupational aspirations.

8. Alexander and Cook (1982) find that class does not account for placement. There is considerable debate on the placement issue. However, there is evidence that heterogeneity by class at the classroom level has positive effects upon academic achievement and adjustment (Rutter, 1980; Rutter, Maughan, Mortimore, Ouston, with Smith, 1979).

9. Sadker and Sadker (1985) as well as others find that teachers are not aware of their gender-specific expectations of students nor do they consciously treat students differently. Yet the girls are consistently treated differently from boys. These findings are analogous to contrasts between parents' self-reports of gender-specific treatment of children and actual parental interaction with boys and girls (see Bush, 1986a).

REFERENCES

Alexander, K. L. & Cook, M. A. (1982). Curricula and coursework: A surprise ending to a familiar story. *American Sociological Review, 47,* 626–640.

American Council on Education. (1984). *The American freshman: National norms for fall, 1984.* University of California at Los Angeles, Graduate School of Education.

Aries, P. (1962). *Centuries of childhood.* New York: Knopf.

Bakan, D. (1971). Adolescence in America: From idea to social fact. In J. Kagan & R. Coles (Eds.), *Twelve to sixteen: Early adolescence.* New York: W. W. Norton.

Bem, S. L. (1983). Gender schema theory and its implications for raising gender-aschematic children in a gender-schematic society. *Signs, 8,* 598–616.

Benedict, R. (1938). Continuities and discontinuities in cultural conditioning. *Psychiatry, 1,* 161–167.

Best, R. (1983). *We've all got scars.* Bloomington: University of Indiana Press.

Block, J. (1984). *Sex role identity and ego development.* San Francisco: Jossey-Bass.

Blyth, D. A., Simmons, R. G., & Bush, D. M. (1977). Transition into early adolescence: A comparison of youth in two educational contexts. *Sociology of Education, 51,* 149–162.

Bowles, S., & Gintis, H. (1976). *Schooling in capitalist society: Educational reform and the contradictions of economic life.* New York: Basic Books.

Braito, R., & Klundt, K. (1984). *Adolescents' views of gender roles and appropriateness of varied family and work conditions.* Paper presented at the meeting of the Western Social Science Association, San Diego, California.

Brooks-Gunn, J., & Petersen, A. C. (Eds.). (1983). *Girls at puberty: Biological and psycho-social perspectives.* New York: Plenum.

Broverman, I., Vogel, S., Broverman, D., Clarkson, F., & Rosenkrantz, P. (1972). Sex-role stereotypes: a current appraisal. *Journal of Social Issues, 28,* 59–78.

Burke, R. J., & Weir, T. (1978). Sex differences in adolescent life stress, social support, and well-being. *Journal of Psychology, 98,* 277–288.

Bush, D. M. (1985). The impact of changing gender role expectations upon socialization in adolescence: Understanding the interaction of gender, age and cohort effects. In A. C. Kerckhoff (Ed.), *Research in sociology of education and socialization* (Vol. 5). Greenwich, CT: JAI Press.

———. (1986a). The impact of family and school on adolescent girls' aspirations and expectations: The public-private split and the reproduction of gender inequality. In J. Figueira-McDonough & R. Sarri (Eds.), *Gender, deviance and social control: Catch-22 strategies in the maintenance of minority status.* Beverly Hills, CA: Sage.

———. (1986b). *Gender and methods of inquiry: Some problems with current conceptions.* Paper presented at the meeting of the Pacific Sociological Association, Denver.

Bush, D. M. & Simmons, R. G. (1981). Socialization processes over the life course. In M. Rosenberg & R. Turner (Eds.), *Social psychology: Sociological perspectives.* New York: Basic Books.

Bush, D. M., Simmons, R. G., & Blyth, D. A. (1985). *The effects of maternal employment upon adolescents' educational and occupational aspirations: Gender role socialization and the reproduction of sex segregation.* Paper presented at the meeting of the American Sociological Association, Washington, DC.

Bush, D. M., Simmons, R. G., Hutchinson, B., & Blyth, D. A. (1978). Adolescent perception of sex roles in 1968 and 1975. *Public Opinion Quarterly, 41,* 459–474.

Chodorow, N. (1978). *The reproduction of mothering: Psychoanalysis and the sociology of gender.* Berkeley, CA: University of California Press.

Cooley, C. H. (1922). *Human nature and the social order* (2nd ed.). New York: Scribner's.

Corder, J. & Stephan, C. W. (1984). Females' combination of work and family roles: Adolescents' aspirations. *Journal of Marriage and the Family, 46,* 391–402.

Deykin, E. Y. (1986). Personal communication, June.

Deykin, E. Y., Perlow, R., & McNamara, J. (1985). Non-fatal suicide and life-threatening behavior among 13–17 year old adolescents seeking emergency medical care. *American Journal of Public Health, 75,* 90–92.

Douvan, E., & Adelson, J. (1966). *The adolescent experience.* New York: Wiley.

Dusek, J. B., & Joseph, G. (1983). The bases of teacher expectancies. *Journal of Educational Psychology, 75*, 327–346.

Eccles, J. S., & Hoffman, L. W. (1984). Sex roles, socialization and occupational behavior. In H. W. Stevenson & A. E. Siegal (Eds.), *Research in child development and social policy* (Vol. 1). Chicago: University of Chicago Press.

Elder, G. H., Jr. (1975). Adolescence in the life cycle: An introduction. In S. Dragastin & G. H. Elder, Jr. (Eds.), *Adolescence in the life cycle: Psychological change and social context*. Washington, DC: Hemisphere.

————. (1980). Adolescence in historical perspective. In J. Adelson (Ed.), *Handbook of adolescent psychology*. New York: Wiley.

Erikson, E. H. (1950). *Childhood and society*. New York: W. W. Norton.

————. (1968). *Identity: Youth and crisis*. New York: W. W. Norton.

————. (1975). *Life history and the historical moment*. New York: W. W. Norton.

Faust, M. S. (1983). Alternative constructions of adolescent growth. In J. Brooks-Gunn & A. C. Petersen (Eds.), *Girls at puberty: Biological and psychological perspectives*. New York: Plenum.

Frieze, I. H., Whitley, B. E., Jr., Hansuy, B. H., & McHugh, M. C. (1982). Assessing the theoretical models for sex differences in causal attributes for success and failure. *Sex Roles, 8*, 333–343.

Gilligan, C. (1982). *In a different voice: Psychological theory and women's development*. Cambridge, MA: Harvard University Press.

Gitelson, I. B., Petersen, A. C., & Tobin-Richards, M. H. (1982). Adolescents' expectancies of success, self-evaluations, and attributions about performance on spatial and verbal tasks. *Sex Roles, 8*, 411–419.

Hall, G. S. (1904). *Adolescence: Its psychology and its relation to physiology, anthropology, sociology, sex, crime, religion, and education*. New York: Appleton.

Hall, R. M., & Sandler, B. R. (1982). *The classroom climate: A chilly one for women?* Washington, DC: The Association of American Colleges.

Herzog, R. R., Bachman, J. G., & Johnston, L. (1983). Paid work, child care, and housework: A national survey of high school seniors' preference for sharing responsibilities between husband and wife. *Sex Roles, 9*, 109–135.

Hill, J. P., & Lynch, M. E. (1983). The intensification of gender-related role expectations during early adolescence. In J. Brooks-Gunn & A. C. Petersen (Eds.), *Girls at puberty: Biological and psychosocial perspectives*. New York: Plenum.

Huston-Stein, A., & Higgins-Trenk, A. (1978). Development of females from childhood through adulthood: Career and feminine orientations. In P. B. Baltes (Ed.), *Life-span developmental psychology* (Vol. 1). New York: Academic Press.

Kagan, J. (1971). A conception of early adolescence. In J. Kagan & R. Coles (Eds.), *Twelve to sixteen: Early adolescence*. New York: W. W. Norton.

Kagan, J., & Coles, R. (Eds.). (1971). *Twelve to sixteen: Early adolescence*. New York: W. W. Norton.

Kanter, R. M. (1977). *Women and men of the corporation*. New York: Basic Books.

Kaufman, D. R., & Richardson, B. L. (1982). *Achievement and women: Challenging the assumptions*. New York: Free Press.

Keith, P. M., & Brubaker, J. H. (1980). Adolescent perceptions of household work: Expectations by sex, age, and employment situation. *Adolescence, 15*, 171–182.

Kett, J. (1977). *Rites of passage: Adolescence in America 1790 to the present*. New York: Basic Books.

Kohn, M. (1969). *Class and conformity*. Homewood, IL: Dorsey Press.

Ladnor, J. (1971). *Tomorrow's tomorrow: The black woman*. Garden City, NY: Anchor Doubleday.

Lever, J. (1978). Sex differences in the complexity of children's play. *American Sociological Review, 43*, 471–482.

Lueptow, L. (1980). Social change and sex role change in adolescent orientations toward life, work, and achievements: 1964–1975. *Social Psychology Quarterly, 43*, 48–59.

Maccoby, E. E. & Jacklin, C. N. (1974). *The psychology of sex differences*. Stanford, CA: Stanford University Press.

Macke, A. S., & Morgan, W. R. (1978). Maternal employment, race, and work orientation of high school girls. *Social Forces, 57*, 187–204.

Marx, K. (1972) [1848]. The 18th Brumaire of Louis Bonaparte. In R. C. Tucker (Ed.), *The Marx-Engels reader*. New York: Norton.

Mead, G. H. (1934). *Mind, self, and society*. Chicago: University of Chicago Press.

Mead, M. (1928). *Coming of age in Samoa*. New York: Morrow.

Neugarten, B. L., & Datan, N. (1973). Sociological perspectives on the life cycle. In P. B. Baltes & K. W. Schaie (Eds.), *Life-span developmental psychology: Personality and socialization*. New York: Academic Press.

Offer, D., Ostrov, E., & Howard, K. I. (1981). *The adolescent: A psychological self-portrait*. New York: Basic Books.

Parsons, J. E., Adler, T. F., & Kaczala, C. M. (1982) Socialization of achievement attitudes and beliefs: Parental influences. *Child Development, 53*, 310–321.

Parsons, J. E., Kaczala, C. M., & Meese, J. L. (1982). Socialization of achievement attitudes and beliefs: Classroom influences. *Child Development, 53*, 322–339.

Parsons, J. E., Meese, J. L., Adler, T. F., & Kaczala, C. M. (1982). Sex differences in learned helplessness. *Sex Roles, 8*, 421–432.

Parsons, T. & Bales, R. F. (1955). *Family, socialization, and interaction process*. Glencoe, IL: Free Press.

Persell, C. (1977). *Education and inequality: The roots and results of stratification in America's schools*. New York: Free Press.

Philipson, I. (1982). Heterosexual antagonisms and the politics of mothering. *Socialist Review, 12*, 55–78.

Powell, G. J., & Fuller, M. (1973). *Black Monday's children: A study of the effect of school desegregation on self-concepts of southern children.* New York: Appleton-Century-Crofts.

Riley, M. W., Johnson, M., & Foner, A. (Eds.). (1972). *Aging and society: A sociology of age stratification.* New York: Russell Sage Foundation.

Rosaldo, M. Z. (1974). Women, culture, and society: A theoretical overview. In M. Z. Rosaldo & L. Lamphere (Eds.), *Women, culture, and society.* Stanford, CA: Stanford University Press.

Rosen, B. C., & Aneshensel, C. S. (1978). Sex differences in the educational-occupational expectation process. *Social Forces, 57,* 164–186.

Rosenbaum, J. E. (1976). *Making inequality: The hidden curriculum of high school tracking.* New York: Wiley.

Rosenberg, M. (1981). The self-concept: Social product and social force. In M. Rosenberg & R. H. Turner (Eds.), *Social psychology: Sociological perspectives.* New York: Basic Books.

Rosenberg, M., & Simmons, R. G. (1972). *Black and white self-esteem: The urban school child.* Washington, DC: American Sociological Association.

Rosenfeld, R. (1980). Race and sex differences in career dynamics. *American Sociological Review, 45,* 583–609.

Rossi, A. S. (1980). Life-span theories and women's lives. *Signs, 6,* 4–32.

Rothschild-Whitt, J. (1979). The collectivist organization: An alternative to rational-bureaucratic models. *American Sociological Review, 44,* 509–527.

Rubin, G. (1975). The traffic in women: Notes in the 'political economy' of sex. In R. Reiter (Ed.), *Toward an anthropology of women.* New York: Monthly Review Press.

Rubin, L. (1976). *Worlds of Pain.* New York: Harper & Row.

———. (1983). *Intimate strangers: Men and women together.* New York: Harper & Row.

Rutter, M. (1980). *Changing youth in a changing society.* Cambridge, MA: Harvard University Press.

Rutter, M., Maughan, B., Mortimore, P., Ouston, J., with Smith, J. (1979). *Fifteen thousand hours: Secondary schools and their effects on children.* London: Open Books.

Sadker, M. P., & Sadker, D. (1982). *Sex equity handbook for schools.* New York: Longman.

———. (1985). Sexism in the schoolroom of the '80s. *Psychology Today, 19* (March), pp. 54–57.

Saltiel, J. (1985). A note on models and definers as sources of influence on the status attainment process: Male-female differences. *Social Forces, 63,* 1069–1075.

Schur, E. M. (1985). *Labeling women deviant: Gender, stigma, and social control.* New York: Random House.

Sewell, W. H., Hauser, R. M., & Wolf, W. C. (1980). Sex, schooling, and occupational status. *American Journal of Sociology, 86,* 551–583.

Sherman, J. (1980). Mathematics, spatial visualization, and related factors:

Changes in girls and boys grades 8–11. *Journal of Educational Psychology,* 72, 476–582.

Siltanen, J. & Stanworth, M. (Eds.), (1984). *Women and the public sphere:* A *critique of sociology and politics.* New York: St. Martin's.

Simmons, R. G., & Blyth, D. A. (1987). *Moving into adolescence: The impact of pubertal change and school context.* Hawthorne, New York: Aldine de Gruyter.

Simmons, R. G., Blyth, D. A., VanCleave, E., & Bush, D. M. (1979). Entry into early adolescence: The impact of puberty, school structure, and early dating on self-esteem. *American Sociological Review, 44,* 948–967.

Simmons, R. G., Brown, L., Bush, D. M., & Blyth, D. A. (1978). Self-esteem and achievement of Black and white adolescents. *Social Problems, 26,* 86–96.

Simmons, R. G., & Rosenberg, F. (1975). Sex, sex-roles and self-image. *Journal of Youth and Adolescence, 4,* 229–258.

Simmons, R. G., Rosenberg, F., & Rosenberg, M. (1973). Disturbance in the self-image at adolescence. *American Sociological Review, 38,* 553–568.

Stack, C. (1974). *All our kin: Strategies for survival in a Black community.* New York: Harper & Row.

Stallard, K., Ehrenreich, B., & Sklar, H. (1983). *Poverty in the American dream: Women and children first.* New York: Institute for New Communications.

Stericker, A. B., & Kurdek, L. A. (1982). Dimensions and correlates of third through eighth graders' sex-role self-concepts. *Sex Roles, 8,* 915–929.

Stinchcombe, A. L. (1964). *Rebellion in a high school.* Chicago: Quadrangle.

Stipek, D. J. (1984). Sex differences in children's attributions for success and failure on math and spelling tests. *Sex Roles, 11,* 969–981.

Stipek, D. H., & Hoffman, J. M. (1980). Children's achievement-related expectancies as a function of academic performance histories and sex. *Journal of Educational Psychology, 72,* 861–865.

Stone, G. & Farberman, H. (1970). *Social psychology through symbolic interaction.* Waltham, MA: Ginn-Blaisdell.

Stryker, S. (1981). Symbolic interactionism: Themes and variations. In M. Rosenberg & R. H. Turner (Eds.), *Social psychology: Sociological perspectives.* New York: Basic Books.

Tanner, J. M. (1961). *Growth at adolescence* (2d ed.). Oxford: Blackwell Scientific Publications.

Thomas, W. I. & Thomas, D. S. (1928). *The child in America.* New York: Knopf.

Thorne, B. (1983). Girls and boys together . . . but mostly apart: Gender arrangements in elementary schools. In W. Hartup & Z. Rubin (Eds.), *Relationships and development.* New York: Lawrence Erlbaum Associates.

Tittle, C. K. (1981). *Careers and family: Sex roles and adolescent life plans.* Beverly Hills, CA: Sage.

Tobin-Richards, M. H., Boxer, A. M., & Petersen, A. C. (1983). The psychological significance of pubertal change: Sex differences in perceptions of self during early adolescence. In J. Brooks-Gunn & A. C. Petersen (Eds.), *Girls at puberty: Biological and psychosocial perspectives.* New York: Plenum.

U.S. Bureau of the Census. (1983). *Statistical abstracts of the United States, 1983.* Washington, DC: U.S. Government Printing Office.

———. (1984). *Money income and poverty status of individuals and families.* Washington, DC: Department of Commerce.

Weber, M. (1947). *A theory of social economic organization.* Glencoe, IL: Free Press.

Weitzman, L. J. (1984). Sex-role socialization: A focus on women. In J. Freeman (Ed.), *Women: A feminist perspective* (3d ed.). Palo Alto, CA: Mayfield.

Westley, W. A., & Elkin, F. (1957). The protective environment and adolescent socialization. *Social Forces, 35,* 243–249.

9

Weight Concerns as Chronic Stressors in Women

Ilana Attie
J. Brooks-Gunn

Among the multitude of stressors encountered by the contemporary American woman is the expectation, from within and without, that she meet an extremely slender ideal for feminine beauty. This ideal has so influenced women that many rate themselves as overweight when indeed they are not. In one survey of over 30,000 readers of *Glamour* magazine, admittedly a sample that may be more likely to adhere to media-inspired body ideals than more nationally representative samples, three-quarters rated themselves as too fat, even though only a fraction actually were overweight. Of those who were underweight based on actuarial data, 45 percent believed themselves to be overweight (Wooley & Wooley, 1984a). In a nationally representative sample of over 8,000 women aged 18 and older, nearly 50 percent rated themselves as overweight (Thornberry, Wilson, & Golden, 1986).

The following discussion focuses on weight-related concerns in white women. Very few studies have been conducted on minority women, although it is believed that the preoccupation with being very thin is less prevalent among black and Hispanic women (Hamilton, Brooks-Gunn, & Warren, 1985; Silber, 1986). In part, this belief is based on the fact that the desire to be thin, even underweight, increases with social class (Stunkard, 1975) and minority women are disproportionately represented in the lower socioeconomic segments of society.

This chapter was prepared under the aegis of the W. T. Grant Foundation and the National Institutes of Health.

Termed by some a "national obsession" (Bruch, 1978), the drive towards thinness is popularly regarded as a desirable situation for women of all weights, rather than a response to powerful cultural influences. While normative, in the sense that most teenage and adult women subscribe to it, the pursuit of the thin ideal is maladaptive from both medical and mental health perspectives. In many women, concern with weight leads to "a virtual collapse of self-esteem and sense of effectiveness" (Wooley & Wooley, 1979, p. 69).

In order to achieve this ideal, women typically diet. In the 1985 Health Insurance Survey, 46 percent of adult women across age and race were currently trying to lose weight, and 85 percent of these were dieting to do so (Thornberry et al., 1986). Even adolescents reflect these trends: over half of white middle-class girls surveyed have been on a diet, again usually in the absence of obesity (Attie, Brooks-Gunn, & Warren, 1985; Nylander, 1971).

Contrary to popular belief, which holds that dieting is a healthy response to sociocultural ideals, the premise to be explored in this chapter is that dieting is not only ineffective but a cause of psychological stress. As we shall see, dieting typically does not result in lower weight, but in fatigue, irritability, chronic hunger, greater reliance on external guidelines for the regulation of food intake, and "counterregulatory" behavior, characterized by uncontrollable urges to binge eat. For some women dieting becomes an addiction; the sense of self-control, virtue, and goodness associated with weight loss becomes necessary to the maintenance of their sense of psychological and physical well-being (Szmukler & Tantam, 1984; Wooley & Wooley, 1985). Our premise is that dieting itself is a stressful condition for many women, in that they strive relentlessly for a weight and shape that cannot be acquired or maintained. Viewed from this perspective, dieting in the service of the cultural ideal is itself a chronic stressor. This is not to say that dieting may not be a response to stress in some instances but that in general, the stereotype of the weight-loss diet as a ticket to self-improvement and stress reduction is a myth. Indeed, although eating patterns may be influenced by life events, the direction of change in eating behavior (overeating, undereating) is likely to be multidetermined.

In this chapter we will examine a variety of factors that have contributed to the current climate of rampant concerns about body shape, unattainable demands for weights below the ideal or norm, and mass dieting. Cultural, social, gender, economic, nutritional, genetic, developmental, and psychological factors in all probability are important determinants, as is illustrated in Figure 1. Based on the work of Smith (1968) and adapted by Parsons, Frieze, and Ruble (1976) to explain sex role behavior, Figure 1 depicts how weight-related concerns may develop and be maintained, even in the face of contradictory evidence (i.e., the case of

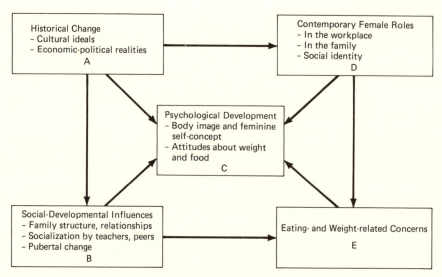

Figure 1. Factors Contributing to Weight-Related Concerns in Women.
(Adapted from Parsons, Frieze, & Ruble, 1976.)

perceiving oneself to be overweight when in fact, one is not). At the societal level, cultural norms and economic-political realities (A) and contemporary social role demands (D) contribute to prescriptions for appropriate weight and body shape. These prescriptions are translated at the
more personal level into social-developmental and family influences on the
child (B), as well as adult self-perceptions (C). Given the pervasiveness of
cultural influences and reinforcing personal experiences, a woman may
never question the validity of her belief that she is overweight or has an
undesirable body. This situation is akin to the observation that sex-role
ideologies in the past have been seen as "normal and irrefutable" because
no other alternatives were ever offered (Bem & Bem, 1970; Parsons et al.,
1976, p. 3). Even if a woman does see alternatives (i.e., acceptance of her
body shape and weight), she may encounter resistance to her perceptions
from peers, spouse, and employer, making it difficult to sustain a contrary
belief.

It is not easy to pinpoint the relative importance of these factors; neither is it possible to make more than inferential statements about the less
proximate factors (i.e., cultural and economic). Given this caveat, we consider possible determinants of weight concerns and dieting behavior from
several perspectives. The first is a cultural historical one, in which we
briefly trace the historical changes in Western body ideals, the impact of
cultural influences on women's beliefs and behaviors, and the effect of
increasing numbers of women in the work force. The second perspective

is developmental in nature and focuses upon the origins of weight concerns and dieting behavior. This perspective is the basis of our research program, and we draw on it to consider the role of cultural ideals in childhood, the effects of the biological changes that transform the young girl's body into that of a woman, and the influence of family socialization practices in the development of weight and body concerns.

Finally, we take issue with the popularly held belief that weight concerns are the domain of overweight individuals, for whom (over)eating is presumably a response to stress or to an inability to manage stressful life events successfully. An alternative view is proposed in which weight concerns and efforts to conform to a certain body shape become a stressor in many women's lives, and may lead to a variety of negative behaviors (e.g., dieting, overeating, drive for thinness, eating disorders). (See Biener, this volume, for a discussion of weight concerns in relation to smoking.) Our primary focus is on weight concerns and dieting behavior, not on the emergence of eating disorders (see Garner, Rockert, Olmsted, Johnson, & Coscina, 1985, and Wooley & Wooley, 1985, for recent reviews of the eating disorder literature). The issue of continuity between dieting and clinical eating disorders is far from resolved (cf. Garner, Olmsted, & Garfinkel, 1983). However, anorexia nervosa and bulimia often begin in the context of restrained eating or dieting, and its frequent companion, binge eating. Accordingly, the factors illustrated in Figure 1 also may play a role in the etiology of eating disorders.[1]

THE RISE OF WEIGHT-RELATED CONCERNS:
POSSIBLE INFLUENCES

The Culture of Thinness

Thinness as a metaphor for beauty and goodness is a fairly recent phenomenon. In their book *The Dieter's Dilemma*, Bennett and Gurin (1982) trace the historical origins of the thin ideal. Emerging just after the turn of this century, the thin feminine figure came to symbolize the then dramatic transformation in the status of women, brought about by a combination of social, economic, and political forces. For the most part, prior to this century, an ample figure was considered both beautiful and an economic asset, as it continues to be in some cultures. Ample body fat made a woman more desirable because it was indicative of health, resistance to disease, and fertility in societies beset with recurrent famines and high infant mortality. For centuries, representations of feminine beauty (known to us through the work of male artists) emphasized a woman's reproductive potential. The prominent belly that dominated images of women in painting from the fifteenth to seventeenth centuries expressed

the fertile ideal. As affection and caring, both within marriage and between mother and child, became increasingly important, the fertile figure
was replaced by the maternal ideal. This ideal, characterized by large
breasts and buttocks, accentuated by a small waist, has lasted until this
century, and continues to appeal to some men in its modern *Playboy* version (Bennett & Gurin, 1982).

The slender female body first appeared in art during the late nineteenth century, a period of contention over female sexuality, health, physiology, and dress (Cott, 1979). As the Victorians cultivated the image of
the passionless, virtuous, yet fertilely plump lady, another woman appeared, one who was sexually free, childless, more dangerous than vulnerable, and *thin*. Through a series of events, including the women's
movement's assault on the double standard and fight for birth control, as
well as the rise of fashion as an industry and of movies as a form of mass
entertainment, women appropriated the image of the femme fatale and
transformed it into a more acceptable, less dangerous form. The new
woman was exemplified in the flapper—carefree, on the move, sexually
free, and androgynously slim. Beginning in the 1920s, the slender, linear
figure was adopted as the prototype for women's fashion; thus, according
to Bennett and Gurin (1982), the original, if implicit message of women's
independence, self-respect, and reproductive control was lost, and thinness became a sign of status and self-mastery. The rapidity with which the
new, linear form replaced the more curvaceous one is startling. In Figures
2 and 3, two covers of *Vogue* depict this change; the first is from 1918 and
the second from 1925. From the 1920s on, no *Vogue* covers have portrayed
women with appreciable breasts or hips.

Although movies and other forms of entertainment have favored one
or the other of the two feminine ideals at different times, architects of
high fashion since the 1920s have tended to define female beauty in extremely slender, linear terms, with the exception of a brief period in the
1950s when postwar, back-to-the home ideology is thought to have revived
the maternal, "hourglass" figure of earlier eras. Thus, the "lean lithe look"
is the benchmark of feminine beauty today, and it has been so for several
decades.[2]

What is particularly troubling, and perhaps startling, is that the cultural emphasis on the lean, lithe look seems to have accelerated in the last
quarter of a century. Attempting to document the shift in cultural attitudes, Garner, Garfinkel, Schwartz, and Thompson (1980) surveyed *Playboy* centerfolds, contestants and winners of the Miss America Pageant, and
dieting articles in six popular women's magazines from 1959 to 1978. Two
major findings emerged. First, women selected to exemplify feminine
beauty, in both its *Playboy* (sensual, maternal) and Miss America (fash-
ionably thin) versions were consistently thinner than corresponding actuarial norms for comparable women in the general population. Second,

Figure 2. Curvaceous Ideal of Feminine Beauty. (Helen Dryden illustration, December 1918. Courtesy VOGUE. Copyright © 1918 [renewed 1946, 1953, 1974, 1981] by The Condé Nast Publications Inc.)

comparing weight within these two groups, both *Playboy* centerfolds and Miss America contestants have become progressively thinner over the past 20 years. At the same time, the average weights of females under 30 have steadily increased, such that the average young woman today is several pounds heavier than her same-age counterpart 20 years ago. This increas-

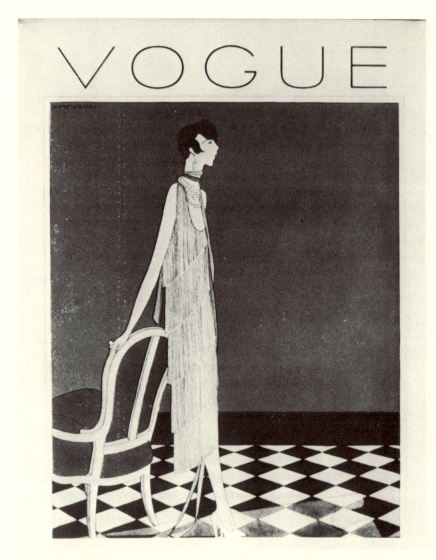

Figure 3. 1925 Flapper. (Harriet Meserole illustration, September 1, 1925. Courtesy VOGUE. Copyright © 1925 [renewed 1946, 1953, 1974, 1981] by The Condé Nast Publications Inc.)

ing discrepancy between ideal and actual weights, coupled with increased attention to dieting in the popular media surveyed, may heighten women's subjective perceptions of being overweight.

Not only have demands for thinness increased, but a corresponding change in body proportions has occurred. The ideal woman today is expected to have a "tubular" form; a relatively small bust and hips, a relatively larger waist. In the study of *Playboy* centerfolds just mentioned, the hip and bust measurements have decreased in the last 20 years, while the waist measurement has increased (Garner et al., 1980).

Importantly, the increasingly tubular and lean bodies portrayed in the 1980s are more characteristic of the prepubertal than postpubertal female. For example, leg length as a proportion of total height decreases throughout puberty for girls, and is larger for adult males than adult females (Faust, 1977). However, an examination of idealized images of women in such socially diverse fashion magazines as *Vogue, Ladies' Home Journal, Seventeen,* and *Cosmopolitan* over the past 20 years indicates that prepubertal body proportions, that is, long-leggedness, are becoming accepted in more and more segments of American society. Specifically, leg lengths more characteristic of prepubertal girls than adult women are now seen not only in high fashion magazines (e.g., *Vogue*) and teenage magazines (e.g., *Seventeen*), but in magazines directed towards young adults (e.g., *Cosmopolitan*). Only magazines directed to mothers (e.g., *Ladies' Home Journal*) may be representing fashion models as more adult in form.

Economic Considerations: Women in the Work Force

When the ideal of thinness first emerged in the post-World War I era, it was heralded as a harbinger of freedom, autonomy, and choice—freedom from traditional roles, autonomy from the family, and choice in reproduction and marriage (Bennett & Gurin, 1982). The persistence of this ideal may be understood in the context of structural changes in the workplace. Specifically, the dramatic increase of women in traditionally male-dominated fields has created pressures on women to compete like men. A demand is placed on women to mimic not only male behavior, but male appearance as well. The "dress for success" notion for women, characterized by dark suits and a lean body shape, may reflect the need to compete with men for power and status. On another level, the thin ideal may serve to deflect the focus away from women's reproductive capacity. Fertility and child rearing are considered incompatible with public sphere—that is, work—values, in that they are believed to siphon off energy and presumably efficiency into the family sphere. This may be one reason why as increasing numbers of women entered the work force, they became portrayed as leaner, less curvaceous, and by implication, less fertile.

Social Influences

On the flip side of the "thin is beautiful" cultural coin is the fear of and prejudice against the obese. As Wooley and Wooley (1979) observe: "Excess body fat is probably the most stigmatized physical feature except skin color, but unlike skin color is thought to be under voluntary control" (p. 69). Fear of body fat has been implicated in the development of various weight-related problems, including chronic dieting associated with the relentless pursuit of thinness, obsessive preoccupation with weight, binge eating as a method of weight control, and poor body image. These problems have been noted in persons of all weight categories, among those with relatively good psychosocial adjustment and others with serious eating disorders. Western culture's dislike and disapproval of body fat is more than an aesthetic preference. This antifat bias functions as a social pressure. It is encountered in many facts of American life, from massive food advertising and diet industries, to idealized bodily images in fashion, entertainment, and art, to public norms of attractiveness operating in the workplace, interpersonal relationships, and socializing institutions.

Popular attributions about obese persons help to shape social stereotypes about excess fat. From early childhood, males and females express markedly negative attitudes toward chubby children and overweight adults, characterizing them as lazy, undisciplined, ugly, stupid, mean, nervous, and socially unappealing (Lerner, 1982). Obese adults are believed to be dependent, anxious, depressed, emotionally immature, and to have little self-control, even though no specific abnormality or personality style has in fact been found to be associated with obesity (McReynolds, 1982).

Stigmatization of fat has at least two enduring effects. The first is the victimization of fat persons themselves. Whether or not they eventually accept dominant cultural views about fatness, fat persons suffer differential treatment on account of their physical appearance, with women suffering more than men. Canning and Mayer (1966) present evidence indicating that the constriction of opportunities may begin relatively early in the lives of overweight females. Their study compared obese and nonobese high school seniors in a middle-class community. Although the groups did not differ on measures of intellectual ability, achievement, or number of applications to college, only 32 percent of obese girls went on to college, compared with 52 percent of nonobese girls. In boys, however, weight status was unrelated to college attendance. The second enduring effect is the social prejudice against obesity which is internalized to some extent by the obese persons themselves, resulting in poor self-esteem (Stunkard & Mendelson, 1967).

Yet, controversy persists over whether obese individuals display eating behaviors and activity levels predisposing them toward weight gain. One group of findings, derived largely from nutritional surveys, reveals the food intake of the obese to be the same as or less than that of lean subjects (Garrow, 1974). When small numbers of obese patients are studied on metabolic services, they show greater caloric intake than patients of normal weight (Coll, Meyer, & Stunkard, 1979). However, studies that compare the eating behavior of obese and nonobese individuals in naturalistic settings show no differences between the two groups in their eating rate, eating style, or caloric consumption (Coll et al., 1979; Stunkard, Coll, Lundquist, & Meyers, 1980). Similarly conflicting findings are reported in studies of physical activity, with some studies showing obese adults to be less physically active, and others showing no difference (Stern, 1984). Recent work suggests an explanation for these findings. Body fat is highly heritable, and because of different genetic set points for weight, obese individuals may remain obese without overeating (Stunkard, Sorensen, Hanis, Teasdale, Chakraborty, Schull, & Schulsinger, 1986).

Of particular interest to us is the possibility that women who are not obese or even overweight may perceive themselves to be so and develop a negative body- and self-image.[3] In this scenario, behavioral expressions of poor self-image, such as social withdrawal, may result in differential treatment, even in the absence of overweight status.

Gender and Self-Perceptions of Weight

Subjective perceptions of being overweight and of attractiveness may be more important determinants of weight- and eating-related problems than actual weight. Teenage and adult women consistently report greater concerns with being overweight than do males, although relative to males the prevalence of obesity is often not higher, and in some age groups and social classes may be considerably lower (Stunkard, 1975). Physical attractiveness is more important to women's, as compared to men's, self-evaluations and evaluations by others (Bar-Tal & Saxe, 1976). Studies that ask men and women to rate body parts, using either a semantic differential or ratings of attractiveness, reveal greater awareness of and concern with bodily appearance among women (Kurtz, 1969), as well as greater affective investment in their bodies (Lerner & Brackney, 1978). For women, feelings of bodily attractiveness are associated with a more positive self-concept (Lerner & Karabenick, 1974), whereas men's self-concepts are more closely tied to feelings of physical effectiveness (Lerner, Orlos, & Knapp, 1976). Physical attractiveness is more likely to influence others' judgments of women's intelligence, education, social class, femininity, and desirability as a dating or marriage partner than corresponding judgments of men (Bar-Tal & Saxe, 1976; Striegel-Moore, Silberstein, & Rodin, 1986). Importantly, research with adolescent and adult samples suggests that males, compared with females, are stronger supporters of stereotypes linking attractiveness in women with positive personality attributes (Downs & Abshier, 1982).

The current cultural emphasis on leanness and physical attractiveness in women extends to widely held stereotypes about the gender-appropriateness of dieting behavior. Using a multidimensional measure of femininity and masculinity with college students, Hawkins, Turell, and Jackson (1983) found self-reported dieting tendencies, but not the percentage of excess body weight, were significantly associated with women's judgments of socially desirable attributes such as expressiveness, selflessness, and concern for others. In men, however, dieting was regarded as a socially undesirable "feminine" trait (i.e., emotional vulnerability), despite other feminine traits having been rated as desirable in males.

DEVELOPMENTAL ORIGINS OF WEIGHT CONCERNS

The study of dieting and weight concerns has been limited by the absence of a developmental approach. Cultural beliefs and social influences have been linked to dieting, albeit in an indirect fashion. Yet developmental origins are not well understood, even though the majority of middle-class adolescent girls report having been on a diet. We propose that weight preoccupation, and behavior directed towards thinness, have emerged as a specifically female mode of psychological adaptation to pubertal change.

Cultural Notions of Attractiveness in Children

Origins of the thin ideal. Cultural notions about what is attractive and desirable are learned before children begin school; by middle childhood, children's attributions of physical attractiveness resemble those made by older adolescents (Cavior & Lombardi, 1973; Faust, 1983). Research using Sheldon's (1942) classification of personality–body type relations, in which subjects choose from among silhouettes depicting ectomorphic (thin), mesomorphic (average), and endomorphic (fat) types reveals that children of both sexes and all body builds express strong preferences for athletic or lean body builds, and dislike of chubby or heavy builds (Staffieri, 1967; 1972).

Research has shown that the mesomorphic male and the ectomorphic female most closely approximate socially shared images of masculinity and femininity, respectively (Guy, Rankin, & Norvell, 1980). Importantly, these body build preferences are associated with peer nominations, interpersonal relationships, and prestige among children and adolescents (Lerner, 1982). Indeed, physical attractiveness has been shown to be more influential than race and ethnicity in determining peer preferences and behavioral attributions among female and male children from black, Anglo, and Mexican backgrounds (Langlois & Stephan, 1977).

Harris (cited in Wooley & Wooley, 1984b) studied body build preferences among males and females from four different ethnic and cultural backgrounds, representing a range of ages (preschool through adulthood) and weights. All subjects expressed more negative attitudes toward fat than normal-weight bodies. Interestingly, kindergarten children expressed unfavorable personality stereotypes about fatness, but did not distinguish fat and thin in terms of attractiveness. The concept that body fat is socially undesirable may develop earlier than the concept that fat is unattractive, providing support for the notion that stigmatization of fat is learned (Wooley & Wooley, 1984b).

Proximate socializers. Through child rearing, parents transmit culturally specific, weight-related values to their children. In one study, expectant parents expressed a powerful aversion toward fat children, and indicated that being fat was worse for girls after age 12 than before (Sherman, cited by Wooley & Wooley, 1984b). How such values are transmitted to children has not been studied directly.

Teachers have been found to treat children differently as a function of attractiveness, a principal component of which is weight. Fourth and sixth graders judged by college students to be physically unattractive were subsequently rated by their teachers as less academically able and less well adjusted than those not rated as unattractive (Lerner & Lerner, 1977). These students actually earned lower grades over a two-year period, in comparison with their more attractive classmates. Other adults working with children also display an aversion toward fat children. In several studies of attitudes towards children with different handicaps, diverse samples of adults, including physicians, nurses, physical and occupational therapists, psychologists, and social workers rated obese children as less likeable than children with a variety of handicaps, deformities, and disfigurements (Goodman, Dornbusch, Richardson, & Hasdorf, 1963; Richardson, Goodman, Hasdorf, & Dornbusch, 1961).

Social Influences in Childhood

In children as well as adults, weight concerns and actual weight are influenced by social class, gender, ethnicity, and family of origin. Social class differences in the incidence of obesity and thinness are established by early childhood, and these differences are smaller for males than females (Stunkard, d'Aquili, Fox, & Filion, 1972). Lower-class females are at greatest risk for the development of obesity during the growing years; this trend is already established by age 6. Across social class, thinness in girls reaches a peak around age 12, the age at which most girls experience a rapid gain in body fat as a consequence of the pubertal growth spurt (Warren, 1983). The accumulation of body fat at puberty is not necessarily indicative of obesity (Brooks-Gunn & Warren, 1985a). However, the incidence of obesity does increase during adolescence, especially among lower-class girls (Stunkard et al., 1972). Few adolescent girls of any class achieve thinness (less than 1 to 2 percent are classified as thin by age 15); yet in adults, over one-third of women in the upper classes are thin (Goldblatt, Moore, & Stunkard, 1965). This is a noteworthy finding, given the lack of success usually reported by adolescents and adults who diet.

Ross and Mirowsky (1983) have documented an independent effect of ethnicity on the prevalence of obesity among both men and women. Like Goldblatt et al. (1965), they found a strong inverse relationship between socioeconomic status and overweight in Anglo and Mexican women, with an absence of social class differences in men of both cultures. Controlling for social class differences, Mexican women were heavier than Anglo women, whereas Anglo men were slightly heavier than Mexican men.

The correlations of weight problems with gender and affluence suggest that sociocultural attitudes about thinness and fatness may be intensified within certain social strata or subcultures. In a representative national sample of youths aged 12 to 17, Dornbusch, Carlsmith, Duncan, Gross, Martin, Ritter, and Siegel-Gorelick (1984) found that body preferences of females differ according to social class status. Controlling for differences in actual levels of fatness, girls in higher social classes showed a much greater desire to be thinner than girls from lower social class backgrounds. Among boys, family income bore little relationship to the desire to be thinner. Other studies suggest that adolescent girls in competitive social environments such as boarding schools, colleges, or vocational schools that emphasize weight and appearance may experience intensified social pressures to meet the thin ideal (Striegel-Moore et al., 1986).

It is only within the last decade that the impact of sociocultural pressures to achieve slimness has begun to spread across class and ethnic lines, affecting adolescents whose values and aspirations diverge from the more traditional ones of their parents (Crisp, 1984). For instance, anorexia nervosa, once considered virtually nonexistent among minority women, is occurring with increasing frequency among girls in upwardly mobile Hispanic and black middle-class families (Silber, 1986).

Family of origin also is a major factor predicting obesity and thinness. Parent-child fatness correlations are high, and these correlations increase with the child's age through age 18, after which time they decrease (Garn, 1985). These family resemblances reflect both genetic (Stunkard et al., 1986) and environmental influences (Garn, 1985). With regard to environmental mediators, types of foods offered in the home, amount of food consumed by parents, and symbols associated with food are most likely absorbed by children through repeated experience. Even familial attitudes about exercise and the amount of time devoted to it probably influence the child directly, and contribute to the parent-child obesity correlations. For example, children who watch more television (and presumably are less active) are more likely to be obese; longitudinal research suggests a causal relationship (Dietz, 1985).

Biological Factors

The fat spurt. As girls mature sexually, they accumulate large quantities of fat in subcutaneous tissue, as indicated by increased skinfold thickness (Young, Sipin, & Roe, 1968). For the adolescent girl, this "fat spurt" is one of the most dramatic physical changes associated with puberty, adding an average of 11 kilograms of weight in the form of body fat. Whereas in girls skinfold thicknesses increase with physical maturation, boys retain the same level of body fat throughout the pubertal period (Gross, 1984). Boys, on the other hand, become increasingly muscular, while girls become less so. Pubertal weight gain, then, reflects fatness in girls, and muscularity in boys. While there may be tremendous variation in the timing of pubertal growth, body fat increases in girls begin to occur around the age of 12 (Warren, 1983), when trends toward thinness begin to disappear.

The increase in fat is a normal developmental phenomenon that occurs around the time of menarche. While a critical amount of fat has been thought to be necessary for menarche, current research suggests that fat accumulation is only one of a number of factors associated with menarche (Brooks-Gunn & Warren, 1985a; Garn, 1980). Girls who are relatively lean due to contextual demands for thinness, such as ballet dancers, are likely to have delayed menarche. These delays are not accounted for by genetic predispositions for late puberty, as inferred from mother-daughter similarities in menarcheal age (Brooks-Gunn & Warren, 1986). Exercise and dieting as well as leanness are implicated in the delays seen in ballet dancers (Brooks-Gunn & Warren, 1985a; Warren, 1980). In addition, a rapid and steep loss of weight contributes to amenorrhea; studies of athletes and of patients with anorexia nervosa suggest a reversion to prepubertal patterns of hormonal secretions (Warren, 1983). The point here is that body fat accumulation is part of the biological, developmental process and is necessary for reproduction (Frisch, 1983).

Timing of maturation. In addition to biological changes, the timing of maturation may play a role in the emergence of weight concerns. Girls who mature early are somewhat more likely to be shorter, heavier for their height, and proportionately shorter-legged when compared with their later maturing peers (Faust, 1977). Importantly, the typical early maturing girl is least likely to conform to the lean, long-legged look depicted in the fashion media as the cultural prototype of feminine beauty. Early maturers are more likely than on-time or late maturers to be dissatisfied with their body shape and weight, to have poorer body images, to have more negative feelings about menarche, and to diet (Blyth, Simmons, & Zakin, 1985; Brooks-Gunn & Warren, 1985b; Bush & Simmons, this volume; Duncan, Ritter, Dornbusch, Gross, & Carlsmith, 1985).

Puberty's relation to weight concerns and dieting. From a psychological standpoint, the process of integrating changes in physical appearance, bodily feelings, and reproductive status may require a fundamental re-organization of the adolescent's body image and other self-representations (Blos, 1962). For girls, but not for boys, body image is intimately bound up with subjective perceptions of weight, and especially with girls' satis-faction with weight; pubescent girls who perceive themselves as under-weight are most satisfied, followed by those who think they are simply average (Tobin-Richards, Boxer, & Petersen, 1983).

These normative biological changes occur in a cultural milieu that does not value the mature female body. As a consequence, one might ex-pect girls to become more dissatisfied with their bodies, more concerned about weight, and more likely to diet as puberty progresses. Data from the National Health Examination Survey indicate that as white girls pro-gress through the pubertal cycle, they express increasing desires to be thin-ner; in boys, however, desires to be thinner were unrelated to physical maturation and occurred in the group who were at the highest percentile for fatness (Dornbusch et al., 1984). This study did not examine the rel-ative contribution of different normative influences to the intensification of dieting seen during early adolescence.

One study examined the relationship between dieting and physical maturation indices (breast development, menarcheal status, and matu-rational timing), chronological age, grade in school, and body image (At-tie et al., 1985). Three hundred and eighty-three white girls in grades seven through ten and their mothers completed questionnaires. One-quarter were dance students, the remainder were private school students not involved with athletics. The major results were that, first, dieting be-havior was influenced by social context. Girls who must control their weight because of professional demands, as in this case dancers had to do, were much more likely to diet than those who do not have such restric-tions, in this case academic students.

Second, dieting increased over the middle adolescent years. As ex-pected, these increases were related to advances in maturational status, specifically menarche and breast development, as well as to timing of mat-uration. Third, dieting behavior was seen not only in girls who were overweight, but in girls who were of normal weight. Thus, dieting in-creased with physical maturation and weight gain, even in girls whose weight was well within the normal range.

Fourth, dancers' dieting behavior was less influenced by physical maturation than was the academic students' behavior, even though breast development and maturational timing did play a role. Part of the reason for the sample differences may be the fact that most dancers maintain low weights during their pubertal development and that most dancers engage in dieting behavior. Finally, body image was more predictive of dieting than maturational status or weight, suggesting that it may mediate the maturation-dieting relationship.

Taken together, these findings suggest that dieting emerges as the body develops and that dieting is not the sole province of girls who are overweight or girls for whom dieting is necessary for professional reasons. The ideal of thinness and the emphasis on the prepubertal "look" (Faust, 1983) are believed to contribute to the increase in dieting behavior at the time of puberty.[4] Because of their desire for conformity and their search for guidelines about how to behave, young adolescents may be particularly susceptible to popular media stereotypes, especially those values and ideals presented by entertainment and fashion industries as vital elements of the "youth culture" (Hamburg, 1980).

Physical and Social Changes Occurring During Early Adolescence

Importantly, for most girls, significant pubertal changes are timed with entry into junior high school. The modal girl reaches the peak of pubertal development in the seventh grade, while the modal boy does so one and one-half to two years later, in the ninth grade (Hill & Lynch, 1983). The work of Simmons and her colleagues (Bush & Simmons, this volume; Simmons, Blyth, & McKinney, 1983; Simmons, Blyth, Van Cleave, & Bush, 1979) reveals that the transition to seventh grade—with the move to a new, impersonal school environment, social pressures to date, and increased achievement demands—is more disruptive, and potentially detrimental to girls' (as compared with boys') self-image and self-esteem. Feelings of uncertainty and sometimes of helplessness with regard to bodily changes, combined with the ambiguity of social demands, appear to heighten feelings of self-consciousness among adolescent girls, driving them towards peer conformity. In contrast to boys, who may welcome the development of their body strength and effectiveness, girls have less clear guidelines for evaluating their individual figure development; at the same time, they are more concerned than their male peers with popularity and looks (Simmons et al., 1979). Taken together, the accumulated evidence suggests that the convergence of novel physical, social, and psychological events during early adolescence may be experienced and dealt with in gender-differentiated ways (Hill & Lynch, 1983).

Family relationships. Developmental and clinical studies have shown that family factors also mediate the adolescent's subjective experience of bodily change (Petersen & Taylor, 1980), as well as their "choice" of behavioral styles of coping, such as compulsive eating or exercise (Yates, Leehey, & Shisslak, 1983). The mother-daughter relationship is considered central to the development of a girl's body image and eating attitudes; less is known about the impact of fathers in this regard. Mothers are believed to influence their adolescent daughters in several days. A mother's comfort with her own body and sexuality, as well as her satisfaction with her role in the family and society, is likely to affect the mother-daughter interaction, and hence the psychological development of her child. In addition, weight obsession and bodily concerns may serve as the battleground for playing out the adolescent's inner struggle to separate from her mother and to "leave home" psychologically. Further, in this period of marked changes in social thought, ideology, and mores concerning women's roles, adolescent girls may receive from the larger society contradictory messages about what it means to be a woman. The resulting stress and confusion—about their identity, their femininity, and their future roles—may be expressed in efforts to control their body shape and weight. While research pertaining to these perspectives is scarce, some representative studies are discussed below.

Woody and Costanzo (1981) interviewed parents of obese and non-obese children and adolescents, finding that parents perceived and treated their obese sons and obese daughters quite differently. Being overweight was seen by parents to be due to overeating by their daughters, but not by their sons. In daughters, overweight and overeating were associated, according to parental reports, with the child's affective responsiveness (positive and negative), emotionality, externality, peer rejection, and parental control of food. None of these relationships was found for boys. These authors speculate that parents take a more active role in altering their daughters' eating behavior, which they view as both problematic and as more susceptible to external influences. One reason for parental efforts to control girls' eating may be their awareness that the psychological and social consequences of being overweight are greater for girls than for boys. The role of such awareness and of other family contextual factors in the development of maladaptive eating patterns deserves further study.

Mothers' feelings about their own bodies may influence their daughters' developing body images and self-concepts. Mothers, like their daughters, experience social pressures to meet the thin, fashionable ideal. Indeed, given their age, mothers' bodies are less likely to fit prevailing cultural aesthetics. Mothers' insecurity about their bodies, as well as conflict around eating may be communicated to their daughters and internalized by them. We have little direct evidence for either the premise that mothers have poor body images, or that their attitudes influence their daughters, either in normal weight or obese children. Young women believe, however, that their mothers dislike their own bodies. In the *Glamour* magazine survey, only 13 percent of the 33,000 readers thought their mothers were satisfied with their bodies. Moreover, in preliminary analyses of our longitudinal study of girls in middle to late adolescence, mothers' self-reported eating attitudes and behavior were related to their daughters' self-reported dieting (Attie, 1987).

Daughters' perceptions of their mothers may turn out to be as influential as actual maternal dieting behavior. Further, the issue may not be how the mother feels about her own body, but how she feels about her daughter's development. At conscious and unconscious levels, mothers transmit cultural ideals and contradictions about notions of gender and femininity (Orbach, 1986). Accordingly, a mother may fail to affirm her daughter's emerging sexual development. Instead, she may convey a deeper sense of physical and social limits—in the way she monitors her daughter's appetite or her changing body shape. In a survey of bulimic behavior in college women, the belief that the mother was critical of the daughter's body was the second strongest predictor of body dissatisfaction and bulimic symptom scores (Debs, Wooley, Harkness-King, & Wooley, 1983, cited in Wooley & Wooley, 1985).

Another perspective on the development of dieting and body image disturbances focuses on the reawakening of separation-individuation issues during adolescence with its developmental demands for identity formation and greater autonomy. Commenting on the mother-daughter relationship during this period, Wooley and Wooley (1985) propose that "dieting may serve simultaneously as identification, differentiation, revenge, and penance" (p. 392). Clinical studies of adolescents with anorexia nervosa suggest that their mothers frequently are unable to tolerate their daughter's efforts to separate and may impede this process through their overinvolvement and intrusiveness. For instance, mothers of anorectic girls have been shown to interfere with their daughters' attempts to establish peer relationships (Lambley, 1983). In the case of anorexia nervosa, the body may become the only arena in which the adolescent girl believes she has control (Bruch, 1973). In our study of normal weight girls, as opposed to girls with eating disorders, low scores on family cohesion, expressiveness, and organization, as reported by mothers, were related to dieting among adolescent daughters (Attie, 1987). These data lend support to the hypothesized role of mothers' perceptions in the development of eating problems, and extend the findings to nonclinical samples who engage in dieting behavior but do not have an eating disorder.

Finally, we know relatively little about how fathers influence their daughters' eating behavior, although recently, the father's role has received greater attention in family interaction studies of patients with eating disorders (Kog, Vandereycken, & Vertommen, 1985). Few studies have addressed the possible impact of paternal attitudes about weight or the father-daughter relationship in the development of eating problems among adolescent girls.

CONSEQUENCES OF WEIGHT-RELATED CONCERNS

The major consequences of weight-related concerns are attempts to alter behavior, most typically in the context of a diet or exercise program. For many women, what begins as a voluntary and seemingly rewarding effort to control weight, that is, the weight loss diet, results in repeated cycles of undereating and overeating, weight fluctuations, and emotional distress.

Dieting

Prevalence. The most pervasive consequence of weight-related concerns is the decision to go on a diet. Dieting (or talking about it) has become a national pastime for women, possibly akin to sports for men (Garner et al., 1985). The dieting industry is big business; no issue of a women's magazine is without an article on dieting tips, and the number of dieting-related articles increased 70 percent from the early 1960s to the late 1970s (Garner & Garfinkel, 1980). Almost all of this media attention is paid to women, even though just as many men as women are obese. And, as noted earlier, one-half to three-quarters of white adolescent girls and adult women report having gone on a diet (Attie et al , 1985; Miller, Coffman & Linke, 1980; Nylander, 1971).

Effects of chronic dieting. Little research has addressed the effects of prolonged caloric restriction in nonclinical samples. A noteworthy exception is the classic study by Keys and his colleagues at the University of Minnesota (Keys, Brozek, Henschel, Mickelsen, & Taylor, 1950), in which 36 male conscientious objectors were placed on an extended semistarvation diet and the psychological, behavioral, and physical effects were carefully documented. Subjects were young, healthy men, who showed high levels of ego strength, emotional stability, and good intellectual ability on several psychological measures obtained early in the study. Following three months of normal eating and activity, the men began a six-month period of semistarvation, in which their food intake was reduced by half—a typical weight reduction technique for women. The experiment concluded with a three-month period of rehabilitation and refeeding.

After losing approximately 25 percent of their original body weight, pervasive effects of semistarvation were seen. First, the men became increasingly preoccupied with food and eating, to the extent that they ruminated obsessively about meals and food, collected recipes and cookbooks, and showed abnormal food rituals, such as excessively slow eating and hoarding of food-related objects. Second, the majority of men suffered some form of emotional disturbance as a result of semistarvation, including depression, hypochondriasis, hysteria, angry outbursts, and in some cases, psychotic levels of disorganization. Symptomatology, as measured by personality tests, was not related to pre-starvation psychological adjustment, and did not always reverse itself during the rehabilitation phase. Third, the men lost their ability to function effectively in work and social contexts, due to apathy, reduced energy and alertness, social isolation, and decreased sexual interest. Fourth, within weeks of reducing their food intake, the men reported relentless hunger, as well as powerful urges to break dietary rules. Some succumbed to eating binges, followed by vomiting and feelings of self-reproach. Ravenous hunger persisted, even following large meals consumed during refeeding; some men found themselves eating continuously, while others engaged in uncontrollable cycles of gorging and vomiting. Other physical symptoms included headaches, gastrointestinal distress, sleepiness, hair loss, as well as physiological changes indicative of the body's attempt to conserve energy (i.e., reduced body temperature, reduced heart and respiratory rate, and decreased basal metabolic rate).

As this study powerfully illustrates, severe and chronic dietary restriction not only disrupts and disturbs regular eating patterns, it also engenders profound psychological, social, and physical changes. Indeed, what were once considered distinctive features of the "obese personality," that is, passivity, anxiety, emotionality, are now recognized as possible sequelae to prolonged and periodic caloric restriction (Polivy & Herman, 1983). The results of this study are thought provoking, given the striking similarities between the disturbed behavior of these experimental subjects and that seen in eating disordered patients who starve themselves. These effects are thought to be related to the body's attempt to defend its preferred body weight in the face of powerful efforts to override this weight (i.e., through starvation). As others have pointed out, much of the behavior thought to cause anorexia nervosa and bulimia may actually be a consequence of starvation (cf., Garner et al., 1985; Wooley & Wooley, 1985). As we elaborate in the following discussion, the normal weight dieter who diets to look or feel better also is vulnerable to disturbed emotional, cognitive, and behavioral patterns by virtue of the constant stress of trying to stay below the body's "natural" or biologically regulated weight (Polivy & Herman, 1983).

Dieting as a chronic stressor. Paradoxically, efforts to lose weight are notoriously ineffective. The large body of research exploring the psychological determinants of eating has led to revisions in theories about weight regulation. The first theories were proposed to explain overeating in the obese. Based upon their research with obese subjects, Schacter and his colleagues (Schachter & Rodin, 1974) proposed the "externality" theory of obesity to explain the behavioral characteristics of "obese eating." Briefly stated, they hypothesized that (1) the eating behavior of obese persons is less responsive to internal physiological states of hunger and satiety than that of normal weight individuals; and (2) the eating behavior of obese individuals is more influenced by salient external cues, such as the smell, sight, and taste of food, time of day, and so on. Schacter extended his theory of environmentally regulated eating in the obese to explain a more pervasive "external" personality style; in short, he proposed that obese individuals are more responsive to any salient stimulus, whether food-related or not. It would follow then, that a person exhibiting such a trait of externality would be likely to eat in an externally induced fashion which in turn would lead to overeating, and eventually to obesity (Rodin & Slochower, 1976).

In an important departure from trait-like theories of externality, Nisbett (1972) theorized that the inclination of overweight people to overeat in response to external cues was really a consequence of their chronic dieting. According to Nisbett's "setpoint" theory, each person has a biologically programmed optimum weight which is regulated by that person's individual setpoint or level of fat storage. Although a person's setpoint is complexly determined by multiple factors, genetic endowment and early feeding experiences may be significant (Coates & Thoresen, 1978).

The notion that body fat is regulated by homeostatic, biological processes has had far-reaching implications for the understanding of weight regulation in both obese and nonobese individuals. Obese persons, under substantial pressure from medical and cultural prescriptions to reduce their weight, may actually be starving themselves by suppressing their weights below their bodies' physiological demands. Theoretically, anyone who, regardless of his or her weight, remains below setpoint as a result of chronic dieting would be susceptible to "external" and other nonphysiological pressures to eat. Being on a diet then, by creating constant hunger and discomfort, renders internal cues virtually useless as a reasonable guide to eating (Wardle & Beinart, 1981).

Attempting to test Nisbett's theory with nonobese persons, Herman and Mack (1975) designed an instrument to distinguish restrained eaters, who are chronically concerned with dieting, from unrestrained eaters, who give little thought to the food they eat. These authors hypothesized that if the chronic restraints of the dieter were experimentally overcome, they would exhibit the externality previously attributed to the condition of obesity. Their predictions were confirmed. Dividing their sample of normal weight and obese college females into restrained and unrestrained eaters, they found that unrestrained eaters conformed to what would be expected from common sense: With increasing amounts of forced preload (ice cream), subjects ate less in a subsequent ad lib (free) consumption period, masked as a taste test. Conversely, restrained eaters tended to overeat following increasing amounts of forced preload. The authors termed this effect "counterregulation."

Extending the restraint paradigm, Polivy (1976) compared the relative influence of cognitive and physiological factors on counterregulatory behavior. Reasoning that restraint must be cognitively mediated, in that one consciously decides to restrict food intake, Polivy manipulated subjects' beliefs about the caloric values of the preloads they had eaten. Although her findings were based on a post hoc regrouping (according to subjects' perceptions about caloric intake), the belief that they had overeaten was sufficient to trigger counterregulatory eating in highly restrained eaters. Likening the dieter's seemingly uncontrolled eating to a naturally occurring eating binge, Polivy (1976) concluded that an eating binge may be triggered by potent cognitions—such as the dieter's perception that the rules had already been broken. Subsequent research has replicated Polivy's (1976) findings with samples of obese and normal weight individuals (Spencer & Fremouw, 1979; Woody, Costanzo, Liefer, & Conger, 1981), supporting the notion that counterregulatory eating and other externally cued responses have a strong cognitive basis.

In a recently proposed theoretical model, Herman and Polivy (1984) term the psychological state of the restrained eater the "what-the-hell-effect" to "capture the dieter's subjective state of caloric abandon" (p. 151). These authors view the regulation of food consumption as taking place within a set of boundaries, rather than about a single point (or setpoint). Integrating physiological and nonphysiological notions into their "field theory" of eating behavior, Herman and Polivy (1984) describe a "range of biological indifference" between the aversive physiological zones of hunger and satiety. When the individual is neither famished nor stuffed, that is, is operating within this zone of biological indifference, psychological and social pressures may override biological factors to control eating behavior. It is within this zone that the chronic dieter constructs his or her "diet boundary," rendering the satiety boundary inadequate as a brake on food consumption. Just as adherence to a diet regimen is cognitively controlled (often in terms of daily "quotas" imposed on food intake), so too the mere belief that one has transgressed one's diet is enough to break the dieter's resolve and trigger counterregulatory consumption. Other psychodynamic factors, such as anxiety, depression, and the belief that alcohol has been consumed, have been shown to disinhibit the restrained eater, leading to greater ad lib consumption (Herman & Polivy, 1975; Polivy & Herman, 1976a, 1976b). The nondieter, unconstrained by any diet boundary (and therefore more responsive to physiologic pressures), responds to affective discomfort and other stressful experiences by decreasing food consumption (Herman & Polivy, 1984).

The work of Herman and Polivy permits an attempt to integrate clinical and laboratory research on eating and its disturbances. Chronic restrained eating is a salient feature of eating among "weight-preoccupied" college students (Hawkins & Clement, 1980), obese individuals (Wooley & Wooley, 1979), patients with anorexia nervosa (Garner et al., 1985), and normal weight patients with bulimia (Mitchell & Pyle, 1981). As would be expected from counterregulatory studies, binge eating patterns are prevalent in substantial proportions of each of these groups of dieters. Accordingly, dieting, not weight status, may account for eating- and weight-related problems in large segments of the population. As stated earlier, attempts to lose weight characterize most dieters, not actual weight loss. Indeed, in our large sample of adolescent girls aged 12 to 16 years, dieting and bulimia scores were positively, not negatively, related to actual weight (Brooks-Gunn & Warren, 1985a).

Importantly, persistent (and often failed) weight loss efforts, counterregulatory behavior, and large weight fluctuations set the stage for disturbance of body image among chronic restrained eaters. Before the culture of mass dieting, women may have developed relatively cohesive and continuous experiences of their bodies, of course, with expectable periods of marked change at puberty and during pregnancy (Wooley & Wooley, 1985). However, in the current cultural climate, women reach adulthood having experienced many body-selves as a result of repeated efforts to modify their bodies to meet prepubertal ideals.

The dieter's dilemma, then, is that he or she relies on perceptual-cognitive signals (e.g., feeling fat, numbers on the scale, "I broke my diet") and affective signals (e.g., anxiety, depression), as opposed to hunger and satiety to guide eating. Recurrent attempts to push the body below its natural weight result in cycles of uncontrollable (counterregulatory) overeating, followed by renewed efforts to gain control through undereating. In this way, dieting becomes a chronic stressor that is self-perpetuating. Concomitant affective states, namely heightened emotionality, increased distractibility, and persistent preoccupation with food, only intensify the stressful experience (Polivy & Herman, 1983).

Increase in Exercise

A possible consequence of weight-related concerns is the fitness movement. More and more women have turned to the road, the pool, and the gym to achieve a pared-down body. However, women's exercise is undertaken primarily in the service of weight control, not physical competence. Over

95 percent of readers surveyed in *Glamour* magazine used exercise in this fashion. With the exception of weight training, in contrast, men's workouts typically are not undertaken primarily for the purpose of achieving a particular body shape.

While exercise has been shown to have laudatory effects, such as increased cardiovascular efficiency and alteration of the body's setpoint, exercise may become an obsession for some. As many as one-third of all cases of anorexia nervosa may be associated with athletic endeavors (Crisp, Hsu, Harding, & Hartshorn, 1980).

Anorexia Nervosa and Bulimia

Perhaps the most alarming outcome associated with the pursuit of thinness through dieting is the rising incidence of weight-related clinical syndromes among adolescent and young adult females (Garner et al., 1985). Anorexia nervosa is an eating disorder characterized by behavior directed toward weight loss, by peculiar attitudes toward food, body image disturbance, and by an implacable refusal to maintain body weight. Occurring predominantly in females (90 to 95 percent), it is one of the few psychiatric disorders that can have an unremitting course resulting in death (Halmi, 1980). Bulimia is an eating disturbance characterized by episodes of uncontrollable overeating, usually followed by vomiting, exercise, or laxative abuse to prevent food absorption. In persons exhibiting this abnormal eating pattern, body weight usually fluctuates within 15 percent of normal weight (American Psychiatric Association, 1980). Like anorexia nervosa, bulimia occurs frequently in weight-preoccupied adolescent and adult women.

Accumulated evidence from clinical studies suggests that some form of binge eating occurs in varying proportions of normal weight, underweight, and obese populations (Wardle & Beinart, 1981). Certain characteristic features of an eating "binge," such as an alternating pattern of dietary restriction and overindulgence in food, are similar across all weight groups. Other features, namely, vomiting and purging, are more common among psychiatric patients with anorexia nervosa and bulimia; they are less frequently mentioned in the literature on obesity. Accordingly, researchers have begun to distinguish "binge eating," which refers to episodes of uncontrollable and excessive eating, from the syndrome of "bulimia," which, in addition to current eating binges, also includes vomiting, as well as a "morbid fear of fatness" (Cooper & Fairburn, 1983). In addition, the relatively recent discovery of bulimic eating patterns among high proportions of anorectic patients (ranging from 30 to 50 percent) has raised the issue of heterogeneity within this diagnostic category (Casper, Eckert, Halmi, Goldberg, & Davis, 1980; Garfinkel, Moldofsky, & Garner, 1980). In an effort to resolve the current controversy over the role of bulimia in this presumed "self-starvation" syndrome, a growing body of research has been focused on the documentation of bulimic (i.e., those with episodes of binging) and restricter (i.e., those who continuously restrict food intake) subtypes of anorexia nervosa, with distinct premorbid, clinical, and prognostic features (Strober, 1981; Strober, Salkin, Burroughs, & Morrell, 1982).

Although good epidemiological data are rare and the possibility of bias exists from referral or exposure factors, available evidence suggests that both anorexia and bulimia have been on the rise over recent decades (Lucas, Beard, Kranz, & Kurland, 1983). While the modal age of onset occurs during adolescence, the risk for developing an eating disorder extends well into adulthood (Pope, Hudson, Yorgelun-Todd, & Hudson, 1984). Some studies suggest that increasing socioeconomic status confers increased vulnerability to the development of eating disorders, independent of race or ethnic background (Andersen & Hay, 1985; Lacey, 1982).[5] In a survey of nine girls' schools in England, the prevalence of anorexia nervosa was 1 in every 200 girls under the age of 16, and 1 in every 100 girls over age 16 (Crisp, Palmer, & Kalucy, 1976). Among groups under vocational pressure to control body weight, such as ballet dancers, the incidence increases severalfold, with estimates ranging from 5 to 7 percent of adolescent and 30 percent in adult dancers (Garner & Garfinkel, 1980; Hamilton, Brooks-Gunn, & Warren, 1986). While bulimia is a less well understood disorder at present, recent prevalence estimates range from around 2 percent in a community based sample (Cooper & Fairburn, 1983) to around 4 or 5 percent in university samples (Katzman, Wolchik, & Braver, 1984; Pyle, Mitchell, Eckert, Halvorson, Neuman, & Goff, 1983). Recent studies show the prevalence of bulimia in high school students to be as high as 5 percent (Crowther, Post, & Zaynor, 1985).

A perplexing, almost perverse concomitant of the rise in clinical eating disorders is the media's portrayal of these life-threatening disorders as glamorous and exciting. Anorexia nervosa is clothed in an aura of goodness associated with self-control, high social standing, independence, and perfectionism (Garner et al., 1983). An increase in the number of women with anorexia nervosa may be a case of social contagion ("me too") and a blurring of the distinction between desiring to be thin and becoming anorectic (Bruch, 1985). While the virtual "discovery" of bulimia in the last decade reflects complex factors including increased exposure, one finds recurrent reports of bulimic patients having been "taught" to vomit by a friend, or having begun to self-induce vomiting after reading about it in the media (Chiodo & Latimer, 1983; Thompson & Schwartz, 1982). In her social history of anorexia nervosa, Brumberg (1985) considers that "what we may be facing is a transformation peculiar to mass culture: the shift of a predominantly psychosomatic disorder into the category of a communicable disease" (p. 95).

The increase in anorexia nervosa in contemporary American culture has raised the question of continuity—between weight obsession and dieting on the one hand, and clinical syndromes of anorexia nervosa and bulimia on the other. Some authors regard anorexia nervosa as a qualitatively distinct syndrome, while others believe that it defines one end of a continuum or spectrum of weight-related concerns. In support of the former view, Garner et al. (1983) found that patients with anorexia nervosa could be distinguished from extremely "weight-preoccupied" women drawn from college and ballet students, not in terms of eating pathology and starvation symptoms, but according to the severity of underlying psychopathology, which was much greater in the anorectic group.

Other investigators believe that chronic, restrained eating may constitute a cumulative stress of such magnitude that dieting in itself may be "a sufficient condition for the development of anorexia nervosa or bulimia" (Wooley & Wooley, 1985, p. 393). According to this perspective, dieting becomes an addiction, maintained by (1) feelings of euphoria associated with successful weight loss, requiring further caloric restriction to maintain the pleasurable, tension-relieving effects; (2) physiologic changes by which the body adapts to food deprivation; and (3) the threat of "withdrawal" symptoms associated with food consumption, including rapid weight gain, physical discomfort, and dysphoria. Furthermore, many women, unable to master the art of starvation, find vomiting and laxative abuse a more effective method of weight control, and thus become bulimic (Wooley & Wooley, 1985). Szmukler and Tantam (1984) have proposed that "starvation dependence," that is, a physiological and psychological "dependence-induced drive to self-starvation" (p. 306), underlies the development of both anorexia nervosa and bulimia.

One question which is particularly germane to the current controversy regarding continuity in eating pathology is whether stressful life events might potentiate the development of an eating disorder in women who are already vulnerable by virtue of the stress of chronic dieting. While research has not addressed this question directly, Strober (1984) has studied the relationship between stressful life events and the occurrence of bulimia in young patients with anorexia nervosa. He found that bulimic anorectics reported nearly twice as many life change events as restrictor anorectics over the 18-month period preceding illness onset, and that these events were more likely to be uncontrollable and undesirable. Whereas for the restricter group, life event changes peaked in the six months prior to onset of illness, bulimic anorectics reported a relatively constant level of stressful events over the 18 months. Strober (1984) advances several speculations to explain these findings. Recognizing the difficulty of extrapolating from animal studies, he notes certain parallels between stress-induced food consumption in animals and the peculiar eating behavior of bulimic (anorectic) individuals. These include a selective preference for highly palatable foods, drivenness and stereotypic behavior in food ingestion, irritability, and heightened arousal levels preceding and during binge episodes. From the perspective of counterregulatory theory, Strober also considers that the chronically stressed bulimic subgroup may be especially susceptible to the disinhibiting effects of aversive life events that occur in the context of stringent dieting and symptoms of self-starvation.

Somewhat paradoxically, the revival of feminist ideology and the radical structural changes in women's lives in the last 20 years have been paralleled by Western culture's reification of the thin ideal as an embodiment of feminine beauty and success. Rather than dismiss this ideal as unattainable, stereotypic, or constraining, society continues to judge women by their adherence to a fairly rigid standard. Indeed, we believe that the current emphasis on thinness for women, and the adherence of so many to the ideal, is an expression of contradiction between the rapidly changing roles for women, and the continuity of traditional self-definition embedded in cultural institutions, and recreated within the family.

The ideal emerged in a period when the weight of American young women increased, the Metropolitan Life Insurance tables were adjusted upwards, and age-related increases in weight were recognized as normal and perhaps sound medically. As a consequence, more and more women do not fit the slender ideal. The paradox—that ideals became lighter and women became heavier—may be understood in part by examining changes in women's roles. The female ideal has become associated with a prepubertal, linear body rather than a postpubertal or rounded body shape. This state of affairs may be linked to the fact that culturally and historically, female attributes and femininity have been considered incompatible with competence, autonomy, or instrumental behavior, by men and women (Broverman, Vogel, Broverman, Clarkson, & Rosenkrantz, 1972). If the female body is perceived as a social marker, then its presence in situations and places requiring instrumental behavior is contradictory. The woman is placed in a double bind, then, as soon as she is in a situation requiring "masculine" behaviors or, more generally, in public as opposed to domestic sphere activities. Unger (1985) presents several contextual examples of the double bind in women's lives which we believe are applicable to an understanding of women's conflicts about their bodies.

First, "an individual is present in a situation in which her femaleness [in this case, her body] is defined as contradictory to other characteristics considered appropriate for that time or place" [in this case, the public sphere] (Unger, 1985, p. 5). As discussed earlier, women's entry into the work force in unprecedented numbers may have contributed to increased pressures to attain thinness, since the female body is perceived as orthogonal to public sphere characteristics such as competence, effectiveness, and competition. Second, a woman's "out-of-place" quality may be marked linguistically, as illustrated by the practice of referring to a woman's body or parts thereof, in public sphere situations. Such references undermine perceptions of a woman as competent, no matter how much they are couched in complimentary terms. Third, a woman becomes a social stimulus because of her female body, even in situations where her presence is "legitimate." While her biological capacity may be irrelevant to her in public sphere situations, it sometimes is seen as salient by others. Finally, the female body may be valued in the private sphere (i.e., in terms of childbearing) but not in the public sphere.

If the female body is a potent social stimulus considered inappropriate in certain sectors of public life (i.e., male spheres), then the rise of the thin ideal it not surprising. Female contours, particularly those associated with the normal accumulations of body fat that occur at puberty, are devalued. The paradox arises when one considers the fact that most women will not be able to conform to the prepubertal ideal and that rather than freeing women from outmoded strictures about desirable body shapes, we have traded one set of constraints for another.

NOTES

1. For example, sociocultural factors have been hypothesized by Garner et al. (1985) and Wooley and Wooley (1985) to influence the incidence of clinical eating disorders. These previous reviews, while taking a similar approach to ours, do not discuss the proximate links between such influences and subsequent disorders. While most cases of anorexia nervosa begin in the context of a diet (sometimes coupled with an exercise regimen), the social and cultural context is more likely to affect a woman's perception of being too heavy and her decision to go on a diet, rather than her development of anorexia nervosa per se. For example, the majority of females in the middle class today have been on diets and wish to weigh less than the ideal for their age and height. However, only a small fraction have a clinical eating disorder. Thus, sociocultural factors influence the development of eating disorders indirectly, via idealized images of attractiveness, body shape, and femininity. More proximate factors have not been studied prospectively in any systematic fashion.

2. Much less has been written about the possible cultural influences on the male's body concept or self-image, in all likelihood because stereotypes about the ideal body are much less rigid for men. Importantly, men's bodies have not been idealized and transformed by media and fashion to the same extent as have women's bodies. Bennett and Gurin (1982) also make an astute observation: "Body fat has played a small role in the masculine image. Most of what we know about the ideals of the past has been filtered to us through the vision of

male artists. What men admire in the bodies of other men has been a muscularity that ranges from slight and lithe to brutish—but that almost always conveys potential for movement and action, whether erotic or competitive" (p. 170).

3. Even the standards are not sacrosanct: The fact that Americans are steadily gaining weight has led to a revision upwards of the original standards. According to the 1959 Metropolitan Life Insurance Company Tables, at least one-half of Americans are overweight, whereas the revised statistics (Society of Actuaries, 1979, pp. 45–69) place one-third of Americans above standard. In most studies, obesity is defined at the 85th percentile of fatness, and leanness is defined at the 15th percentile cutoff (Garn, 1985).

4. It is important to remember that eating patterns may influence the timing and course of puberty itself. Delayed puberty, as well as a high incidence of menstrual disturbances (amenorrhea, irregular cycles), occurs frequently in girls who are involved in athletics and those under vocational pressure to maintain low body weight (Frisch, 1983; Warren, 1983). In a four-year longitudinal study of ballet dancers, Warren (1980) found the mean age of menarche to be 15.4 years, which was significantly older than age-matched controls, whose mean age of menarche (12.5 years) was similar to the average age in the United States (12.8 years). The ballet dancers also displayed a significant asynchrony in the progression of pubertal growth, with breast development and menarche remarkably delayed, while pubic hair development was unaffected. These differences are hypothesized to be a consequence of the fact that breast development and menarche are estrogen-dependent, while pubic hair development is androgen-dependent. In a series of studies, the later age of menarche for dancers was related to leanness, exercise, and dieting (Brooks-Gunn, Warren, & Hamilton, 1986; Hamilton, Brooks-Gunn, & Warren, 1985, 1986).

5. Some investigators have considered the possibility of a genetic vulnerability to develop an eating disorder. For instance, twin studies reveal that 44 to 50 percent of monozygotic twins are concordant for anorexia nervosa. Regrettably, comparable series of dizygotic twins are not available. In a recent review of this literature, Scott (1986) argues for further research to elucidate a possible diathesis-stress (genotype-environment) model of eating disorders.

REFERENCES

American Psychiatric Association. (1980). *Diagnostic and statistical manual of mental disorders* (3rd ed.). Washington, DC: American Psychiatric Association.

Andersen, A. E., & Hay, A. (1985). Racial and socioeconomic influences in anorexia nervosa and bulimia. *International Journal of Eating Disorders, 4,* 479–488.

Attie, I. (1987). *Development of eating problems in adolescence: A follow-up of girls at risk.* Unpublished doctoral thesis, Catholic University.

Attie, I., Brooks-Gunn, J., & Warren, M. P. (1985). *Developmental antecedents of restrained eating: The impact of pubertal change.* Paper presented at the Biennial Meeting of the Society for Research in Child Development, Toronto.

Bar-Tal, D., & Saxe, L. (1976). Physical attractiveness and its relationship to sex-role stereotyping. *Sex Roles, 2,* 123–133.

Bem, S. D., & Bem, D. J. (1970). Case study of a nonconscious ideology: Training the woman to know her place. In D. J. Bem (Ed.), *Beliefs, attitudes, and human affairs.* Belmont, CA: Brooks/Cole.

Bennett, W., & Gurin, J. (1982). *The dieter's dilemma: Eating less and weighing more.* New York: Basic Books.

Blos, P. (1962). *On adolescence.* New York: Free Press.

Blyth, D. A., Simmons, R. G., & Zakin, D. F. (1985). Satisfaction with body image for early adolescent females: The impact of pubertal timing within different school environments. *Journal of Youth and Adolescence, 14,* 207–225.

Brooks-Gunn, J. (1986). Pubertal processes and girls' psychological adaptation. In R. Lerner & T. T. Foch (Eds.), *Biological-psychosocial interactions in early adolescence: A life-span perspective.* Hillsdale, NJ: Lawrence Erlbaum.

Brooks-Gunn, J., & Warren, M. P. (1985a). Measuring physical status and timing in early adolescence: A developmental perspective. *Journal of Youth and Adolescence, 14,* 163–189.

———. (1985b). The effects of delayed menarche in different contexts: Dance and nondance students. *Journal of Youth and Adolescence, 14,* 285–300.

———. (1986). Genetic and environmental contributions to delayed puberty. Unpublished manuscript.

Brooks-Gunn, J., Warren, M. P., & Hamilton, L. H. (1986). The relationship of eating disorders to amenorrhea in ballet dancers. Unpublished manuscript.

Broverman, I. K., Vogel, S. R., Broverman, D. M., Clarkson, F. E., & Rosenkrantz, P. S. (1972). Sex-role stereotypes: A current appraisal. *Journal of Social Issues, 28,* 59–78.

Bruch, H. (1973). *Eating disorders.* New York: Basic Books.

———. (1978). *The golden cage.* Cambridge: Harvard University Press.

———. (1985). Four decades of eating disorders. In D. M. Garner & P. E. Garfinkel (Eds.), *Handbook of psychotherapy for anorexia nervosa and bulimia.* New York: Guilford Press.

Brumberg, J. J. (1985). "Fasting girls": Reflections on writing the history of anorexia nervosa. In A. B. Smuts & J. W. Hagen (Eds.), History and research in child development. *Monographs of the Society for Research in Child Development, 50* (4–5, Serial No. 211).

Canning, H., & Mayer, J. (1966). Obesity—Its possible effect on college acceptance. *New England Journal of Medicine, 275,* 1172–1174.

Casper, R. C., Eckert, E. D., Halmi, K. A., Goldberg, S. C., & Davis, J. M. (1980). Bulimia: Its incidence and clinical importance in patients with anorexia nervosa. *Archives of General Psychiatry, 37,* 1030–1035.

Cavior, N., & Lombardi, D. A. (1973). Developmental aspects of judgment of physical attractiveness in children. *Developmental Psychology, 8,* 67–71.

Chiodo, J., & Latimer, P. R. (1983). Vomiting as a learned weight-control technique in bulimia. *Journal of Behavior Therapy and Experimental Psychiatry, 14,* 131–135.

Coates, T. J., & Thoresen, C. E. (1978). Treating obesity in children and adolescents: A review. *American Journal of Public Health, 68,* 144–151.

Coll, M., Meyer, A., & Stunkard, A. J. (1979). Obesity and food choices in public places. *Archives of General Psychiatry, 36,* 795–797.

Cooper, P. J., & Fairburn, C. G. (1983). Binge-eating and self-induced vomiting in the community: A preliminary study. *British Journal of Psychiatry, 142,* 139–144.

Cott, N. F. (1979). Passionlessness: An interpretation of Victorian sexual ideology, 1790–1850. In N. F. Cott & E. H. Pleck (Eds.), *A heritage of her own: Toward a new social history of American women.* New York: Simon & Schuster.

Crisp, A. H. (1984). The psychopathology of anorexia nervosa: Getting the "heat" out of the system. In A. J. Stunkard & E. Stellar (Eds.), *Eating and its disorders.* New York: Raven Press.

Crisp, A. H., Hsu, L. K. G., Harding, B., & Hartshorn, J. (1980). Clinical features of anorexia nervosa. A study of a consecutive series of 102 female patients. *Journal of Psychosomatic Research, 24,* 171–191.

Crisp, A. H., Palmer, R. S., & Kalucy, R. S. (1976). How common is anorexia nervosa? A prevalence study. *British Journal of Psychology, 128,* 545–559.

Crowther, J. H., Post, G., & Zaynor, L. (1985). The prevalence of bulimia and binge eating in adolescent girls. *International Journal of Eating Disorders, 4,* 29–42.

Dietz, W. H. (1985). Do we fatten our children at the television set? Obesity and television viewing in children and adolescents. *Pediatrics, 75,* 807.

Dornbusch, S. M., Carlsmith, J. M., Duncan, P. D., Gross, R. T., Martin, J. A., Ritter, P. L., & Siegel-Gorelick, B. (1984). Sexual maturation, social class, and the desire to be thinner among adolescent females. *Developmental and Behavioral Pediatrics, 5,* 308–314.

Downs, A. C., & Abshier, G. R. (1982). Conceptions of physical appearance among young adolescents: The interrelationships among self-judged appearance, attractiveness stereotyping, and sex-typed characteristics. *Journal of Early Adolescence, 2,* 255–265.

Duncan, P. D., Ritter, P. L., Dornbusch, S. M., Gross, R. T., & Carlsmith, J. M. (1985). The effects of pubertal timing on body image, school behavior, and deviance. *Journal of Youth and Adolescence, 14,* 227–235.

Faust, M. S. (1977). Somatic development of adolescent girls. *Monographs of the Society for Research in Child Development, 42* (1, Serial No. 169).

——. (1983). Alternative constructions of adolescent growth. In J. Brooks-Gunn & A. C. Petersen (Eds.), *Girls at puberty: Biological and psychosocial perspectives.* New York: Plenum.

Frisch, R. E. (1983). Fatness, puberty, and fertility. In J. Brooks-Gunn & A. C.

Petersen (Eds.), *Girls at puberty: Biological and psychosocial perspectives.* New York: Plenum.

Garfinkel, P. E., Moldofsky, H., & Garner, D. M. (1980). The heterogeneity of anorexia nervosa: Bulimia as a distinct subgroup. *Archives of General Psychiatry, 37,* 1036–1040.

Garn, S. M. (1980). Continuities and change in maturational timing. In O. G. Brim, Jr. & J. Kagan (Eds.), *Constancy and change in human development.* Cambridge: Harvard University Press.

———. (1985). Continuities and changes in fatness from infancy through childhood. *Current Problems in Pediatrics, 15,* 1–47.

Garner, D. M., & Garfinkel, P. E. (1980). Sociocultural factors in the development of anorexia nervosa. *Psychological Medicine, 10,* 647–656.

Garner, D. M., Garfinkel, P. E., Schwartz, D., & Thompson, M. (1980). Cultural expectations of thinness in women. *Psychological Reports, 47,* 483–491.

Garner, D. M., Olmsted, M. P., & Garfinkel, P. E. (1983). Does anorexia nervosa occur on a continuum: Subgroups of weight-preoccupied women and their relationship to anorexia nervosa. *International Journal of Eating Disorders, 2,* 11–20.

Garner, D. M., Rockert, W., Olmsted, M. P., Johnson, C., & Coscina, D. V. (1985). Psychoeducational principles in the treatment of bulimia and anorexia nervosa. In D. M. Garner & P. E. Garfinkel (Eds.), *Handbook of psychotherapy for anorexia nervosa and bulimia.* New York: Guilford Press.

Garrow, J. S. (1974). *Energy balance and obesity in man.* New York: Elsevier.

Goldblatt, P. B., Moore, M. E., & Stunkard, A. J. (1965). Social factors in obesity. *Journal of the American Medical Association, 192,* 1039–1044.

Goodman, N., Dornbusch, S. M., Richardson, S. A., & Hasdorf, A. H. (1963). Variant reactions to physical disabilities. *American Sociological Review, 28,* 429–435.

Gross, R. T. (1984). Patterns of maturation: Their effects on behavior and development. In M. D. Levine & P. Satz (Eds.), *Middle childhood: Development and dysfunction.* Baltimore: University Park Press.

Guy, R. F., Rankin, B. A., & Norvell, M. J. (1980). The relation of sex-role stereotyping to body image. *Journal of Psychology, 105,* 167–173.

Halmi, K. A. (1980). Eating disorders. In H. I. Kaplan, A. M. Freedman, & B. J. Sadock (Eds.), *Comprehensive textbook of psychiatry* (Vol. 3). Baltimore: Williams and Wilkins.

Hamburg, B. A. (1980). Early adolescence as a life stress. In S. Levine & H. Ursin (Eds.), *Coping and health.* New York: Plenum.

Hamilton, L. H., Brooks-Gunn, J., & Warren, M. P. (1985). Sociocultural influences on eating disorders in female professional dancers. *International Journal of Eating Disorders, 4,* 465–477.

———. (1986). Nutritional intake of female dancers: A reflection of eating problems. *International Journal of Eating Disorders, 5,* 925–934.

Hawkins, R. C., & Clement, P. F. (1980). Development and construct validation of a self-report measure of binge-eating tendencies. *Addictive Behaviors, 5,* 219–226.

Hawkins, R. C., Turell, S., & Jackson, L. J. (1983). Desirable and undesirable masculine and feminine traits in relation to students' dieting tendencies and body image dissatisfaction. *Sex Roles, 9,* 705–718.

Herman, C. P., & Mack, D. (1975). Restrained and unrestrained eating. *Journal of Personality, 43,* 647–660.

Herman, C. P., & Polivy, J. (1975). Anxiety, restraint, and eating behavior. *Journal of Abnormal Psychology, 84,* 666–672.

———. (1984). A boundary model for the regulation of eating. In A. J. Stunkard & E. Stellar (Eds.), *Eating and its disorders.* New York: Raven Press.

Hill, J. P., & Lynch, M. E. (1983). The intensification of gender-related role expectations during early adolescence. In J. Brooks-Gunn & A. C. Petersen (Eds.), *Girls at puberty: Biological and psychosocial perspectives.* New York: Plenum.

Katzman, M. A., Wolchik, S. A., & Braver, S. L. (1984). Prevalence of frequent binge eating and bulimia in a nonclinical college sample. *International Journal of Eating Disorders, 3,* 53–62.

Keys, A., Brozek, J., Henschel, A., Mickelsen, O., & Taylor, H. L. (1950). *The biology of human starvation.* Minneapolis: University of Minnesota Press.

Kog, E., Vandereycken, W., & Vertommen, H. (1985). Towards a verification of the psychosomatic family model: A pilot study of ten families with an anorexia/bulimia nervosa patient. *International Journal of Eating Disorders, 4,* 525–538.

Kurtz, R. M. (1969). Sex differences and variations in body attitudes. *Journal of Consulting and Clinical Psychology, 33,* 625–629.

Lacey, J. (1982). The bulimic syndrome at normal body weight: Reflections on pathogenesis and clinical features. *International Journal of Eating Disorders, 2,* 59–65.

Lambley, P. (1983). *How to survive anorexia.* London: Muller.

Langlois, J. H., & Stephan, C. (1977). The effects of physical attractiveness and ethnicity on children's behavioral attributions and peer preferences. *Child Development, 48,* 1694–1698.

Lerner, R. M. (1982). Children and adolescents as producers of their own development. *Developmental Review, 2,* 342–370.

Lerner, R. M., & Brackney, B. (1978). The importance of inner and outer body parts attitudes in the self concept of late adolescents. *Sex Roles, 4,* 225–238.

Lerner, R. M., & Karabenick, S. A. (1974). Physical attractiveness, body attitudes, and self-concept in late adolescents. *Journal of Youth and Adolescence, 3,* 307–316.

Lerner, R. M., & Lerner, G. V. (1977). Effects of age, sex, and physical attractiveness on child-peer relations, academic performance, and elementary school adjustment. *Developmental Psychology, 13,* 585–590.

Lerner, R. M., Orlos, J. B., & Knapp, J. R. (1976). Physical attractiveness, physical effectiveness, and self-concept in late adolescents. *Adolescence, 11,* 313–326.

Lucas, A. R., Beard, C. M., Kranz, J. S., & Kurland, L. T. (1983). Epidemiology of anorexia nervosa and bulimia. *International Journal of Eating Disorders, 2,* 85–91.

McReynolds, W. T. (1982). Toward a psychology of obesity: Review of research on the role of personality and level of adjustment. *International Journal of Eating Disorders, 2,* 37–57.

Miller, T., Coffman, J., & Linke, R. (1980). Survey on body image, weight, and diet of college students. *Journal of the American Dietetic Association, 77,* 561–566.

Mitchell, J. E., & Pyle, R. L. (1981). The bulimic syndrome in normal weight individuals: A review. *International Journal of Eating Disorders, 1,* 61–73.

Nisbett, R. E. (1972). Eating behavior and obesity in men and animals. *Advances in Psychosomatic Medicine, 7,* 173–193.

Nylander, I. (1971). The feeling of being fat and dieting in a school population: An epidemiologic interview investigation. *Acta Socio-Medica Scandinavica, 3,* 17–26.

Orbach, S. (1986). *Hunger strike: The anorectic's struggle as a metaphor for our age.* New York: Norton.

Parsons, J. E., Frieze, I. H., & Ruble, D. N. (1976). Introduction. *Journal of Social Issues, 32,* 1–5.

Petersen, A. C., & Taylor, B. (1980). Puberty: Biological change and psychological adaptation. In J. Adelson (Ed.), *Handbook of adolescent psychology.* New York: Wiley.

Polivy, J. (1976). Caloric perception and regulation of intake in restrained and unrestrained subjects. *Addictive Behavior, 1,* 237–243.

Polivy, J., & Herman, C. P. (1976a). The effects of alcohol on eating behavior: Disinhibition or sedation? *Addictive Behaviors, 1,* 121–125.

———. (1976b). Clinical depression and weight change: A complex relation. *Journal of Abnormal Psychology, 85,* 338–340.

———. (1983). *Breaking the diet habit: The natural weight alternative.* New York: Basic Books.

Pope, H. G., Hudson, J. I., Yorgelun-Todd, D., & Hudson, M. (1984). Prevalence of anorexia nervosa and bulimia in three student populations. *International Journal of Eating Disorders, 3,* 53–62.

Pyle, R. L., Mitchell, J. E., Eckert, E. D., Halvorson, P. A., Neuman, P. A., & Goff, G. M. (1983). The incidence of bulimia in freshman college students. *International Journal of Eating Disorders, 2,* 79–85.

Richardson, S. A., Goodman, N., Hasdorf, A. H., & Dornbusch, S. M. (1961). Cultural uniformity in relation to physical disabilities. *American Sociological Review, 26,* 241–247.

Rodin, J., & Slochower, J. (1976). Externality in the non-obese: Effects of environmental responsiveness on weight. *Journal of Personality and Social Psychology, 33,* 338–344.

Ross, C. E., & Mirowsky, J. (1983). Social epidemiology of overweight: A substantive and methodological investigation. *Journal of Health and Social Behavior, 24,* 288–298.

Schachter, S., & Rodin, J. (1974). *Obese humans and rats.* Potomac, MD: Lawrence Erlbaum.

Scott, D. W. (1986). Anorexia nervosa: A review of possible genetic factors. *International Journal of Eating Disorders, 5,* 1–20.

Sheldon, W. H. (1942). *The varieties of temperament: A psychology of constitutional differences.* New York: Harper.

Silber, T. J. (1986). Anorexia nervosa in blacks and hispanics. *International Journal of Eating Disorders, 5,* 121–128.

Simmons, R., Blyth, D. A., & McKinney, K. (1983). The social and psychological effects of puberty on white females. In J. Brooks-Gunn & A. C. Petersen (Eds.), *Girls at puberty: Biological and psychosocial perspectives.* New York: Plenum.

Simmons, R., Blyth, D. A., Van Cleave, E. F., & Bush, D. M. (1979). Entry into early adolescence: The impact of school structure, puberty, and early dating on self-esteem. *American Sociological Review, 44,* 948–967.

Smith, M. B. (1968). A map for the analysis of personality and politics. *Journal of Social Issues, 24,* 15–28.

Society of Actuaries, Committee on Mortality. (1979). *Build and blood pressure study* (Vol. 1). Chicago: Society of Actuaries.

Spencer, J. A., & Fremouw, W. J. (1979). Binge eating as a function of restraint and weight classification. *Journal of Abnormal Psychology, 88,* 262–267.

Staffieri, J. R. (1967). A study of social stereotype of body image in children. *Journal of Personality and Social Psychology, 7,* 101–104.

——. (1972). Body build and behavioral expectancies in young females. *Developmental Psychology, 6,* 125–127.

Stern, J. S. (1984). Is obesity a disease of inactivity? In A. J. Stunkard & E. Stellar (Eds.), *Eating and its disorders.* New York: Raven Press.

Striegel-Moore, R. H., Silberstein, L. R., & Rodin, J. (1986). Toward an understanding of risk factors for bulimia. *American Psychologist, 41,* 246–263.

Strober, M. (1981). The significance of bulimia in juvenile anorexia nervosa: An exploration of possible etiologic factors. *International Journal of Eating Disorders, 17,* 833–840.

——. (1984). Stressful life events associated with bulimia in anorexia nervosa: Empirical findings and theoretical speculations. *International Journal of Eating Disorders, 3,* 3–16.

Strober, M., Salkin, B., Burroughs, J., & Morrell, W. (1982). Validity of the bulimia-restricter distinction in anorexia nervosa: Parental personality characteristics and female psychiatric morbidity. *Journal of Nervous and Mental Disease, 170,* 345–351.

Stunkard, A. J. (1975). From explanation to action in psychosomatic medicine: The case of obesity. *Psychosomatic Medicine, 37,* 195–236.

Stunkard, A. J., d'Aquili, E. E., Fox, S., & Filion, R. D. L. (1972). Influence of social class on obesity and thinness in children. *Journal of the American Medical Association, 221,* 579–584.

Stunkard, A. J., Coll, M., Lundquist, S., & Meyers, A. (1980). Obesity and eating style. *Archives of General Psychiatry, 37,* 1127–1129.

Stunkard, A. J., & Mendelson, M. (1967). Obesity and body image: 1. Characteristics of disturbances in the body image of some obese persons. *American Journal of Psychiatry, 123,* 1296–1300.

Stunkard, A. J., Sorensen, T. I. A., Hanis, C., Teasdale, T. W., Chakraborty, R., Schull, W. J., & Schulsinger, F. (1986). An adoption study of obesity. *New England Journal of Medicine, 314,* 193–198.

Szmukler, G. I., & Tantam, D. (1984). Anorexia nervosa: Starvation dependence. *British Journal of Medical Psychology, 57,* 303–310.

Thompson, M. G., & Schwartz, D. M. (1982). Life adjustment of women with anorexia nervosa and anorexia-like behavior. *International Journal of Eating Disorders, 1,* 47–60.

Thornberry, O. T., Wilson, R. W., & Golden, P. (1986). Health promotion and disease prevention provisional data from the National Health Interview Survey: United States, January–June, 1985. *Vital and Health Statistics of the National Center for Health Statistics, 119,* 1–16.

Tobin-Richards, M. H., Boxer, A. M., & Petersen, A. C. (1983). The psychological significance of pubertal change: Sex differences in perceptions of self during early adolescence. In J. Brooks-Gunn & A. C. Petersen (Eds.), *Girls at puberty: Biological and psychosocial perspectives.* New York: Plenum.

Unger, R. K. (1985). *Between the "no longer" and the "not yet": Reflections on personal and social change.* Paper presented at the First Carolyn Wood Sherif Memorial Address, American Psychological Association, Los Angeles.

Wardle, J., & Beinart, H. (1981). Binge-eating: A theoretical review. *British Journal of Clinical Psychology, 20,* 97–109.

Warren, M. P. (1980). The effects of exercise on pubertal progression and reproductive function in girls. *Journal of Clinical Endocrinological Metabolism, 51,* 1150–1157.

———. (1983). Physical and biological aspects of puberty. In J. Brooks-Gunn & A. C. Petersen (Eds.), *Girls at puberty: Biological and psychosocial perspectives.* New York: Plenum.

Woody, E. Z., & Costanzo, P. R. (1981). The socialization of obesity-prone behavior. In S. S. Brehm, S. M. Kassin, & F. X. Gibbons (Eds.), *Developmental social psychology: Theory and research.* Oxford: Oxford University Press.

Woody, E. Z., Costanzo, P. R., Liefer, H., & Conger, J. (1981). The effects of taste and caloric perceptions on eating behavior of restrained and unrestrained subjects. *Cognitive Therapy and Research, 5,* 381–390.

Wooley, S. C., & Wooley, O. W. (1979). Obesity and women—I. A closer look at the facts. *Women's Studies International Quarterly, 2,* 69–79.

———. (1984a). 33,000 women tell how they really feel about their bodies. *Glamour,* February.

———. (1984b). Should obesity be treated at all? In A. J. Stunkard & E. Stellar (Eds.), *Eating and its disorders*. New York: Raven Press.

———. (1985). Intensive outpatient and residential treatment for bulimia. In D. M. Garner & P. E. Garfinkel (Eds.), *Handbook of psychotherapy for anorexia nervosa and bulimia*. New York: Guildford Press.

Yates, A., Leehey, K., & Shisslak, C. M. (1983). Running—An analogue of anorexia? *New England Journal of Medicine, 308,* 251–255.

Young, C. M., Sipin, S. S., & Roe, D. A. (1968). Density and skinfold measurements: Body composition of pre-adolescent girls. *Journal of American Dietetic Association, 53,* 25.

PART IV

COPING
AND
ADAPTATION

10

Gender Differences in the Social Moderators of Stress

Deborah Belle

Involvement in supportive human relationships has been hypothesized to protect stressed individuals against a variety of ills, from depression (Belle, 1982a; Brown, Bhrolchain, & Harris, 1975; Pearlin & Johnson, 1977) to complications of pregnancy (Barrera & Balls, 1983; Nuckolls, Cassell, & Kaplan, 1972) to ill health following job loss (Gore, 1978). Emotionally intimate, confiding relationships appear to be particularly powerful in some circumstances (Brown et al., 1975; Lowenthal & Haven, 1968), while less intimate connections with acquaintances, workmates, and neighbors are often also associated with positive outcomes (Miller & Ingham, 1976; Pearlin & Johnson, 1977). Theorists have argued that members of our social networks can provide us with social support resources such as assistance in problem solving and reassurance of worth, and can support a "repertoire of satisfactory social identities" (Hirsch, 1981, p. 163) that are critical to our self-concept and self-esteem. Such resources, in turn, help to prevent demoralization in times of stress, increase our options when confronting change and loss, and often facilitate a more active style of problem solving (Antonucci & Depner, 1982; Cobb, 1976; Hirsch, 1981).

Social networks can also have negative impacts on individuals, as several recent studies have demonstrated (Belle, 1982a, 1982b; Cohler & Lieberman, 1980; Eckenrode & Gore, 1981; Fiore, Becker, & Coppel, 1983; Fischer, 1982; Kessler & McLeod, 1984; Riley & Eckenrode, 1986; Rook,

1984; Wahler, 1980). The theoretical links between the social network and stress reactions have been less fully developed than those between the social network and beneficial social support.

Research does suggest that networks can create or exacerbate psychological distress when network members convey disrespect or disapproval, betray confidences, or fail to fulfill expectations for aid (Belle, 1982a; Fiore et al., 1983; Wahler, 1980), when network members place heavy demands on individuals to provide assistance and support (Cohler & Lieberman, 1980; Stack, 1974), and when the stressful life circumstances of network members produce a "contagion of stress" (Wilkins, 1974) from sufferer to network member (Eckenrode & Gore, 1981; Belle, 1982a). As I have argued elsewhere, "one cannot receive support without also risking the costs of rejection, betrayal, burdensome dependence, and vicarious pain" (Belle, 1982a, p. 143). Studies that have separated the social network into stressful and supportive components have found evidence that the stressful components are actually more strongly related to mental health status than are the supportive ones (Belle, 1982a; Fiore, Becker, & Coppel, 1983; Rook, 1984).

Furthermore, research suggests that the supportive aspects of social ties are more pronounced among those from subgroups favored with high levels of personal resources, such as income, education, and internal locus of control (Eckenrode, 1983; Lefcourt, Martin, & Saleh, 1984; Sandler & Lakey, 1982), while the costs of social ties are greater among those with fewer such resources (Belle, 1983; Riley & Eckenrode, 1986). For instance, in a recent study of the impact of social ties on women with differing levels of material and psychological resources, Riley and Eckenrode found that maintaining a large support network was beneficial only for the women with higher levels of resources. Such networks actually appeared more harmful than helpful for low-resource women, who presumably had greater difficulty in responding to the needs of network members and who were more distressed by the stressful experiences of network members than were high-resource women.

While research on the social network as a stress moderator has proliferated in recent years, gender differences in this area have received little attention. This is surprising, since gender differences in interpersonal behavior and interpersonal relationships are evident throughout the life cycle, suggesting that men and women differ in the ways they participate in social relationships and in the resources they seek in such relationships. Throughout life, the norms for appropriate male behavior tend to promote self-reliance and inhibit emotional expressiveness, self-disclosure, and help-seeking (DePaulo, 1982; Jourard, 1971; Lowenthal & Haven, 1968), while females are encouraged to value close relationships and even to define themselves in terms of the close relationships in which they participate (Chodorow, 1974; Gilligan, 1982; Miller, 1976). Given such differences, it is likely that social moderators of stress function differently for males and females.

Existing research on social moderators of stress sheds little light on gender differences. Studies often investigate the impact of social support within a single sex group, usually in relation to a stressful situation which is entirely or disproportionately experienced by one sex or the other. Researchers often focus on women in their reproductive and family roles, for example, and on men in their roles as economic providers. Thus, we have studies of the importance of support for women who experience pregnancy and childbirth (Barrera, 1981; Barrera & Balls, 1983; Feiring & Taylor, n.d.; Nuckolls, Cassel, & Kaplan, 1972; Turner & Noh, 1982), single parenthood (Colletta, 1979; McLanahan, Wedemeyer, & Adelberg, 1981; Stack, 1974; Weinraub & Wolf, 1983), battering (Butehorn, 1985; Mitchell & Hodson, 1986), widowhood (Bankoff, 1983; Hirsch, 1980), the myocardial infarction of the spouse (Finlayson, 1976), or depression (Belle, 1982a; Brown et al., 1975), and we have studies of men experiencing occupational stress (LaRocco, House, & French, 1980; LaRocco & Jones, 1978) and job loss (Gore, 1978). Several studies consider the importance of social support in enhancing women's maternal behavior (Abernethy, 1973; Crnic, Greenberg, Ragozin, Robinson, & Basham, 1983; Crockenberg, 1981; Feiring & Taylor, n.d.; Longfellow, Zelkowitz, Saunders, & Belle, 1979; Wahler, 1980; Weinraub & Wolf, 1983), while no comparable research tradition has investigated men's behavior with their children in relation to the social support resources these fathers receive.

Women appear to be overrepresented as subjects in social support studies, just as males are overrepresented in most stress research (Makosky, 1980). For instance, in Benjamin Gottlieb's edited volume, *Social networks and social support* (1981), three of the book's eleven chapters present new data on entirely female research populations (working-class mothers, pregnant adolescents, women experiencing marital disruption), while no chapters present data on solely male populations. Perhaps the very concept of social support is more compatible with cultural images of female psychological functioning.

Even when male and female responses to the same stressor (e.g., divorce) are investigated, the specific stress factors which might be moderated by social support may well differ for men and women. In the case of divorce, for instance, women are more likely than men to be faced with daunting child care responsibilities and extremely limited financial resources, while men are more likely than women to experience rootlessness and painful loss of day-to-day contact with their children (Brown & Fox, 1979; Hetherington, Cox, & Cox, 1978; Ross & Sawhill, 1975).

Given the sparsity of existing research on gender differences in the social moderators of stress, this chapter reviews what is known about gender and (1) participation in social networks, (2) mobilization of social support in times of psychological distress, (3) response to network members who experience stress reactions, and (4) the positive and negative implications of involvement in social networks. The review is limited almost entirely to research from Western industrialized societies and to studies completed in the last twenty years. Within these constraints, this chapter highlights several findings which suggest that there are gender differences in the ways males and females relate to their social networks in times of stress, and argues that further research to elucidate these gender differences would also help to unravel some of the central theoretical confusions within the social support–social network research tradition.

PARTICIPATION IN SOCIAL NETWORKS

Some researchers have characterized male participation in social networks across the life cycle as more "extensive" but less "intensive" than that of females. There is ample evidence that males tend to participate in more activity-focused relationships than do females, while females at all ages maintain more emotionally intimate relationships than do males.

Several studies have reported a tendency for boys to play in groups of three or more, which allows for more elaborated games and team sports, and for girls to prefer dyadic interaction, with its opportunities for emotional intimacy (Lever, 1976; Tietjen, 1982; Waldrop & Halverson, 1975). Bryant (1985) found that school-aged boys knew and interacted with more adults than did girls, and tended to interact with more peers as well. Tietjen (1982) reported that boys had a larger circle of friends than did girls. Bryant (1985) also found, however, that girls were more likely than boys to engage in intimate talks with peers and tended to have more such talks with adults—and even with pets! During adolescence, girls have been found to report more intimacy in friendship than do boys (Hunter & Youniss, 1982; Kon & Losenkov, 1978) and to disclose more about themselves than do boys (Dimond & Munz, 1967; Rivenbark, 1971).

There is some evidence that men have more acquaintances than do women, while women have more friends than do men. Booth (1972) and Miller and Ingham (1976) found that adult men had larger networks (including close friends and acquaintances) than women, while Weiss and Lowenthal (1975) discovered that the women in their sample had more friends than did the men. However, Caldwell and Peplau (1982) found no differences between male and female unmarried college students in the numbers of friends named.

The relative size of men's and women's networks seems to be strongly affected by many factors. Fischer (1982) found, for instance, that having children restricted the social involvements of mothers more than those of fathers. Mothers more than fathers differed from childless adults in having fewer friends and associates, fewer social activities, less reliable social supports, and more localized networks. Age and ill health, however, restricted the size of men's networks more than those of women. Social class and employment status have also been shown to affect differentially the size of men's and women's networks (Booth, 1972; Depner & Ingersoll, 1982; Lowenthal & Haven, 1968).

While the relative size of men's and women's networks varies with many factors, women's greater investment in close, confiding relationships seems to endure throughout life. In their cross-cultural research, Whiting and Whiting (1975) found that girls seek more help from others in early childhood and offer more help and support to others in the preadolescent years than do boys. Candy, Troll, and Levy (1981), in an exploration of friendship among women from age 14 to 80, were struck by the consistency with which disclosing private feelings and offering emotional and instrumental support were named as functions of women's friendships. Booth and Hess (1974) found that women's interactions were more dyadic and intimate and that women seemed to have more close personal relationships than did men. In middle age and old age, women are more likely than men to have close relationships (Depner & Ingersoll, 1982) and confidants (Lowenthal & Haven, 1968).

While women's relationships tend to emphasize emotional intimacy, men's friendships tend to center around shared activities and experiences, such as sports (Caldwell & Peplau, 1982; Weiss & Lowenthal, 1975), repeating the gender differences observed in childhood.

MOBILIZATION OF SUPPORT IN TIMES OF STRESS

Throughout the life cycle, females show a greater propensity to mobilize social supports in times of stress. Females are more likely than males to seek out such support, to receive such support, and to be pleased with the support they receive. In childhood, girls are more likely than boys to seek help when facing problems (Nelson-LeGall, Gumerman, & Scott-Jones, 1983) and are more likely to confide their experiences to at least one other person than are boys (Belle & Longfellow, 1984). In a study of 8- to 15-year-old children whose parents had divorced, Wolchik, Sandler, and Braver (1984) found that girls reported more family members who provided emotional support and positive feedback and more individuals from outside the family who provided advice, goods and services, and supportive feedback than did boys. Girls also felt more positively than did boys about the individuals who provided this support.

Among adolescents, girls name more informal sources of support, such as friends and other adults, than do boys (Cauce, Felner, & Primavera, 1982) and are more likely to turn to their peers for support than are boys (Burke & Weir, 1978). Among college students, females report more available helpers, receive more support, and rate other people more helpful in dealing with problematic events than do males (Cohen, McGowan, Fooskas, & Rose, 1984).

Women facing stress have been found to seek out more sources of both formal and informal support than do men. Women experiencing divorce are more likely to turn to at least one other person for help, to turn to multiple categories of helpers, to participate in Parents Without Partners (a mutual support group), and to utilize professional counseling (Brown & Fox, 1979; Chiriboga, Coho, Stein, & Roberts, 1979). Divorced women are also more likely than divorced men to turn to their own children, friends, and doctors for support (Chiriboga et al., 1979).

These patterns were also found in a general study of help-seeking (Veroff, Kulka, & Douvan, 1981; Veroff, Douvan, & Kulka, 1981). Women were more likely than men to utilize both formal and informal sources of help, more likely than men to turn to more than one friend or family member in times of crisis, and more likely to turn to friends and to children in times of unhappiness.

What is most striking about men's mobilization of support is that it is so heavily focused on one support provider—the wife. Among an elderly population sample, wives were the most frequently mentioned confidants of men, while women were about twice as likely as men to mention a child or other relative and more likely to name a friend as a confidant (Lowenthal & Haven, 1968). Veroff, Douvan, and Kulka (1981) found that married men were more likely than married women to turn solely to their spouses in times of stress. Even following divorce, men were significantly more likely than women to report that in the ideal situation the most helpful person to them would be their spouse (Chiriboga et al., 1979).

Not only do men and women tend to differ in their utilization of potential support figures in times of stress, there is also suggestive evidence for gender differences in the particular support resources sought by men and women. Brown and Fox (1979) reported that among divorcing men and women who had sought counseling, men were more likely than women to report that counseling improved their communication skills, while women were more likely than men to say they found emotional support from the counseling. In a projective study with college students, only women envisioned a troubled person who confided in a friend as gaining relief from stress, enhanced insight, or strength through sharing her worry with the friend (Mark & Alper, 1985). Men, on the other hand, typically depicted the friend giving advice or the two friends working on a solution to the problem together. However, "none of the men imagined any kind of self-enhancement, growth, strengthening, or relief as a result of confiding" (p. 86).

The disposition to utilize support resources in times of difficulty has been linked to psychological femininity as assessed by Bem's measure of gender-role orientation (Vaux, Burda, & Stewart, in press). McMullen and Gross (1983), who conducted a major review of gender differences in help-seeking, concluded that "our culture has included help-seeking among the behaviors that are designated as more appropriate for females than males" (p. 251). Men may regard help-seeking as a threat to their competence or independence, while women may view help-seeking as a means of creating or sustaining interpersonal relationships, and thus a desirable experience in its own right (DePaulo, 1982).

Men may also refrain from help-seeking because of explicit social sanctions against such behavior, particularly in the workplace. Weiss (1985) found in an interview study of upper-income men in administrative and business-related occupations that the occupational setting seemed to prohibit or punish the display of emotions other than anger. "Failing to maintain the proper facade of self-assurance could be penalized in the world of work" (p. 57). For the men Weiss studied, this prohibition often seemed to extend beyond the workplace into the home, so that men concealed their "weaker" emotions from their wives and even from themselves.

McMullen and Gross (1983) have also argued that because help-seeking has been considered a feminine activity, and because the male role is more highly valued in our culture, there has probably been "a general cultural devaluation of this activity and the person who seeks help" (p. 252). As men and women increasingly move away from such traditional sex role norms, we may well see a lessening of the stigma against seeking help in times of stress and more appropriate help-seeking by both men and women (McMullen & Gross, 1983).

RESPONSE TO NETWORK MEMBERS
WHO EXPERIENCE STRESS

> Women's place in man's life cycle has been that of nurturer, caretaker, and helpmate, the weaver of those networks of relationships on which she in turn relies (Gilligan, 1982, p. 17).

Just as females are more frequent utilizers of social support, they appear to be utilized more often than males as *providers* of social support when others are under stress. Fischer (1982) found that while men and women tended to name persons of their own gender for most support, women were named disproportionately as counselors and companions by both men and women. In their family roles as wives, mothers, and "kin keepers," and in their community roles as neighbors and friends, women provide considerable social support to others. What has sometimes been called women's "expressive function" (Parsons & Bales, 1955) can also be viewed as the provision of social support to others (Vanfossen, 1981).

Within marriage, husbands more than wives report being understood and affirmed by their spouses (Campbell, Converse, & Rodgers, 1976; Vanfossen, 1981), and husbands have generally been found to confide in their wives more frequently than wives do in their husbands (Lowenthal & Haven, 1968; Warren, 1975). However, in one study of male professionals and their wives, Burke, Weir, and Harrison (1976) discovered that wives disclosed problems to their spouses more often than husbands did to their wives. In a study of upper-income married men, Weiss (1985) found that, while husbands typically told their wives little of the events of the workday, men did communicate their feelings about their work through their moods and through the "leakage" of information, such as overheard telephone conversations. Thus wives could often guess the issues which were preoccupying their husbands, while at the same time they were discouraged from talking about them. Whatever the extent or nature of their confiding behavior, husbands are much more likely than wives to rely solely on the spouse as confidant, as discussed above (Veroff, Douvan, & Kulka, 1981).

While adult gender roles are changing to some extent, mothers still retain more responsibility for the care of children than do fathers, and are still named more frequently as confidants by children (Belle & Longfellow, 1984) and adolescents (Rivenbark, 1971). Hunter and Youniss (1982) found that mothers exceeded both fathers and friends as sources of intimacy and nurturance to children at the fourth-grade level, and studies have shown that mothers are major sources of advice, guidance, and intimacy to their adolescent children as well (Kandel & Lesser, 1972; Kon & Losenkov, 1978). Even when children are themselves adult, mothers may be more knowledgeable about and more emotionally involved in children's problems than are fathers (Loewenstein, 1984).

A striking piece of evidence for the importance of females as support providers comes from a study of 7- and 10-year-old children who were asked to name the ten individuals who were most important to them (Bryant, 1985). Each child in the study had a sibling who was two to three years older than the interviewed child. Not only were more older sisters (95 percent) than older brothers (73 percent) named among the children's "top ten," but these older sisters were represented more frequently on "top ten" lists than any other figures, including mothers and fathers. However, Furman and Buhrmester's recent study of fifth- and sixth-grade children (1985) did not confirm the salience of the older sister as support figure. In their study both older and same-sex siblings were named as particularly important support figures. Instrumental aid was actually seen as coming more frequently from brothers than sisters.

Studies of black families, white working-class families, white ethnic families, and low-income families emphasize the importance of the instrumental assistance and emotional support shared among female kin, friends and neighbors, particularly around child rearing (Belle, 1982a; Cohler & Lieberman, 1980; McAdoo, 1980; Stack, 1974; Young & Willmott, 1957). The importance of such female networks in ensuring day-to-day survival and maintaining family solidarity has been noted by many.

There is also evidence that females tend to be more supportive friends than are males. Wheeler, Reis, and Nezlek (1983) found that among both male and female college seniors, loneliness was negatively related to the amount of time spent with females, while time spent with males did not appear to buffer loneliness. Only when the "meaningfulness" of interactions with males was taken into consideration did contact with males appear to stave off loneliness. In an ingenious role-play study of friendships (Caldwell & Peplau, 1982), women who role-played a friend calling to congratulate another on a recent success made more supportive statements than did men. They were more likely than men to say they were happy for the successful person, were more likely to express enthusiasm for the friend's success, and were more likely to ask about the friend's own feelings than were men role-playing the same conversation. Perhaps, however, this study's criteria for supportiveness simply reflect a feminine style of support provision. It would be interesting to know whether other, more indirect statements, such as humor, irony, or mock criticism actually served to convey support between male role-players.

In addition to the support women provide informally to their husbands, children, other relatives, neighbors, and friends, many women are professionally involved in the provision of support to those under stress. Many predominantly female occupations, such as teaching, nursing, and social work, require empathic attention to the needs of others and the ability to provide emotional support to those in distress. While a full discussion of women's professional involvement in providing social support is beyond the scope of this chapter, it should be noted that many women "already gave at the office" when they come home to provide support to members of their informal social networks.

What accounts for the tendency of both males and females to turn to females disproportionately in times of stress and for women to offer support to so many others? Wheeler et al. (1983) have argued that women are simply more effective as social partners than are men. Men, in contrast, tend to lack training in supportiveness skills (Bernard, 1971), so that their attempts at providing social support are not as effective as those of women. Whiting and Whiting (1975) have shown that across diverse cultures infants tend to elicit nurturant behavior from those in contact with them, and that girls consistently spend more time than boys close to home and in the company of mothers and infants. Girls thus have more ample opportunities than do boys to practice nurturant behaviors and to come to feel comfortable and adept in a nurturing role.

Miller (1976) has argued that women's socialization and especially their subordinate status, which requires attention to others, better prepares them "to first recognize others' needs and then to believe strongly that others' needs can be served" so much so that women organize their lives around the principle of nurturing others and promoting their growth. This is consistent with Gilligan's argument (1982) that women's moral sense tends to presume responsibility for the well-being of others.

Bernard (1971) has argued that the supportive or "stroking" function (first outlined in work by R. F. Bales on emotional-expressive behavior in groups) in which one shows solidarity, raises the status of others, gives help, rewards, agrees, concurs, complies, understands, and passively accepts, is the quintessential female function. "No matter what job a woman is doing or what role she is performing, high or low, the supportive function is assumed to be part of it. Indeed, the behaviors that constitute stroking . . . add up to a description of the ideal-typical woman wherever she is found" (p. 90). Women are simply expected to engage in "stroking" and are punished if they do not do so. "Men do not expect support from men; they are nonplussed when it is not forthcoming from women" (p. 94).

POSITIVE AND NEGATIVE IMPLICATIONS OF INVOLVEMENT IN SOCIAL NETWORKS

The research reviewed earlier in this chapter certainly gives rise to the expectation that the moderating effects of social networks and supports may function differently for men and women. As indicated, women tend to (1) maintain more emotionally intimate relationships than do men, (2) mobilize more social supports in times of stress than do men while relying less heavily than men on the spouse as a source of social support, and (3) provide more frequent and more effective social support to others than do men. The remainder of this chapter considers some possible consequences of such gender differences in social networks and social supports.

Women Maintain More Emotionally Intimate Relationships Than Do Men

Two lines of research evidence suggest that important consequences flow from the differential investment by men and women in close, confiding, and intimate relationships. One line suggests that the preferred patterns

of network involvement may actually be differentially beneficial to males and females over the life course. In her study of social support in middle childhood, Bryant (1985) found that boys appeared to derive benefits from the extensive, casual involvements they typically preferred, rather than from intensive, intimate involvements, while the reverse was true for girls. Specifically, casual involvement with many adults was positively linked to social perspective-taking skill, internal locus of control, and empathy for boys, while such involvements were negatively related to social perspective-taking skill and internal locus of control among girls. Intimate involvements with adults predicted positive socioemotional development for girls, but not for boys. Similarly, Waldrop and Halverson (1975) found that social maturity and facility with peers had very different correlates for boys and girls. Boys who were more socially at ease, spent more hours with peers, and were judged to find peers more important to them differed from boys with less social facility chiefly in the *numbers* of friendships they had. Girls who were more socially at ease, spent more hours with peers, and were judged to find peers more important to them differed from other girls chiefly in the *intensity* and *intimacy* of the friendships they had. Interestingly, peer sociability at age 2½ tended to predict these very different patterns of social involvement at age 7½ for boys and girls. While these longitudinal results are striking, they do not prove that boys and girls find different types of social involvements inherently beneficial. The findings may also be interpreted as suggesting that socially adept boys and girls are more successful than their less accomplished peers in determining the kind of social relationships that are considered socially appropriate for their gender.

Among adults, Miller and Ingham (1976) reported that for women, having a good confidant and having a sizeable array of acquaintances were both associated with positive outcomes, while for men, only the acquaintanceship measure was associated with well-being. The authors note, however, that this gender difference may have resulted from the small sample size for men. Additional evidence about the relative importance to men and to women of casual versus intimate relationships would add to our understanding of this issue.

A very different line of research suggests that women's propensity for intimate social involvements may predispose women to the "contagion of stress" that is felt when troubling life events afflict those to whom they are emotionally close. Dohrenwend (1976) found, for instance, that when men and women were asked to list recent events that had occurred to themselves, family members, and other people important to them, a higher proportion of the events women reported had happened to family members or friends rather than to the respondents themselves. Eckenrode and Gore (1981) reported that women whose relatives and friends experienced stressful life events such as burglaries and illnesses found these events stressful to themselves, and reflected this vicarious stress in their own poor health. Kessler and McLeod (1984) argue that this sensitivity to the undesirable life events of others actually accounts for women's greater vulnerability to stressful life events in comparison to men. Wethington, McLeod, and Kessler (this volume) were able to show that while men are distressed by events that happen to their children and spouses, women are distressed not only by these events but by events which occur to other members of the social network. Thus, it is women's greater "range of caring" that seems to expose them to additional vicarious stress.

Women Mobilize More Varied Social Supports in Times of Stress Than Do Men

Research on bereavement provides the most impressive evidence that men's and women's differential investment in social support figures has consequences for their well-being. In particular, a man's heavy investment in his wife as confidant and support figure may account for the higher mortality rates of widowers versus widows in the months and years following bereavement. In one large-scale prospective study which matched widowed adults to married persons on race, sex, year of birth, and place of residence, mortality rates for widowed women were virtually no different from those for married women, while male mortality rates were significantly higher for widowers than for married men (Helsing & Szklo, 1981). Similarly, Berkman and Syme (1979) found in a nine-year follow-up study of almost 7,000 adults that marriage was much more protective for men than for women, even after mortality statistics were adjusted for self-reported physical health status at the time of the initial survey, for socioeconomic status, health practices such as smoking, alcoholic beverage consumption, obesity and physical activity, and a cumulative index of health practices. Stroebe and Stroebe (1983) concluded from their literature review on sex differences in the health risks of the widowed that men are more vulnerable to mental and physical health sequelae, and that the most adequate explanation for the greater vulnerability of men focuses on their lack of alternate support figures following the death of the spouse.

While men appear particularly vulnerable when they lose a spouse to death, other research suggests that differences in the actual supportiveness of the spouse when alive may be more important to women than to men. Husaini, Neff, Newbrough, and Moore (1982) studied the stress-buffering properties of social support among rural married men and women and found that various aspects of the marital relationship (marital satisfaction, spouse satisfaction, spouse as confidant) were more powerfully associated with mental health status among women than among men.

Why should the mere presence of a wife be beneficial, while only the supportiveness of a husband is protective? Such a finding is reminiscent of previously discussed research on gender differences in the supportiveness of friends. Loneliness among college students was negatively related to the amount of time spent with females but only with the reported "meaning-fulness" of time spent with males. Such findings are open to different inter-pretations but may reflect a ceiling effect: the average wife (or female friend) may provide such a high level of support that further increments in supportiveness make little difference to health and mental health out-comes. It may also be that since the role of wife is so central to a woman's social status and self-concept, a nonsupportive spouse is particularly dev-astating to a woman's well-being.

To complicate matters further, Vanfossen (1981) has shown that the mental health impact of spouse support varies for men and women de-pending on what facets of marital support are considered, and also de-pending on the employment status of the wife. Specifically, emotional intimacy and affirmation from spouses are crucial to the emotional well-being of married men and nonemployed wives, while equity in the marital relationship and affirmation from the spouse are particularly important to employed wives.

When we turn from the marital relationship to other network ties, there is evidence that men and women may be differentially protected by their involvements. In their prospective study of mortality, Berkman and Syme (1979) found that overall the protective effects of social contacts were stronger for women than for men. While, as discussed earlier, marriage was much more protective for men, it was women who benefited more from contact with friends and relatives and from involvement in formal and informal groups. Holahan and Moos (1981) reported that the quality of family relationships was associated with well-being for women but not for men, while the quality of work relationships was more strongly related to well-being for men than for women.

Women Provide More Frequent and More Effective Social Support to Others Than Do Men

Several authors have pointed to women's heightened vulnerability to stress resulting from women's propensity to take care of needy and stressed net-work members. Fischer (1982) found that women, especially mothers of young children, were much more likely than others to report too many demands from members of their households.

> In general women and parents, especially parents of infants and toddlers, were most likely to feel pressed by their households, but the combination of being a woman and being a parent was especially

deadly. . . . The general point is clear: children demand and women respond to those demands, as well as to the demands of others (p. 136).

Similarly, Cohler and Lieberman (1980) discovered that among first and second generation adult members of three European ethnic groups, the women who were more involved with relatives and friends experienced *more* psychological distress than their less involved peers, while network involvement among the men was either unrelated to mental health or showed small positive associations with morale. Cohler and Lieberman note that, particularly within the ethnic communities they studied, women are socialized from childhood to care for others. Such socialization may then contribute to the contagion of stress women experience from the disasters and disappointments of others. In addition to the vicarious pain they feel, women may also find themselves burdened with new tasks and obligations to aid the suffering individual. The close contact experienced in such kin-keeping may then keep the sufferer's pain vivid to the person who aids him or her.

Women's specialization as support providers and men's relative neglect of this activity may also have consequences for cross-sex friendships and for romantic and marital relationships. In a male-female relationship, the female may experience a "support gap" (Belle, 1982b) when she receives less support from a significant male figure than she provides to him. If the flow of supportive provisions is highly unequal, and if the woman is heavily involved in providing support to children, needy friends, or relatives while receiving little support in return, the result may well be demoralization and depression.

This review has suggested that there are pervasive gender differences in the ways men and women construct their networks and utilize them in times of stress, and that these differences have consequences for men's and women's well-being. Many challenges remain, however, before a full understanding of these issues is achieved.

One topic which has not yet received the attention it deserves is the question of what supportive provisions men and women (and boys and girls) actually desire in their interpersonal encounters, and how these different provisions then relate to the outcomes of the supportive experience. If men receiving counseling during their marital breakups believe they have found help with communication skills, while women point to the emotional support they received, perhaps the single term "support" is too *global* to capture the diverse provisions men and women perceive and receive in other situations as well. Studies have shown that boys and girls tend to prefer different styles of personal networks, but little research has addressed the specific provisions that boys and girls find in their preferred types of networks or the ways in which boys and girls come to value the specific experiences they can find in such networks.

While most network studies emphasize the benefits to be gained by network involvement, a new line of research is demonstrating that the costs of network ties may, if anything, be greater than the benefits. Studies have also shown, as noted earlier, that the costs and benefits of networks are not distributed randomly among the population, but tend to vary with gender and with access to personal resources (which also tends to vary with gender).

In addition to the gender differences in network involvements that have been discussed thus far, it is important to note the impact of society-wide inequalities in access to crucial resources as these affect men's and women's utilization of support resources. A growing body of research has shown, ironically, that those most in need of supportive provisions from their social networks are those least likely to receive them, while they are also most likely to experience the costs of network involvement (Belle, 1983; Eckenrode, 1983; Lefcourt, Martin, & Saleh, 1984; Riley & Eckenrode, 1986; Sandler & Lakey, 1982). In American society at large, women are more likely than men to fall into the ranks of the impoverished, to hold relatively powerless positions in the workplace, and to lack the independent resources that can give bargaining advantages within marriage. Research to date has not examined the importance of access to such material and psychological resources along with gender in predicting the impact of network involvements.

An examination of gender differences in the social moderators of stress has exposed complexities and confusions in our current theoretical models of social support which associate social ties with exclusively positive outcomes. Close attention to women's experience has suggested several plausible mechanisms by which networks may exacerbate or may relieve stress. If such mechanisms are valid, then they should apply as well to men whose networks and style of network involvement match those more typically associated with women. Men, for instance, who experience strong emotional identification with the sorrows of others and men who feel strong community or personal imperatives to care for distressed and needy network members should be more susceptible than men without such patterns to the contagion of psychological distress and its vicarious pain. Men who maintain intimate emotional ties with persons other than the spouse should be more resilient following bereavement than men who confide only in their wives. Pursuing the leads that have been discovered could lead to clarification and enrichment of our ideas about the social moderators of stress for both men and women.

REFERENCES

Abernethy, V. (1973). Social network and response to the maternal role. *International Journal of Sociology of the Family, 3,* 86–92.

Antonucci, T., & Depner, C. (1982). Social support and informal helping relationships. In T. Wills (Ed.), *Basic processes in helping relationships*. New York: Academic Press.

Bankoff, E. A. (1983). Social support and adaptation to widowhood. *Journal of Marriage and the Family, 45,* 827–839.

Barrera, M. (1981). Social support in the adjustment of pregnant adolescents: Assessment issues. In B. H. Gottlieb (Ed.), *Social networks and social support*. Beverly Hills, CA: Sage.

Barrera, M., & Balls, P. (1983). Assessing social support as a prevention resource: An illustrative study. *Prevention in Human Services, 2,* 59–74.

Belle, D. (1982a). Social ties and social support. In D. Belle (Ed.), *Lives in stress: Women and depression*. Beverly Hills, CA: Sage.

———. (1982b). The stress of caring: Women as providers of social support. In L. Goldberger & S. Breznitz (Eds.), *Handbook of stress: Theoretical and clinical aspects*. New York: Free Press.

———. (1983). The impact of poverty on social networks and supports. *Marriage and Family Review, 5,* 89–103.

Belle, D., & Longfellow, C. (1984). *Turning to others: Children's use of confidants*. Paper presented at the annual meeting of the American Psychological Association, Toronto.

Berkman, L. F., & Syme, L. (1979). Social networks, host resistance, and mortality: A nine-year follow-up study of Alameda County residents. *American Journal of Epidemiology, 109,* 186–204.

Bernard, J. (1971). *Women and the public interest*. Chicago: Aldine.

Booth, A. (1972). Sex and social participation. *American Sociological Review, 37,* 183–193.

Booth, A., & Hess, E. (1974). Cross-sex friendship. *Journal of Marriage and the Family, 36,* 38–47.

Brown, G., Bhrolchain, M., & Harris, T. (1975). Social class and psychiatric disturbance among women in an urban population. *Sociology, 9,* 225–254.

Brown, P., & Fox, H. (1979). Sex differences in divorce. In E. Gomberg & V. Franks (Eds.), *Gender and disordered behavior: Sex differences in psychopathology*. New York: Brunner/Mazel.

Bryant, B. (1985). The neighborhood walk: Sources of support in middle childhood. *Monographs of the Society for Research in Child Development, 50* (3, Serial No. 210).

Burke, R. J., & Weir, T. (1978). Sex differences in adolescent life stress, social support, and well-being. *Journal of Psychology, 98,* 277–288.

Burke, R. J., Weir, T., & Harrison, D. (1976). Disclosure of problems and tensions experienced by marital partners. *Psychological Reports, 38,* 531–542.

Butehorn, L. (1985). *Effects of the social network on the battered woman's decision to stay in or leave the battering relationship*. Unpublished doctoral dissertation, Boston University.

Caldwell, M. A., & Peplau, L. A. (1982). Sex differences in same-sex friendship. *Sex Roles, 8,* 721–732.

Campbell, A., Converse, P., & Rodgers, W. (1976). *The quality of American life: Perceptions, evaluations, and satisfactions.* New York: Russell Sage.

Candy, S. G., Troll, L. W., & Levy, S. G. (1981). A developmental exploration of friendship functions in women. *Psychology of Women Quarterly, 5,* 456–472.

Cauce, A. M., Felner, R. D., & Primavera, J. (1982). Social support in high-risk adolescents: Structural components and adaptive impact. *American Journal of Community Psychology, 10,* 417–428.

Chiriboga, D. A., Coho, A., Stein, J. A., & Roberts, J. (1979). Divorce, stress and social supports: A study in help-seeking behavior. *Journal of Divorce, 3,* 121–135.

Chodorow, N. (1974). Family structure and feminine personality. In M. Rosaldo & L. Lamphere (Eds.), *Women, culture, and society.* Stanford: Stanford University Press.

Cobb, S. (1976). Social support as a moderator of life stress. *Psychosomatic Medicine, 38,* 300–314.

Cohen, L. H., McGowan, J., Fooskas, S., & Rose, S. (1984). Positive life events and social support and the relationship between life stress and psychological disorder. *American Journal of Community Psychology, 12,* 567–587.

Cohler, B. M., & Lieberman, M. A. (1980). Social relations and mental health: Middle-aged and older men and women from three European ethnic groups. *Research on Aging, 2,* 445–469.

Colletta, N. (1979). Support systems after divorce: Incidence and impact. *Journal of Marriage and the Family, 41,* 837–846.

Crnic, K. A., Greenberg, M. T., Ragozin, A. S., Robinson, N. M., & Basham, R. B. (1983). Effects of stress and social support on mothers and premature and full-term infants. *Child Development, 54,* 209–217.

Crockenberg, S. B. (1981). Infant irritability, mother responsiveness, and social support influences on the security of infant-mother attachment. *Child Development, 52,* 857–865.

DePaulo, B. (1982). Social-psychological processes in informal help seeking. In T. A. Wills (Ed.), *Basic processes in helping relationships.* New York: Academic Press.

Depner, C., & Ingersoll, B. (1982). Employment status and social support: The experience of the mature woman. In M. Szinovacz (Ed.), *Women's retirement: Policy implications of recent research.* Beverly Hills, CA: Sage Yearbooks in Women's Policy Studies, Vol. 6.

Dimond, R. E., & Munz, D. C. (1967). Ordinal position of birth and self-disclosure in high school students. *Psychological Reports, 21,* 829–833.

Dohrenwend, B. S. (1976). *Anticipation and control of stressful live events: An exploratory analysis.* Paper presented to the annual meeting of the Eastern Psychological Association, New York City.

Eckenrode, J. (1983). The mobilization of social supports: Some individual constraints. *American Journal of Community Psychology, 11,* 509–528.

Eckenrode, J., & Gore, S. (1981). Stressful events and social support: The significance of context. In B. Gottlieb (Ed.), *Social networks and social support.* Beverly Hills, CA: Sage.

Feiring, C., & Taylor, J. (n.d.). *The influence of the infant and secondary parent on maternal behavior. Toward a social systems view of infant attachment.* Unpublished paper, University of Pittsburgh.

Finlayson, A. (1976). Social networks as coping resources: Lay help and consultation patterns used by women in husbands' post infarction career. *Social Science and Medicine, 10,* 97–103.

Fiore, J., Becker, J., & Coppel, D. B. (1983). Social network interactions: A buffer or a stress? *American Journal of Community Psychology, 11,* 423–439.

Fischer, C. (1982). *To dwell among friends: Personal networks in town and city.* Chicago: University of Chicago Press.

Furman, W., & Buhrmester, D. (1985). Children's perceptions of the personal relationships in their social networks. *Developmental Psychology, 21,* 1016–1022.

Gilligan, C. (1982). *In a different voice.* Cambridge, MA: Harvard University Press.

Gore, S. (1978). The effect of social support in moderating the health consequences of unemployment. *Journal of Health and Social Behavior, 19,* 157–165.

Gottlieb, B. (Ed.). (1981). *Social networks and social support.* Beverly Hills, CA: Sage.

Helsing, K. J., & Szklo, M. (1981). Mortality after bereavement. *American Journal of Epidemiology, 114,* 41–52.

Hetherington, E., Cox, M., & Cox, R. (1978). The aftermath of divorce. In J. H. Stevens, Jr., & M. Mathews (Eds.), *Mother-child father-child relationships.* Washington, DC: National Association for the Education of Young Children.

Hirsch, B. J. (1980). Natural support systems and coping with major life changes. *American Journal of Community Psychology, 8,* 159–172.

———. (1981). Social networks and the coping process: Creating personal communities. In B. H. Gottlieb (Ed.), *Social networks and social support.* Beverly Hills, CA: Sage.

Holahan, C., & Moos, R. (1981). Social support and psychological distress: A longitudinal analysis. *Journal of Abnormal Psychology, 90,* 365–370.

Hunter, F. T., & Youniss, J. (1982). Changes in functions of three relations during adolescence. *Developmental Psychology, 18,* 806–811.

Husaini, B. A., Neff, J. A., Newbrough, J. R., & Moore, M. C. (1982). The stress-buffering role of social support and personal competence among the rural married. *Journal of Community Psychology, 10,* 409–426.

Jourard, S. (1971). Some lethal aspects of the male role. In J. Pleck & J. Sawyer (Eds.), *Men and masculinity.* Englewood Cliffs, NJ: Prentice-Hall.

Kandel, D. B., & Lesser, G. S. (1972). *Youth in two worlds: U.S. and Denmark.* San Francisco: Jossey-Bass.

Kessler, R. C., & McLeod, J. D. (1984). Sex differences in vulnerability to undesirable life events. *American Sociological Review, 49,* 620–631.

Kon, I. S., & Losenkov, V. A. (1978). Friendship in adolescence: Values and behavior. *Journal of Marriage and the Family, 40,* 143–155.

LaRocco, J. M., House, J. S., & French, J. R. P., Jr. (1980). Social support, occupational stress, and health. *Journal of Health and Social Behavior, 21,* 202–218.

LaRocco, J. M., & Jones, A. P. (1978). Co-worker and leader support as moderators of stress-strain relationships in work situations. *Journal of Applied Psychology, 63,* 629–634.

Lever, J. (1976). Sex differences in the games children play. *Social Problems, 23,* 478–487.

Lefcourt, H. M., Martin, R. A., & Saleh, W. E. (1984). Locus of control and social support: Interactive moderators of stress. *Journal of Personality and Social Psychology, 47,* 378–389.

Loewenstein, S. F. (1984). *Fathers and mothers in midlife.* Presentation to the Family Track Seminar of the Boston University Department of Psychology, Boston.

Longfellow, C., Zelkowitz, P., Saunders, E., & Belle, D. (1979). *The role of support in moderating the effects of stress and depression.* Paper presented at the biennial meeting of the Society for Research in Child Development, San Francisco.

Lowenthal, M. J., & Haven, C. (1968). Interaction and adaptation: Intimacy as a critical variable. *American Sociological Review, 33,* 20–30.

Makosky, V. (1980). Stress and the mental health of women: A discussion of research and issues. In M. Guttentag, S. Salasin, & D. Belle (Eds.), *The mental health of women.* New York: Academic.

Mark, E. W., & Alper, T. G. (1985). Women, men, and intimacy motivation. *Psychology of Women Quarterly, 9,* 81–88.

McAdoo, H. (1980). Black mothers and the extended family support network. In L. Rodgers-Rose (Ed.), *The black woman.* Beverly Hills, CA: Sage.

McLanahan, S. S., Wedemeyer, N. V., & Adelberg, T. (1981). Network structure, social support, and psychological well-being in the single-parent family. *Journal of Marriage and the Family, 43,* 601–612.

McMullen, P. A., & Gross, A. E. (1983). Sex differences, sex roles, and health-related help-seeking. In B. DePaulo, A. Nadler, & J. Fisher (Eds.), *New directions in helping* (Vol. 2). New York: Academic Press.

Miller, J. (1976). *Toward a new psychology of women.* Boston: Beacon.

Miller, P. M., & Ingham, J. G. (1976). Friends, confidants, and symptoms. *Social Psychiatry, 11,* 51–58.

Mitchell, R., & Hodson, C. (1986). Coping and social support among battered women: An ecological perspective. In S. Hobfoll (Ed.), *Stress, social support and women.* New York: Hemisphere.

Nelson-Le Gall, S., Gumerman, R. A., & Scott-Jones, D. (1983). Instrumental help-seeking and everyday problem-solving: A developmental perspective. In B. DePaulo, A. Nadler, & J. Fisher (Eds.), *New directions in helping* (Vol. 2). New York: Academic Press.

Nuckolls, K. B., Cassel, J., & Kaplan, B. H. (1972). Psychosocial assets, life crisis and the prognosis of pregnancy. *American Journal of Epidemiology, 95,* 431–441.

Parsons, T., & Bales, R. (1955). *Family, socialization, and interaction process.* New York: Free Press.

Pearlin, L., & Johnson, J. (1977). Marital status, life-strains, and depression. *American Sociological Review, 42,* 704–715.

Riley, D., & Eckenrode, J. (1986). Social ties: Subgroup differences in costs and benefits. *Journal of Personality and Social Psychology, 51,* 770–778.

Rivenbark, W. H. (1971). Self-disclosure patterns among adolescents. *Psychological Reports, 28,* 35–42.

Rook, K. S. (1984). The negative side of social interaction: Impact on psychological well-being. *Journal of Personality and Social Psychology, 46,* 1097–1108.

Ross, H., & Sawhill, I. (1975). *Time of transition: The growth of families headed by women.* Washington, DC: Urban Institute.

Sandler, I. N., & Lakey, B. (1982). Locus of control as a stress moderator: The role of control perceptions and social support. *American Journal of Community Psychology, 10,* 65–80.

Stack, C. (1974). *All our kin: Strategies for survival in a Black community.* New York: Harper & Row.

Stroebe, M. S., & Stroebe, W. (1983). Who suffers more? Sex differences in health risks of the widowed. *Psychological Bulletin, 93,* 279–301.

Tietjen, A. (1982). The social networks of preadolescent children in Sweden. *International Journal of Behavioral Development, 5,* 111–130.

Turner, R. J., & Noh, S. (1982). *Psychological distress in women: A longitudinal analysis of the roles of social support and life stress.* Paper presented at the National Conference on Social Stress, University of New Hampshire.

Vanfossen, B. E. (1981). Sex differences in the mental health effects of spouse support and equity. *Journal of Health and Social Behavior, 22,* 130–143.

Vaux, A., Burda, P., & Stewart, D. (in press). Orientation towards utilizing support resources. *Journal of Community Psychology.*

Veroff, J., Douvan, E., & Kulka, R. (1981). *The inner American: A self-portrait from 1957–1976.* New York: Basic Books.

Veroff, J., Kulka, R., & Douvan, E. (1981). *Mental health in America: Patterns of help-seeking from 1957 to 1976.* New York: Basic Books.

Wahler, R. (1980). The insular mother: Her problems in parent-child treatment. *Journal of Applied Behavior Analysis, 13,* 207–219.

Waldrop, M., & Halverson, C. (1975). Intensive and extensive peer behavior: Longitudinal and cross-sectional analysis. *Child Development, 46,* 19–26.

Warren, R. (1975). *The work role and problem coping: Sex differentials in the use of helping systems in urban communities.* Paper presented to the annual meeting of the American Sociological Association, San Francisco.

Weinraub, M., & Wolf, B. M. (1983). Effects of stress and social supports on mother-child interactions in single- and two-parent families. *Child Development, 54,* 1297–1311.

Weiss, L., & Lowenthal, M. (1975). Life-course perspectives on friendship. In M. L. Lowenthal, M. Thurnher, & D. Chiriboga (Eds.), *Four stages of life.* San Francisco: Jossey-Bass.

Weiss, R. S. (1985). Men and the family. *Family Process, 24,* 49–58.

Wheeler, L., Reis, H., & Nezlek, J. (1983). Loneliness, social interaction, and sex roles. *Journal of Personality and Social Psychology, 45,* 943–953.

Whiting, B., & Whiting, J. (1975). *Children of six cultures.* Cambridge, MA: Harvard University Press.

Wilkins, W. (1974). Social stress and illness in industrial society. In E. Gunderson & R. Rahe (Eds.), *Life stress and illness.* Springfield, IL: Charles C. Thomas.

Wolchik, S. A., Sandler, I. N., & Braver, S. L. (1984). *The social support networks of children of divorce.* Paper presented at the American Psychological Association meeting, Toronto.

Young, M., & Willmott, P. (1957). *Family and kinship in East London.* London: Routledge and Kegan Paul.

11

Sex Differences in Cognitive Coping with Stress

Suzanne M. Miller
Nicholas Kirsch

Gender has often been cited as playing an important role in individuals' choice of coping strategies (that is, their response to stress in a particular situation) and coping styles (that is, their characteristic modes of dealing with stress). Common sense suggests that the physiological and environmental/cultural differences of being male or female should impact on levels of stress and subsequent adaptation. Despite this, and in spite of the recent plethora of literature concerning stress and its ill effects, there is surprisingly little in the literature on gender differences. Further, almost nothing is known about the cognitive factors that may underlie or exacerbate the effects of gender.

This chapter will attempt to distill and clarify the evidence pertaining to gender differences in stress responses, particularly as they relate to cognitive dimensions such as coping strategies and styles. Specifically, we will address the following two questions: (1) Is there evidence for sex differences either in cognitive response strategies and/or in dispositional coping styles?; and (2) What are the nature and consequences—the differential adaptiveness—of these alternative strategies and styles? We begin by presenting the major cognitive strategies and styles and the evidence

The research reported in this chapter was partially supported by the Robert Wood Johnson Foundation and by Temple University Grant-In-Aid of Research.

for and against sex differences in these coping patterns. We emphasize what is known and point out what is unknown or suspected, with a view to specifying critical empirical areas for future research. Finally, we conclude by summarizing how the data bear on the potential causes and development of gender effects.

WHY INVESTIGATE SEX DIFFERENCES IN COPING?

In spite of the many methodological problems with the reporting and assessing of psychological disorders, one finding that remains virtually uncontested is that women in Western cultures have higher rates of affective and anxiety disorders than do men, in both clinical and nonclinical populations (Amenson & Lewinsohn, 1981; Briscoe, 1982; Cleary, this volume; Dohrenwend & Dohrenwend, 1969; Hammen & Padesky, 1977; Jenkins, 1985; Miller & Ben Joseph, 1987a; Silverman, 1968; Weissman & Klerman, 1977). There are countless plausible explanations for this finding, and undoubtedly the true causes are many and interrelated (see Weissman & Klerman, 1977, for a thorough discussion of hypothesized causes).

Some of the recent investigations of psychopathology among college students and homogeneous young adult populations have found equivalent rates of morbidity in males and females—at least for depression—thus casting some doubt on the widely held belief that women are universally more depressed than men (Hammen & Padesky, 1977; Jenkins, 1985; Parker & Brown, 1979). If valid, two possible explanations for these divergent findings are (1) a developmental hypothesis—that is, sex differences in mental illness and concomitant coping change as a function of age so that the findings of equivalent male and female rates of depression (and anxiety) arise because the subjects are not yet at the age where these states are manifest; or (2) a sociological hypothesis—that is, the failure to find differences between male and female depression (and anxiety) scores is evidence that women are not inherently more prone to depression. Rather, changes in social climate and cultural conditions may result in a cohort effect, such that depression is equally likely in younger—but not older—men and women (Hammen & Padesky, 1977).

Given the significant differences in psychological morbidity, particularly among adult men and women, it becomes relevant and intriguing to explore whether there are significant gender differences in cognitive coping styles and strategies. To the extent that cognitive coping mechanisms are presumed to be important factors underlying vulnerability to anxiety and depression (Beck, 1976; Seligman, 1975), adult females should be found to display more maladaptive cognitive coping patterns than males.

THE EVIDENCE

The evidence on sex differences in cognitive coping styles and strategies comes from a wide range of theories and research.[1] Three major criteria were used for inclusion or exclusion of studies. First, we included studies that dealt specifically with coping cognitions in psychologically stressful situations and their implications for anxiety and depression. Such situations could be naturalistic, experimentally contrived, or hypothetical. Accordingly, studies were excluded if they focused on cognitive skills (e.g., problem-solving ability, verbal or math ability, etc.), cognitive strategies in nonstressful situations (e.g., decision-making and risk-taking studies), and social behaviors (e.g., love, conformity, etc.). As Deaux (1984) has argued, the nature of a situation is a critical determinant of an individual's cognitive perception of and response to that situation. Thus it is not unlikely that there will be discrepancies between the findings in this chapter and others, where situations of a different nature are the focus. A further criterion for inclusion was that the study had to focus on nonclinical groups. Since it is likely that clinically depressed and anxious subjects generally are characterized by maladaptive cognitive styles/strategies—regardless of gender—we omitted such populations (see Miller & Kirsch, 1986 for a full review).

A final criterion was that studies specifically reported analyses of gender differences. It was disappointing to find that a majority of the studies of cognitive coping and stress that would otherwise meet our criteria did not report on sex differences.[2]

Our discussion is organized in terms of the following six types of thought patterns: (1) negative self-evaluations, negative expectancies, and negative thoughts; (2) irrational thoughts, cognitive distortions, and information processing and recall; (3) causal attributions, including work on locus of control and perception of control; (4) self-monitoring and self-regulation studies, including research on delay of gratification, punishment, and self-control; (5) information seeking and avoidance; and (6) emotion-focused, problem-focused, and appraisal-focused coping.

We begin each section by describing briefly the theoretical rationale underlying each of these patterns; we then evaluate the findings with respect to such dimensions as the validity and reliability of the coping measures, the situational variables that were accounted for, comparability between the different studies, and generalizability to other populations. We end each section by evaluating the similarities and discrepancies in the data and by pointing out gaps to be filled by future research.

NEGATIVE SELF-EVALUATIONS, NEGATIVE EXPECTANCIES, AND NEGATIVE THOUGHTS

The work reviewed in this section is divided into three categories pertaining to negative views of the self, the future, and the world. The framework underlying many of these studies is Beck's (1976) cognitive theory of depression. Drawing on extensive clinical work, Beck's theory postulates a "negative cognitive triad" that depicts the depressed individual's views of the self, the world, and the future all as negative and as harbingers of depressed affect (Beck, 1976).

Other studies explore Bandura's (1977) self-efficacy theory, which is concerned with how a person's self-appraised coping ability influences subsequent feelings and actions in particular situations (Bandura, 1977, 1979, 1983). Self-efficacy expectations such as "I can perform at a competent level" need to be distinguished from outcome expectations such as "What will result from my actions." Bandura's theory postulates that positive self-efficacy is associated with higher motivation and effort, while low self-efficacy produces little initiative or output of energy. In contrast to Beck's theory, which is more specific to depression, Bandura's view implicates low self-efficacy expectations as precursors of both anxiety and depression (Bandura, 1979).

Negative Self-Evaluations

Negative self-evaluations refer to the depressed individual's view of him- or herself as inadequate, incompetent, deficient, and incapable of attaining any worthwhile fulfillment.

The studies reviewed here pertain not only to Beck's construct of negative self-appraisals and Bandura's self-efficacy view, but also to several other perspectives, including work on self-esteem, self-worth, and self-punitiveness. Only two of the eleven studies of negative self-evaluation reported finding any sex differences (Funabiki, Bologna, Pepping, & FitzGerald, 1980; Siegel, 1985).[3] Both studies used college populations, and in both cases females exhibited a more negative sense of self-worth than did males. In one study, Seigel (1985) asked normal, anxious, and depressed college freshmen to predict how they felt their roommates would evaluate them. Only the depressed students predicted that their roommates would evaluate them more negatively than their roommates actually did. Women were significantly more likely than men to show this pattern of negative bias. Seigel also found depressed women to be more self-derogatory than depressed men, suggesting that an overall negative response bias may dominate in women of college age. Although males and females showed equal rates of depression in this study, the negative bias characteristic of females may be a predisposing factor for later (more serious) depression. If so, then interventions designed to modify self-esteem would be warranted before depression becomes full-blown.

Similarly, Funabiki et al. (1980) found that undergraduate women were more likely than men to make self-deprecatory statements. Further, the number of self-deprecatory statements correlated with higher depression scores on the Beck Depression Inventory (BDI). As in the Seigel (1985) study, equal rates of depression were found among college-aged men and women, supporting the view that negative thinking in college-age populations may be a harbinger of future depression, particularly among women. These two studies had several weaknesses, however: they used self-report measures administered in hypothetically nonstressful settings to assess coping styles and were correlational in nature.

Of the other studies on self-evaluation, most were correlational and focused on generalized self-report statements, although a few of these studies also employed observer ratings of self-evaluation. Others assessed actual coping strategies employed during experimentally contrived "stressful" situations. In any event, none of the other studies in this area replicated or substantiated the results of Seigel (1985) or Funabiki et al. (1980) (although several employed similar populations and measures—e.g., Tabachnik, Crocker, & Alloy, 1983). Thus it seems likely that differential self-evaluations play at best a weak and inconsistent role in explaining gender effects in coping with stress.

Negative Expectations

According to Beck's cognitive theory, depressed individuals have a pessimistic outlook for the future, they expect negative outcomes in all their endeavors, and thus are often loath to take any action to change their predicament. In their negative view of the future, they pessimistically think today's pain and suffering will continue and worsen. Aspirations are short-lived because failure is the felt destiny. Overall, the evidence reviewed gives almost no indication that there are sex differences in adults' expectations of future success or failure in stressful episodes. Of the seven adult studies in this area, only one (Rosenfield & Stephan, 1978) yielded any sex differences.[4] In this study, males exhibited higher expectations for success than females on a task of figuregram matching. It is difficult to reconcile the results of this study with the results of other research. One possible methodological explanation is the relatively nonstressful nature of the task (figuregram matching) used by Rosenfield and Stephan. If this is a robust finding, then higher incidence of depression among women may not be the result of a maladaptive coping set in response to stressful episodes, but rather of a negative cognitive bias operative during more neutral or ambiguous events. The other studies either assessed expectancies of success and failure with self-report measures that asked subjects to imagine how they would cope in stressful situations, or had subjects perform "stressful" tasks in which they then estimated their degree of success/failure on the just completed task or reported their expected success/failure on future tasks of a similar nature.

In contrast to the preceding literature on adults, two studies of children found that boys and girls differ in their expectancies of success and failure (Dweck, Goetz, & Strauss, 1980). In the first study, 80 fifth-grade boys and girls completed four trials of an educational task in which failure was experimentally induced. After each trial they were given failure feedback and then asked their expectations for success/failure on the upcoming trial. For the fifth trial, the task, the experimenter, or both were changed for most subjects. Results from the children's expectancies of success or failure for the fifth trial revealed that when something was changed about the task, boys had higher expectancies for success than girls. This finding, the authors suggest, demonstrates that girls generalize their failure from one situation to another, while boys view the situations as distinct and independent in terms of what is required to succeed.

In the second study by Dweck et al. (1980), fourth, fifth, and sixth graders reported their expected grades for the next report card, three weeks away. This was done at two different times, before the fall report card and before the winter report card. Comparing these predictions with the actual grades revealed that (1) boys had higher expectations than girls before the first report card even though girls had received better grades on the last (spring) report cards, and (2) before receiving the second report card, girls' expectations of performance were equal to those of the boys, which were at the same high level as before the fall report cards. Girls' grades were significantly higher than boys' grades on both report cards, which probably explains the girls' rise in expectations between fall and winter. Boys' expectations in the winter were seemingly undaunted by their fall grades, which were below their expected grades.

Overall, the data from these experiments suggest that girls' expectations of future performance are affected more by past or present failures than by past or present successes whereas boys' expectations of future performance do not seem to be negatively affected by present or past failures.

The authors hypothesize that girls' "pessimistic" coping strategies lead to "lowered persistence, deterioration of problem-solving strategy in the face of difficulty, [and] avoidance of the area in which failure has taken place" (p. 452) and are detrimental to their school performance. It is difficult to integrate these findings with the general trend of the adult data discussed above. One highly speculative hypothesis that may account for the discrepancy is that these cognitive strategies are more accessible, or rather, measurable in young girls than in adults. Over the course of adolescence and young adulthood, these strategies may evolve into styles that are much more subtle, difficult to measure, and increasingly intertwined with other aspects of the person.

Negative Views of the World

Beck's (1976) cognitive theory postulates that depressed individuals have a negative world view in which they perceive environmental demands as insatiable and life events as obstacles that block the pathway to happiness. The evidence for gender differences in negative views is very weak. We found only five studies that reported looking for effects of gender. The only study that found any significant sex differences showed that college women reported more elation than college men in response to positive (hypothetical) situations, yet there were no sex differences in response to negative (hypothetical) situations (Kuiper & MacDonald, 1983).[5] This finding hardly suggests a negative bias in women's world views that might help explain their disproportionate incidence of affective disorders. However, one potentially interesting hypothesis suggested by this finding is that women's cognitions during stress are more likely to go to extremes and to fluctuate more widely than are men's.

The studies in this area used several different approaches to examining negative thoughts, including the self-reporting of negative thoughts during imagined or experimentally contrived events and the recalling of negative thoughts from past real-life events. Based on the absence of sex differences in these studies, it appears that males and females are not characterized by differential world views. It should be noted, however, that no studies of children's negative thinking were reviewed. Considering the data of Dweck et al. (1980) discussed above, investigations of children's positive and negative thoughts may be useful.

In sum, many studies have assessed cognitive coping traits, styles, and strategies pertaining to aspects of the negative cognitive triad (negative views of the self, the world, and the future), self-efficacy, and related constructs. A wide array of coping measures were employed using a variety of subject populations in both natural and laboratory settings, yet relatively few of the studies reported finding any significant gender differences.

IRRATIONAL THOUGHTS, COGNITIVE DISTORTIONS, AND INFORMATION PROCESSING

Distorted and/or irrational cognitions as well as negatively biased information processing are often implicated as causes of depression, anxiety, and other psychological disorders. For example, axiomatic in Beck's theory is that depression is maintained by preexisting "schemas" which ensure that all information is processed and appraised in a negative fashion (Beck, 1976; Beck, Rush, Shaw, & Emery, 1979; Kuiper & MacDonald, 1983). Similarly, in Ellis's (1962) view, depression is the result of illogical jumps in thinking (often in the form of catastrophizing) that prove to be maladaptive. An example might be the dysphoric college student who exclaims, "My girlfriend tells me I'm too dependent . . . she must be right, I'm just a helpless little baby." This is the opposite of even-handed, accurate perceptions of reality, and task-oriented thinking.

Irrational Thoughts and Cognitive Distortions

In research in this area, here again very few gender effects emerge. Only two of the nine studies of irrational thoughts and cognitive distortion reported finding significant sex effects.[6] Furthermore, the generalizability of these few positive studies appears to be limited. Chan & Tsoi (1984) found that female Chinese college students scored significantly higher than their male counterparts on the Chinese version of the Cognitive Distortion Questionnaire (CDQ). The CDQ consists of eight stories which subjects read and then rate for the thoughts, feelings, and expectations of the central character. The extent to which a subject's ratings conform to objective norms determines his/her cognitive distortion score. Therefore, scores on the CDQ are based on projections and do not directly reflect the subject's own cognitive distortions while coping with stress. These results are further compromised by the fact that depression scores on the BDI were significantly higher than BDI means of American college students, with Chinese males evidencing slightly higher levels of depression than Chinese females. Hence the cross-cultural generalizability of these findings is unclear.

With children, Kogan (1971) found boys in high pressure (stressful) task situations were more likely to guess on questions where they did not know the answer, even though subjects were penalized for guessing. The result was even stronger among boys who were highly anxious or defensive, although it is unclear whether this distortion of outcome probabilities was the cause or effect of anxiety and defensiveness. This finding dovetails nicely with the conclusion of Dweck et al. (1980) that boys do not generalize failure from one situation to another; they are "optimistic" whereas girls may be "sadder but wiser." That is, girls may be more cognizant of the odds against success, subsequently discarding many "risky" options in an attempt to avoid failure. If these findings are borne out by future research, they may implicate a specific cognitive component that is consistent with boys' higher incidence of conduct disorders (they fail to see potential failure) and girls' predisposition to helplessness (they overgeneralize failure).

Information Processing

In the area of information processing and recall, only one out of ten studies found any sex differences, showing that induced mood has a stronger distortive effect on women's word recall than on men's (Clark & Teasdale, 1985).[7] College students were shown pleasant and unpleasant words while in a normal mood. Half the subjects were then induced to be happy, whereas sadness was induced in the other half. Subjects then recalled words from those presented during the earlier normal mood. Females in the "happy" mood condition recalled more of the pleasant words than did the "happy" males. Conversely, females in the "sad" mood recalled more of the unpleasant words than did the "sad" males. These results may indicate that women's cognitions fluctuate more or are more plastic than are men's, although the differential adaptiveness of these opposing patterns remains unclear. Clark and Teasdale's second (1985) experiment, in part a manipulation check of the first study, further clouds these results. Apparently, the words displayed to subjects in the first experiment were found to be used more often in real life by women than by men. This phenomenon may have artifactually inflated women's recall of the words in the first study. Hence, this study needs to be replicated, using sexually undifferentiated words, before any conclusions can be drawn.

The studies reported in this section represent a wide range of experimental approaches, using a variety of cognitive measures on several distinct subject populations. Most of these studies assessed self-reports of one's own or other's thoughts and cognitions, typically not in relation to particular stressful events. Other studies, particularly those examining information processing and recall, used analog designs in which words or information were presented to subjects and then recall was assessed for errors or distortions. Taken together, the evidence presented suggests few if any sex differences in irrational thoughts, cognitive distortions, or information processing and recall while coping with stress.

CAUSAL ATTRIBUTIONS, LOCUS OF CONTROL, AND PERCEPTIONS OF CONTROL

The Reformulated Learned Helplessness model of depression posits three main attributional dimensions that are relevant in depression (Abramson, Seligman, & Teasdale, 1978). Individuals who are prone to chronic, generalized, and self-blaming depressions tend to make internal, stable, and global attributions for the cause of failure. Conversely, the cause of success tends to be attributed to external, unstable, and specific factors. The "locus of control" model (Lefcourt, 1982; Rotter, 1966) postulates that internalizers (those who tend to see events as determined by themselves) and externalizers (those who tend to attribute causality externally) are differentially prone to depression. Finally, "perceptions of control" focuses on a person's subjective appraisals of whether he or she has any influence in a given situation. Of the many studies reviewed here, few demonstrate clear sex differences in causal attributions, locus of control, or perceptions of control.[8]

In a series of field and laboratory-based experiments with children, Dweck and her colleagues found sex differences when assessing either attributional styles or strategies. Specifically, girls tended to attribute failure to internal, stable factors such as lack of ability, while boys tended to attribute failure to external factors such as the teacher, or to unstable factors such as effort (Dweck & Bush, 1976; Dweck & Goetz, 1977; Dweck & Reppucci, 1973). Furthermore, following failure feedback, subjects who made external attributions (usually boys) were more likely to work persistently and improve performance on the tasks, while internalizers (usually girls) were more prone to helplessness ("Since I lack the ability to succeed, why keep trying") and to suffer concomitant decrements in performance on the school-type tasks. In contrast, several conceptually similar studies failed to find sex differences (Diener & Dweck, 1980; Fisher, Rolf, Hasazi, & Cummings, 1984; Licht & Dweck, 1984; Rothbaum, Wolfer, & Visintainer, 1979).

Doherty and Baldwin (1985), in a longitudinal study of normal adults, found that sex differences in causal attributions developed over an eight-year period. Specifically, although no differences emerged in the earlier years of the study, women in the later years were more likely to endorse external attributions than men were. It is hard to account for these results. The authors hypothesized that a "cultural shift" had occurred whereby women who had entered the workplace in the late 1970s began to be made aware of the constraints on their abilities and so became more external in their attributions. This is a highly speculative and broad hypothesis that is difficult to reconcile with other findings. Furthermore, this study used the Internal-External Locus of Control Scale (Rotter, 1966), which collapses items across positive and negative events, stressful and nonstressful events, controllability and internality, and internal, stable, and global attributions. Since these dimensions appear to be differentially related to anxiety and depression, it would seem important to keep them methodologically distinct (Miller & Seligman, 1982).

One final study found sex differences in causal attributions, but the results are difficult to interpret (Amenson & Lewinsohn, 1981). Consistent with the attributional models, internal attributions for failure and external attributions for success were associated with depression in a community sample. Unexpectedly, however, men were higher on both of these attributions than were women. Further, women were found to be more depressed than men as assessed by clinical interviews and self-report. Contrary to the Reformulated Learned Helplessness Model, this study suggests that while men—not women—may have the insidious attributional style, they do not suffer the concomitant depressive consequences.

The inconsistent and weak sex effects obtained in studies of causal attributions of adults are compatible with the findings and conclusions of Rosenfield and Stephan (1978). They found that men, on a task presented to them as masculine, made internal attributions for success and external attributions for failure. However, when the identical task was described as feminine, males made the opposite attributions. Women showed a similar pattern: that is, when the task was deemed feminine, females made internal attributions for success and external attributions for failure, whereas when the identical task was deemed masculine, female subjects made external attributions for success and internal attributions for failure. Results also showed that motivation for the task ("ego involvement") and, to a lesser extent, expectancies of failure accounted for men's and women's different attributions. Not surprisingly, females had higher motivation on tasks described as feminine, while males had higher motivation on tasks described as masculine. The authors conclude that gender, in and of itself, is not a useful predictor of a person's causal attributions and that other factors, such as ego involvement, may be more pivotal. Indeed, to the extent that ego involvement is linked to the gender specificity of the task, one would expect females generally to display a negative attributional pattern in a variety of nondomestic situations typically considered to be masculine in nature (see also Deaux, 1984; Lenney, 1977).

In sum, the research that assesses causal attributions, locus of control, and perceptions of control during stressful episodes suggests no consistent differences between males and females. Studies included here used different research methodologies (e.g., self-reported attributions and control perceptions in actual or imagined stressful events, attributions and perceptions generated during experimentally contrived stressful events, and observer ratings of subjects' attributions and perceptions) as well as a variety of subject populations (e.g., community populations, college students). If causal attributions and control perceptions do in fact play a role in depression and related emotional disorders, the relevant theories and methodologies need to be modified to account for the lack of sex effects. Interestingly, Martin, Abramson, and Alloy (1984) found that female— but not male—college students rated another person's control over a laboratory task as higher than their own control over the same task. Differential perceptions of one's own control relative to that of others may represent an avenue for future research.

INFORMATION SEEKING AND AVOIDANCE

When individuals are threatened with aversive events, there are two alternative informational modes of coping that they can employ. "Monitoring" involves being alert for and sensitized to threat-relevant information, whereas "blunting" involves cognitive avoidance and transformation of threat-relevant cues (Miller, 1979a, 1980a, 1981, 1987, in press). Recent research in this area suggests that blunters often fare better during uncontrollable stressful events than their monitoring counterparts. One explanation is that individuals can most successfully reduce stress by "tuning out," that is, by engaging in distraction and related psychological techniques (Averill & Rosenn, 1972; Bandura, 1977, 1979, 1983; Cohen & Lazarus, 1973; Miller, 1987, in press; Miller & Mangan, 1983; Phipps & Zinn, 1986). Of the fifteen studies in this area, only three found significant sex differences (Stone & Neale, 1984; Viney & Westbrook, 1982; Watkins, Weaver, & Odegaard, 1986).[9]

In a study by Watkins et al. (1986), female coronary patients undergoing highly stressful cardiac catheterization were significantly more likely than male patients to be characterized by a blunting coping style, as assessed by the Miller Behavioral Style Scale (MBSS). Similarly, Viney and Westbrook (1982) found that chronically ill females indicated that they more often engaged in "escape-focused" coping strategies than did chronically ill men. Finally, Stone and Neale (1984) found, in a community sample, that women indicated using "distraction" coping strategies to cope with chronic stressors significantly more often than did men.

Taken together, of the studies reporting sex differences, women are more likely than men to blunt out stress-relevant information in a variety of situations. The bulk of these studies used the MBSS to assess coping style and/or assessed the use of coping strategies in specific situations. To the extent that women blunt in response to uncontrollable stressors, this may represent an adaptive coping strategy or style (Miller, 1979b, 1980b). However, most studies failed to demonstrate such a sex difference. More studies are needed that assess information-seeking strategies and styles of males and females during both controllable and uncontrollable situations, to determine whether one group is more adaptively flexible than the other.

SELF-MONITORING AND SELF-REGULATION

Self-blame and self-punitiveness are two prominent features in most descriptions of emotional disorders, particularly depression (Carver & Ganellen, 1983). In coping with stress, depressed individuals tend to be guilt ridden and to describe themselves as worthless and inadequate (Beck, 1976; Seligman, 1975). Of the six studies in this area, three reported sex differences. However, the results of these studies are not consistent with each other.

One study by Parker and Brown (1979) compared the coping of general medical patients with those of outpatient depressives. Subjects were provided with a checklist of behaviors, and indicated which ones they would engage in to cope with two hypothetical stressful situations. The results indicated that women were more likely than men to engage in self-consolation behaviors, such as "Spend money on yourself, seek warmth, listen to music." Moreover, men more often than women indicated engaging in "reckless" behaviors (akin to self-punishment) when coping with stress, such as "Do something to gain the attention of others, be reckless in some activity, drink alcohol." However, in a follow-up study using a slightly refined version of the coping behavior checklist, the findings on greater recklessness in men were not replicated (Parker & Brown, 1982).

Carver and Ganellen (1983) found that college females engaged in more self-criticism in response to hypothetical failures than did college males. Moreover, females tended to overgeneralize self-critical statements—for example, "If I can't do this well, I can't do anything well," and such overgeneralization was found to account for a high percentage of the variance in depression scores.

Finally, in two studies by Gotlib (1981, 1982), no sex differences were found in either self-administered rewards or punishments. Both studies compared normal subjects with depressed and nondepressed psychiatric inpatients. In the first study, self-reward and punishment were assessed as follows: Subjects performed word recall/recognition tasks and after each task indicated whether they thought, "That was a good choice, keep up the good work," or else, "That wasn't a good choice, I didn't do very well that time." If neither of these cognitions was appropriate the subject could pass. In the second study, subjects viewed prerecorded tapes of themselves debating various issues with another subject. While viewing the tape, at various intervals, each subject indicated whether his or her cognitions were self-rewarding, self-punishing, or neither, according to similar criteria as described above. Although the two psychiatric groups were higher on self-punishment and lower on self-reward than the nonpatient group, males and females did not differ from each other.

Overall, females appear to be more self-consoling (Parker & Brown,

1979) and self-critical (Carver & Ganellen, 1983) than males. However, the two groups do not appear to differ in self-administered rewards or punishments (Gotlib, 1981, 1982). These apparent discrepancies may be due to the fact that the studies are actually tapping subtly different constructs. Self-consolation, as assessed by Parker and Brown (1979), appears to involve the use of distraction and reassurance in the face of hypothetical threats, while self-criticism, as assessed by Carver and Ganellen (1983), involves self-evaluations in response to hypothetical failure. In contrast, self-reinforcement and self-punishment, as assessed by Gotlib (1981, 1982), appear to be more related to ongoing self-evaluations of actual performance, where performance outcome is ambiguous. Thus, it is conceivable that males and females might differ in the first two cognitions (self-consolation and self-criticism), but not in the latter (self-reinforcement and self-punishment). Taken together, the literature reviewed here suggests that there may be sex differences in self-monitoring. However, further research is needed to document the precise nature of these effects as well as their relation to depressive pathology.

Self-Control

Conceptually, self-control involves the processes of successfully maximizing positive events (delay of gratification) and minimizing negative events. Previous research suggests that the same cognitive dimensions that are adaptive when dealing with threatening situations (e.g., how information is processed) are also operative when dealing with the frustration of waiting for deferred rewards. Further, some research with adults suggests that those who are more prone to depression may be less able to wait successfully for preferred but delayed rewards than those who are not depressed (Rehm & Plakosh, 1975). This may be because depressives have negative expectations about the future and thereby are pessimistic about the value of waiting for deferred outcomes. The data in this area are conflicting as to sex differences. Out of seven studies involving adults or college students, only one found sex differences.

Wertheim and Schwarz (1983) assessed delay of gratification by obtaining subjects' self-reports of whether they would prefer an immediate but small reward or a delayed but larger reward. To assess delay of punishment, these authors presented three neutral tasks and three punishing tasks to subjects who then indicated the three tasks they preferred to undertake. The underlying assumption was that choosing to do the three punishing tasks immediately, thereby avoiding an aversive delay interval, was the more adaptive response. Among males—but not females—higher depression was in fact associated with immediate gratification and postponement of punishment. However, males in this study were found to be more depressed than females, which may account for the sex differences in these coping strategies. That is, depression rather than gender may have caused males to opt for immediate rewards and delayed punishment.

The delay of gratification by children has been extensively studied by Mischel and his colleagues (Mischel, 1968, 1973, 1974, 1979, 1984; Mischel, Ebbeson, & Zeiss, 1972; Mischel & Moore, 1973). One study reported looking for sex effects but failed to find any (Mischel & Moore, 1973). Two later studies of self-control in childhood both found sex differences. Humphrey (1982) and Kendall, Zupan, and Braswell (1981) found that girls scored higher than boys on "self-control." In the study by Kendall et al. (1981), children's self-control was measured by a 33-item Self-Control Rating Scale (SCRS), which attempts to tap disruptive behaviors. Humphrey (1982) utilized a revised version of this scale along with children's self-reports.

The evidence suggests that boys may show less self-control than girls as assessed in terms of disruptive, "acting out" behaviors, but not when measured by delay of gratification tasks. This brings into question the existence of a single unitary self-control construct and suggests that sex differences observed here may be related more to "externalizing" problems, such as conduct disorders, than to "internalizing" problems such as delay of gratification, depression, and anxiety. These findings are consistent with results of studies in children showing higher rates of externalizing disorders in boys than in girls (Eme, 1979; Rutter, Tizzard, Yule, Graham, & Whitmore, 1976).

EMOTION-FOCUSED, PROBLEM-FOCUSED, AND APPRAISAL-FOCUSED COPING

Problem-focused coping refers to attempts to modify or eliminate the source of stressors by taking instrumental actions, such as devising plans and strategies for getting admitted to graduate school. In contrast, emotion-focused coping refers to attempts to control stressor-related emotions and maintain affective equilibrium, such as commiserating with peers about the anticipatory anxiety revolving around applying to graduate school (Billings & Moos, 1984; Folkman & Lazarus, 1980). The usual method of determining an individual's strategy is to have the person complete a checklist, questionnaire, or interview indicating the strategies that he or she (1) actually remembers having employed during a recent stressful episode, (2) would use during a hypothetically described stressful episode, or (3) is currently using, here and now, to cope with a stressful situation.

Some evidence suggests that actively confronting a problem (problem-focused coping) is less likely to result in depression than is emotional regulation of a problem (emotion-focused coping) (Billings & Moos, 1981, 1984; Pearlin & Schooler, 1978). Other research suggests that while problem-focused coping may be more adaptive in changeable (controllable) situations, such as trying to get a job in times of economic expansion, emotion-focused coping strategies may be more adaptive in uncontrollable situations that must be accepted, such as being laid off from work due to economic recession (Coyne, Aldwin, & Lazarus, 1981; Lazarus & Folkman, 1984; Stone & Neale, 1984; Viney & Westbrook, 1982). A common cultural belief is that men more often use, and are more proficient with "problem-focused" coping strategies, while women more often rely on, and are more proficient with "emotion-focused" coping strategies (Stone & Neale, 1984). Six of the seven studies did in fact find significant gender differences. However, the nature and direction of these effects is somewhat controversial.

Billings and Moos (1981) studied a community sample of adults and found that while women scored higher than men on emotion-focused coping, the two groups did not differ in the use of problem-focused coping. In contrast, one study found evidence that whereas men relied more on problem-focused coping strategies during particular situations such as work, no significant sex differences emerged in the use of emotion-focused coping strategies (Folkman & Lazarus, 1980).

These discrepancies may be partially resolved by considering variations in the measures used to assess coping. In all the above studies, subjects were asked to choose a recent stressful life event and to indicate and describe the strategies they actually employed while coping with it. However, in the study by Billings and Moos (1981), the dimensions assessed included only the type and frequency of responses used and the perceived stressfulness of the sampled event. In contrast, Folkman & Lazarus (1980) used the Ways of Coping Questionnaire (WCQ), which, in addition to the above, also assesses whether the event in question is perceived to be controllable, uncontrollable, or requiring more information. There gender effects only emerged in the latter two categories. It is possible, then, that Billings and Moos failed to find sex differences in the use of problem-focused coping strategies because their subjects tended spontaneously to recall controllable situations. However, this explanation does not resolve inconsistencies in the data on emotion-focused coping.

Two related studies looked only at problem-focused coping. Viney and Westbrook (1982) asked chronically ill medical patients to indicate how they coped with their illness by rank-ordering six different coping strategies (supplied on cards by the experimenter). Men more often than women used "action strategies," defined as "flexible reality-oriented strategies." These seem conceptually similar to the definition of problem-focused coping proposed by other investigators and the study thus supports the findings of Folkman and Lazarus (1980). Finally, Shannan, DeNour, and Garty

(1976) found that among subjects with terminal renal failure, a highly debilitating and presumably stressful condition, men more often than women used active coping strategies, assessed in a sentence completion format. Interestingly, in a group of normal, healthy, and apparently non-stressed control subjects, no sex differences were found in this coping dimension, suggesting that differences may only be activated under conditions of threat.

One methodological weakness common to all the above studies is the retrospective and global nature of situations assessed. As such, important dynamics of the coping process may be forgotten or inadvertently edited out during the summarization process. To overcome these inadequacies, Stone and Neale (1984) used a prospective design in which they asked a community sample to complete a daily coping response checklist, consisting of 55 coping strategies, as well as open-ended essays describing how they were coping. Every stressor noted by the respondent was assessed for perceived controllability, desirability, changeability, meaningfulness, and whether or not it was expected. Results showed that men more often than women reported using "direct-action" strategies whereas women were more likely to use "catharsis." Further, for both sexes, problem-focused strategies were more often employed in controllable situations and emotion-focused strategies were more likely in uncontrollable situations.

Unfortunately, the Stone and Neale study has several limitations due to problems of validity and reliability of the coping measure, including reliance on self-report indices and overlapping of coping response categories. Additionally, the reflection and introspection entailed in daily completion of open-ended items may actually have a major effect on the ongoing coping process. Further, the study does not address the issue of which coping strategy is more adaptive and under what situations. Finally, as with previous studies, this work relies on subjective perceptions of variables, such as control, without independent measurements or manipulations of these factors. Conceivably control perceptions may be a consequence rather than a cause of strategy choice, and the main distinction between males and females may well reside in the perceptual domain.

In a different vein, Frank, McLaughlin, and Crusco (1984) asked college students to complete the Defense Mechanism Inventory (DMI), which assessed self-reported defense mechanisms used to cope with ten hypothetical situations. Results indicated males more often externalized conflict onto other persons or onto the environment (i.e., expressed anger to others and attributed their own negative intent to others), while women more often internalized conflict against the self (i.e., blamed themselves). Although these findings must be viewed with caution (the measure is unvalidated and situational variables were not taken into account), externalizing may represent a form of problem-focused coping whereas internalizing may represent a form of emotion-focused coping.

Appraisal-Focused Coping

Appraisal-focused coping refers to the way in which an individual defines and redefines the meaning of a stressful situation (Billings & Moos, 1984). This coping style has received relatively little attention in recent studies, perhaps due to confusions in the nature of the construct itself (cf. Krantz, 1983; Stone & Neale, 1984). Not surprisingly, results in this area have been mixed. Two of the six studies found sex differences.[10] Jemmot, Croyle, and Ditto (1984) asked subjects to estimate how often they became ill and found that while men's estimates were accurate, women overestimated their illness rates in comparison with their actual medical records. However, there were no sex differences in how subjects perceived the severity of their illnesses (see also Miller & Brody, 1985). Similarly, Kessler, Brown, and Broman (1981) found that among people experiencing symptoms of generalized psychological distress, women were more likely to appraise their condition as an emotional problem requiring special attention. Men, on the other hand, tended to view their distress as a problem not requiring any extraordinary action. These findings, if robust, could help explain the higher rates of female psychological morbidity and help-seeking. Of course, life expectancy differentials suggest that men's strategies may catch up with them and may be more deleterious in the long run. On the other hand, Stone and Neale (1984) found no sex differences in the appraisal-focused coping strategies of a sample of community adults. Stattin (1984) also failed to find sex differences in how adolescents appraised anxiety-provoking situations.

To summarize, it appears that the categories of emotion-focused and problem-focused coping may yield significant sex differences in how people cognitively cope with stress. Many of the studies found that men tend to cope with stress by using strategies that work directly to alter the stressful environment, whereas women may possibly use strategies that modify their emotional response. Further, it is possible that women appraise threatening events as more stressful than men do. However, given the methodological constraints of these studies, further research is needed before firm conclusions can be drawn. In particular, it will be important to vary systematically parameters of the aversive event, such as its controllability, while measuring corresponding perceptions of control along with strategy choice and affective level.

The present chapter explored the relation between gender and cognitive coping patterns under stress. A wealth of evidence suggests that compared to males, females have higher rates of anxiety and depression—the two major emotional responses to stressful situations. Most current theoretical perspectives emphasize the pivotal role of cognitive factors in accounting for these stress responses. Since women appear to be more vulnerable to stressors than their male counterparts, one would expect that they are characterized by more insidious and maladaptive cognitive coping patterns. To examine this possibility, we reviewed over 200 studies pertaining to six major theoretically derived cognitive categories. In general, the literature provides at best equivocal support for the existence of sex differences in cognitive coping with stress.

The strongest positive results are found in the domain of problem-focused coping, where a high proportion of studies (six of seven) obtained significant differences. Specifically, males are more likely to use problem-focused coping strategies than females, particularly at work, in uncontrollable situations, and in situations requiring more information. To the extent that problem-focused coping taps such attributes as aggressiveness and achievement-striving, this finding is consistent with previous investigations of male-female differences (Maccoby & Jacklin, 1974). Unfortunately, the bulk of these studies used retrospective, self-report instruments. Further, while a lack of problem-focused coping skills among females could well underlie helplessness and depressive symptomatology, these states were not assessed. It will be important to explore these effects in future work, using more direct observations and systematically measuring and manipulating core situational variables (e.g., control, chronicity) and affective responses (e.g., anxiety, depression).

A second area showing weaker support for sex differences has to do with self-monitoring. Three of seven studies showed that females tend to be both more self-critical and more self-consoling than males. These results must be interpreted with caution. First, although self-critical patterns appear to be maladaptive and associated with depression, the differential adaptiveness of self-consoling versus nonconsoling patterns is unclear. Further, these three studies relied on hypothetical, self-report scales. When more direct measures were obtained and related to ongoing performance, these results were not borne out (Gotlib, 1981, 1982). Finally, these studies did not consider situational variations such as type of event, chronic versus acute stressor, perceived controllability, and so forth. Hence, the generalizability and adaptational significance of such patterns remain elusive.

There is little support for the existence of gender differences in the categories of negative self-evaluations/expectations/thoughts; cognitive distortion/irrational cognitions/information processing; attributions/control perceptions; and information seeking. The few positive effects that do emerge are found primarily in work on cognitive strategies in children. In a series of studies, Dweck and her colleagues showed that boys are less likely to generalize failure and tend to make more external and unstable attributions for failure than girls. Consistent with this finding, girls tend to show less persistence in the face of failure compared to boys and to be more susceptible to helplessness-inducing experiences (Dweck & Bush,

1976; Dweck & Reppucci, 1973). However, given the relative paucity of research on children along with the existence of contradictory results in other childhood studies, these findings must be viewed with caution. If they are replicated in future research, it will be important to try to reconcile this work with the bulk of the adult literature, which shows no gender differences. It appears likely that the cause of this discrepancy may well involve a confluence of developmental, psychosocial, and biological factors, in addition to methodological differences, such as the use of direct "talking-one's-thoughts-out-loud" measures that can be obtained more easily with young children than with adults.

How can we account for the general lack of positive findings? One possibility that would salvage the cognitive perspectives on stress is that significant effects fail to emerge due to limitations in the design and methodology of the studies. As it stands, far too much of the research relies on often unvalidated self-report instruments to measure affective reactions, coping patterns, perceived situational variables, and self-regulatory adaptiveness. Further, assessments of anxiety and depression are often too global, collapsing across the two states. Similarly, questionnaire assessments of coping style too often fail to specify the nature of the event in question with regard to such critical factors as its controllability, predictability, chronicity, and so forth. Finally, such measures are rarely obtained in conjunction with concurrent measures of actual coping strategy. These problems are particularly evident in the categories of cognitive distortions and irrational thoughts. Given the current theoretical emphasis on person-by-situation interactions, more studies are needed that will simultaneously manipulate important situational parameters and measure coping style along with ongoing coping strategies (Miller, 1981, 1987, in press; Miller & Green, 1985; Mischel, 1973, 1979, 1981).

Perhaps one of the main problems with past research is that it has overlooked the most likely domains for the existence of sex differences. For example, a compelling and robust finding in the literature, at least with young children, is that males and females differ in their use of aggression, with the former tending to be more aggressive—particularly more physically aggressive—than the latter (Maccoby & Jacklin, 1974). Stress researchers have primarily focused on anxiety and depression in their study of responses to threat. Yet, might there not be gender differences in dysfunctional approaches to stress which involve the prototypic features of aggression, such as acting out? Two major questions arise: If we were to investigate explicitly sex differences in the adult use of aggression, would we find them? If so, how is male versus female aggression cognitively represented as a potential mode for coping with stress?

A second, although less likely, reason for the lack of sex differences is that the differential rates of anxiety and depression are simply artifacts of response biases, with males tending to underreport or suppress such symptomatology. To the extent that males are socialized to underreport these states, their incidence of depression and anxiety should be higher when assessed by clinical interviews or tasks that indirectly tap these syndromes than by self-report instruments. However, this does not appear to be the case (Amenson & Lewinsohn, 1981; Phillips & Segal, 1969; Weissman & Klerman, 1977). In the absence of demonstrated symptomatology, one must assume either that the individual is symptom free or that the symptoms are really there, but suppressed and transformed. This latter supposition harkens back to such concepts as "masked" depression to account for the nonoccurrence of depressive pathology. However, it is our view that such constructs are too vague and distant from the phenomenon under study to be of much value (see also Phillips & Friedlander, 1982). A more conceptually challenging possibility is that sex differences in anxiety and depression are cognitively derived, but the traditional theories do not tap the relevant cognitions. Alternatively, it may be that the cognitive level is not the route for sex differences. This view suggests that while the cognitive categories under consideration can be causes of depression and anxiety, they are neither necessary nor sufficient for these states to occur. Accordingly, the higher incidence of such pathology in females may be due to some other etiological factor, such as a higher incidence of life stresses, biological predisposition, and so forth.

In conclusion, the available evidence shows that females are more prone to psychological distress than males are, yet do not consistently demonstrate any underlying cognitive characteristic that would account for this difference. If this effect is borne out in future research, we may have to look elsewhere for the origins of female vulnerability.

NOTES

1. The literature review draws on a variety of sources, primarily journal articles, but also book chapters, manuscripts, presentations, and dissertations. The bulk of journal articles are from *Journal of Personality and Social Psychology, Journal of Consulting and Clinical Psychology, Journal of Abnormal Psychology,* and *Cognitive Therapy and Research.* The vast majority of the literature is from the late 1970s until the present, although some papers from as early as the 1960s were also included.

2. There are three possible explanations of why a study would fail to report sex effects: (1) sex differences were not considered (i.e., sex of subject was not included in analyses of group differences); (2) sex differences were in fact found, but reported elsewhere, in a different article from the same study or; (3) sex differences were looked for and not found but these negative results were not reported, probably due to space considerations. It is our opinion that the first two possibilities occur only rarely, and therefore in the bulk of the studies where sex differences were not reported, it would seem safe to

assume that, in fact, no sex differences were found. However, erring on the sides of caution and in the interests of space, such studies are not reviewed here (see Miller & Kirsch, 1986 for a full review).

3. The following studies of negative self-evaluations found no sex differences: Amenson & Lewinsohn (1981); Blatt, Quinlan, Chevron, McDonald, & Zuroff (1982); Fenigstein, Scheier, & Buss (1975); Heppner, Baumgardner, & Jackson (1985); Hirsch, Moos, & Reischel (1985); Kanfer & Zeiss (1983); Tabachnik, Crocker, & Alloy (1983); Underwood, Froming, & Moore (1977); Wright & Mischel (1982).

4. The following studies of negative expectations in adults found no sex differences: Amenson & Lewinsohn (1981); Garber & Hollon (1980); Golin, Jarrett, Stewart, & Drayton (1980); Kernis, Zuckerman, Cohen, & Spadafora (1982); McNitt & Thornton (1978); Viney & Westbrook (1982).

5. The following studies of negative views of the world found no sex differences: Deffenbacher & Hazaleus (1985); Harrell & Ryon (1983); Hollon & Kendall (1980); Oliver & Baumgart (1985).

6. The following studies of irrational thoughts and cognitive distortions found no sex differences: Amenson & Lewinsohn (1981); Davison, Feldman, & Osborn (1984); Deffenbacher & Hazaleus (1985); Hamilton & Abramson (1983); Johnson, Petzel, Hartney, & Morgan (1983); Oliver & Baumgart (1985). Sarason (1984) reported more cognitive distortions in female than male college students, but significance levels were not given.

7. The following studies of information processing found no sex differences: Brunstein & Olbrich (1985); Chanowitz & Langer (1981); Gotlib (1981); Hammen (1977); Harvey, Winters, Weintraub, & Neale (1981); Hasher, Rose, Zacks, Sanft, & Doren (1985); Ingram (1984); Swann, Jr. & Read (1981); Wells, Hoffman, & Enzle (1984).

8. The following studies of causal attributions and perceptions of control found no sex differences: Alloy & Abramson (1982); Amenson & Lewinsohn (1981); Brewin & Harris (1985); Cutrona, Russell, & Jones (1985); Diener & Dweck (1980); Dweck, Davidson, Nelson, & Enna (1978); Garber & Hollon (1980); Hamilton & Abramson (1983); Hammen, Krantz, & Cochran (1981); Heppner, Baumgardner, & Jackson (1985); Martin, Abramson, & Alloy (1984); Moore, Strube, & Lacks (1984); Mukherji, Abramson, & Martin (1982); Peterson, Semmel, von Baeyer, Abramson, Metalsky, & Seligman (1982); Rippere (1976); Rothbaum, Wolfer, & Visintainer (1979); Seligman, Abramson, Semmel, & von Baeyer (1979); Underwood, Froming, & Moore (1977); Weiner, Graham, Stern, & Lawson (1982).

9. The following studies of information seeking and avoidance found no sex differences: Burstein & Meichenbaum (1979); Carver, Antoni, & Scheier (1985); Cassileth, Zupkis, Sutton-Smith, & March (1980); Efran, Chorney, Ascher, & Lukens (1981); Gard & Edwards (1986); Houston, Fox, & Forbes (1984); Miller (1987); Miller & Ben Joseph (1987b); Miller & Brody (1985); Miller, Leinbach, & Brody (1985); Mullen & Suls (1982); Parker & Brown (1979, 1982).

10. The following studies of appraisal-focused coping found no sex differences: Kaslow, Rehm, & Siegel (1984); Mitchell, Cronkite, & Moos (1983); Stattin (1984); Stone & Neale (1984).

REFERENCES

Abramson, L. Y., Garber, I., Edwards, N. B., & Seligman, M. E. P. (1978). Expectancy changes in depression and schizophrenia. *Journal of Abnormal Psychology, 87,* 102–109.

Abramson, L. Y., Seligman, M. E. P., & Teasdale, J. D. (1978). Learned helplessness in humans: Critique and reformulation. *Journal of Abnormal Psychology, 87,* 49–74.

Alloy, L. B., & Abramson, L. Y. (1982). Learned helplessness, depression, and the illusion of control. *Journal of Personality and Social Psychology, 42,* 1114–1126.

Amenson, C. S., & Lewinsohn, P. M. (1981). An investigation into the observed sex difference in prevalence of unipolar depression. *Journal of Abnormal Psychology, 90,* 1–13.

Averill, J. R., & Rosenn, M. (1972). Vigilant and nonvigilant coping strategies and psychophysiological stress reactions during the anticipation of electric shock. *Journal of Personality and Social Psychology, 23,* 128–141.

Bandura, A. (1977). *Social learning theory.* Englewood Cliffs, NJ: Prentice-Hall.

————. (1979). Self-efficacy: An integrative construct. Invited address presented at meeting of the Western Psychological Association, San Diego.

————. (1983). Self-efficacy determinants of anticipated fears and calamities. *Journal of Personality and Social Psychology, 45,* 464–469.

Beck, A. T. (1976). *Cognitive therapy and the emotional disorders.* New York: International Universities Press.

Beck, A. T., Rush, A. J., Shaw, B. F., & Emery, G. (1979). *Cognitive theory of depression.* New York: Guilford.

Billings, A. G., & Moos, R. H. (1981). The role of coping responses and social resources in attenuating the stress of life events. *Journal of Behavioral Medicine, 4,* 139–157.

————. (1984). Coping, stress, and social resources among adults with unipolar depression. *Journal of Personality and Social Psychology, 46,* 877–891.

Blatt, S. J., Quinlan, D. M., Chevron, E. S., McDonald, C., & Zuroff, D. (1982). Dependency and self-criticism: Psychological dimensions of depression. *Journal of Consulting and Clinical Psychology, 50,* 113–124.

Brewin, C. R., & Harris, J. (1985). Induced mood and causal attributions: Further evidence. *Cognitive Therapy and Research, 9,* 225–229.

Briscoe, M. (1982). Sex differences in psychological well-being. *Psychological Medicine, 12,* Monograph Supplement 1.

Brunstein, J. C., & Olbrich, E. (1985). Personal helplessness and action control: Analysis of achievement-related cognitions, self-assessments, and performance. *Journal of Personality and Social Psychology, 48,* 1540–1551.

Burstein, S., & Meichenbaum, D. (1979). The work of worrying in children undergoing surgery. *Journal of Abnormal Child Psychology, 7,* 121–132.

Carver, C. S., Antoni, M., & Scheier, M. F. (1985). Self-consciousness and self-assessment. *Journal of Personality and Social Psychology, 48,* 117–124.

Carver, C. S., & Ganellen, R. J. (1983). Depression and components of self-punitiveness: High standards, self-criticism, and overgeneralization. *Journal of Abnormal Psychology, 92,* 330–337.

Cassileth, B. R., Zupkis, R. V., Sutton-Smith, K., & March, V. (1980). Information and participation preferences among cancer patients. *Annals of Internal Medicine, 92,* 832–836.

Chan, C., & Tsoi, M. M. (1984). The BDI and stimulus determinants of cognitive related depression among Chinese college students. *Cognitive Therapy and Research, 8,* 501–508.

Chanowitz, B., & Langer, E. J. (1981). Premature cognitive commitment. *Journal of Personality and Social Psychology, 41,* 1051–1063.

Clark, D. M., & Teasdale, J. D. (1985). Constraints on the effects of mood on memory. *Journal of Personality and Social Psychology, 48,* 1595–1608.

Cohen, F., & Lazarus, R. S. (1973). Active coping processes, coping dispositions, and recovery from surgery. *Psychosomatic Medicine, 35,* 375–389.

Coyne, J. C., Aldwin, C., & Lazarus, R. S. (1981). Depression and coping in stressful episodes. *Journal of Abnormal Psychology, 90,* 439–447.

Cutrona, C. E., Russell, D., & Jones, R. D. (1985). Cross-situational consistency in causal attributions: Does attributional style exist? *Journal of Personality and Social Psychology, 47,* 1043–1058.

Davison, G. C., Feldman, P. M., & Osborn, C. E. (1984). Articulated thoughts, irrational beliefs, and fear of negative evaluation. *Cognitive Therapy and Research, 8,* 349–362.

Deaux, K. (1984). From individual differences to social categories: Analysis of a decade's research on gender. *American Psychologist, 39,* 105–116.

Deffenbacher, J. L., & Hazaleus, S. L. (1985). Cognitive, emotional, and physiological components of test anxiety. *Cognitive Therapy and Research, 9,* 169–180.

Diener, C. I., & Dweck, C. S. (1980). An analysis of learned helplessness: II. The processing of success. *Journal of Personality and Social Psychology, 39,* 940–952.

Doherty, W. J., & Baldwin, C. (1985). Shifts and stability in locus of control during the 1970's: Divergence of the sexes. *Journal of Personality and Social Psychology, 48,* 1048–1053.

Dohrenwend, B. P., & Dohrenwend, B. S. (1969). *Social status and psychological disorder: A causal inquiry.* New York: Wiley.

Dweck, C. S., & Bush, E. S. (1976). Sex differences in learned helplessness: I. Differential debilitation with peer and adult evaluators. *Developmental Psychology, 12,* 147–156.

Dweck, C. S., Davidson, W., Nelson, S., & Enna, B. (1978). Sex differences in learned helplessness: II. The contingencies of evaluative feedback in the classroom, and III. An experimental analysis. *Developmental Psychology, 14,* 268–276.

Dweck, C. S., & Goetz, T. E. (1977). Attributions and learned helplessness. In J. H. Harvey, W. Ickes, & R. F. Kidd (Eds.), *New directions in attribution research* (Vol. 2). Hillsdale, NJ: Lawrence Erlbaum Associates.

Dweck, C. S., Goetz, T. E., & Strauss, N. L. (1980). Sex differences in learned helplessness: IV. An experimental and naturalistic study of failure generalization and its mediators. *Journal of Personality and Social Psychology, 38*, 441–452.

Dweck, C. S., & Reppucci, N. D. (1973). Learned helplessness and reinforcement responsibility in children. *Journal of Personality and Social Psychology, 25*, 109–116.

Efran, J., Chorney, R. L., Ascher, L. M., & Lukens, M. D. (1981). *The performance of monitors and blunters during painful stimulation.* Paper presented at the meeting of the Eastern Psychological Association, New York.

Ellis, A. (1962). *Reason and emotion in psychotherapy.* New York: Lyle Stuart.

Eme, R. F. (1979). Sex differences in childhood psychopathology. *Psychological Bulletin, 86*, 574–595.

Fenigstein, A., Scheier, M. F., & Buss, A. H. (1975). Public and private self-consciousness: Assessment and theory. *Journal of Consulting and Clinical Psychology, 43*, 522–527.

Fischer, M., Rolf, J. E., Hasazi, J. E., & Cummings, L. (1984). Follow-up of preschool epidemiological sample: Cross-age continuities and predictions of later life adjustment with internalizing and externalizing dimensions of behavior. *Child Development, 55*, 137–150.

Folkman, S., & Lazarus, R. S. (1980). An analysis of coping in a middle-aged community sample. *Journal of Health and Social Behavior, 21*, 219–239.

Frank, S. J., McLaughlin, A. M., & Crusco, A. (1984). Sex role attributes, symptom distress, and defensive style among college men and women. *Journal of Personality and Social Psychology, 47*, 182–192.

Funabiki, D., Bologna, N. C., Pepping, M., & FitzGerald, K. (1980). Revisiting sex differences in the expression of depression. *Journal of Abnormal Psychology, 89*, 194–202.

Garber, J., & Hollon, S. D. (1980). Universal vs. personal helplessness in depression: Belief in uncontrollability or incompetence? *Journal of Abnormal Psychology, 89*, 56–66.

Gard, D., & Edwards, P. W. (1986). *Pretreatment sensitization and chemotherapy-related nausea and vomiting.* Paper presented at the meeting of the Society of Behavioral Medicine, San Francisco.

Golin, S., Jarrett, S., Stewart, M., & Drayton, W. (1980). Cognitive theory and the generality of pessimism among depressed persons. *Journal of Abnormal Psychology, 89*, 101–104.

Gotlib, I. (1981). Self-reinforcement and recall: Differential deficits in depressed and nondepressed psychiatric inpatients. *Journal of Abnormal Psychology, 90*, 521–536.

———. (1982). Self-reinforcement and depression in interpersonal interaction: The role of performance level. *Journal of Abnormal Psychology, 91*, 3–13.

Hamilton, E., & Abramson, L. Y. (1983). Cognitive patterns and major depressive disorder: A longitudinal study in a hospital setting. *Journal of Abnormal Psychology, 92*, 173–184.

Hammen, C. L. (1977). Effects of depression, feedback, and gender on selective exposure to information about the self. *Psychological Reports, 40*, 403–408.

Hammen, C. L., Krantz, S. E., & Cochran, S. D. (1981). Relationship between depression and causal attributions about stressful life events. *Cognitive Therapy and Research, 5,* 351–358.

Hammen, C. L., & Padesky, C. A. (1977). Sex differences in the expression of depressive responses on the Beck Depression Inventory. *Journal of Abnormal Psychology, 86,* 609–614.

Harrell, T. H., & Ryon, N. B. (1983). Cognitive-behavioral assessment of depression: Clinical validation of the Automatic Thoughts Questionnaire. *Journal of Consulting and Clinical Psychology, 51,* 721–725.

Harvey, P., Winters, K. C., Weintraub, S., & Neale, J. M. (1981). Distractibility in children vulnerable to psychopathology. *Journal of Abnormal Psychology, 90,* 298–304.

Hasher, L. H., Rose, K. C., Zacks, R. T., Sanft, H., & Doren, B. (1985). Mood, recall, and selectivity effects in normal college students. *Journal of Experimental Psychology: General, 114,* 104–118.

Heppner, P. P., Baumgardner, A., & Jackson, J. (1985). Problem-solving self-appraisal, depression, and attributional style: Are they related? *Cognitive Therapy and Research, 9,* 105–113.

Hirsch, B. J., Moos, R. H., & Reischel, T. (1985). Psychosocial adjustment of adolescent children of a depressed, arthritic, or normal parent. *Journal of Abnormal Psychology, 94,* 154–164.

Hollon, S. D., & Kendall, P. C. (1980). Cognitive self-statements in depression: Development of an Automatic Thoughts Questionnaire. *Cognitive Therapy and Research, 4,* 383–395.

Houston, B. K., Fox, J. E., & Forbes, L. (1984). Trait anxiety and children's state anxiety, cognitive behaviors, and performance under stress. *Cognitive Therapy and Research, 8,* 631–641.

Humphrey, L. L. (1982). Children's and teachers' perspectives on children's self-control: The development of two rating scales. *Journal of Consulting and Clinical Psychology, 50,* 624–633.

Ingram, R. E. (1984). Toward an information-processing analysis of depression. *Cognitive Therapy and Research, 8,* 443–478.

Jemmott, J. B., III, Croyle, R. T., & Ditto, P. H. (1984). *Subjective judgements of illness prevalence and seriousness.* Paper presented at meeting of the Society of Behavioral Medicine, Philadelphia.

Jenkins, R. (1985). New horizons: Sex differences in minor psychiatric morbidity. *Psychosomatic Medicine,* Monograph Supplement 7.

Johnson, J. E., Petzel, T. P., Hartney, L. M., & Morgan, R. A. (1983). Recall of importance ratings of completed and uncompleted task as a function of depression. *Cognitive Therapy and Research, 7,* 51–56.

Kanfer, R., & Zeiss, A. M. (1983). Depression, interpersonal standard setting, and judgments of self-efficacy. *Journal of Abnormal Psychology, 92,* 319–329.

Kaslow, N. J., Rehm, L. P., & Siegel, A. W. (1984). Social-cognitive and cognitive correlates of depression in children. *Journal of Abnormal Child Psychology, 12,* 605–620.

Kendall, P. C., Zupan, B. A., & Braswell, L. (1981). Self-control in children:

Further analysis of the Self-Control Rating Scale. *Behavior Therapy, 12,* 667–681.

Kernis, M. H., Zuckerman, M., Cohen, A., & Spadafora, S. (1982). Persistence following failure: The interactive role of self-awareness and the attributional basis for negative expectancies. *Journal of Personality and Social Psychology, 43,* 1184–1191.

Kessler, R. C., Brown, R. C., & Broman, C. L. (1981). Sex differences in psychiatric help seeking: Evidence from four large surveys. *Journal of Health and Social Behavior, 22,* 49–64.

Kogan, N. (1971). Educational implications of cognitive styles. In G. Lesser (Ed.), *Psychology and educational practice.* Glenview, IL: Scott Foresman.

Krantz, S. E. (1983). Cognitive appraisals and problem-directed coping: A prospective study of stress. *Journal of Personality and Social Psychology, 44,* 638–643.

Kuiper, N. A., & MacDonald, M. R. (1983). Schematic processing in depression: The self-based consensus bias. *Cognitive Therapy and Research, 7,* 469–484.

Lazarus, R. S., & Folkman, S. (1984). *Stress, appraisal, and coping.* New York: Springer.

Lefcourt, H. M. (1982). *Locus of control: Current trends in theory and research.* Hillsdale, NJ: Erlbaum.

Lenney, E. (1977). Women's self-confidence in achievement settings. *Psychological Bulletin, 84,* 1–13.

Licht, B. G., & Dweck, C. S. (1984). Determinants of academic achievement: The interaction of children's achievement orientations with skill area. *Developmental Psychology, 20,* 628–636.

Maccoby, E. E., & Jacklin, C. N. (1974). *The psychology of sex differences.* Stanford, CA: Stanford University Press.

Martin, D. J., Abramson, L. Y., & Alloy, L. B. (1984). Illusion of control for self and others in depressed and nondepressed college students. *Journal of Personality and Social Psychology, 46,* 125–136.

McNitt, P. C., & Thornton, D. W. (1978). Depression and perceived reinforcement: A reconsideration. *Journal of Abnormal Psychology, 87,* 137–140.

Miller, S. M. (1979a). Coping with impending stress: Psychophysiological and cognitive correlates of choice. *Psychophysiology, 16,* 572–581.

———. (1979b). Controllability and human stress: Method, evidence and theory. *Behavior Research and Therapy, 17,* 287–304.

———. (1980a). When is a little information a dangerous thing? Coping with stressful life-events by monitoring vs. blunting. In S. Levine & H. Ursin (Eds.), *Coping and health.* New York: Plenum.

———. (1980b). Why having control reduces stress: If I can stop the roller coaster I don't want to get off. In J. Garber & M. Seligman (Eds.), *Human helplessness: Theory and applications.* New York: Academic Press.

———. (1981). Predictability and human stress: Towards a clarification of evidence and theory. In L. Berkowitz (Ed.), *Advances in experimental social psychology* (Vol. 14). New York: Academic Press.

———. (1987). Monitoring and blunting: Validation of a questionnaire to assess styles of information-seeking under threat. *Journal of Personality and Social Psychology, 52,* 345–353.

———. (in press). To see or not to see: Cognitive informational styles in the coping process. In M. Rosenbaum (Ed.), *Learned resourcefulness: On coping skills, self-regulation and adaptive behavior.* New York: Springer.

Miller, S. M., & Ben Joseph, H. (1987a). *Gender differences in affective variables.* Unpublished manuscript, Temple University.

———. (1987b). The relation between monitoring and self-criticism on self-regulation and self-criticism. Unpublished manuscript, Temple University.

Miller, S. M., & Brody, D. S. (1985). *Coping with stress by monitoring vs. blunting: Implications for health.* Paper presented at the meeting of the American Psychological Association, Los Angeles.

Miller, S. M., & Green, M. L. (1985). Coping with stress and frustration: Origins, nature, and development. In M. Lewis & C. Saarni (Eds.), *Socialization of emotions.* New York: Plenum.

Miller, S. M., & Kirsch, N. (1986). The role of gender in cognitive responses to stress. Unpublished manuscript, Temple University.

Miller, S. M., Leinbach, A., & Brody, D. S. (1985). *Coping style in hypertensives: Implications for treatment.* Paper presented at the meeting of the Society of Behavioral Medicine, New Orleans.

Miller, S. M., & Mangan, C. E. (1983). Interacting effects of information and coping style in adapting to gynecologic stress: Should the doctor tell all? *Journal of Personality and Social Psychology, 45,* 223–236.

Miller, S. M., & Seligman, M. E. P. (1982). The reformulated model of helplessness and depression: Evidence and theory. In R. J. Neufeld (Ed.), *Psychological stress and psychopathology.* New York: McGraw-Hill.

Mischel, W. (1968). *Personality and assessment.* New York: Wiley.

———. (1973). Toward a cognitive social learning reconceptualization of personality. *Psychological Review, 80,* 252–283.

———. (1974). Processes in delay of gratification. In L. Berkowitz (Ed.), *Advances in experimental social psychology* (Vol. 7). New York: Academic Press.

———. (1979). On the interface of cognition and personality: Beyond the person-situation debate. *American Psychologist, 34,* 740–754.

———. (1981). A cognitive social learning approach to assessment. In T. V. Merluzzi, C. R. Glass, & M. Genest (Eds.), *Cognitive assessment.* New York: Guilford Press.

———. (1984). Convergences and challenges in the search for consistency. *American Psychologist, 39,* 351–364.

Mischel, W., Ebbeson, E. B., & Zeiss, A. R. (1972). Cognitive and attentional mechanisms in delay of gratification. *Journal of Personality and Social Psychology, 21,* 204–218.

Mischel, W., & Moore, B. (1973). Effects of attention to symbolically presented rewards on self-control. *Journal of Personality and Social Psychology, 28,* 172–179.

Mitchell, R. E., Cronkite, R. C., & Moos, R. H. (1983). Stress, coping, and depression among married couples. *Journal of Abnormal Psychology, 92,* 433–448.

Moore, J., Strube, M. J., & Lacks, P. (1984). Learned helplessness: A function of attribution style and comparative performance information. *Personality and Social Psychology Bulletin, 10,* 526–535.

Mukherji, B. R., Abramson, L. Y., & Martin, D. J. (1982). Induced depressive mood and attributional patterns. *Cognitive Therapy and Research, 6,* 15–21.

Mullen, B., & Suls, J. (1982). "Know thyself": Stressful life changes and the ameliorative effect of private self-consciousness. *Journal of Experimental Social Psychology, 18,* 43–55.

Oliver, J. M., & Baumgart, E. P. (1985). The dysfunctional attitude scale: Psychometric properties and relation to depression in an unselected adult population. *Cognitive Therapy and Research, 9,* 161–167.

Parker, G., & Brown, L. B. (1979). Repertoires of responses to potential precipitants of depression. *Australia and New Zealand Journal of Psychiatry, 13,* 327–333.

———. (1982). Coping behaviors that mediate between life events and depression. *Archives of General Psychiatry, 39,* 1386–1391.

Pearlin, L. I., & Schooler, C. (1978). The structure of coping. *Journal of Health and Social Behavior, 19,* 2–21.

Peterson, C., Semmel, A., von Baeyer, C., Abramson, L. Y., Metalsky, G. I., & Seligman, M. E. P. (1982). The attributional style questionnaire. *Cognitive Therapy and Research, 6,* 287–299.

Phillips, D., & Segal, B. (1969). Sexual status and psychiatric symptoms. *American Sociological Review, 34,* 58–72.

Phillips, I., & Friedlander, F. (1982). Conceptual problems in the study of depression in childhood. In L. Grinspoon (Ed.), *Psychiatry 1982: Annual review.* Washington, DC: American Psychiatric Association.

Phipps, S., & Zinn, A. B. (1986). Psychological response to amniocentesis: II. Effects of coping style. *American Journal of Medical Genetics, 25,* 143–148.

Rehm, L. P., & Plakosh, P. (1975). Preference for immediate reinforcement in depression. *Journal of Behavior Therapy and Experimental Psychiatry, 6,* 101–103.

Rippere, V. (1976). Antidepressive behavior: A preliminary report. *Behavior Research and Therapy, 14,* 289–299.

Rosenfield, D., & Stephan, W. G. (1978). Sex differences in attributions for sex-typed tasks. *Journal of Personality, 46,* 244–259.

Rothbaum, F., Wolfer, J., & Visintainer, M. (1979). Coping behavior and locus of control in children. *Journal of Personality, 47,* 118–135.

Rotter, J. B. (1966). Generalized expectancies for internal vs. external control of reinforcements. *Psychological Monographs, 80* (Whole No. 609).

Rutter, M., Tizzard, J., Yule, W., Graham, P., & Whitmore, K. (1976). Research Report Isle of Wight Studies, 1964–1974. *Psychological Medicine, 6,* 313–332.

Sarason, I. G. (1984). Stress, anxiety, and cognitive interference: Reactions to tests. *Journal of Personality and Social Psychology, 46,* 929–938.

Seigel, S. J. (1985). *Interpersonal perceptions and consequences of depressive-significant other interactions: A naturalistic study of college roommates.* Unpublished Master's thesis, Northwestern University.

Seligman, M. E. P. (1975). *Helplessness: On depression, development and death.* San Francisco: Freeman.

Seligman, M. E., Abramson, L. Y., Semmel, A., & von Baeyer, C. (1979). Depressive attributional style. *Journal of Abnormal Psychology, 88,* 242–247.

Shannan, J., DeNour, A. K., & Garty, I. (1976). Effects of prolonged stress on coping style in terminal renal failure patients. *Journal of Human Stress, 2,* 19–26.

Silverman, C. (1968). *The epidemiology of depression.* Baltimore: Johns Hopkins University Press.

Stattin, H. (1984). Developmental trends in the appraisal of anxiety-provoking situations. *Journal of Personality, 52,* 46–57.

Stone, A. A., & Neale, J. M. (1984). New measure of daily coping: Development and preliminary results. *Journal of Personality and Social Psychology, 46,* 892–906.

Swann, Jr., W. B., & Read, S. J. (1981). Acquiring self-knowledge: The search for feedback that fits. *Journal of Personality and Social Psychology, 41,* 1119–1128.

Tabachnik, N., Crocker, J., & Alloy, L. B. (1983). Depression, social comparison, and the false-consensus effect. *Journal of Personality and Social Psychology, 45,* 668–699.

Underwood, B., Froming, W. J., & Moore, B. S. (1977). Mood, attention, and altruism: A search for mediating variables. *Developmental Psychology, 13,* 404–414.

Viney, L. L., & Westbrook, M. T. (1982). Coping with chronic illness: The mediating role of biographic and illness-related factors. *Journal of Psychosomatic Research, 26,* 595–605.

Watkins, L. O., Weaver, L., & Odegaard, V. (1986). Preparation for cardiac catheterization: Tailoring the content of instruction to coping style. *Heart and Lung, 15,* 382–389.

Weiner, B., Graham, S., Stern, P., & Lawson, M. E. (1982). Using affective cues to infer causal thoughts. *Developmental Psychology, 18,* 278–286.

Weissman, M. M., & Klerman, G. L. (1977). Sex differences and the epidemiology of depression. *Archives of General Psychiatry, 34,* 98–111.

Wells, G. L., Hoffman, C., & Enzle, M. E. (1984). Self- versus other-referent processing at encoding and retrieval. *Personality and Social Psychology Bulletin, 10,* 574–584.

Wertheim, E. H., & Schwarz, J. C. (1983). Depression, guilt, and self-management of pleasant and unpleasant events. *Journal of Personality and Social Psychology, 45,* 884–889.

Wright, J. C., & Mischel, W. (1982). The influence of affect on cognitive social learning person variables. *Journal of Personality and Social Psychology, 43,* 901–914.

12

Stress Responses and Personality

Suzanne C. Ouellette Kobasa

"Why are there only twenty women executives?" I wondered as I assembled the data from an initial study of stress (Kobasa, 1979). The primary aim of the study was to understand how personality served as a buffer or moderator in the stress-illness relationship. I had also hoped, however, to look at gender differences in this process—to consider whether personality functioned as a resource for stress resistance in the same way for the men and women executives of a midwestern utility company. Unfortunately, there were only 20 women out of nearly 900 subjects—not enough for a meaningful comparison.

In the ten years that have passed since then, a great deal of work has been done on moderator variables in the stress process—that is, variables that serve to buffer the negative effect of stressors. Some studies, by no means the majority, have included personality variables but only a small subset of these have considered gender differences. Before turning to the research literature, however, I decided to obtain some firsthand impressions of how women construe the stress in their lives and how they understand what influences whether they stay healthy or fall sick under stress. Having heard and read reflections from men on these issues, I was curious about the differences that gender might make for developing a model of stress resistance. I conducted open-ended interviews and group discussions with women lawyers, so as to compare their experiences with what had been learned from largely male groups.

In this chapter interviews with groups of women lawyers will introduce a general model for studying personality, stress, and stress resistance. Following the depiction of the model and of the distinctive place of personality within it, the chapter turns to a review of the available relevant literature on the major personality variables that have been studied as buffers of the negative effects of stress: control, self-concept, Type A, and hardiness. Studies of female, male, and combined groups are considered; some of these specify gender differences, most do not.

NOTES FROM A FOCUS GROUP

Seeking to understand how women lawyers perceive for themselves the impact of work-related stress in their lives, I invited a group to talk freely about their jobs. The women gathered around the table varied in law specialty, stage in law career, age group, and life style.

The women unanimously agreed that the term "stressful" is applicable to many aspects of a lawyer's life. With regard to their work, they brought up such issues as: the struggle to make partner in their firms; the often poor match between the realities of practicing law and that for which law school had prepared them; the amount of work required of them on a daily basis; the ethical dilemmas encountered in their practices; and the seemingly sexist and discriminatory acts of their older male colleagues. With regard to life outside of work, the women talked about the pressures introduced into their lives by a variety of life changes: the onset of illness in one or both of their parents; meeting someone who provoked them to reevaluate their single and unattached life style; a first baby at age 40. The discussion also revealed concerns and stressful events that, according to all present, simultaneously involved several areas of life that cannot be strictly classified under a single social science label such as "work stress," "family stress," or "personal stress." Examples included the corporate lawyer's balancing of responsibilities to her big city firm and to her aging parents in a faraway small town, the trial lawyer's difficulties in fostering a new yet potentially long-term relationship while also meeting her formidable professional goals, the 40-year-old's decision to have a child and not to cut back on her many commitments in her active civil rights practice.

Consensus also characterized the group's portrayal of the negative effects that the stressfulness of women lawyers' lives can have on both physical and psychological health. Referring to their own experiences and those of other women lawyers they know, the women described numerous and varied warning signs that stress was reaching excessively high levels. The most salient complaints were weekly migraine headaches, trouble sleeping at night, temper outbursts, difficulty in becoming pregnant, feelings of depression, and frequent nocturnal trips to the bathroom.

The long discussion, however, was not always so bleak in its portrayal of the women lawyers' experiences. When I asked, "Does stress always mean trouble for your health and well-being?" some of the participants provided a more optimistic story, citing incidents in which a woman lawyer dealt with what most people would agree to be high levels of stress without falling sick. Examples of resiliency or resistance in the face of stress ranged from depictions of very specific coping stategies to broad statements on individuals' philosophies of life.

One participant appeared to have read every book ever published on techniques of stress management. She described her meditation program and her athletic club membership as her keys to health in a life that included partnership in a major downtown firm, four children under the age of fifteen, and a struggling artist husband. Another woman argued that it was the availability of social resources that made the difference between her friend's success under stress and her own debilitation. She depicted her friend as someone who had a mentor within her firm guiding her efforts and a lover at home supporting all her professional and personal achievements: her ability to talk with and receive advice from both had gotten her through a lengthy and difficult trial without even one sleepless night. The same group member described herself, on the other hand, as someone who hoped to succeed in her firm despite the lack of a confidant in her personal life and senior partners who represented only obstacles. She clearly saw good advice and emotional support from others as important stress buffers. Without them, she explained to the group, she felt doomed to suffer anxiety and urinary tract infections whenever she took on a new case.

Her comments provoked other participants to nominate the specific things that they thought one might do for oneself or obtain from others in order to resist the negative health effects of stress. The list of secret weapons in the war with stress included taking a time management course, cutting red meats from one's diet, taking in an au pair helper, and signing up for biofeedback treatments.

At that point, however, two women expressed their fear that any attempt to find the single best solution to the women lawyers' stress problems would be futile. For them, there was no magic bullet. Rather, one characterized as her "bottom line" in facing stress the ability always to know and feel that she was doing what she had chosen to do both in work and in the other areas of her life; although this ability might express itself through a variety of specific behaviors that someone else might label stress management techniques, what was critical for her was that it represented an active and self-determined stance. The other woman depicted as fundamental to effective coping a clear and consistent awareness of one's values and priorities. A third participant noted the importance of realizing that one has the capacity or skills to express one's values and priorities. Finally, a fourth contributor noted her agreement with William James' belief that one can successfully respond to any changes in and demands from one's environment if one also feels that the environment values one's efforts and offers room for autonomous activity.

CONCEPTUALIZING PERSONALITY AS A SOURCE OF DIFFERENCES IN WOMEN'S RESPONSES TO STRESS

The summary of the focus group with women lawyers demonstrates the complexity of the stress process in women's lives. Even a cursory review of these qualitative data indicates that to understand how women react to stress requires more than just recording the sources of stress in their environments and the assumed consequences of these for women's physical and mental health. One also needs to consider what it is that increases or lessens the likelihood that stressors will lead to illness. In other words, one wants to understand those factors that serve as moderators of stress or, using the phrase that I prefer, as stress-resistance resources. Figure 1 presents the minimum requirements of a model for guiding stress research. Each component or box in the model is filled in with an example or two from the discussion with women lawyers.

Under the heading "Stress-Resistance Resources" are three types of moderators of environmental stressors that work together to create a buffer between those stressors and negative stress consequences. According to this

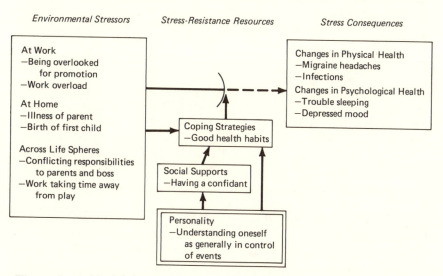

Figure 1. A Model for Research on Stress Resistance with Examples for Major Components.

model, there is no direct and inevitably positive association between increases in stressor levels and a worsening of physical and mental health. The box labeled "Coping Strategies" refers to specific ways of perceiving, interpreting, and acting in the face of stressors that minimize their threat and lessen the degree of negative arousal evoked. The women lawyers' exercise or meditation, their use of time management techniques, and their health-related habits such as regular physical exercise are all relevant to this component of the model. The box labeled "Social Supports" refers to all of those resources for managing stressors that one obtains through interactions with others: turning to a mentor at work for advice, enjoying the emotional support of an intimate, and having someone to take over household chores are all examples of using others either to resolve or minimize a stressful situation.

The third and, for this chapter, most important, stress-resistance resource is "Personality." When stress researchers refer to personality, they have in mind something distinctive to the individual, as opposed to the environment or social context in which he or she resides (Kobasa, 1979; Kobasa, Maddi, & Kahn, 1982). The emphasis is on personality as a general predisposition to respond in particular ways. In asking about the relationship between personality and environmental stressors such as life events, stress researchers consider what it is that the individual *brings to* the encounter with stress. The women lawyers' references to their overall approaches to life and the degree to which they express self-determination, clarity about values and priorities, personal competence, and an ability to have a meaningful impact on the world all point to the critical role played by personality in the stress process.

It is also typically assumed that personality refers to something about the individual that is persistent, demonstrating consistency across time and a variety of situations. Some stress researchers may choose to focus on personality characteristics that are cardinal, that is, those that fundamentally influence all domains of an individual's life. Others may select characteristics that are restricted to shaping behavior in only selected spheres. All, however, generally assume that the aspects of personality to be considered in stress research are constituents of that which Allport called the "Johnian quality of John and the Marian quality of Mary" (Allport, 1961).

Evidence exists for all of the following as major sources of stress resistance: control; a self-concept that reflects high self-esteem and low self-denigration; the absence of the Type A behavior pattern, that is, being Type B; and hardiness. Each of these is defined below. The more of each of these that one has, the less likely one is to suffer psychological or physical debilitation due to environmental stressors.

As one reviews the data, however, one notes the varying strengths of the findings. Not all of the studies employ the most appropriate methodology. With respect to design, one wishes to find longitudinal-prospective approaches, which require the researcher to collect baseline levels of stress consequence or outcome variables. It is only when effects are found for stress and stress-resistance resources *while* initial levels of outcome variables are controlled that one can speculate on causal influences on health. Too often, however, stress and personality researchers have relied on retrospective designs and concurrent data collection. With regard to statistics, the preferred technique is to use multiple regression analyses in which the cross-product term (environmental stressor × personality characteristic) is entered into the equation after the main effect terms for stressor and personality.[1] Here one again finds many studies falling short of the ideal: in most early (and some recent) studies, researchers created subgroups in their sample and compared the correlation between stressors and stress outcomes for subjects high on the personality characteristic with the correlations of those low on the characteristic. Without knowing the level of stressors or stress outcomes for each of the groups, however, it is impossible to make meaningful interpretations of their findings. Cohen and Edwards (1986), in a recent review paper, argue articulately for the statistical inappropriateness and uninterpretability of these studies.

Other issues that one should keep in mind in evaluating personality and stress studies concern the stress outcome. Although claims are usually made for the impact of stressors and stress-resistance resources on health in general, outcome variables are often restricted to psychological concerns, such as depression and anxiety. Fewer studies include physical illness (for example, onset of infection) or physiological processes (for example, increase in cholesterol level) as outcomes. Another concern is the nature of the group under study. In the area of personality and stress, investigations involving convenience samples of college students still outnumber those of adults in real-life settings. Here too we need to know more about the level of stress students experience compared to that of adults.

These comments are not intended to dissuade the reader from a concern with personality and its impact on stress responses. An equally cautionary introduction could accompany a discussion of social support or coping as stress-resistance resources. In fact, recent papers by Kasl (e.g., 1985) make clear that most aspects of the field of "stress and disease" contain fundamental problems yet to be resolved. In reviewing the current state of the art, we find not only areas where one may have gone wrong in the past, but also justification for continued and more sophisticated effort in the future.

The personality characteristics selected for review here are those for which at least two studies support its effectiveness as a moderator of environmental stressors and at least one study allows a statement about gender differences. These criteria require the exclusion of personality variables such as private self-consciousness (e.g., Mullen & Suls, 1982) and sensation seeking (e.g., Smith, Johnson, & Sarason, 1978).[2]

WHAT WE NOW KNOW ABOUT PERSONALITY AND STRESS RESPONSES

The studies are reviewed in two groups: (1) those which involve as subjects either men only or a combined group not analyzed by gender, and (2) those which involve only women or a combined group subdivided expressly for the purpose of observing gender differences. In this way we can evaluate the importance of gender in the case of each personality characteristic.

Control

The notion that individuals who perceive themselves as having control over events in their lives cope more effectively than do individuals who place others or fate in charge has generated more research on personality as a stress-resistance resource than has any other individual difference concept. Put in precise social learning terms, some researchers predict that under stress, individuals who hold a generalized *internal* locus of control belief that events are contingent upon their behavior will show less debilitation than those who have a generalized *external* locus of control belief that events are contingent upon external factors. Other researchers use "mastery" or "personal competence," terms more familiar to humanistic and ego psychology.

Furthermore, control is the personality characteristic around which the most intriguing gender differences emerge. In a review that essentially ignores gender, Cohen and Edwards (1986) concluded that control is the personality characteristic with the most consistent and strongest evidence for stress buffering. However, focusing on studies in which women have been observed closely or in which gender differences were elaborated challenges their conclusion. Contradictory findings and perplexing results emerge as one begins to consider whether or not control works in the same way for women as it does for men.

Studies of men and combined groups. The earliest support for the control prediction is a study by Johnson and Sarason (1978). Using concurrent data from 124 college students, they found that only those with external locus of control experienced anxiety and depression in the face of stressful life events. Four years later, Sandler and Lakey (1982) obtained similar results using a smaller college sample and the fatalism dimension of the Rotter scale (Mirels, 1970): although there was a positive relationship between life events and psychological symptoms for all students, those with an external locus showed a stronger association.

Both the Johnson and Sarason and Sandler and Lakey studies, however, rely on subgrouping correlations, the problem noted above, and do not present critical information such as the mean levels of symptoms for each of the subgroups. Somewhat more reassuring, at least on statistical grounds, are those studies employing regression techniques. Lefcourt, Miller, Ware, and Sherk (1981), for example, apply hierarchical regression analyses in three cross-sectional studies of college students. Using both the Rotter scale and the Multidimensional-Multiattributional Causality Scale (MMCS) of Lefcourt, von Bayer, Ware, and Cox (1979), they demonstrated the impact of different measures of control on the relationship between life events and general mood disturbance. Evidence of a buffering effect was found for both generalized internal control and locus of control specific to affiliations with others.

Generalizing the control notion to a group of 965 married adults, Husaini, Neff, Newbrough, and Moore (1982) demonstrated, in seven out of eight separate regression analyses, that adults who have a sense of "personal competence" are less likely to experience depression when dealing with life events. In one of the few stress studies involving minority groups, Wheaton (1982) further elaborates the control notion for adults. In a random sample of 132 Anglo-Americans and 108 Mexican-Americans, taking into account sex, education, church attendance, social desirability, and physical problems, regression analyses showed that individuals who tend not to accept personal outcomes as inevitable, unchangeable, and predetermined experienced fewer symptoms of depression when confronted with acute life events (but not with chronic stressors).

Although most studies focus on control and its direct influence upon the coping process, a few have considered its indirect effects, demonstrating how control mediates the effectiveness of social support as a stress-resistance resource. Sandler and Lakey (1982) found that having support was more beneficial for students with an internal locus of control than for externals. Among internals, the greater the support, the weaker the link between stress and psychological symptoms. Among externals, support made no difference: the likelihood of negative stress consequences was as great for externals with support as for externals without support. These findings are supported by other work that benefits from the use of regression analysis (e.g., Husaini et al., 1982).

Much of the research evidence drawn from studies of men or combined groups appears to support the claim that individuals with a personal sense of control (assessed as either internal locus of control, low fatalism, or personal competence) are more likely to stay healthy under stress. The reader should note, however, that there are contradictory findings. Krause and Stryker (1984), for example, in a longitudinal study of over 2000 middle-aged men, suggest the complicated possibility that control acts as a buffer only when it exists to a moderate degree; too much control or too little may not be helpful. Two longitudinal studies, McFarlane, Norman, Streiner, and Roy (1983) and Nelson and Cohen (1983), failed to show any stress-buffering effect by control. These two studies, however, are exceptions. One can conclude from the bulk of the work on control that, in general, adults who have an internal sense of control are less likely than those with an external locus of control to become ill in the face of life stressors.

Women and gender differences. In a study of 300 married women, Krause (1985) obtained results similar to those on men and combined groups. Krause also, however, makes a unique contribution in this investigation by taking into account subjects' possible tendency to present themselves in a socially desirable way. In other words, Krause recognizes that women might have a tendency to minimize both their reports of negative events in their lives, such as divorce or financial problems, as well as their experience of negative effects such as symptoms of depression. He hypothesized that social desirability attenuates the interaction effect between stress and control beliefs. Through a statistical procedure, he controlled for the effects of social desirability on depression. In so doing he found that locus of control buffered the effects of stress on depressive symptoms. In fact, he noted that the impact of stress on depression was approximately 60 percent stronger for women with external control beliefs.

In studies that involve explicit comparisons of men and women, findings emerge that are less straightforward. Toves, Schill, and Ramanaiah (1981), for example, redid the earliest control study by Johnson and Sarason and found internal locus of control to be a stress-resistance resource for men only. Similarly, Lefcourt (1982) described subdividing his subjects and finding that being internal versus external in control had no impact on how women responded to stressors. His male students, on the other hand, enjoyed the buffering effect: those who were internal showed less of a stressor/distress connection than those who were external.

A third study, however, offers a very different picture. Husaini et al. (1982), in the study described above, decided deliberately to take up the question of gender differences in stress resistance. In investigations of differential responsiveness to stressors, they saw a potential explanation for the often reported gender difference in psychiatric symptoms (a difference that has women suffering more distress). They pursued this idea by comparing the extent to which personal competence and social support protect women, in comparison to men, from depression in the face of stressful events.

Although their results were many and not equally strong, one can conclude that for both men and women, there were direct influences from life events and personal competence on depression. With regard to the stress-buffering offered by personal competence, regression results portrayed this personality style as slightly *more* effective for women. In addition, one finds for both men and women a conditioning of social support effects by personality. Most striking were the results for both men and women that showed that when individuals are feeling low in personal competence, some forms of social support have a negative effect on health. For example, for men and women under high stress, higher support from friends when one is feeling low in competence leads to higher vulnerability to stressors. Husaini and colleagues interpreted this interaction between stress-resistance resources with the suggestion that higher social support may pose to individuals with less competence a serious ego threat, and thereby provoke greater depression.

In trying to make sense of the inconsistency between the study by Husaini et al. (1982) and the Toves et al. (1981) and Lefcourt studies, one should note that Husaini et al. have the advantages of adult married subjects and not students, a significantly larger sample, and a more complex research design. The most appropriate conclusion to be drawn across these studies is that the case for control in women is not settled. It should not, however, be dismissed as a stress-resistance resource in women; results are convincing enough to justify additional study.

Finally, important data on women and control appear in the now-classic study by Pearlin and Schooler (1978) of the relationships among life strain in various role areas, general psychological resources, specific coping responses, and emotional distress. Drawing on a large-scale study of 2300 individuals, they find that there is a "pronounced imbalance between the sexes in their possession and use of effective mechanisms" (p. 15). "Mastery," assessed as the extent to which one sees one's life chances as being under one's control in contrast to being fatalistically ruled, is one of the general resources or personality characteristics that buffers the emotional impact of chronic stressors in their study. According to Pearlin and Schooler, mastery is found predominantly among the males in the sample. The authors suggest that this difference has to do with socialization patterns, which less adequately prepare women to confront the environmental stressors of life.

Given the work reviewed above, it is safe to conclude that although there are some similarities, control does not always "work" as a stress-resistance resource in the same way for men and women. Exactly how and why control has a different impact across gender are still unclear. One possibility is that women do not have "enough" of this personality resource. It may be that there are thresholds for control, that is, a certain amount may be necessary for effective stress buffering, and that women's typical levels do not reach this certain amount. Another possibility is that one kind of control works for men and another works for women. Contrasting the Husaini et al. and Pearlin and Schooler studies with those of Lefcourt and Toves, Schill, and Ramanaiah one can argue for a difference between control conceived of as (1) a sense of personal competence or mastery, and that defined as (2) generalized expectancies regarding control within oneself (rather than in others or fate) over a variety of personal, interpersonal, and broad sociopolitical domains. It may be that the former—that is, feeling effective in what it is that one has to do in life—is more important for women's stress resistance than it is for men's. The latter, more important for men, appears dependent on believing that one holds securely within oneself general influence over all of life's arenas.

A third possibility may be that we are not measuring control as well in women as in men. Men may be more willing to endorse items indicating that they have control over various aspects of their lives. Women, in contrast, may have a tendency to minimize the relationship between any action they might take and any significant changes in social and political affairs. As Krause showed, when one is sensitive to the issue of social desirability and uses techniques to reduce the bias in measurement, the stress-buffering effects of control, not previously apparent among women, become so.

Self-Concept

This aspect of personality concerns the degree to which individuals hold positive views and reject negative views about themselves: respectively, the presence of self-esteem and the absence of self-denigration. In depictions of the stress and coping process, investigators emphasize the importance of how one evaluates oneself. How threatened one feels is dependent upon how one evaluates not only the seriousness of the stressful situation but one's resources to meet it. The general prediction is that individuals high in self-esteem and low in self-denigration will be less likely to suffer debilitation than those low in self-esteem and high in self-denigration. As the studies reviewed below demonstrate, this prediction holds as strongly for women as it does for men.

Studies of men and combined groups. There is one major study that provides data on males, females, and gender differences: the Pearlin and Schooler investigation introduced above. Working with a combined group of over 2000 subjects, they found in a series of regression analyses that the presence of favorable attitudes toward the self and the absence of negative attitudes significantly moderates the negative emotional impact of life strains in the role areas of marriage, parenting, household economics, and occupation. Comparing the relative efficacy of the two self-concept resources with each other and with mastery, their third personality moderator, Pearlin and Schooler found a fairly clear ordering in the efficacy of personality characteristics. Freedom from self-denigration emerged as the most potent protector against stress-related debilitation, followed by mastery and self-esteem.

Women and gender differences. With regard to women, gender differences, and self-concept, the Pearlin and Schooler study offers a message as pessimistic as the one they provided for mastery. Women are lower on self-esteem and higher on self-denigration than are men. Again, sex differences emerge to identify women as less well-equipped to deal with life stress.

Two studies involved only women and generally support the depiction of self-concept as a stress-resistance resource. So, although positive views of self may be weaker in women, they appear strong enough to buffer the negative effects of stressors. Nuckolls, Cassel, and Kaplan (1972) included self-esteem in their composite measure of psychosocial assets (along with marital adjustment, family relationships, friendship patterns, and feelings about pregnancy). They found that women who had high stressful life event scores before and during their pregnancies and who were also low on psychosocial assets had more delivery complications recorded in their charts than any other subgrouping of subjects. Similar findings were reported from a more statistically sophisticated, longitudinal study of women and self-esteem (Hobfoll & Leiberman, 1987). Observing 99 Israeli women who had experienced either a normal delivery, a caesarean section, a preterm delivery of an infant weighing less than two kilograms, or a spontaneous abortion, Hobfoll and Leiberman found self-esteem to be an effective stress-resistance resource both at the time of the obstetrical event and three months later: women with higher self-esteem showed less depression and anxiety.

The studies of self-concept, although far fewer than those of control, suggest that the self-concept operates as effectively as a stress-resistance resource for women as it does for men. Gender differences do appear to exist in the degree to which women and men equally possess self-esteem and self-denigration (Pearlin & Schooler, 1978). Future work, therefore, should attempt to establish how the self-concept might be enhanced in women so as to increase their resiliency in the face of stress.

Type A Behavior Pattern

The Type A behavior pattern refers to a combination of psychological characteristics that includes extreme competitiveness, achievement striving, high job involvement, time urgency, and hostility. Type B refers to the absence of this pattern. In general, the research literature characterizes individuals high in Type A as stress-prone and likely to suffer negative health consequences. Glass (1977) conceptualizes demanding environments as provoking the Type A pattern in susceptible individuals, thereby increasing their psychophysiological responses to these environments.

With regard to gender differences, when one controls for socioeconomic, occupational, or educational factors, the incidence of Type A is comparable for women and men, and being Type A appears to be as bad for women's health as it is for men's. Closer examination of specific studies, however, reveals that gender is relevant to how one measures the effects of Type A, conceptualizes its determinants, assesses which aspects of Type A are to be conceptualized, and determines exactly what aspects of Type A are detrimental for health.

Studies of men and combined groups. Much of the work on Type A consists of field studies which document the main effect of Type A on physical health, as opposed to the interaction effect that one typically seeks in studies of stress resistance. There are also, however, a smaller number of field studies that do consider Type A in its reaction to stressful environments. Caplan and Jones (1975), for example, studied 122 male students during a computer shutdown. Gathering data immediately before the shutdown and five months later, they gained limited support for the stress resistance of Type A. Specifically, the one analysis that involved perceptions of change in workload, anxiety, and Type A showed that Type A students had a greater positive correlation between perceived change in workload and anxiety than Type B students. No other analysis was significant. A study by Suls, Gastorf, and Witenberg (1979) is also only marginally supportive of the moderating power of Type A. Using 125 undergraduates as subjects, the investigators found that students scoring high on Type A showed a stronger association between anxiety and undesirable and unexpected events for which personal control is indeterminable than Type B students. No other significant results emerge, however, in this study that involved several subgrouping comparisons. Finally, a study of 339 managers by Ivancevich, Matteson, and Preston (1982) offers the advantage of a nonstudent sample, but not that of a consistently compelling set of findings. In about a third of their subgrouping analyses, they showed that managers who are high on Type A suffered more from the negative consequences of stress. They argue that Type B moderates the negative impact of quantitative workload on systolic and diastolic blood pressure, and the impact of role conflict on systolic pressure.

Findings of studies in which Type A is considered as a stress-resistance factor are, in summary, not as clear-cut as those which show direct links between Type A and health. One should also note, however, that the former group did not employ the most sophisticated approaches now available to the evaluation of environmental stressors or stress moderation.

Women and combined groups. Using a design similar to that which they used in their study of managers, Ivancevich and colleagues studied 57 women nurses in the field. They evaluated the moderating power of Type A with regard to a number of job stressors (quantitative and qualitative work load, time pressure, physician relations, supervisor relations, and role conflicts). The stress outcomes that they considered in their cross-sectional approach included both psychological and physiological outcomes: job satisfaction; serum cholesterol and triglycerides; systolic and diastolic blood pressure; and percent body fat. Although only seven of their sixty subgrouping analyses were significant, the investigators suggest that being Type B protects one from the negative effects of stress. More specifically, Type A nurses show a greater association between serum cholesterol and time pressures, role conflict, and quantitative overload, and between systolic blood pressure and quantitative overload than do Type B nurses.

MacDougall, Dembroski, and Krantz (1981) offer a fascinating laboratory study of the differences between men and women with regard to what elicits a negative Type A stress response. Tests such as reaction time performance and reactions to immersion in cold water, which have been found to provoke differential cardiovascular activity in Type A and Type B men, failed to so so with women. In other words, in response to the standard laboratory stressors, the cardiovascular reaction of Type A women was the same as that for Type B women. When the stressor was changed to include an interpersonal stressor of a competitive nature, however, one finds differences between the two female groups. When women were forced to interact with others in the context of an oral history quiz, Type A women showed greater heart rate and higher systolic pressure than Type B women.

On the basis of the Type A studies that fit the stress and stress-resistance model assumed in this chapter, little can be said about gender differences. The MacDougall, Dembroski, and Krantz study does suggest that men and women may differ with regard to the type of stressor with which personality interacts. In their study, one observes the stress buffering of Type B in women when they are confronting an interpersonal stressor and not when they encounter the instrumental laboratory task typically used in studies of men. Apart from this study, however, one can only conclude that Type A has similar effects for men and women as they deal with stressors.

One also has to emphasize that there have been very few studies that have looked at Type A in interaction with specific environmental stressors. Again, most studies look only at the direct effects of Type A on health and not the indirect or resistance effects. Results on Type A and women from the Framingham Heart Study (one of the two major field studies documenting a main effect of Type A on health), however, suggest that stress-resistance studies might be very revealing.

In documenting the effects of Type A, Haynes and Feinleib (1980) note that all of the following increase women's risk for coronary heart disease: being a clerical worker, having demanding family responsibilities, working with an unsupportive boss, living with a blue-collar husband, and lacking job mobility. Each of these occupational and socioeconomic characteristics might be translated into sets of environmental stressors. It appears that, for the Framingham women, it is not only being Type A, but being Type A while also contending with a number of serious stressors that puts one at risk for heart disease. The Framingham results suggest a number of interesting personality and stress-resistance hypotheses.

Hardiness

Like the Type A behavior pattern, hardiness is a constellation of psychological characteristics, containing expressions of commitment, control, and challenge. *Commitment* is the ability to believe in the truth, importance, and interest value of who one is and what one is doing; and thereby, the tendency to involve oneself fully in the many situations of life, including work, family, interpersonal relations, and social institutions. *Control* refers to the tendency to believe and act as if one can influence the course of events. Persons with control seek explanations with an emphasis on their own responsibility and not simply in terms of others' actions or fate. *Challenge* is based in the belief that change, rather than stability, is the normative mode of life. Persons with challenge seek out change and new experiences, approaching them with cognitive flexibility and tolerance for ambiguity. The basic hardiness proposition is that among persons facing significant environmental stressors, those high in hardiness will be significantly less likely to fall ill, either mentally or physically, than those who lack hardiness and display alienation, powerlessness, and threat in the face of change.

As was noted at the beginning of this chapter, in references to my own work, hardiness studies are essentially studies of personality and stress resistance in men. There are only a few published studies of hardiness and women, and a formal test of gender differences across the various data sets that now exist is not yet completed. What is known is presented here in the spirit of encouraging more research on personality and stress resistance.

Studies of men and combined groups. Building upon retrospective work, Kobasa, Maddi, and Kahn (1982) conducted a prospective/longitudinal study with 259 male middle-level business executives. These executives from whom personality, stressful life event, and general physical health data had been collected in 1975 provided yearly stressor and illness reports for the next two years. A hardiness score was created for each subject from the 1975 data by creating a composite from the five scales (out of an original fifteen) that appeared—on conceptual and, later, empirical grounds—

to be the best indicators of the hardiness construct. These scales were the Work, Self, and Powerlessness subscales from the Alienation versus Commitment Test (Maddi, Kobasa, & Hoover, 1979), the Rotter Internal Locus of Control Scale (1966), and the Security Scale from the California Life Evaluation Schedule (Hahn, 1966).

In the face of stressful life events, and when baseline physical illness level was controlled, executives lower in hardiness were more likely to become ill than were those with higher hardiness scores. In addition, the stress-buffering effect of hardiness was particularly strong when the executives were under high stress. In other words, hardiness protects male executives from experiencing negative health outcomes when faced with negative life events, and the protection is especially strong when the life events are especially stressful.

Other hardiness studies have examined the joint effects of personality with other stress-resistance resources (exercise, family medical history, objective social assets, and perceived social supports) in male executive groups (Maddi & Kobasa, 1984). In general, the results show hardiness to be independent of these other moderators and to combine additively with them in boosting stress resistance. An important exception to this conclusion, however, emerged in a study of hardiness and perceived family support (Kobasa & Puccetti, 1983). Interestingly, among executives facing high levels of stress, only those high in hardiness appear to benefit from family support, that is, from feeling that they are part of a cohesive family in which they can freely express their emotions. The executives reporting the most physical symptoms were those scoring high on stressful events, low on hardiness, and high on family support. One interpretation of these results is that for executives who are feeling alienated from what is going on in their work lives, out of control, and no longer challenged, the family's offer of support becomes an opportunity for retreat or withdrawal. Additionally, the executives under study were confronting stressors having primarily to do with work. It may very well be that feelings of emotional expressivity and cohesiveness in the family do not provoke the kind of coping that these executives needed to engage in. A third possibility draws on the study by Husaini et al. (1982) reviewed earlier that provides similar social support and personality findings. It may be that for the low hardy male executive a "supportive" wife may unwittingly pose an ego threat by making her husband feel dependent on her. His feelings of inadequacy and his likelihood of falling ill are increased by her attempts to help.

In a hardiness study involving a combined group, Nowack (1986) examined the buffering effects of both hardiness and Type A, using daily life hassles as his measure of environmental stressors and psychological distress and burnout as his stress outcomes. His subjects were 193 human service employees, 68 percent of whom were women. Since outcome data were collected at baseline, Nowack was able to control for prior levels of distress and burnout. Hardiness was associated with lower levels of psychological distress and burnout, and for subjects under stress, higher levels of hardiness were associated with lower levels of burnout.

Women and gender differences. Two studies offer some support for generalizing hardiness effects to women, while a third study suggests the opposite conclusion. In a dissertation, Hill (1982) examined relationships among environmental stressors, hardiness, coping styles, and psychiatric symptoms. Her subjects were 99 white, employed, well-educated, middle-class women; about half were married and the majority had either one or no children. Using prospective data collection, she observed women's coping styles across a number of career and interpersonal events and evaluated the extent to which (a) coping styles were shaped by personality hardiness as opposed to situational determinants, (b) coping styles and hardiness were related to psychiatric symptomatology, and (c) hardiness had an indirect effect on symptoms through its effect on coping styles. Results relevant to hardiness were that when prior symptoms are controlled, stressful life events, lack of hardiness, and an incompetent coping style are all linked with later symptoms. Hill interprets her analysis to show that hardiness works directly to reduce symptoms, rather than working mainly through its effect on coping.

Additional support for at least part of the hardiness notion comes from a study of women and depression by Ganellen and Blaney (1984). Using a slightly different assessment of hardiness and analyzing the three component scales separately, they found main effects for commitment to self and vigorousness and interaction effects between commitment to self and stressful life events in the predicted direction.

Using 82 female secretaries as their subjects, Schmied and Lawler (1986) found no support for the hardiness moderator hypothesis. Moreover, neither hardiness nor Type A had a main effect on a general physical illness score. A surprising finding was that Type B women with high stress, not Type A women, had high illness scores. The authors propose a number of explanations for their findings and the differences between them and those gained in studies of men. First, they speculate that hardiness in women may be best conceptualized and measured by constructs other than the ones currently employed. Second, they suggest that the difference they observe in women may have to do with their occupational setting. Schmied and Lawler's subjects were secretaries. The early hardiness work involved executives and professionals.

Elaborating on this point, one might speculate that occupational settings serve to enhance or stifle the stress-resistance effect of personality. Business executives may find themselves in jobs that allow them to exercise, and perhaps even to grow in, commitment, control, and challenge. Secretaries, on the other hand, may confront jobs which limit their expression of hardiness. It may indeed be the case, for example, that some bosses enjoy personal expressions of control at the expense of their secretaries' sense of control. This speculation points toward a hardiness study in which one measures occupational receptivity or encouragement of hardiness, along with individuals' general predisposition toward hardiness and environmental stressors.

LEARNING MORE ABOUT PERSONALITY, GENDER, AND STRESS RESPONSES

In bringing the questions of gender differences to the study of personality and stress response, two basic points emerge. The first is that the available studies depict women, as well as men, as benefiting from personality as a source of stress resistance. Although sex differences do emerge as one reviews individual projects, the general picture is that the more women feel in control, have high self-esteem and low self-denigration, are Type B rather than Type A, and express hardiness, the less likely are they to fall ill under stress. The second lesson points to the value of certain methodological improvements in our conducting of stress-resistance research. In trying to make sense of gender differences, we find that there are some approaches that are more useful than others. The discussion of control, for example, points up the importance of controlling for measurement bias, as well as the possibility of there being thresholds that control must meet in order to function as a buffer. In studies of self-concept, one finds the value of changing one's designs to allow for studies seeking to enhance self-esteem in subjects. The Type A literature suggests the usefulness of studies that directly assess stressors along with behavior pattern, as well as the use of different laboratory techniques for men and women. Similarly, hardiness studies of women tell us that in order better to see the effect of personality, we may need to consider different measurement scales.

Another conclusion that one can draw is that there are too few studies of the kind reviewed in this chapter. The neglect of personality in studies of stress among women and stress and gender differences is somewhat surprising given numerous studies showing that women suffer more symptoms under the impact of stressors, and given the theme prevalent in the psychological and sociological literatures that depicts women as having been socialized in a way that keeps them from developing resilient personalities (e.g., Radloff, 1980). While little boys are being taught to be oriented toward problem solving, independent and in control; little girls are learning how to express emotions, be sensitive toward others, and act in a dependent way. Both the available data on stress outcomes and the long-standing socialization themes should generate more investigations of the impact of gender on stress-resistance processes.

One explanation for the lack of studies may be the inadequacy of current paradigms. We need, for example, to reconceptualize the personality characteristics we propose as stress-resistance resources. We need to ask ourselves at this point in the development of our field if we are looking at the right variables, rather than assume that because a variable "worked" in a study of men or a combined group, it is also applicable to women.

Our choice of personality variables should be guided by a coherent theoretical framework that we make explicit for our reader. More expansive theorizing is likely to provoke the need for more complex personality hypotheses. Rather than continuing to do single variable studies, we need to turn toward a whole person or personological approach to stress resistance.

A related recommendation is the elaboration of a contextual focus. Future researchers need to develop ways of systematically studying stress resistance as that which occurs within a variety of interpersonal, small group, sociopolitical and cultural contexts. Varying contexts, furthermore, may facilitate or hinder the expression of those personality characteristics that one nominates as stress-resistance resources. In some jobs or relationships, it may be easier for a woman to express hardiness than in others. For example, a study by Cronkite and Moos (1984) suggests that the relationships among an individual's self-esteem, coping response, and later functioning under stress are critically dependent upon his or her partner's corresponding coping level. Finally, our intention as stress researchers is not only to understand personality-based stress resistance but to enhance it. These recommendations will help us to advance our intervention efforts.

NOTES

1. The cross-product term is an index of the difference between the slope of the stressor-stress outcome relationship for persons high in the personality characteristic and the slope of the relationship for persons low in the resource; thereby, it indicates the effectiveness of the proposed stress-resistance resource.

2. Other concerns led to the exclusion of the personality-related characteristics of coping styles (e.g., the approach versus avoidance coping strategies in Cronkite and Moos, 1984) and social skills (e.g., the individual difference factors of social competence, social anxiety, and self-disclosure in Cohen, Sherrod, and Clark, 1986).

REFERENCES

Allport, G. W. (1961). *Pattern and growth in personality.* New York: Holt, Rinehart, and Winston.

Caplan, R. D., & Jones, K. W. (1975). Effects of work load, role ambiguity, and

Type A personality on anxiety, depression, and heart rate. *Journal of Applied Psychology, 60,* 713–719.

Cohen, S., & Edwards, J. R. (1986). Personality characteristics as moderators of the relationship between stress and disorder. In R. W. J. Neufeld (Ed.), *Advances in the investigation of psychological stress.* New York: Wiley.

Cohen, S., Sherrod, D. R., & Clark, M. S. (1986). Social skills and the stress-protective role of social support. *Journal of Personality and Social Psychology, 50,* 963–973.

Cronkite, R. C., & Moos, R. H. (1984). The role of predisposing and moderating factors in the stress-illness relationship. *Journal of Health and Social Behavior, 25,* 372–393.

Ganellen, R. J., & Blaney, P. H. (1984). Hardiness and social support as moderators of the effects of life stress. *Journal of Personality and Social Psychology, 47,* 156–163.

Glass, D. C. (1977). *Behavior patterns, stress, and coronary disease.* Hillsdale, NJ: Lawrence Erlbaum.

Hahn, M. E. (1966). *California life goals evaluation schedule.* Palo Alto, CA: Western Psychological Services.

Haynes, S. G., & Feinleib, M. (1980). Type A behavior and the incidence of coronary heart disease in the Framingham Heart Study. *Advances in cardiology.* Basel, Switzerland: Karger Press.

Hill, L. A. (1982). Personality and coping style as mediators of the stress and mental health relationship of employed women. Unpublished doctoral dissertation, University of Chicago.

Hobfoll, S. E., & Leiberman, J. R. (1987). Personality and social resources in immediate and continued stress resistance among women. *Journal of Personality and Social Psychology, 52,* 18–26.

Husaini, B., Neff, J., Newbrough, J. R., & Moore, M. C. (1982). The stress-buffering role of social support and personal competence among the rural married. *Journal of Community Psychology, 10,* 409–426.

Ivancevich, J. M., Matteson, M. T., & Preston, C. (1982). Occupational stress, Type A behavior and physical well being. *Academy of Management Journal, 25,* 373–391.

Johnson, J. H., & Sarason, I. (1978). Moderator variables in life stress research. In I. G. Sarason & C. D. Spielberger (Eds.), *Stress and anxiety* (Vol. 6). New York: Wiley.

Kasl, S. (1985). Environmental exposure and disease: An epidemiological perspective on some methodological issues in health psychology and behavioral medicine. In A. Bawn & J. Singer (Eds.), *Advances in environmental psychology: Methods and environmental psychology* (Vol. 5). Hillsdale, NJ: Lawrence Erlbaum.

Kobasa, S. C. (1979). Stressful life events, personality, and health: An inquiry into hardiness. *Journal of Personality and Social Psychology, 37,* 1–11.

Kobasa, S. C., Maddi, S. R., & Kahn, S. (1982). Hardiness and health: A prospective study. *Journal of Personality and Social Psychology, 42,* 168–177.

Kobasa, S. C., & Puccetti, M. C. (1983). Personality and social resources in stress resistance. *Journal of Personality and Social Psychology, 45,* 839–850.

Krause, N. (1985). Stress, control beliefs, and psychological distress: The problem of response bias. *Journal of Human Stress, 11,* 11–19.

Krause, N., & Stryker, S. (1984). Stress and well-being: The buffering role of locus of control beliefs. *Social Science and Medicine, 18,* 783–790.

Lefcourt, H. M. (1982). *Locus of control* (2nd ed.). New York: Academic Press.

Lefcourt, H. M., Miller, R. S., Ware, E. E., & Sherk, D. (1981). Locus of control as a modifier of the relationship between stressors and moods. *Journal of Personality and Social Psychology, 41,* 357–369.

Lefcourt, H. M., von Bayer, C. L., Ware, E. E., & Cox, D. J. (1979). The Multidimensional-Multiattributional Causality scale: The development of a goal specific locus of control scale. *Canadian Journal of Behavioral Science, 11,* 286–304.

MacDougall, J. M., Dembroski, T. M., & Krantz, D. S. (1981). The effects of types of challenge on pressor and heart rate responses in Type A and B women. *Psychophysiology, 18,* 1–9.

Maddi, S. R., & Kobasa, S. C. (1984). *The hardy executive.* Hillsdale, IL: Dow Jones–Irwin.

Maddi, S. R., Kobasa, S. C., & Hoover, M. (1979). An alienation test. *Journal of Humanistic Psychology, 19,* 73–76.

McFarlane, A., Norman, G., Streiner, D., & Roy, R. (1983). The process of social stress: Stable, reciprocal, and mediating relationships. *Journal of Health and Social Behavior, 24,* 160–173.

Mirels, H. L. (1970). Dimensions of internal versus external control. *Journal of Consulting and Clinical Psychology, 34,* 226–228.

Mullen, B., & Suls, J. (1982). "Know thyself": Stressful life changes and the ameliorative effect of private self-consciousness. *Journal of Experimental Social Psychology, 18,* 43–55.

Nelson, D. W., & Cohen, L. H. (1983). Locus of control and control perceptions and the relationship between life stress and psychological disorder. *American Journal of Community Psychology, 11,* 705–722.

Nowack, K. (1986). Type A, hardiness, and psychological distress. *Journal of Behavioral Medicine, 9,* 537–548.

Nuckolls, K. B., Cassel, J., & Kaplan, B. H. (1972). Psychological assets, life crisis and the prognosis of pregnancy. *American Journal of Epidemiology, 95,* 431–441.

Pearlin, L. I., & Schooler, C. (1978). The structure of coping. *Journal of Health and Social Behavior, 19,* 2–21.

Radloff, L. (1980). Risk factors for depression: What do we learn from them? In M. Guttentag, S. Salasin, & D. Belle (Eds.), *The mental health of women.* New York: Academic Press.

Rotter, J. B. (1966). Generalized expectancies for internal versus external control of reinforcement. *Psychological Monographs: General and Applied, 80,* 1 (Whole No. 609).

Sandler, I. N., & Lakey, B. (1982). Locus of control as a stress moderator: The role of control perceptions and social support. *American Journal of Community Psychology, 10,* 65–80.

Schmied, L. A., & Lawler, K. A. (1986). Hardiness, Type A behavior and the stress-illness relation in working women. *Journal of Personality and Social Psychology, 51,* 1218–1223.

Smith, R. E., Johnson, J. G., & Sarason, I. G. (1978). Life change, the sensation seeking motive, and psychological distress. *Journal of Consulting and Clinical Psychology, 46,* 348–349.

Suls, J., Gastorf, J. W., & Witenberg, S. H. (1979). Life events, psychological distress and the Type A coronary-prone behavior pattern. *Journal of Psychosomatic Research, 23,* 315–319.

Toves, C., Schill, T., & Ramanaiah, N. (1981). Sex differences, internal-external locus of control, and vulnerability to life stress. *Psychological Reports, 49,* 508.

Wheaton, B. (1982). A comparison of the moderating effects of personal coping resources in the impact of exposure to stress in two groups. *Journal of Community Psychology, 10,* 293–311.

13

Gender Differences in the Use of Substances for Coping

Lois Biener

Substance use is a common behavioral response to psychological distress. In some situations it may be an effective one. The frequent prescription of psychotropic drugs by physicians testifies to the widespread belief that chemical alteration of emotional states is the most appropriate remedy for some stress reactions. When symptoms such as anxiety or depression interfere with effective functioning, their reduction may sometimes be a necessary first step in active management of problematic situations. These benefits notwithstanding, if one routinely resorts to alcohol, drugs, or tobacco in order to deal with life's stressors, problems are likely to result. Habitual use of some substances produces behavioral changes that interfere with daily functioning and leads to deterioration in familial and social relationships. Furthermore, some substances are highly addictive. Continuous use brings social stigma and poses serious, even lethal health risks. Trying to break the habit becomes a stressor in itself. Hence, rather than ameliorate psychological distress, substance use often exacerbates it.

The question addressed by this chapter is whether men and women differ in their use of alcohol, prescription psychotropics (i.e., stimulants, sedatives, tranquilizers, and pain killers), or cigarettes in response to life's stressors. These are the substances used by a large proportion of the general population. In order to investigate the question, we must first understand the purposes served by using these substances and how their value as coping devices may differ for men and women.

This work was partially supported by NSRA fellowship MH 17058, awarded to Lois Biener, and by NCI Grant #38309, awarded to David B. Abrams and Michael J. Follick.

Substance use can potentially serve two distinct functions related to stress. First, alcohol, drugs, and tobacco may reduce the negative feelings that accompany the perception of stressful situations. This is the function that comes most readily to mind—the utility of drugs for what Lazarus and Folkman (1984) call "emotion-focused coping." To the extent that men and women differ in their perceived need to manage unpleasant emotions, they will differ in their likelihood of choosing to use a substance. It is important to realize, however, that substances may also function as a "problem-focused coping" strategy (Lazarus & Folkman, 1984). That is, they may be used to alter aspects of the stressful situation. Their pharmacological properties may make them useful for achieving a variety of goals—people often use caffeine to stay awake, alcohol to get to sleep, cigarettes to concentrate. We can see, then, that gender will affect the likelihood of using a substance in response to a stressor to the extent that (1) men and women differ in their perceived need for emotion-focused coping and (2) men and women confront problems that are differentially amenable to change through the use of alcohol, drugs, or tobacco.

Regardless of the target of the coping efforts, however, alternative behaviors are possible. In addition to substance use, there are many alternative "emotion-focused" coping strategies (cf. Lazarus & Folkman, 1984). Cognitive reappraisal—for example, minimizing the importance of the situation or thinking that things could be worse—can reduce negative affect. Meditating, exercising, or confiding in a friend are other emotion-focused strategies that can reduce negative affect. Likewise, the goals achieved with the help of drugs can also be achieved without them. To explore gender differences in substance use one must ask whether gender would affect the choice of one emotion-focused coping strategy over another. Can gender help explain, for example, what makes a drink, a pill, or a cigarette appear to be easier to use or more effective than venting one's anger or pouring one's heart out to a friend? Answering this question requires consideration of all possible coping strategies and specification of how gender affects their accessibility, effectiveness, and the skill with which they are used. This broad inquiry is beyond the scope of this chapter, but is undertaken somewhat in the chapters in this volume on use of social support (Wethington, McLeod, & Kessler; Belle), the chapter on cognitive coping (Miller & Kirsch), and in the concluding chapter. What will be covered here is how gender affects the choice among substances. I shall propose that when faced with a coping task, women and men will differ in the tendency to consider using a particular substance to the extent that gender norms influence (1) opportunities for exposure to the substance and (2) the perceived appropriateness of regular use.

Simply examining differential rates of use of a substance is not sufficient for determining gender differences in its use as a device for affect management. First, since substance use is often socially disapproved behavior, it is reasonable to expect a certain amount of concealment. Second, not all substance use is a response to the experience of distress. Sometimes the purpose is purely recreational; sometimes drugs are prescribed for medical problems unrelated to alteration of mood. Furthermore, the addictive properties of substances often lead to continued use to avoid the stress of withdrawal. Hence, mere comparison of prevalence indexes would not indicate relative use of substances for affect management.

Simply asking men and women how often they use alcohol, drugs, or cigarettes in response to negative feelings would seem the most straightforward research technique, and is, in fact the predominant one. It assumes, however, that people are conscious of their motivations and willing to share them honestly with researchers. It has been observed that women are more likely than men to report symptoms of physical and emotional discomfort (Pennebaker, 1982), and are more likely to interpret generalized feelings of malaise and distress as psychiatric problems requiring treatment (Kessler, Brown, & Broman, 1981). It would be reasonable to assume, therefore, that women would be more likely than men to acknowledge distress as a motivator for substance use.

Furthermore, even if we could establish that a particular substance was being used as a coping device more often by one gender than the other, without controlling for simultaneous use of other substances, this might tell us little about gender differences in the general tendency to use substances for coping. As I shall argue below, the choice among substances is influenced by gender in several ways.

With all these caveats in mind, I shall proceed to examine sex differences in use of alcohol, prescription psychotropic drugs, and cigarettes. For each, sex differences in prevalence will be reviewed and evidence for differential use in response to psychological distress will be presented. Where differences are found, the possible reasons for them will be explored by examining the likelihood of gender-specific norms affecting exposure and sanctions for regular use. Where these explanations are not sufficient (i.e., in the case of cigarettes), sex differences in motivation for use of the substance will be examined.

GENDER DIFFERENCES IN ALCOHOL AND DRUG USE FOR COPING

Differential Prevalence

A number of recent reviews have examined sex differences in the use of alcohol (Ferrence, 1980; Fillmore, 1984; Leland, 1982). The overwhelming consensus is that alcohol is used more often and more heavily by men than by women. In spite of the concern that drinking problems among women have been increasing and going unnoticed, there is no evidence in studies of trends since the 1960s that the gender ratio is converging. More women than men abstain from drinking (41 vs. 24 percent) and there are three to four times as many heavy drinkers, problem drinkers, and alcoholics among males compared to females. The gender differences are similar across ethnic groups, but for heavy drinking the difference is greater for whites than for blacks. The smaller sex ratio for blacks relative to whites is due more to the lower prevalence of heavy drinkers among black men (14 percent of blacks vs. 21 percent of whites) rather than to differences in heavy drinking among women (7 percent of blacks vs. 5 percent of whites) (Leland, 1982).

It has been postulated that as sex roles become liberalized and women begin to take on occupational roles similar to men, they will lose their relative immunity to alcohol problems. Several studies have examined the prevalence of drinking in various subgroups of women to see whether certain role combinations were more typical of people with drinking problems. Some studies have suggested that employed married women were more likely to be heavy drinkers than married women not working outside the home (Johnson, 1982; Parker, Parker, Wolz, & Harford, 1980). However, more recent national survey data do not support these findings (Wilsnack, Wilsnack, & Klassen, 1984). The data do indicate that employed women are less likely to be totally abstinent than nonemployed women, but this pattern need not indicate greater stress-related drinking in the employed group. It could be due to their greater opportunity to drink, to their greater exposure to alcohol, as well as to less traditional attitudes toward drinking.

The only consistent evidence of a change over time is in the increase in drinking among adolescent girls. However, as Thompson and Wilsnack (1984) point out, the convergence in sex ratios for alcohol use and problem drinking among adolescents must be interpreted with caution. The greatest increases in girls' drinking occurred between the 1940s and 1970s, with few changes since the 1970s. The convergence reflects both increases in girls' drinking and some stabilization or decline in boys' drinking. Although more girls are using alcohol now than 30 years ago, they still make up only a small fraction of adolescent problem and heavy drinkers. Nevertheless, since use of a substance as a coping device requires previous exposure to its effects, this increase in exposure among young girls may presage eventual resort to alcohol in times of stress—all other things remaining equal (e.g., barring negative physiological reactions and social change that increases availability of other coping responses).

The patterns of use of psychotropic drugs obtained by prescription (i.e., stimulants, sedatives, tranquilizers, analgesics) are almost the mirror image of alcohol use. Data collected in the late 1970s indicated that 55 percent of women had used a prescription psychotropic at some point in their lives while only 37 percent of men had done so (Fidell, 1982). Cooperstock and Sims (1971) surveyed records of a representative sample of pharmacies in Toronto and found that 69 percent of all prescriptions for mood-modifying drugs were written for women. Cafferata, Kasper, and Bernstein (1983) surveyed a random sample of households to determine correlates of obtaining prescription psychotropics. They found that twice as many women as men obtained such prescriptions and that women use these drugs more frequently and for longer periods of time than men.

This preponderance of females among users of mood-modifying drugs has been apparent for many years in both the United States and other countries (Balter, Levine, & Manheimer, 1974; Cooperstock, 1978, 1979) and is specific to drugs obtained by prescription. Illicit use of psychotropics (i.e., use of prescription drugs obtained without prescription and illegal substances such as heroin, other opiates, cocaine, hallucinogens, inhalants, marijuana, and hashish) occurs much more rarely than legal drug use in the general population, and sex differences for this type of substance use are similar to the pattern found for alcohol. In virtually every category and age group, use by males exceeds that of females. Furthermore, the sex differences do not seem to be changing over time (Ferrence & Whitehead, 1980). The link between women and prescription drug usage is underlined by the fact that prior to the passage of the Harrison Narcotics Act in 1914, twice as many women as men were addicted to opiates (such as Lydia Pinkham's Female Tonic) which were freely dispensed for "female troubles" (Marsh, Colten, & Tucker, 1982).

Sex Differences in Initial Exposure and Reinforcements for Continued Use

What can we make of these mirror image sex differences in the use of alcohol versus prescription psychotropic drugs? A comprehensive reading of the relevant literature suggests that the major reason for the sex differences in use patterns is differential routes to substance use.

Compared to men, women are much less likely to have been exposed to alcohol during adolescence. Some argue that norms for appropriate behavior proscribe the use of alcohol by females and result in greater disapproval of drunkenness in women than in men (Gomberg, 1982). The data on this issue are sparse and contradictory (see Leland, 1982 for review). It seems more accurate to say that women *believe* that drunkenness is more socially disapproved for women than for men, but when asked to make evaluative judgments of specific individuals, the gender of the problem drinker tends not to matter (cf. Biener, 1983). Furthermore, there is reason to believe that women's expectations about the effect alcohol will have on them can result in increased rather than reduced distress (Abrams & Wilson, 1979).

Lemle (1984) proposes that sex differences in alcohol use are due to its prescription for males rather than its proscription for females. He argues that drinking is a prime expression of the traditional male sex role. In support of this hypothesis, he points to the fact that men are more likely than women to drink with same-sex friends; that drinking is a predominant activity at athletic events; and that male, but not female, heavy drinkers increase their consumption in the presence of heavy drinking models. Lemle argues that alcohol provides an accepted way for men to socialize together. It is a means of symbolically demonstrating one's manliness, both to oneself and to others. Heavy drinking, in particular, exemplifies an unconventional, risk-taking style which is accepted, if not expected, in men. In this context, the previously mentioned change in patterns of abstinence and drinking among adolescent girls suggests that earlier double standards in tolerance of rebellious behavior may be abating (Thompson & Wilsnack, 1984).

Differential use of prescription psychotropic drugs can also be attributed to sex differences in norms and expectations. Cooperstock's (1971) model provides an explanation for this phenomenon.

> Women are permitted greater freedom than men to express feelings, perceive their feelings more readily, and hence recognize emotional difficulties. This . . . recognition enables the woman to define her difficulties within a medical model and thus bring them to the attention of her physician. The physician, representing the society that sanctions this freer expression, expects female patients to behave in this way, and thus expects them to require a higher proportion of mood-altering drugs than the less expressive male patients. (p. 238)

Cooperstock's model has been supported empirically through studies of sex differences in symptom recognition and help seeking (Kessler et al., 1981; Pennebaker, 1982) and through studies of physician expectations (see Fidell, 1980).

It is reasonable to ask whether women are encouraged to define their conflicts in terms of individual physical or emotional illness rather than in terms of the sexual inequities inherent in our culture. By prescribing mood-altering drugs, the physician helps alleviate women's symptoms without drawing attention to the causes behind them. A poignant example of how this might work is the response of a woman explaining her use of tranquilizers:

> I take it to protect the family from my irritability because the kids are kids. I don't think it's fair for me to start yelling at them because their normal activity is bothering me. My husband says I overreact. . . . I'm

an emotional person, more so than my husband who's an engineer and very calm and logical—he thinks . . . but because I overreact is no reason for the family to suffer from my irritability. . . . So I take the Valium to keep me calm. . . . Peace and calm. That's what my husband wants because frankly the kids get on his nerves, too. But he will not take anything. . . . He blows his top. . . . When I blow my top I am told to settle down. When he does it, it's perfectly alright. . . . And this I have resented over the years, but I've accepted it. I'm biding my time. One of these days I'm going to leave the whole kit and kaboodle and walk out on him. Then maybe I won't need any more Valium. (Cooperstock & Lennard, 1979, p. 336, ellipses in original)

Sex Differences in Alcohol and Drug Use in Response to Distress

The fact of greater use of alcohol by men and greater use of prescription psychotropics by women need not indicate a greater propensity by either sex to use substances for coping with distress. Rather the sex differences in use probably reflect the differential likelihood that men and women will be exposed to the two substances and rewarded or sanctioned for continued use. In sum, the sex differences in the use of alcohol and prescription psychotropics are not inconsistent with the hypothesis that men and women are equally likely to resort to substance use for coping, and that the sex difference is merely in the choice of substances.

This hypothesis is supported by two studies that investigate use of both alcohol and prescription drugs in response to distress. Timmer, Veroff, and Colten (1985) investigated the relationship between economic, marital, and job stressors and the tendency to use drugs and alcohol. Using a national probability sample survey, they asked, "When you feel worried, tense, or nervous, do you ever drink alcoholic beverages (take medicines or drugs) to help you handle things?" More men than women reported using alcohol to relieve tension (29 vs. 16 percent). More women than men reported using drugs to relieve tension (34 vs. 24 percent). This study does not provide information on the rates of using both substances or neither substance, so it is difficult to determine the total rates of substance coping for women versus men.

More complete information is provided by Parry, Cisin, Balter, Mellinger, and Manheimer (1974). In a national survey conducted in the early 1970s, they asked about the use of alcohol and drugs in response to feeling "nervous or upset or a little blue and depressed." They found that about 70 percent of men and women reported using neither of the substances for coping. Women were twice as likely to use drugs only (19 percent of women vs. 9 percent of men); men were more than twice as likely to use alcohol only (16 percent of men vs. 6 percent of women); and 3 to 4 percent of each group reported using both substances to cope. This study shows that people who use substances to cope tend to choose between alcohol and drugs. For men the choice is more likely to be alcohol; for women the choice is more likely to be prescription drugs. Furthermore, there seems to be little difference in the proportion of men and women who cope by turning to either or both of these substances.

GENDER DIFFERENCES IN CIGARETTE SMOKING

Differential Prevalence of Cigarette Smoking

In contrast to the analysis of alcohol and drug use, interpreting sex differences in cigarette smoking is more straightforward. While smoking by women was once frowned upon, gender-based barriers to smoking seem to have vanished in white and black populations in the United States.[1] Epidemiological surveys over the past 30 years demonstrate that the proportion of women who smoke is approaching that of men. For example in 1955, 52 percent of adult men smoked compared to 25 percent of adult women. In 1983, the proportion of male smokers dropped to 35 percent while the proportion of women smokers had risen to 30 percent (Stoto, 1986). In some groups of professionals, the rate of smoking among women even surpasses that of men (Dicken & Bryson, 1978; Eyres, 1973; Sorenson & Pechacek, 1986; USDHHS, 1980).

The growing awareness of the health risks associated with cigarette smoking has brought about increasing efforts to promote smoking cessation and to prevent initiation of cigarette use. The Surgeon General of the United States has announced the goal of creating a smoke-free society by the year 2000. Efforts aimed to meet that goal are apparent in the creation of a special division within the National Cancer Institute devoted to the study of smoking behavior and in the allocation of $150 million for research and innovative programs on smoking cessation and prevention. The convergence in the proportion of male and female smokers and the alarming increase in incidence of lung cancer among women have led to a particular concern with smoking among women.

The convergence in the proportion of males and females currently smoking is due to a number of different factors, one of which is product development and marketing. The introduction of filtered and low tar cigarettes has made smoking physiologically easier for women to tolerate (Silverstein, Feld, & Kozlowski, 1980). Carefully targeted advertising has helped to make smoking attractive to women (USDHHS, 1980). A second factor involves changes over the past few decades in the initiation of smoking. Although recent data suggest that initiation of smoking among adolescents is on the decline (Cleary, Hitchcock, Semmer, Flinchbaugh, & Pinney, 1986), until 1979 a higher proportion of adolescent girls were starting to smoke than used to be the case (USDHEW, 1977; USDHHS, 1980). The increase may have been due to a reduction in double standards for adolescent behavior, as discussed earlier in the context of increased alcohol use among girls. Compared to nonsmokers, teenage girls who smoke are more likely to be self-confident, socially and sexually experienced, and rebellious against authority (USDHEW, 1977).

A third reason for the convergence in male and female smoking rates is that women are quitting at a slower rate than men. Although some analyses suggest a recent trend toward equivalent cessation (Waldron, 1987), others indicate that the quit rate is lower for women than for men within virtually every age group (Stoto, 1986). Women smokers seem to be more resistant to quitting than men. In population surveys women smokers are less likely to report being interested in quitting (Blake, Pechacek, Klepp, Folsom, Jacobs, & Mittelmark, 1984; Frerichs, Aneshensel, Clark, & Yokopenic, 1981). Furthermore, compared to men who have quit smoking, women quitters are more likely to relapse (Gritz, 1980). A number of hypotheses have been put forward to account for the lower rate of quitting in women. Since one explanation assumes that the experience of unhealthy symptoms is what motivates quitting, and since most current female smokers started smoking later in life than males (Harris, 1983), it takes longer for the women to experience these symptoms. If one controls for amount of time smoking, the sex difference may disappear (Gritz, 1980). As of this writing, such an analysis has not been carried out. Furthermore, recent statistics on female and male adolescent smokers who start smoking at about the same age show the same sex difference in quitting as is seen in adults (Cleary et al., 1986). The explanation for women's lower rate of quitting that is most relevant to this chapter maintains that women, more than men, rely on cigarettes as a method for dealing with negative affect, and that this reliance makes them either less motivated or less able to stop smoking.

Sex Differences in Smoking in Response to Psychological Distress

There has been some empirical verification of the notion that women are more likely than men to use cigarettes to cope with negative affect. Women are more likely to *say* that they smoke in response to negative affect and that stressful events trigger relapse when they have quit smoking (Frith, 1971; USDHHS, 1980). It's hard to know whether these reports are accurate or are due to women's greater propensity to report negative experiences. There is only one published laboratory study that attempted to manipulate affect and observe smoking behavior in male and female college students (Ikard & Tomkins, 1973). The authors showed 39 male and 15 female smokers a funny film and an upsetting film. The students were categorized into those who smoked only during the funny film, only during the upsetting film, during both films or during neither film. Results showed that a greater proportion of the women than the men smoked only during the upsetting film (79 vs. 36 percent). This study supports the hypothesis that women are more likely than men to be negative-affect smokers. However, it relies on a small select sample. More research is needed that directly manipulates affect and observes differential smoking by men and women.

If we allow that the weight of existing evidence, however flawed, indicates that women are more likely than men to smoke in response to stressful experiences, we can go on to speculate about why that might be the case. There are several potential explanations, each of which would make cigarettes more useful to women than to men. The first attributes greater reliance on cigarettes for coping to the consequences of the social subordination of women. The second explanation attributes women's greater reliance on cigarettes to gender differences in the biochemical actions of nicotine, which may moderate the relationship between cigarette smoking and affective state. The third explanation suggests that smoking may be more useful as a problem-focused coping strategy for women because of the particular problems women experience. There is some empirical support for each of these explanations, but definitive studies remain to be carried out.

Sex Differences in Smoking Associated with Subordinate Social Status

Emotion-focused coping is likely to be used when the individual views the stressor as one that he or she is incapable of changing—when the aim of coping is to accept and adjust to the situation (cf. Lazarus & Folkman, 1980; Stone & Neale, 1984). Given the relatively low status of women in most occupational situations (see LaCroix & Haynes, this volume) and women's family roles, which emphasize their relationships with others rather than their individual achievements, it is reasonable to propose that women are, in fact, more likely to lack control over stressful situations. Hence, stressors experienced by women may be particularly amenable to emotion-focused coping. Furthermore, since traditional socialization practices reinforce female passivity and unassertiveness, it would not be surprising that even controllable situations would often be seen as unchangeable and that the goal of coping would be adaptation. Applying this explanation to smoking, one would predict that for any given level of environmental stressors, women will be more likely than men to find cigarette smoking an effective coping device.

A number of studies have demonstrated that smoking rates are related to environmental stressors in both men and women (Linsky, Colby, & Straus, 1986; Tagliacozzo & Vaughn, 1982). A study by Biener, Abrams, Follick, and Hitti (1986) suggests that the aforementioned higher rate of smoking among female compared to male professionals may be partially due to their greater likelihood of holding stressful jobs. A convenience sample of 700 hospital employees responded to a survey on smoking habits and job characteristics. Employees were categorized as either professional (physicians, registered nurses, managers, psychologists, etc.) or nonprofessional (technicians, clerical workers, service and maintenance personnel) using criteria established by the Bureau of the Census (U.S. Department of Commerce, 1971). As expected, the rate of smoking was higher for female professionals than for males (28 vs. 17 percent). Using the model of job strain developed by Karasek (1979), the authors queried the employees on their experience of two types of job characteristics that have been linked to perceived stress and to physical illness—psychological demand and control over aspects of the work situation. Karasek has shown that workers most at risk for stress-related illness are those who experience low control in the face of high demands (see LaCroix and Haynes, this volume, for a discussion of Karasek's model). As might be expected, professionals of both sexes reported significantly more demand than nonprofessionals. One might also expect that professionals of both sexes would report more control than nonprofessionals. This pattern was true for the men, but there was no difference in level of control reported by professional and nonprofessional women. Furthermore, women at both job levels reported less control than men. Forty percent of the professional women characterized their jobs as being of the high-strain type—high in demand and low in control. Only 15 percent of the professional men reported this combination of job characteristics.

Biener et al. (1986) found that controlling for age, demand and control significantly predicted smoking status for professional women. Women reporting high-strain jobs were more likely to be smokers than those in low-strain jobs. Demand and control did not predict smoking status for professional men. However the relative absence of high strain and of smoking among the professional men leaves the meaning of this finding somewhat ambiguous.

A similar relationship was observed in a large-scale study of white-collar workers in Sweden (Karasek, Lindell, & Gardell, in press). In that study over 8000 workers responded to a survey assessing work characteristics, family characteristics, health behaviors, and physical illness. The association between job and family factors and health outcomes was examined separately for men and women. One of the few sex differences the authors discovered in predictors of health behaviors was that for women there was a stronger association between job factors and smoking. In sum, it seems plausible that high demand in the context of low control is contributing to the relatively high level of smoking in professional women. The lower level of smoking in professional men may be due to their greater control, to less of a tendency to use cigarettes in response to strain, or both.

Sex Differences in Pharmacological Effects of Nicotine

While the precise mechanism is unclear, it has been demonstrated quite reliably that nicotine regulates the smoker's mood. (See Gilbert, 1979 for a review of research on the effects of nicotine on emotion.) Hughes (1985) deprived smokers of cigarettes and provided them with either nicotine gum or a placebo. He then assessed their emotional state by means of the smokers' self-report and their spouses' report. Compared to smokers receiving nicotine gum, those who received the placebo reported higher levels of anger and tension. Furthermore, spouses of smokers in the placebo condition rated them as being more irritable and anxious than did spouses of smokers in the nicotine gum condition.

Schachter (1978) reviewed evidence indicating that it is not that nicotine makes people calm or better able to handle irritations. Rather, it is the absence of nicotine, once one has become habituated, that makes people anxious and more vulnerable to behavioral disruption. Several studies compared the mood and performance of nonsmokers to smokers who had or had not been deprived of cigarettes. Each one showed that in the presence of environmental irritants (e.g., noise or electric shock) undeprived smokers and nonsmokers performed and felt equally well. However, smokers who were deprived of cigarettes showed marked deficits in mood and performance.

An intriguing speculation that surfaces periodically in the literature implies that compared to men, women smokers may experience sharper declines in their blood nicotine level when they are stressed. The reduction in blood nicotine level is inferred from the amount of unmetabolized nicotine found in urine of laboratory subjects. The metabolism of nicotine is apparently affected by the acid/base balance in the body. It has been demonstrated that by giving smokers an acidifying agent, the amount of unmetabolized nicotine excreted will be increased. Since smokers adjust their rate of smoking to maintain a constant level of nicotine in the blood (Schachter, 1978), the more rapidly that level declines, the more one will have an urge for additional cigarettes. Schachter, Kozlowski, and Silverstein (1977) confirmed this by increasing the acidification in smokers (lowering their urinary pH) and demonstrating a consequent increase in number of cigarettes smoked. The pH of urine is lowered by numerous factors—

nutrition, drugs, and most interestingly, distress (Schachter, 1978). Hence the stress-smoking connection makes sense physiologically, because if stress lowers bodily pH and causes more rapid reduction in the blood nicotine level, the urge to smoke will increase. If the experience of distress is more apt to produce nicotine excretion in women smokers than in men, one would expect that it would lead women to smoke more when stressed.

The speculation that changes in urinary pH produce greater excretion of nicotine in women than in men derives from two studies. Silverstein, Kelly, Swan, and Kozlowski (1982) gave nonsmoking college students substances that would produce either acidic or alkaline conditions before having them smoke a cigarette. They then asked subjects to volunteer to smoke another cigarette. Female subjects whose urine had been acidified were significantly more willing to smoke again than those whose urine had been alkalyzed. There was no difference, however, for males. Presumably, the females in the acid condition had metabolized less nicotine, were less negatively affected by it, and more willing to smoke again for the sake of science. The second study that suggests sex differences in metabolism of nicotine was done by Beckett, Gorrod, and Jenner (1971). In that study the urine of smokers and nonsmokers was maintained at an acid pH. Subjects were injected with nicotine and the rate of excretion of nicotine was measured. Female nonsmokers excreted nicotine more rapidly than male nonsmokers and female smokers excreted nicotine more rapidly than a subgroup of male smokers.

Clearly we need more systematic research on the relationship between gender, distress, and the metabolism of nicotine. Studies remain to be done that manipulate the urinary pH of female and male smokers (as opposed to nonsmokers) and observe any differential excretion of nicotine. If the speculations outlined here are confirmed, they imply that cigarette smoking may be more chemically addictive for women than for men. Once habituated to nicotine, women may have greater difficulty quitting because the experience of distress may trigger acute withdrawal symptoms including cravings for nicotine, irritability, and anxiety. If men are less likely to excrete nicotine when they feel distress, they may also experience less reinforcement from smoking in response to distress and hence find it easier to give up cigarettes. It is interesting to note that among smokers trying to quit, women are more likely than men to describe themselves as addicted to cigarettes (Eiser & Van Der Pligt, 1986).

Sex Differences in Use of Cigarettes as Problem-Focused Coping

The pharmacological properties of cigarettes are believed to have two effects that may make them particularly useful for women. One relates to the effects on the ability to screen out extraneous input in order to focus on a cognitive task. The other relates to the role of nicotine in weight control.

Cigarettes and cognitive performance under stressful conditions. One of the attractions of smoking may be nicotine's ability to enhance performance by reducing attention to potentially stressful distractors (Gilbert, 1979). Research on cognitive styles has consistently demonstrated that women tend to be more field dependent than men. That is, they are more responsive to extraneous stimuli when performing certain types of cognitive tasks (Frieze, Parsons, Johnson, Ruble, & Zellman, 1978). Hence, the distraction-filtering effect of cigarettes may be more useful for women than for men, and withdrawal of nicotine may be accompanied by more cognitive disruption in women. Although contradictory findings have been reported (Svikis, Hatsukami, Hughes, Carroll, & Pickens, in press), results supportive of this hypothesis were obtained by Knott (1984a). Knott had male and female smokers and nonsmokers perform a reaction time task while being subjected to different types of distractors. Smokers were required to abstain from tobacco for 12 hours prior to testing. Female smokers made decisions more slowly and with more errors than female nonsmokers under two of the three types of distraction conditions. The performance of male smokers and nonsmokers, however, did not differ.

In another study (Knott, 1984b) male and female smokers and nonsmokers were exposed to high-intensity auditory stimuli (an unpleasant experience). Their skin conductance was recorded. Compared to nonsmokers, smokers had higher resting skin conductance levels and responded more strongly to the unpleasant noise. This effect was stronger in female than in male smokers. It is not clear from the report whether the hyperresponsivity in female smokers was due simply to individual differences that preceded (and perhaps prompted) initiation of smoking or to the fact that the smokers were experiencing withdrawal, since they were not permitted to smoke during the three-hour morning testing session. This research suggests, however, that female smokers may respond more strongly to aversive stimuli than either male smokers or nonsmokers of either sex.

Cigarettes and weight control. Smokers as a group tend to weigh less than nonsmokers, and quitting smoking is often accompanied by significant weight gains (Rodin & Wack, 1984). Research by Grunberg, Winders, and Popp (1987) suggests that biological differences may be responsible for weight gain among women who quit smoking. However, comparisons of weight gain in men and women who quit smoking have not indicated differences by sex (Hall, Ginsberg, & Jones, 1986; Rodin & Wack, 1984). Even if males and females are equally likely to lose weight while smoking and to regain it after quitting, the differential importance of body weight would lead women to find weight loss due to smoking more rewarding and weight gain due to quitting more punishing than men. (See Attie & Brooks-Gunn, this volume, for a discussion of the quest for thinness as a stressor.) Indeed, weight concerns play a very important role in women's smoking behavior. Gritz (1986) reviewed evidence that teenage girls are much more likely than teenage boys to believe that smoking controls weight. The prevalence of this belief in girls rises with age and closely mirrors the rise in girls' smoking. Furthermore, women are more likely than men to report that fear of weight gain keeps them from giving up cigarettes (USDHHS, 1980). Biener, Abrams, and Follick (1986) found that compared to male participants, women entering smoking cessation programs were significantly less confident that they would be able to resist the urge to smoke when they wanted to avoid eating; among smokers who did not enroll in treatment, women were significantly more worried than men that quitting smoking would lead to weight gain.

This chapter has addressed the question of whether there is a gender difference in the tendency to use alcohol, prescription drugs, or cigarettes as a means of coping with life's stressors. I have argued that drinking alcohol, taking drugs, or smoking cigarettes in response to the experience or anticipation of stress can be best understood as particular examples of the more general process of coping. The decision to use a substance, like the decision to try to change the situation or to confide in a friend, is affected by (a) the perceived goal of the coping process and (b) the number and perceived effectiveness of other strategies in one's behavioral repertoire. Gender will have an impact on behavior because gender affects both the goals of the coping process as well as the particular coping strategies people learn to use.

The differential patterns of use of alcohol (used more often by men) and prescription drugs (used more often by women) can be most reasonably attributed to differences in social norms affecting exposure to each of these substances as well as to norms affecting perceived appropriateness of continued use. Studies that examine the use of either or both alcohol and prescription drugs (Parry et al., 1974; Timmer et al., 1985) suggest that similar proportions of males and females turn to one or the other of these substances in response to stress.

As regards cigarettes, however, there are fewer gender-related factors affecting exposure or differentially sanctioning their use. The research reviewed here suggests that after being exposed to cigarettes, women may be more likely than men to smoke in response to feelings of distress. Women's reliance on cigarettes is probably multiply determined. Research findings, while scanty, are consistent with the hypothesis that female biology may result in women having increased cravings for cigarettes during stressful or demanding situations. In addition, the need to conform with social ideals of feminine thinness adds to the motivation to use cigarettes for their anorectic properties and undermines motivation to quit. Further, the subordinate status of women at the workplace and in the family results in their frequently having less power than men to change stressful situations, and at the same time their roles as nurturer and caretaker proscribe acting against others with expressions of anger, irritation, or hostility. Hence, women may be more likely than men to rely on cigarettes to reduce negative affect.

It is not only women who suffer from the effects of coping through substance use. The role that alcohol plays in defining masculinity may increase the likelihood that men will resort to drinking to handle stress. The health risks associated with regular use of alcohol, drugs, and cigarettes are sufficiently serious to warrant a major public health initiative to curtail their use. Continued exploration of the ways traditional gender roles increase the likelihood of substance use may be an important step in reducing the damage done by substance use as a coping strategy.

NOTE

1. It is likely that smoking among women is still frowned upon among some ethnic minorities in the United States. Prevalence of smoking has been shown to be substantially lower in Mexican American and Asian samples than in white women. (Gritz, 1986; Hazuda, Stern, Haffner, Gaskill, & Gardner, 1982).

REFERENCES

Abrams, D. B., & Wilson, G. T. (1979). Effects of alcohol on social anxiety in women: Cognitive versus physiological processes. *Journal of Abnormal Psychology, 88,* 161–172.

Balter, M. B., Levine, J., & Manheimer, D. J. (1974). Cross-national study of the extent of anti-anxiety/sedative drug use. *New England Journal of Medicine, 290,* 769–774.

Beckett, A. H., Gorrod, J. W., & Jenner, P. (1971). The effect of smoking on nicotine metabolism in vivo in man. *Journal of Pharmacy and Pharmacology, 23,* 625–675.

Biener, L. (1983). Perceptions of patients by emergency room staff: Substance abusers versus non-substance abusers. *Journal of Health and Social Behavior, 24,* 264–275.

Biener, L., Abrams, D. B., & Follick, M. J. (1986). *Sex differences in participants of a worksite smoking cessation program.* Unpublished manuscript, Brown University, Providence.

Biener, L., Abrams, D. B., Follick, M. J., & Hitti, J. (1986). *Gender differences in smoking and quitting.* Paper presented at the Society of Behavioral Medicine, San Francisco.

Blake, S. M., Pechacek, T., Klepp, K. I., Folsom, A., Jacobs, D., & Mittelmark, M. (1984). *Gender differences in smoking cessation strategies.* Paper presented at the Society for Behavioral Medicine, Philadelphia.

Cafferata, G. L., Kasper, J., & Bernstein, A. (1983). Family roles, structure, and stressors in relation to sex differences in obtaining psychotropic drugs. *Journal of Health and Social Behavior, 24,* 132–143.

Cleary, P. D., Hitchcock, J. L., Semmer, N., Flinchbaugh, L. J., & Pinney, J. M. (1986). *Adolescent smoking: Research and health policy.* Discussion Paper Series, Institute for the Study of Smoking Behavior and Policy, Cambridge, MA.

Cooperstock, R. (1971). Sex differences in the use of mood-modifying drugs: An explanatory model. *Journal of Health and Social Behavior, 12,* 238–243.

———. (1978). Sex differences in psychotropic drug use. *Social Science and Medicine, 12B,* 179–186.

———. (1979). A review of women's psychotropic drug use. *Canadian Journal of Psychiatry, 24,* 29–33.

Cooperstock, R., & Lennard, H. L. (1979). Some social meanings of tranquilizer use. *Sociology of Health and Illness, 1,* 331–346.

Cooperstock, R., & Sims, M. (1971). Mood modifying drugs prescribed in a Canadian city: Hidden problems. *American Journal of Public Health, 65,* 5.

Dicken, C., & Bryson, R. (1978). Psychology in action, the smoking of psychology. *American Psychologist, 33,* 504–507.

Eiser, J. R., & Van Der Pligt, J. (1986). "Sick" or "hooked": Smokers' perceptions of their addiction. *Addictive Behaviors, 11,* 11–15.

Eyres, S. J. (1973). Public Health Nursing Section Report of the 1972 APHA Smoking Survey. *American Journal of Public Health, 63,* 846–852.

Ferrence, R. G. (1980). Sex differences in the prevalence of problem drinking. In O. J. Kalant (Ed.), *Alcohol and drug problems in women.* New York: Plenum.

Ferrence, R. G., & Whitehead, P. C. (1980). Sex differences in psychoactive drug use: Recent epidemiology. In O. J. Kalant (Ed.), *Alcohol and drug problems in women.* New York: Plenum.

Fidell, L. S. (1980). Sex role stereotypes and the American physician. *Psychology of Women Quarterly, 4,* 313–331.

———. (1982). Gender and drug use and abuse. In I. Al-Issa (Ed.), *Gender and psychopathology.* New York: Academic Press.

Fillmore, K. M. (1984). "When Angels Fall": Women's drinking as cultural preoccupation and as reality. In S. C. Wilsnack & L. J. Beckman (Eds.), *Alcohol problems in women.* New York: Guilford Press.

Frerichs, R. R., Aneshensel, C. S., Clark, V. A., & Yokopenic, P. (1981). Smoking and depression: A community survey. *American Journal of Public Health, 71,* 637–640.

Frieze, I. H., Parsons, J. E., Johnson, P. B., Ruble, D. N., & Zellman, G. L. (1978). *Women and sex roles: A social psychological perspective.* New York: W. W. Norton.

Frith, C. (1971). Smoking behavior and its relation to the smoker's immediate experience. *British Journal of Social Clinical Psychology, 10,* 73–78.

Gilbert, D. G. (1979). Paradoxical tranquilizing and emotion-reducing effects of nicotine. *Psychological Bulletin, 86,* 643–660.

Gomberg, E. S. (1982). Historical and political perspective: Women and drug use. *Journal of Social Issues, 38,* 9–23.

Gritz, E. (1980). Problems related to use of tobacco by women. In O. J. Kalant (Ed.), *Alcohol and drug problems in women.* New York: Plenum.

———. (1986). Gender and the teenage smoker. In B. A. Ray & M. C. Braude (Eds.), *Women and drugs: A new era for research.* National Institute of Drug Abuse Research Monograph 65. (DHHS Publication No. ADM 86–1447).

Grunberg, N. E., Winders, S. E., & Popp, K. A. (1987). Sex differences in nicotine's effects on consummatory behavior and body weight in rats. *Psychopharmacology, 91,* 221–225.

Hall, S. M., Ginsberg, D., & Jones, R. T. (1986). Smoking cessation and weight gain. *Journal of Consulting and Clinical Psychology, 54,* 342–346.

Harris, J. E. (1983). Cigarette smoking among successive birth cohorts of men and women in the United States during 1900–80. *Journal of the National Cancer Institute, 71,* 473–479.

Hazuda, H. P., Stern, M. P., Haffner, S. M., Gaskill, S. P., & Gardner, L. I. (1982). Work status and women's protection against coronary heart disease. Paper presented at the annual meeting of the American Public Health Association, Montreal.

Hughes, J. R. (1985). *The relationship between smoking and mood: Role of smoking in affect regulation.* Symposium presented at the Society for Behavioral Medicine meetings, New Orleans.

Ikard, F. F., & Tomkins, S. (1973). The experience of affect as a determinant of smoking behavior: A series of validity studies. *Journal of Abnormal Psychology, 81,* 172–181.

Johnson, P. B. (1982). Sex differences, women's roles and alcohol use: Preliminary national data. *Journal of Social Issues, 38,* 93–116.

Karasek, R. (1979). Job demands, job decision latitude, and mental strain: Implications for job redesign. *Administrative Science Quarterly, 24,* 285–305.

Karasek, R., Lindell, J., & Gardell, B. (In press.) Work and non-work correlates of illness and behavior in male and female Swedish white collar workers. *Journal of Occupational Medicine.*

Kessler, R. C., Brown, R. C., & Broman, C. L. (1981). Sex differences in psychiatric help seeking: Evidence from four large surveys. *Journal of Health and Social Behavior, 22,* 49–64.

Knott, V. J. (1984a). Noise and task induced distraction effects on information processing: Sex differences in smokers and non-smokers. *Addictive Behaviors, 9,* 79–84.

———. (1984b). Electrodermal activity during aversive stimulation: Sex differences in smokers and non-smokers. *Addictive Behaviors, 9,* 195–199.

Lazarus, R. S., & Folkman, S. (1980). An analysis of coping in a middle-aged community sample. *Journal of Health and Social Behavior, 21,* 219–239.

———. (1984). *Stress, appraisal, and coping.* New York: Springer.

Leland, J. (1982). Gender, drinking and alcohol abuse. In I. Al-Issa (Ed.), *Gender and psychopathology.* New York: Academic Press.

Lemle, R. (1984). *Alcohol and masculinity: A review and reformulation of sex role, dependency, and power theories of alcoholism.* Paper presented at the American Psychological Association, Toronto.

Linsky, A. S., Colby, J. P., & Straus, M. A. (1986). *Social stress, smoking behavior and mortality from cancer of the respiratory system: A macro social analysis.* Paper presented to the Second National Conference on Social Stress Research, University of New Hampshire, Durham.

Marsh, J. C., Colten, M. E., & Tucker, M. B. (1982). Women's use of drugs and alcohol: New perspectives. *Journal of Social Issues, 38,* 1–8.

Parker, D., Parker, E. S., Wolz, M. W., & Harford, T. C. (1980). Sex roles and alcohol consumption: A research note. *Journal of Health and Social Behavior, 21,* 43–48.

Parry, H. J., Cisin, I. H., Balter, M. B., Mellinger, G. D., & Manheimer, D. J. (1974). Increasing alcohol intake as a coping mechanism for psychic distress. In R. Cooperstock (Ed.), *Social aspects of the medical use of psychotropic drugs.* Toronto: Alcoholism and Drug Addiction Research Foundation of Ontario.

Pennebaker, J. W. (1982). *The psychology of physical symptoms.* New York: Springer-Verlag.

Rodin, J., & Wack, J. T. (1984). The relationship between cigarette smoking and body weight: A health promotion dilemma? In J. D. Mattarazzo, S. M. Weiss, J. A. Herd, N. E. Miller, & S. M. Weiss (Eds.), *Behavioral health: A handbook of health enhancement and disease prevention.* New York: Wiley.

Schachter, S. (1978). Pharmacological and psychological determinants of smoking. *Annals of Internal Medicine, 88,* 104–114.

Schachter, S., Kozlowski, L. T., & Silverstein, B. (1977). Effects of urinary pH on cigarette smoking. *Journal of Experimental Psychology: General, 106,* 13–19.

Silverstein, B., Feld, S., & Kozlowski, L. T. (1980). The availability of low-nicotine cigarettes as a cause of cigarette smoking among teenage females. *Journal of Health and Social Behavior, 21,* 383–388.

Silverstein, B., Kelly, E., Swan, J., & Kozlowski, L. T. (1982). Physiological predisposition toward becoming a cigarette smoker: Experimental evidence for a sex difference. *Addictive Behaviors, 7,* 83–86.

Sorenson, G., & Pechacek, T. (1986). Occupational and sex differences in smoking and smoking cessation. *Journal of Occupational Medicine, 28,* 360–364.

Stone, A. A., & Neale, J. M. (1984). New measure of daily coping: Development and preliminary results. *Journal of Personality and Social Psychology, 46,* 892–906.

Stoto, M. A. (1986). Changes in adult smoking behavior in the United States: 1955–1983. Discussion Paper Series, Institute for the Study of Smoking Behavior and Policy, Cambridge, MA.

Svikis, D. S., Hatsukami, D. K., Hughes, J. R., Carroll, K. M., & Pickens, R. W. (In press.) Sex differences in the tobacco withdrawal syndrome. *Addicitive Behaviors.*

Tagliacozzo, R., & Vaughn, S. (1982). Stress and smoking in hospital nurses. *American Journal of Public Health, 72,* 441–448.

Thompson, K. M., & Wilsnack, R. W. (1984). Drinking problems among female adolescents. In S. C. Wilsnack & L. J. Beckman (Eds.), *Alcohol problems in women.* New York: Guilford Press.

Timmer, S. G., Veroff, J., & Colten, M. E. (1985). Life stress, helplessness, and the use of alcohol and drugs to cope: An analysis of national survey data. In S. Shiffman & T. A. Wills (Eds.), *Coping and substance use.* London: Academic Press.

U.S. Department of Commerce, Bureau of the Census (1971). *1970 Census of Population. Alphabetical Index of Industries and Occupations.* Washington, DC: U.S. Government Printing Office.

U.S. Department of Health, Education and Welfare, Public Health Service (USDHEW) (1977). *Cigarette smoking among teenagers and young women* (DHEW Publication No. NIH 77-1203). Washington, DC: U.S. Government Printing Office.

U.S. Department of Health and Human Services (USDHHS) (1980). *The health consequences of smoking for women, a report of the surgeon general* (USDHHS Publication No. HH 5396). Washington, DC: U.S. Government Printing Office.

Waldron, I. (1987). Patterns and causes of gender differences in smoking. (Unpublished manuscript.)

Wilsnack, R. W., Wilsnack, S. C., & Klassen, A. D. (1984). Women's drinking and drinking problems: Patterns from a 1981 national survey. *American Journal of Public Health, 74,* 1231–1238.

Conclusion

The lesson of this volume is that gender affects the stress process in many ways and at many points. Being male or female influences both the input side of the process, by determining whether a situation will be perceived as stressful, and the output side, by influencing both choices among coping responses and the long-term health implications of stress reactions. For the most part, we believe the effects of biological sex are mediated through the psychological and social consequences of being male or female. Further, the impact of sex on the stress process will be conditioned by the extent to which an individual has experienced socialization patterns consistent with traditional gender norms and the extent to which one identifies with traditional notions of masculinity and femininity. The more traditional one's socialization experiences and the more fully one internalizes traditional gender schema, the greater the impact of one's sex.

The contributions assembled in this volume describe how an individual's gender will affect various stages of the stress process. We provide here an integration by focusing on the basic elements: situations conducive to stress, responses to perceived stress, and long-term outcomes.

SITUATIONS CONDUCIVE TO STRESS

Situations are conducive to stress when they involve threats to an individual's well-being. Although no situation is stressful until it is perceived as such, some situations are likely to be perceived as threatening by everyone; others are threatening only in the context of individuals' unique goals and values. We call the former *objectively stressful situations* and the latter *subjectively stressful situations.* Being male or female influences the frequency and type of exposure to both kinds of situations.

Objectively Threatening Situations

There are situations that are objectively stressful because they jeopardize human survival. Men and women are differentially at risk for encountering such situations. To start with some very obvious examples, men are more likely to encounter the stress of military combat; only women encounter the stress of pregnancy and childbirth. The objective stressfulness of situations is also a function of the extent to which they limit personal autonomy and block access to and control over resources. The chapters in the second section of this book indicate that in both occupational and family domains, women's roles are more likely than men's to be associated with low control over outcomes.

Aneshensel and Pearlin present data showing that women move into and out of the labor force more frequently than men. This discontinuity in women's employment is due, in part, to the demands of women's family roles and to the fact that jobs held by women, because of their low status and low security, are tempting to leave. Women, therefore, are more likely to experience the stress of changes in employment status—that is, being laid off, moving to another job, or entering and reentering the labor force. Moreover, women's jobs are notably low paying; women earn less than two-thirds of what men earn for similar jobs. The discontinuities and economic disparities, in and of themselves, constitute an important source of gender differences in objective conditions conducive to stress. Further, they have contributed to the feminization of poverty. Poverty, as we all know, is a major stressor.

LaCroix and Haynes document the pervasiveness of occupational segregation. Approximately half of the working men and women in the United States are employed in jobs primarily held by members of their own gender. This means that men and women hold different kinds of jobs. Men are more likely than women to encounter the stressor of physical risks associated with their occupation. Women, on the other hand, tend to have less power and authority than men at the workplace, and this disparity in power is an important stressor.

Turning to family roles, many of the chapters illustrate women's relative lack of control. Barnett and Baruch argue that the situations faced by wives and mothers are very different from those faced by husbands and fathers. Consider the maternal role. The role of mother is notorious for its incessant demands. We believe it is also inherently low in control. The role of father has traditionally been low in demands and high in control.

By virtue of the perquisites of the breadwinner role, the traditional father is protected from excessive demands of children. He need not drive them to early morning hockey games, stay home when they are sick, or interrupt his meetings to comfort a crying baby. At the same time, he has control over the family's resources and therefore can dispense or withhold them as he sees fit. In addition, mothers are held and hold themselves responsible for the happiness of their children. If their children "turn out" well, they have done a good job. If they turn out poorly, both parents—and many professionals—tend to lay blame at the mother's not the father's feet. In reality, neither parent has much power to affect many aspects of their children's welfare. Accidents, drug use, academic talent are for the most part out of a parent's control.

The role of wife can also diminish control over one's life. By virtue of their position both in the family and in the larger society, wives typically have been more affected by events occurring in their husbands' lives than vice versa. Whereas this is true of wives in general, it may be especially true for nonemployed wives, thereby accounting in part for the high incidence of stress reactions among full-time housewives. For example, a woman's husband is transferred and she has to relocate. If there are children involved, her job is also to support them through their adjustments. If the woman is not employed she has no colleagues at the new location with whom to affiliate. Compared to the distress of the husband, that of the wife is relatively invisible and perhaps for that reason more pernicious. When the husband's pain is the focus of attention, there is no mechanism for acknowledging and resolving the distress of the wife. A powerful illustration of the way these effects operate comes from the current farm crisis. Most of the attention given to this problem has focused on the losses experienced by the men.

> As the auctioneer's gavel signals the foreclosure of yet another farm in the Midwest, the television camera picks out the seamed face of the farmer, head bowed in defeat. The woman at his side, who shared the burdens of the so-called "family farm," is ignored. (Turkington, 1986, p. 18).

As one farm wife put it:

> They were the farmers, and we were just the wives. If you asked our men, we never had any real pain at all through this. They think they suffered more than we did. (p. 18)

The tremendous silent burden of these stressors on the farm wives is reflected by research suggesting that the fate of the farm family "rests in the hands of the rural wife. If she remains strong, the family stays together. If she crumbles, the family will probably dissolve" (p. 18).

Another important facet of female nonwork roles is their embeddedness in supportive networks composed of family and community members. The chapters by Belle and by Wethington, McLeod, and Kessler suggest that women's embeddedness may itself be stressful. Embeddedness exposes one to events that demand responses; these events are, by definition, not under one's control. Women suffer from other people's problems. A neighbor's mother dies and she needs someone to comfort her. A close relative loses her job and needs help while looking for another job. Thus involvement in social networks, while potentially offering a woman coping resources, can yield a net loss in terms of control.

Subjectively Threatening Situations

Threats to one's survival and to one's sense of control can be seen as threats to well-being regardless of unique values, goals, and resources. We refer here to gender differences in subjective sources of stress—specifically, those conditions that differ in stressfulness for men and women because they constitute a threat to sex-linked goals and values.

Gender norms prescribe particular behaviors for males and females and proscribe others. They push people into rather narrow patterns that may not suit their unique characteristics. Expectations that all women will be nurturant and dependent, and conform to particular standards of feminine beauty mean that when women see themselves as something else, that perception will be a stressor. Similarly, if men must be strong, fearless, and competent, then the inevitable experiences of weakness, fear, and incompetence will be stressors for men.

Adolescence, according to several authors, is the period in which boys and girls most strongly experience the enormous power of sex-role standards to shape both their perceptions of and also their responses to perceived stress. For girls, adolescence marks a major discontinuity. As they think about their futures, girls must confront the fact that the sex-role standard by which they will be measured constrains them in many ways; they are moving into society's devalued sex role. Differences in how boys and girls cope with the demands of dating illustrate some of these gender-related propensities. Especially for girls, adolescence is characterized by a shift in concerns from achievement to popularity. Dating is the mark of success; popular girls date, unpopular girls don't. Ostensibly girls who are successful in this arena ought to be high in self-esteem. Yet the opposite is true, according to Bush and Simmons. Girls who date, especially if they are early maturing and are in junior high school environments, suffer decreases in self-esteem relative to other groups of girls. Success at dating may actually signal movement from a focus on self and autonomy to a focus on pleasing others and loss of autonomy and control. For boys, dating marks success in attracting females, an important aspect of the male role. Success in the male role, however, has no implications for loss of autonomy and control. Not surprisingly, therefore, boys who date suffer no loss in self-esteem.

Attie and Brooks-Gunn, in their discussion of weight concerns, point out that physical attractiveness is more important for females than for males. The pernicious effects of these concerns, although present before adolescence, take on a new vigor at this time. Weight concerns are associated both with women's self-evaluation and with evaluation by others. The authors argue that women's greater obligation to be physically attractive is responsible for widespread dieting behavior, even among those who are not overweight. They show how dieting itself is an important chronic source of stress.

Janoff-Bulman and Frieze, in their discussion of reactions to victimization, point out that an experience of sexual abuse is seen as stressful for different reasons according to the gender of the victim. For men, the experience undermines one's sense of masculinity by demonstrating the victim's vulnerability and weakness. For women, the experience undermines one's ability to trust. The differing nature of stressors helps to make sense of the differing reactions to abuse by men (aggression) and women (withdrawal).

RESPONSE TO STRESSFUL CONDITIONS

According to Lazarus and Folkman (1984), the perception of a stressor is the outcome of two cognitive processes. The first, termed "primary appraisal," is the process by which a person decides whether or not a situation is potentially threatening. The second, "secondary appraisal," involves an assessment of the resources one has for coping with the threat. If one perceives that one's resources can effectively reduce the threat, less stress is experienced than if one perceives that one has inadequate resources. It is in part because men and women differ in their position in the social hierarchy, and consequently in the nature of the coping resources they possess, that they differ in their perception of the threat inherent in various situations.

Pearlin and Schooler (1978) define coping as "any response to external life strains that serves to prevent, avoid or control emotional distress" (p. 3). They categorize responses into three groups: (1) those that modify the situation—for example, negotiation of conflicts, coercive influence, or other direct alterations of the environment; (2) responses that control the meaning of the problem—for example, positive comparisons or selective ignoring; and (3) responses that function to manage emotional distress—for example, emotional discharge, substance use, and helpless resignation. Lazarus and his colleagues label the first category "problem-focused coping" and the second two categories "emotion-focused coping." Studies show rather consistently that women are more likely than men to use emotion-focused coping and less likely to use direct action (see Miller & Kirsch, this volume). Pearlin and Schooler (1978) found that use of emotion-focused responses entailing selective ignoring of problems in response to the strains of marriage and parenting tended to exacerbate psychological distress.

Emotion-focused coping techniques are likely to be used when the individual perceives the stressor as one that cannot be changed; the coping task is defined in terms of needing to accept and adjust to the situation (cf. Folkman & Lazarus, 1980; Stone & Neale, 1984). The possibility of change is often an objective characteristic of an event or situation, and in those cases where it is minimal, emotion-focused coping is likely to be the most effective way to manage distress. We believe, however, that the perception of changeability is often a function of the social consensus of people close to the individual as well as his or her appraisal of personal resources (power, money, problem-solving skills, social supports). For a given stressful situation, there will be some degree of variation in the extent to which it is perceived as changeable. Consider a worker in conflict with a supervisor. The worker's willingness and ability to negotiate an acceptable resolution to the conflict depends on several factors: status in the workplace, experience in conflict resolution, perception of the appropriateness of one's position in the conflict, and the availability of equally attractive jobs should the attempt at conflict resolution fail. The identical conflict could be perceived as unchangeable by an isolated machine operator and changeable by a shop steward.

Given the relatively low status of women in most occupational situations and the socialization patterns that have traditionally reinforced lack of assertiveness, it is not surprising that women, more often than men, see stressful situations as unchangeable, leaving adaptation as the goal of coping. Such perceptions may explain why women tend to turn to others for support more often than men. While social support can be used in the service of problem-focused coping, it is often used as an opportunity for emotional expression and self-enhancement, as Belle points out. In the absence of perceiving the power to change the situation, women may resort to self-consoling behaviors like smoking, eating, or shopping; or to self-changing behavior like dieting, exercise, or other self-improvement programs. (See the chapter by Biener in this volume.)

Long-Term Outcomes

Men and women are vulnerable to different long-term disorders. As Cleary's chapter demonstrates, women benefit in terms of longevity and relative immunity from coronary heart disease (CHD). Men, in contrast, suffer less from anxiety and depression. The stressors men and women confront and their responses to those stressors may be responsible for the differential health outcomes.

Suppression of emotion and cardiovascular disease. Given the pervasive evidence that fewer stressors are associated with male social roles, how can we account for men's shorter life span and greater vulnerability to acute, life-threatening diseases—the first paradox noted in the introduction? Adherence to the culturally prescribed behaviors and norms for men, that is, the male gender role, we believe may be a major cause of men's health disadvantage. The cultural role to which men aspire predisposes them to patterns of emotional and behavioral responsivity which are associated with poor physical health.

The notion that the male sex role may be hazardous to men's health is not a new idea (see, for example, Waldron, 1986). In this volume, the chapters by Biener and by Cleary point to some of the behavioral factors that are responsible for men's shorter life span, such as greater risk taking and more use of cigarettes and alcohol. Cleary also suggests that genetic factors may be partially responsible. A somewhat different approach is taken by Polefrone and Manuck. Their analysis focuses on gender differences in physiological reactivity to stressors, a hypothesized mediator of the relationship between environmental stressors and coronary heart disease (CHD). On the one hand, they provide evidence that female reproductive hormones, by reducing cardiovascular responsivity to environmental stressors, may be partially responsible for lower female vulnerability to CHD. They suggest, however, that responsivity to stressors is also a function of one's ego involvement in the outcome of the stressful situation, which often varies with gender. Evidence supporting this proposition includes studies showing that when confronted with "achievement-related" tasks, males secrete higher levels of epinephrine than females. Studies of cardiovascular responsivity to such stressors as electric shocks, video games, and difficult cognitive tasks also tend to show higher responsivity among males, though somewhat less consistently. In contrast, in a situation likely to be equally, if not more, involving for women— accompanying one's child to the hospital—epinephrine excretion was as high in mothers as in fathers.

This research could be interpreted as meaning that the female protection against CHD is due at least in part to women's relatively lower concern with achievement-relevant tasks; even though women might have stressful jobs, it may not matter as much to them whether they do well or poorly. Therefore, this argument goes, their cardiovascular systems are less taxed by the stressors they encounter. Such an interpretation, however, is unwarranted. It assumes that the "true" indicator of concern is physiological responsivity. It is equally plausible, however, that cognitive/verbal responses are valid indicators. Indeed, we believe that physiological responsivity to a stressor depends less on ego involvement in the outcome than on whether one suppresses or expresses negative emotional reactions to the threatening situation. When such reactions are aroused, if not discharged directly through overt emotional displays, they will be discharged indirectly through physiological reactivity.

A potential solution then emerges to the paradox of greater female longevity in the context of stressful social roles. The key is the differential social appropriateness of emotional expressivity for men and women. To the extent that men accept the traditional gender-role norm that to be masculine is to be stoic, strong, competent, and fearless, they will find it difficult to accept and express feelings of distress, weakness, incompetence, and fear. Since these feelings are bound to be evoked in the day-to-day course of events, particularly in situations where evaluation of one's competence is an issue, men will repeatedly suppress these feelings, and in doing so suffer a physiological cost.

Evidence linking suppression of emotional response to poor health comes from several quarters. Rieker, Edbril, and Garnick (1985) found that concealment of emotions was an important predictor of sexual impairment in men treated for testis cancer. Pennebaker and O'Heeron (1984) interviewed men and women who had lost their spouses to accidents or suicide and found that a year after the loss, those who kept their grief to themselves showed many more health problems than those who had confided in someone.

Studies of the relationships among self-report of affect, facial displays of emotion, and measures of physiological reactivity (such as skin conductance and heart rate) also provide some evidence for suppression as a potential mediator of health risks. Notarius, Wemple, Ingraham, Burns, and Kollar (1982) reviewed this work and reported their own results demonstrating that compared to highly expressive subjects, those who were rated as minimally expressive during a stressful interpersonal encounter showed significant increases in heart rate.

The work of Frankenhaeuser and her colleagues, discussed by Polefrone and Manuck, shows that in spite of a lower level of physiological reactivity during stressful experiences, females were more likely than males to report more psychological distress. Men, although they performed no better than women, reported stronger feelings of task-related success and satisfaction in contrast to dissatisfaction, and also secreted more stress hormones. Reflecting on these findings, the investigators suggested that the psychoneuroendocrine mechanisms involved in adaptation and coping differ in the two genders. They proposed that the physiological costs of adaptation may be greater for men, and the psychological costs greater for women (Frankenhaeuser, Von Wright, Collins, Von Wright, Sedvall,

& Swahn, 1978). We further propose that there may be a causal link between the two modes of responding to stress—suppressing the expression of psychological distress may result in physiological reactivity.

It is interesting to note that among the studies reviewed by Polefrone and Manuck, the only study in which the epinephrine excretion was as high in females as in males was one in which women would be as likely as men to suppress their negative emotional responses: in that study, as noted above, parents were observed bringing their child to the hospital. In such a situation, women might well try as much as men to hide their fear and concern in order to avoid frightening their child.

There is one negative emotion that is expressed more by men than by women and is consistent with male gender norms—the expression of anger (Frost & Averill, 1982; Hyde, 1986). It may be, however, that anger is the one emotion that yields no physiological benefit in its expression. While there is evidence that suppression of anger is related to elevated blood pressure for men as well as women, it is not necessarily true that anger expression is associated with decreased physiological or cardiac reactivity. Manuck, Morrison, and Bellack (1986) found that hypertensive men differed from normotensives in exhibiting problems with assertion: in the face of anger they were either hyperassertive or nonassertive. Hyperassertion was defined by hostile-aggressive expressions of anger; nonassertiveness by both the denial and suppression of anger. Hyperassertion, in addition to lacking physiological benefit, may push people away, leaving the enraged person isolated and cut off from confidant relationships. Having a confidant is one of the best buffers against the negative health outcomes, including cardiovascular disease, often associated with occupation-based stress and negative life events (Belle, this volume; House, 1981).

Lack of control and depression. The persistent female excess in depression and anxiety is another gender-related long-term stress outcome. Insights from various chapters shed some light on the paradox of women's higher risk for these outcomes in the context of their greater expressivity and social embeddedness. The key to untangling this paradox may be the amount of control one has over important events in one's life. The importance of a sense of control for mental health has been widely recognized in the clinical and research literature. Reflection on the contributions in this volume suggests that women's greater tendency toward depression may be due both to socialization into a gender role that encourages relinquishing of control to others and to their occupancy of social roles that provide less opportunity for control. The female gender role prescribes dependence, nonassertiveness, and subordination of one's needs to those of others. Neither the perception that one has control over one's life nor the ability to take control is part of the standard to which most women are socialized. Indeed, the price of being a fully socialized female in our culture may be a predisposition to feelings of lack of control and ultimately to depression.

Ironically, emotional expressivity, the very trait we propose improves women's cardiovascular health, may contribute to depression in some people. Kobasa's research on the combined effects of family support and personality resources suggests an underlying process. She found that among male executives low in hardiness (that is, those who felt alienated and lacking in control), having a family situation that allowed for more rather than less expression of feelings was associated with more severe stress reactions. Perhaps other people's consoling reactions to expressions of psychological distress ("How terrible for you!"; "Take it easy. Have a tranquilizer and everything will work out for the best") invite those who feel ineffective and out of control to accept and adapt to stressful situations. As Kobasa indicates, women are more likely than men to be low in the mastery component of hardiness. At the same time their gender role facilitates expressivity and encourages the development of social ties. Hence women may be more likely than men to experience depression as a consequence of expressivity.

On the other hand, men's traditional lack of expressivity may have an unanticipated benefit, predisposing men to deal with their problems on their own rather than by engaging with others, and may contribute to their tendency toward problem-focused coping, bolstering feelings of efficacy and control and thereby reducing the risk of depression. (See Nolen-Hoeksema, 1987 for an elaboration of this point.) In sum, in comparison to men, women's greater depression seems to be due to their relative lack of control, influenced by the lower social status of women, norms of the female gender role, and the demands of the social roles they occupy.

DIRECTIONS FOR FUTURE RESEARCH

Each chapter in this volume points to ways in which introducing considerations of gender changes and enriches understanding of the stress process. Progress in elucidating gender differences, however, has been hampered by several methodological problems. Major among these is the issue of whether traditional, controlled laboratory studies are by their nature unsuitable for examining gender differences in stress reactions. The aim of such studies is to assess the effect of gender on stress reactions by controlling all the independent variables except gender and then measuring changes in the outcome variables of interest. The intent is to present female and male subjects with identical stressors. Often this aim is served by presenting subjects with such cognitive tasks as anagrams, and assessing performance. It is likely that the tasks used in these situations have so little real world significance that generalizations beyond the laboratory are highly questionable. Further, there is abundant evidence that men and women differ with respect to which real world situations they perceive as stressful. Thus the task for researchers is to identify gender-relevant situations that are perceived as equally stressful and then to examine stress reactions.

In addition, gender may exert its influence on the stress process only within certain levels of perceived stress. Under conditions of very high or very low perceived stress, there may be no gender differences. When the building is on fire, everyone runs out. Conversely, when the perceived stress is low, individual differences may account for more variance in stress reactions than gender differences. Thus, to study gender differences, one needs to identify stressors that are perceived as moderately stressful. More progress will be made in understanding gender differences in the stress process if experimental studies utilize gender-relevant stimuli that are perceived as equally and moderately stressful.

Finally, as Aneshensel and Pearlin note, although employed men and women may be thought of as occupying the paid employee role, in reality their roles are quite dissimilar. Studies of the effect of social role occupancy on gender differences in perceptions of stress and stress reactions often fail to take into account these important differences that are masked by similar role terms. Thus employed women and men, and married women and men, cannot be assumed to occupy similar roles. It may be possible, however, to move from a concern with role occupancy to a focus on the nature of roles. For example, we know that the dimensions of control and demand are important in understanding the stressfulness of roles. Thus, men and women who are employed in jobs with similar levels of control and demand might be thought of as having similar roles. Future research might study the effects of gender on stress reactions among men and women who occupy social roles characterized by similar levels of these two dimensions.

In sum, the contributions in this volume point strongly to the conclusion that aspects of both male and female roles are dangerous to health— the prohibition against vulnerability in men; the barriers to gaining power and control in women. Stress researchers should investigate whether men who are able to express feelings of vulnerability are at lower risk for coronary heart disease and whether assertive women are less likely to become depressed. Continued examination of these aspects of gender roles should produce knowledge that can improve the mental and physical health of both women and men.

REFERENCES

Folkman, S., & Lazarus, R. S. (1980). An analysis of coping in a middle-aged community sample. *Journal of Health and Social Behavior, 21*, 219–239.

Frankenhaeuser, M., Von Wright, M., Collins, A., Von Wright, J., Sedvall, G., & Swahn, C. (1978). Sex differences in psychoneuroendocrine reactions to examination stress. *Psychosomatic Medicine, 40*, 334–343.

Frost, W. D., & Averill, J. R. (1982). Differences between men and women in the everyday experience of anger. In J. R. Averill (Ed.), *Anger and aggression: An essay on emotion*. New York: Springer-Verlag.

House, J. S. (1981). *Work, stress, and social support*. Reading, MA: Addision-Wesley.

Hyde, J. S. (1986). Gender differences in aggression. In J. S. Hyde & M. C. Linn (Eds.), *The psychology of gender*. Baltimore, MD: Johns Hopkins University Press.

Lazarus, R. S., & Folkman, S. (1984). *Stress, appraisal, and coping*. New York: Springer Publishing Co.

Manuck, S. B., Morrison, R. L., & Bellack, A. S. (1986). Psychological factors in hypertension. In *Hypertension: Psychophysiological, biobehavioral, and epidemiological aspects*. (NIH 86-2704.) Washington, DC: U.S. Government Printing Office.

Nolen-Hoeksema, S. (1987). Sex differences in unipolar depression: Evidence and theory. *Psychological Bulletin, 101*, 259–282.

Notarius, C. I., Wemple, C., Ingraham, L. J., Burns, T. J., & Kollar, E. (1982). Multichannel responses to an interpersonal stressor: Interrelationships among facial display, heart rate, self-report of emotion, and threat appraisal. *Journal of Personality and Social Psychology, 43*, 400–408.

Pearlin, L. I., & Schooler, C. (1978). The structure of coping. *Journal of Health and Social Behavior, 19*, 2–21.

Pennebaker, J. W., & O'Heeron, R. C. (1984). Confiding in others and illness rate among spouses of suicide and accidental-death victims. *Journal of Abnormal Psychology, 93*, 473–476.

Rieker, P. P., Edbril, S. D., & Garnick, M. B. (1985). Curative testis cancer therapy: Psychosocial sequelae. *Journal of Clinical Oncology, 3*, 1117–1126.

Stone, A. A., & Neale, J. M. (1984). New measure of daily coping: Development and preliminary results. *Journal of Personality and Social Psychology, 46*, 892–906.

Turkington, C. (1986). Farm women and stress. *APA Monitor, 17*, 18.

Waldron, I. (1986). What do we know about causes of sex differences in mortality? A review of the literature. *Population Bulletin of the United Nations*, No. 18–1985, pp. 59–76.

Author Index

Subject Index